# Introduction to Learning Disabilities

## A Psycho-Behavioral Approach

DANIEL P. HALLAHAN and JAMES M. KAUFFMAN
University of Virginia

Prentice-Hall, Inc., Englewood Cliffs, New Jersey

*Library of Congress Cataloging in Publication Data*

HALLAHAN, DANIEL P. (date).
  Introduction to learning disabilities.

  (Prentice-Hall special education series)
  Bibliography: p. 267.
  Includes index.
  1. Learning disabilities.   I. Kauffman, James
M., joint author.   II. Title.   [DNLM: 1. Ed-
ucation, Special.   2. Learning disorders.   LC4661
H181i]
LC4704.H34        371.9        75–29498
ISBN 0–13–485524–8

PRENTICE-HALL SPECIAL EDUCATION SERIES
William M. Cruickshank, Series Editor

Printed in the United States of America

10   9   8   7

Prentice-Hall International, Inc., *London*
Prentice-Hall of Australia, Pty. Ltd., *Sydney*
Prentice-Hall of Canada, Ltd., *Toronto*
Prentice-Hall of India Private Limited, *New Delhi*
Prentice-Hall of Japan, Inc., *Tokyo*
Prentice-Hall of Southeast Asia (Pte.) Ltd., *Singapore*

# Contents

# 9 Language Disabilities   179

# 10 Social-Emotional Disabilities   221

# Preface

With the rapid expansion of the field of learning disabilities, its "growing pains" have become evident. Especially painful have been the lack of competent teachers, the frequent lack of appropriate services for children, and the strident, sometimes bitter, controversies regarding theory and practice. As with any new movement within education, the specialty of learning disabilities is fraught with fads and frills. In a field so young, and serving a population so greatly in need of services, many are tempted to believe in "solutions" before their value has been proved.

It is time for a rational look at many aspects of this newest and now largest area of special education. Indeed, the definition of "learning disabilities" itself demands close scrutiny. With the growing awareness that categorical separation of exceptional children may not in many respects be warranted, it is imperative that questions be raised regarding the "uniqueness" of the learning disabilities category. It is our premise that children identified as learning disabled, educable mentally retarded, and emotionally disturbed have a great deal in common—more characteristics in common, in fact, than they have those that are unique. For this reason students of mental retardation and emotional disturbance, as well as the rising tide of professionals concerned with noncategorical special education, should find this book of interest.

This book does remain, however, first and foremost an introductory book in *learning disabilities*. The basic characteristics, assessment techniques, and remedial methods associated with the field are introduced. Rather than reducing the scope of the area of learning disabilities, we have actually broadened it to incorporate *any* child who has a specific learning problem, whether he be labeled learning disabled, emotionally disturbed, or educable mentally retarded.

We have maintained a developmental, empirical, behavioral orientation in this book. The major remedial procedures associated with the area of learning disabilities are presented, but we have also given special attention to the methods of applied behavior analysis or behavior modification along with many practical examples of teaching techniques that are based on empirical data. We believe that deviant childhood learning must be understood within the context of normal child development; hence, our frequent discussion of normal development and its implications for comprehending the problems of the learning disabled. Consequently, both experienced and novice teachers will, we believe, find this volume to be of value.

We would like to acknowledge the assistance of Elizabeth D. Heins in the preparation of this manuscript. We are also grateful to Cyndy Kelly, Caroline Jones, Ann Mercer, Linda Wilberger, and Susan Powers for their typing of the manuscript.

D. P. H.

J. M. K.

# Historical Roots

# 1

The field within special education that has experienced the fastest growth and expansion has undoubtedly been that of learning disabilities. Capturing the interest and attention of professionals and laymen alike, this burgeoning sphere of work and study has quickly gathered in its ranks individuals from a wide variety of backgrounds. Professionals from every sector of special education—general educators, physical educators, neurologists, ophthalmologists, optometrists, pediatricians, physical therapists, psychologists, and a host of others—have all taken an active interest in the "learning disabilities explosion."

While this ground swell of interest has resulted in the rapid formation of professional and parent groups and services for children, it has not been without its problems. When so many individuals from diverse backgrounds congregate, a certain amount of confusion is inevitable. One example of it is evidenced by the numerous terms used interchangeably to describe the same child. Within the literature and within the field, "learning disabilities," "minimal brain injury," "minimal brain dysfunction," "specific learning disabilities," "psychoneurological learning disabilities," "perceptual disabilities," "educational handicaps," "reading disabilities," "underachievement," and at least a dozen other labels have been used synonymously.

## HISTORICAL DEVELOPMENT
## OF THE FIELD
## OF LEARNING DISABILITIES

One of the primary reasons for the current confusion in the field of learning disabilities with regard to such basic considerations as definition and
classification is the field's rather unique evolution. Other special education
professionals have traditionally developed their practices, for the most
part, from a common source. Concern for the special educational needs
of the mentally retarded, emotionally disturbed, deaf, and blind, for
example, came about primarily through the physicians' treatment of
children with these handicaps. Medical personnel, in other words, were
the first professionals to be confronted with the problems of children now
served under the auspices of special education. Once a group of children
was defined as deviant by the medical profession, a distinct sphere of
special education, with its own techniques and philosophy, was created
by educators in order to address the learning problems of the children
involved. The medical profession, with its long history of established procedures, thus enabled most areas of exceptionality to be built upon a
common core of ideas and directions.

  In contrast, the development of learning disabilities as a field of
special education did not follow the usual course. Although the medical
profession was involved in the initial identification of learning disabled
children, the field of learning disabilities, unlike other sectors of special
education, lacked the "advantage" of developing within a unified framework of thinking. Instead, the concepts, ideas, and directions of this
"new" field were, and continue to be, fostered almost exclusively within
widely varied educational circles. It is undoubtedly true that in the best
of all possible worlds a field of special education should be established by
the educational profession, but it is unfortunately true also that the educational profession of the early 1960s was not prepared to accept the chal-
lenge of developing this new area of exceptionality. Special education, in
particular, began to assert itself as an entity apart from general education
and, especially, from medicine. With the rapid expansion both of federal
legislation and of university training programs, special education was
beginning to flex its muscles as a national power. It was within this
professional and legal flux of the early 1960s that the speciality of learning disabilities *presumably* was formed.

  Within this historical context of educational instability, learning
disabilities has become known as the avant-garde field of specialization.
The field itself was to be the prototype of all that should be "good" about
any aspect of special education. With zeal characteristic of any new

movement, the people in learning disabilities tended to discard associations with the past and severed their ties with other divisions of special education. This isolationist tendency doubtless was the single most significant cause of today's confusion regarding definition and terminology. Because existing terminology belonged to the past, the "young" field of learning disabilities in its quest for new frontiers created for itself the task of reclassification.

Despite the efforts of learning disabilities specialists to foster a trend of separatism, however, it is our basic tenet that the present-day field of learning disabilities has its roots firmly implanted within both the area of emotional disturbance and, particularly, in the area of mental retardation (this idea has been further developed elsewhere; Cruickshank & Hallahan, 1973; Hallahan & Cruickshank, 1973). In fact, the theoretical rationale and many of the teaching methods now advocated by learning disabilities teachers have a long history within emotional disturbance and mental retardation. Furthermore, it is not coincidental that the teaching methods for learning disabilities are the same as those used for many years with the retarded. Although few teachers today are aware of these associations, the methods and concepts they have considered to be under the exclusive domain of learning disabilities actually have an established precedent within the area of mental retardation.

The situation is most unfortunate. Not only has recognition not been given the truly pioneering efforts of previous theoreticians and practitioners, but ignorance of these historical roots has contributed significantly to the myriad present-day misunderstandings regarding the definition of learning disabilities. In the hope of clarifying the issue of definition and differential diagnosis, we have included the following historical perspective on the emergent nature of the field of learning disabilities.

To emphasize the evolutionary and emergent quality of the field now referred to as "learning disabilities," we have presented the following historical account in a basic flow chart. Numerous other significant figures and events naturally could have been cited, but the following traces the *major* lines of development with regard to the basic orientation and definition of the field. (For a more detailed analysis of this historical background, the reader is referred to Chapter 3 of Hallahan & Cruickshank, 1973.)

Kurt Goldstein was one of the foremost behavioral scientists to take advantage of the physical disabilities of soldiers suffering from head

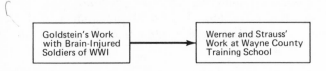

wounds incurred during World War I. Much of what Goldstein learned about his brain-injured soldiers, whom he referred to as "traumatic dements," formed the basis of his now classic work *The Organism* (Goldstein, 1939), which dealt with broad issues of human development. Although Goldstein did not have at his disposal today's methods of rigorous experimentation, he studied the behavior of the soldiers within a clinical framework. Through careful observation, he was able to identify the following five behavioral characteristics in his patients: forced responsiveness to stimuli, figure-background confusion, hyperactivity, meticulosity, and catastrophic reaction.

With regard to forced responsiveness to stimuli, Goldstein noted that his patients seemed driven to respond to all salient objects in their surroundings. They were easily distracted by other people and objects in their environment. While awareness of events in the immediate environment can be considered critical to one's well-being, the extent to which Goldstein's patients spent their time in these activities made their behavior truly pathological. Reacting indiscriminately to various stimuli, they seemed unable to distinguish the essential from the inessential.

Figure-background confusion can be viewed as a special case of forced responsiveness to stimuli. Because Goldstein was a disciple of the German school of Gestalt psychology, he was interested in the perception of form and the perceptual figure-ground relationships of his patients. Whereas the normal reader is able to perceive this book, as he is reading it, as a figure distinct from the background of the desk on which it may rest, and whereas he also is able to focus his attention on a word or on a simple group of words in the midst of the hundreds of words on the facing page, Goldstein's patients would have had great difficulty with the activity of reading. Unable to inhibit response to any stimuli, they would react nearly equally to "background" and "figure" stimuli alike. Such behavior impeded their ability to form essential figure-background relationships.

Another possible manifestation of their overresponsiveness to stimuli was the extreme motor activity of Goldstein's patients. Again, it was the frequency and apparent aimlessness of their movement which distinguished it as hyperactivity rather than productive exploration of the environment.

According to Goldstein, the other two characteristics—meticulosity and catastrophic reaction—were intimately interwoven, with the former used as a defense against the latter. Catastrophic reaction, hypothesized Goldstein, resulted from the chaotic existence of living in a world of bizarre perceptions, wherein the soldiers frequently lost contact with reality and experienced a total emotional breakdown analogous to a severe temper tantrum. Goldstein posited that the meticulous life-style of these brain-injured individuals was a defensive ploy to prevent cata-strophic reactions from occurring. When the soldiers became very rigid in their everyday living habits, and when they spent a great deal of effort in structuring their time schedules and the objects in their environment, they merely were protecting themselves from a damaging break in rou-tine. Without such a self-imposed structure, the soldiers presumably would be at the mercy of their own gross misperceptions.

It was these germinal investigations of Goldstein that laid the foun-dation for the two most important figures in the evolution of the field of learning disabilities: Alfred Strauss and Heinz Werner. Strauss, a neuro-psychiatrist and associate professor at the University of Heidelberg, and Werner, a developmental psychologist and associate professor at the Uni-versity of Hamburg, emigrated from Germany to the United States after Hitler's rise to power. Both subsequently continued their work at the Wayne County Training School in Northville, Michigan. Though each man successfully pursued lines of research and practice peculiar to his own interests (Werner, for example, with his *Comparative Psychology of Mental Development* (1948), became one of the leading theorists of developmental psychology), it was their many years of collaboration which contributed to the chain of events that eventually led to the field of learning disabilities as we know it today.

Through a series of investigations with purportedly brain-injured, mentally retarded children (Strauss & Werner, 1942; Werner & Strauss, 1939b; 1940; 1941) Werner and Strauss replicated the results that Gold-stein had reported with brain-injured adults. In particular, they found the retarded children whom they classified as brain-injured (*exogenous* mentally retarded) to display more forced responsiveness to stimuli than the retarded children who revealed no indication of brain injury (*en-dogenous* mentally retarded).

This work of Werner and Strauss did not go without criticism. Specifically, the procedures used to form their exogenous and endogenous groups were attacked as being inappropriate (Sarason, 1949). One way in which an individual could be classified as exogenous (brain-injured) was on the basis of behavior alone. Even if no direct evidence of a lesion was obtained through neurological tests and there was no indication of brain damage in the medical history of the individual, (e.g., abnormal birth), a child was classified as exogenous if he displayed behavior clinically observed to occur in brain-damaged individuals. Although Werner and Strauss could be faulted on the grounds of having formed their exogenous group on other than stringent neurological evidence, the case against them would not have been so damaging had they used, for classification purposes, behaviors other than those on which they eventu-ally were to compare the exogenous and endogenous subjects (e.g., forced responsiveness to stimuli). Circular logic is evident in their comparing in experimental tests the two groups—exogenous and endogenous—on behaviors used to place the children differentially into one· or the other group in the first place.

While the numerous criticisms of others certainly weaken the inference drawn by Werner and Strauss that brain damage is a *cause* of distractibility and hyperactivity, these faults do not negate the fact that these two researchers did find evidence of a sizable subgroup of retarded children who did exhibit a forced responsiveness to stimuli. It is important to point out here that up until this time mental retardation was perceived as a relatively homogeneous state. All retardates were considered to be alike, and consequently no differential or individual educational or psychological programming was initiated on their behalf. Dispelling the long-standing notion that there were no individual differences among the retarded, the work of Werner and Strauss, therefore, had revolutionary impact.

It was their concern for taking heed of individual differences that prompted Werner and Strauss to make educational recommendations for their exogenous children. Significant studies that initiated these educational recommendations were those of Strauss and Kephart (1939) and Kephart and Strauss (1940), who found that after admission to Wayne County Training School, the IQs of the endogenous children increased over the years, whereas those of the exogenous declined. Concluding that the institutional regime was inappropriate for the exogenous group, Werner and Strauss (1940) and Strauss (1943) recommended an educational program to combat the major deviant psychological characteristics of the exogenous group. Keeping in mind the tendency in these children to overreact to stimuli in the environment, they suggested a diminution of inessential stimuli in favor of an increase in saliency of materials essential to learning.

These experimental investigations of Werner and Strauss, together with subsequent papers dealing with educational practices, provided the basis for the now classic volumes—*Psychopathology and Education of the Brain-Injured Child* (Strauss & Lehtinen, 1947) and *Psychopathology and Education of the Brain-Injured Child: Progress in Theory and Clinic* (Vol. 2) (Strauss & Kephart, 1955). Both volumes, but especially the first, became the educational handbook for teachers of mentally retarded and brain-injured children. The educational techniques detailed by Strauss and Lehtinen for the brain-injured, mentally retarded child are still espoused within present-day methods books for the learning disabled child.

To evaluate adequately the impact of research begun by Werner and Strauss would be difficult indeed. Not only did they provide a most crucial link (in terms of influencing people and future events) in the evolution of the field eventually called "learning disabilities," but also they proposed a notable conceptual frame of reference with regard to the role of psychological diagnosis in education. Basing educational recommendations on the *particular* behavioral pathology of the child, they advocated educational programming that has the same orientation as "prescriptive teaching" (Peter, 1965)—a term that is practically the byword of contemporary professionals in the field of learning disabilities. The concept of diagnosing strengths and weaknesses and then constructing an educational prescription on this diagnostic information is a core strategy of the field of learning disabilities.

Under the influence of Werner and Strauss, the Wayne County Training School was on the "cutting edge" of research and practice. The institution therefore attracted numerous young scholars launching their careers. Consequently, in addition to creating research and educational concepts, Werner and Strauss influenced the eventual development of the field of learning disabilities because of the effect their ideas had on other individuals with whom they were in close professional contact.

One such individual was William Cruickshank. Though Cruickshank has been recognized for many years as a leader in the field of special education, perhaps his most significant work in terms of the evolution of learning disabilities has gone relatively unrecognized by special education professionals. In 1957 he published the results of a major study in which he replicated the work of Werner and Strauss, and Goldstein before them, with cerebral palsied children of near-normal, normal, and above-normal intelligence (Cruickshank, Bice, & Wallen, 1957). This study formed a conceptual bridge between lowered and normal intelligence. Finding that cerebral palsied children of normal intelligence exhibited poor figure-ground relationships, presumably due to distractibility, as did the exogenous mentally retarded children of Werner and Strauss, Cruickshank facilitated the needed (in terms of eventual development of the learning disability field) transfer of concern to children of normal intelligence.

Cruickshank's research project with cerebral palsied children is significant because it was the first major extension of the research of Werner and Strauss to children with normal intelligence, and his Montgomery County (Maryland) Project is important because it was the first formalized attempt to implement the educational recommendations of Werner and Strauss with children of normal intelligence (see Cruickshank, 1976). In the late 1950s, Cruickshank initiated a demonstration-pilot study that

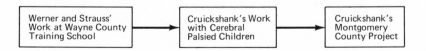

Werner and Strauss' Work at Wayne County Training School → Cruickshank's Work with Cerebral Palsied Children → Cruickshank's Montgomery County Project

culminated in *A Teaching Method for Brain-Injured and Hyperactive Children* (Cruickshank, Bentzen, Ratzeburg, & Tannhauser, 1961). In this project, Cruickshank and his colleagues included children who ranged in tested IQ from educable retarded to normal, and extended the principles of a highly structured program within a classroom devoid of distracting stimuli.

Although the details of the Montgomery County Project will not be discussed until a later chapter, it is important to note here that many of the children included in the project classrooms would otherwise have been placed in classes for the emotionally disturbed or the educable mentally retarded. More importantly, from the extensive case histories of the children, it is also apparent that many of them would today be placed in programs for the learning disabled. The study thus serves as a link among educable mental retardation, emotional disturbance, and learning disabilities.

As the following passage reveals, among the greatest problems encountered by individuals associated with the Montgomery County Project were those of terminology and classification.

The authors of this study and the members of the Diagnostic Team struggled for many hours to obtain a meeting of the minds regarding definitions. They were hindered by the stereotypes of the several professions and by the literature which employed such terms as *brain injury, brain damage,* and *brain disorder.* The traditional medical classifications of cerebral palsy, aphasia, epilepsy, and others, and the literature pertaining to each, carry further implications for definitions and contain somewhat different definitions.

The children about whom this monograph is concerned are those who are defined as hyperactive, with or without diagnosis of brain damage. Specific brain injury is difficult to delineate in every instance. While neurological examination and pediatric history in over half the cases supported the fact that brain injury was undoubtedly present, the Diagnostic Team members were frequently reluctant to agree that brain injury or other form of central nervous system disorder did actually exist. The diagnostic and clinical data accumulated on the individual children, however, fell into a pattern or "clustering" which made it possible to describe the children in terms of behavioral and learning disorders. A group decision to include a child in the study was made on this basis.

Thus, children who demonstrated hyperactivity, dissociative tendencies, perseveration, figure-background reversals, and angulation problems in combination or as separate psychological characteristics; children who indicated traditional organic characteristics in pattern and scatter analysis on intelligence tests; and children who demonstrated these characteristics in appropriate ways in pediatric examinations, in neurological, audiological, and psychiatric examinations; as well as in the psychological examinations, were included in the group. Hyperactivity, in traditional terms, often applies to those children who are characterized by emotional disturbances and gross manifestations of behavior disorders. While some children in the population of the current study were characterized by these factors, hyperactivity is herein defined to include much more subtle deviations in behavior, and is more specifically considered to be related to matters of short attention span, visual and auditory distractibility, and disturbances in perception leading to dissociative tendencies.* (Cruickshank, et al., 1961, pp. 9–10)

The Montgomery County Project thereby provided a rationale for employing Werner and Strauss's concepts with children of normal intelligence. In fact, by including children who tested as retarded in the same classroom with children who tested as normal, Cruickshank was one of the first educators to recognize that differential grouping of children should be based on information other than IQ levels. The mental age rather than the IQ of the child, as well as important behavioral characteristics (e.g., hyperactivity, figure-background problems, and so forth), should be the primary criteria used for educational grouping. This concern for the specific behavioral characteristics of the nonlearning child was no doubt generated by the same concern of Werner and Strauss and is a central theme of learning disabilities today.

At about the same time as Cruickshank's publication of the Montgomery County Project two other contributions destined to be significant aspects of the backbone of learning disabilities were made by former staff members of Wayne County Training School—Newell Kephart's *Slow Learner in the Classroom* (1960; 2nd ed., 1971) and S. A. Kirk, J. J. McCarthy, and W. D. Kirk's *Illinois Test of Psycholinguistic Abilities* (1961: rev. ed., 1968).

Whereas Cruickshank elaborated upon Werner and Strauss's and Strauss and Lehtinen's concepts of reduced environmental stimuli and

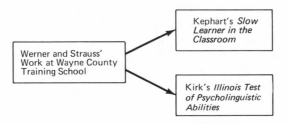

* W. M. Cruickshank, F. A. Bentzen, F. H. Ratzeburg, & M. T. Tannhauser, *A Teaching Method for Brain-Injured and Hyperactive Children* (Syracuse: Syracuse University Press, 1961), pp. 9–10. Reprinted by permission.

structured educational programming, Kephart emphasized perceptual-motor training. Kephart's *Slow Learner*, in which he provided numerous techniques for teachers to use in training perceptual-motor skills of "slow learning" children (soon to be referred to as "learning disabled"), quickly became a classic as a methods book. Primarily because of the work of such individuals as Kephart, and Cruickshank to a lesser extent, the field of learning disabilities has a perceptual-motor orientation. Owing to the assumption, first advocated by Werner and Strauss and later emphasized by Kephart, that perceptual and perceptual-motor development is the basis for later conceptual learning, most educational tests, materials, and programs for the learning disabled are perceptual-motor in nature rather than being oriented toward other aspects of development, such as language (Hallahan & Cruickshank, 1973).

One individual who did give some visibility to the language disabilities of learning disabled children was Samuel Kirk. After many years of work and experimentation with retarded children, Kirk and his colleagues published the experimental edition of the *Illinois Test of Psycholinguistic Abilities* (Kirk, McCarthy, & Kirk, 1961). Built upon the communications model of C. E. Osgood (1957), the ITPA considers (1) channels of communication (auditory-vocal and visual-motor); (2) psycholinguistic processes (reception, organization, and expression); and (3) levels of organization (representational and automatic). Each of the various subtests of the ITPA fits within the three dimensions of the Osgood model.

Development of the ITPA was significant in furthering the concept of differential abilities inherent in contemporary learning disability literature. This instrument was devised with the intent of enabling a teacher to construct a blueprint of the child's particular strengths and weaknesses before structuring his educational program. The uniqueness of the ITPA is its educational orientation; subsequent pamphlets and manuals drawing on the test offer specific educational recommendations for disabilities in specific skill areas (Bush & Giles, 1969; Karnes, 1968; Kirk & Kirk, 1971). While research has offered only partial support for the basic rationale of the ITPA (Hallahan & Cruickshank, 1973), the educational focus of the test, as well as its attempt to assess different areas of ability, has made its construction an extremely important historical event for the field of learning disabilities. The ITPA provided further rationale for the concern for differential abilities and held the promise of an instrument for assessing these various abilities. The ITPA will be discussed further in Chapter 9.

As previously stated, professional literature by the early 1960s was beginning to reflect a new concern for the child of average intelligence with learning problems—the same learning problems evidenced by a

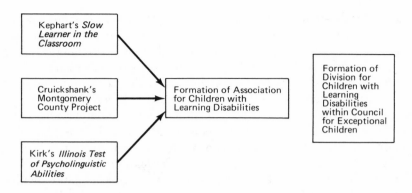

sizable proportion of mentally retarded children. The formation of the parent organization, the Association for Children with Learning Disabilities (ACLD), in 1963, coupled with the creation a few years later of a Division for Children with Learning Disabilities within the professional organization known as the Council for Exceptional Children, provided the formal confirmation of this new field of special education.

The actual acceptance of the term "learning disabilities" was the result of a meeting of parents in Chicago in 1963. Up until that time, these concerned parents, confused by the professional literature which was using interchangeably some two or three dozen terms (e.g., dyslexia, reading disabilities, perceptual handicaps, minimal brain injury), had not been able to mount a concerted effort on behalf of their children. This problem existed despite the fact that in the early 1960s the potential impact of parent organizations on legislation for services, research, and professional training was perhaps at its height, and parent groups representing other areas of special education already had scored many victories for their children (Cruickshank, 1967). Seeking an identity of their own, the parents at this meeting pressed for a suitable label for their children. In his address to the group, Samuel Kirk suggested that the term should be educationally rather than etiologically based. Kirk's term, "learning disabilities," was accepted, and the Association for Children with Learning Disabilities was formally established the following year (see Kirk, 1976).

Though the formation of ACLD provided a rallying point for parents of children who had been denied services, the orientation of the group has been a factor in the current confusion regarding the definition of learning disabilities. Perhaps fearful of the stigma attached to the retarded, ACLD has tended to disassociate itself from the area of mental retardation. The result has been that the shared characteristics of retarded and learning disabled children and the similarities in services and educational programming for the two groups—the heritage of the field of learning disabilities—have been ignored. This zeal to create a separate category with no conceptual ties to other areas has been a primary factor in the rampant confusion regarding the definition of learning disabilities.

Formation of the parent and professional organizations completes our flow chart of the *major* events and individual contributions relative to the development of the field of learning disabilities. Other events and people obviously could have been included; only the basic skeletal framework has been outlined. The final composite of the chart is presented in Figure 1.1. The main conclusion to be drawn from this figure, specified in the section labeled "Identification of Population," is that the field of learning disabilities evolved gradually from a preoccupation with the mentally retarded to a concern for children of normal intelligence. The point to be emphasized is that the brain-injured adults of Goldstein; the exogenous, retarded children of Werner and Strauss; the brain-injured children of normal intelligence of Cruickshank; the slow learners, "minimally brain-injured," emotionally disturbed, or hyperactive children with normal intelligence of Cruickshank, Kephart, and Kirk; and the learning disabled children of the ACLD and the present-day field all have, in general, a great deal in common with regard to psychological and behavioral characteristics. The children in each of these groups have evidenced problems in functioning in specific areas of ability.

### Other Historical Figures

The influence of Goldstein, Strauss, and Werner was primarily in the visual perceptual and visual-motor realm. Because these figures have been the most influential, the learning disabilities field has a heavy perceptual and perceptual-motor flavor. There were, however, others who played an important part in developing the field of learning disabilities.

As Wiederholt (1974) has delineated in his thorough review, a historical line of development that emphasizes the spoken language disabilities of children can be traced back to the work of such individuals as Broca (1861), Jackson (1915), Wernicke (1908), and Head (1926). These individuals influenced the work of such people as Myklebust, Kirk, and Eisenson whom we will discuss in Chapter 9. Concern for disorders of written language received its impetus from the landmark work of Hinshelwood (1917) and Orton (1937).

## APPLIED BEHAVIOR ANALYSIS
## AND LEARNING DISABILITIES

In addition to the fact that work in other areas of special education has contributed to the evolution of learning disabilities, the emergence of this new specialization also has been influenced during the past decade by

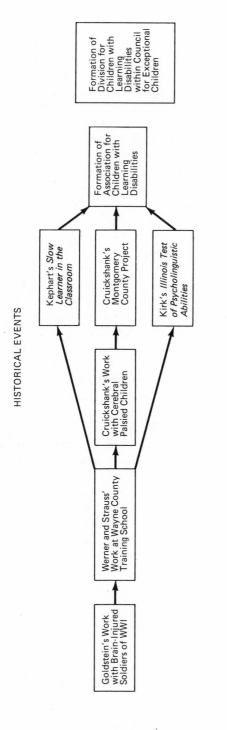

HISTORICAL EVENTS

Goldstein's Work with Brain-Injured Soldiers of WWI

Werner and Strauss' Work at Wayne County Training School

Kephart's *Slow Learner in the Classroom*

Cruickshank's Work with Cerebral Palsied Children

Cruickshank's Montgomery County Project

Kirk's *Illinois Test of Psycholinguistic Abilities*

Formation of Association for Children with Learning Disabilities

Formation of Division for Children with Learning Disabilities within Council for Exceptional Children

IDENTIFICATION OF POPULATION

Adults; Brain-Injured

Children; Exogenous (Presumed Brain-Injured); Retarded

Children; Brain-Injured; Normal in Intelligence

Children; Slow Learners; "Minimally Brain-Injured"; Hyperactive; Behavior Disordered; Emotionally Disturbed; Normal in Intelligence

Children; Learning Disabled; Normal in Intelligence

FIGURE 1.1.
*Major historical events in the evolution of the field of learning disabilities.*

applied behavior analysis,* an approach to measurement and remediation of specific disabilities and learning problems of children. The development of applied behavior analysis is, in our view, intimately related to the growth of the field of learning disabilities for three reasons. First, the application of applied behavior analysis to education can be viewed as an extension and elaboration of the highly structured, directive approach found by Strauss and Lehtinen (1947), Cruickshank et al. (1961), Zimmerman and Zimmerman (1962), Haring and Phillips (1962), and others to be successful with retarded, brain-injured, and emotionally disturbed children.** Second, current methods of applied behavior analysis have had a profound influence on the development of educational methodology for all handicapped children. Third, the concern of applied behavior analysis for specification of abilities is congruent with the emphasis of the field of learning disabilities. As we have already indicated, children considered mentally retarded, brain-injured, emotionally disturbed, slow learning, learning disabled, and so forth, share many common psychological and behavioral characteristics. These children are similar also in their responses to educational and behavior management techniques. Consequently, a synopsis of the growth of behavior modification methods in special education provides the basis for understanding sound educational methodology for children with learning disabilities, a behavioral theme to which we will return in each succeeding chapter.

Concurrently with and immediately following Cruickshank's Montgomery County Project with hyperactive and brain-injured children, other individuals were establishing similar educational procedures for emotionally disturbed children. In the late 1950s and early 1960s, Richard J. Whelan, a teacher and Director of Education at the Menninger Clinic's Southard School in Topeka, Kansas, was pioneering the use of a highly

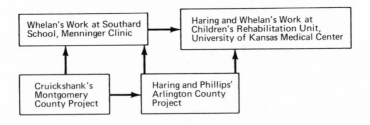

* The terms applied behavior analysis and behavior modification are considered synonymous.

** It is not being suggested here that these persons provided the foundation for the development of applied behavior analysis, but that a structured approach represented a simple application of the behavior principles expounded by B. F. Skinner and an elementary form of behavior modification methodology.

structured classroom environment for severely emotionally disturbed children. Over a period of about ten years, he had found that academic learning difficulties were a prominent feature of disturbed children's behavior and that academic progress was often a harbinger of significant change in the child's social and emotional behaviors (Whelan, 1974). In addition, he found that social and emotional disorders could profitably be viewed as learning problems and that, like academic behaviors, these problems could be resolved by carefully structuring the child's environment, as suggested by the work of B. F. Skinner and other pioneer behaviorists. As a result, Whelan formulated for emotionally disturbed children an educational program involving both behavior management and academic remediation. The earlier work and writing of Strauss, Lehtinen, and Cruickshank, as well as of Skinner, clearly influenced Whelan's work and so it is not surprising that he was later to join forces with one of Cruickshank's students.

The combined academic remediation-behavior management emphasis of a highly structured approach to teaching disturbed children was also evident in the Arlington County (Virginia) Project of Norris G. Haring and E. Lakin Phillips (Haring & Phillips, 1962). A student of Cruickshank's, Haring was greatly influenced in his thinking by the Montgomery County Project (Haring, 1974b). He and Phillips compared, in an experimental study, the relative efficacy of three types of classroom arrangements for emotionally disturbed children: (1) a regular classroom with consultative help for the regular classroom teacher; (2) a special class with a permissive (i.e., relatively nondirective, nonstructured) approach; and (3) a special, highly structured class patterned along many of the same dimensions prevalent in the classes of the Montgomery County Project. The Haring and Phillips study indicated that the highly structured approach was the most effective. "Highly structured" meant that the child's environment was very predictable and that academic tasks were carefully tailored to fit the child's level of achievement. Because many of the children with whom they worked exhibited emotional lability, poor work habits, and short spans of attention, emphasis was placed on appropriate conduct, task completion, gradually longer periods of attention to tasks, and positive consequences for the desired pupil responses. That their educational methods augured well for the evolution of an effective approach to teaching for all children, including those that today are labeled "learning disabled," was indicated by their description of a structured classroom: "A structured classroom is one in which clear direction, firm expectations, and consistent follow-through are paramount; this is presumably a healthy state of affairs for normal children, as well as necessary for optimal growth of emotionally disturbed children" (Haring & Phillips, 1962, p. 80).

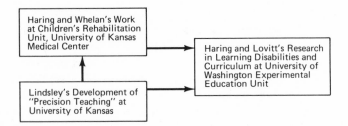

Beginning in 1962, Haring and Whelan worked together at the Children's Rehabilitation Unit of the Kansas University Medical Center. During several years of experimentation, they refined their ideas and created educational methods more firmly rooted in learning research (e.g., Haring & Whelan, 1965; Whelan & Haring, 1966; Whelan, 1966). Haring, in particular, was influenced by Ogden R. Lindsley, who also joined the Kansas University faculty in the early 1960s, and his functional analysis of behavior (e.g., Lindsley, 1964). Lindsley's techniques of measurement and analysis of behavior, which are known as "precision teaching," continue to influence the work of Haring and his colleagues at the University of Washington as well as many other educational researchers and practitioners. A student of Haring and Lindsley at Kansas University in the 1960s, Thomas C. Lovitt has been particularly instrumental in turning the methods of precision teaching and applied behavior analysis toward learning disabilities and curriculum research (e.g., Haring & Lovitt, 1967; Lovitt, 1967, 1968, 1970, 1973, 1973a, 1976). He, along with Haring and others at the University of Washington's Experimental Education Unit, have been focusing their attention recently upon ways in which instructional methods and remediation of academic deficits can be improved (Haring & Hayden, 1972; Lovitt, 1976).

Also during the 1960s, Frank M. Hewett was designing a systematic, structured educational program for children with learning and behavior problems (Hewett, 1974). His experiences at the Fernald School and the Neuropsychiatric Institute School at the University of California at Los Angeles supplied the foundation for his design of an "engineered classroom" in which basic learning principles are applied to the management

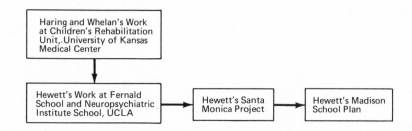

of behavior and to academic instruction. Hewett's Santa Monica Project (Hewett, 1968) involved the use of his engineered classroom approach with educationally handicapped children in public schools. Undoubtedly, the Montgomery County Project of Cruickshank et al., the Arlington Project of Haring and Phillips, the work of Haring and Whelan at Kansas, and the work of O. I. Lovaas at UCLA influenced Hewett's thinking. However, he appears to have come to many of his ideas independently, and he continues to find new techniques for using behavior modification principles in teaching educationally deficient children. Some of his more recent work has involved the "Madison Plan" (Hewett, Taylor, & Artuso, 1970), which includes methods for reintegrating educationally handicapped children with their normal peers.

The decade of the 1960s was a time in which a number of individuals in child psychology and child development made substantial contributions to the scientific analysis of behavior based on Skinner's work in operant conditioning (Skinner, 1953). Chief among these individuals were Donald M. Baer, Wesley C. Becker, Sidney W. Bijou, Jay Birnbrauer, R. Vance Hall, Todd R. Risley, and Montrose M. Wolf who, along with their colleagues at the Universities of Washington, Kansas, and Illinois, researched methods of teaching a variety of handicapped children, including the retarded, disturbed, and learning disabled (cf. Bijou & Baer, 1967; Risley & Baer, 1973). While it is true that many other persons were instrumental in the development of behavior modification in the 1960s and the interrelationships among behavior modifiers are quite complex (see Goodall, 1972), the individuals mentioned here were particularly important in the historical development of applied behavior analysis in special education (and the field of learning disabilities in particular) not only because of their obvious leadership as theoreticians and researchers (e.g., Becker, 1971, 1973; Bijou & Baer, 1961; Baer, Wolf, & Risley, 1968; Hall, 1971), but also because of their special interests in handicapped children and classroom applications of behavior principles. Their work certainly affected the thinking of Haring, Hewett, Lovitt, and Whelan. More important, however, is the fact that the work of these individuals has had a pervasive influence on the field of special education —it has delineated the methodology of applied behavior analysis and has included pioneer studies in which specific skills were taught to handicapped children of nearly every description.

The growth and development of behavioral methods from the relatively simple, structured approach of Cruickshank, Haring, and Whelan

> Baer, Becker, Bijou, Birnbrauer, Hall, Risley, and Wolf develop applied behavior analysis at University of Washington, University of Kansas, and University of Illinois

to the more precise behavior analysis methods now being applied with all types of handicapped children are depicted in Figure 1.2. It should be noted again that behavior management and instructional programming methods are not peculiar to children labeled mentally retarded, emotionally disturbed, or learning disabled (see also Bricker & Bricker, 1975; Lent, 1975). The basic principles and methods of applied behavior analysis and task analysis that apply across special education labels will be outlined in Chapter 5.

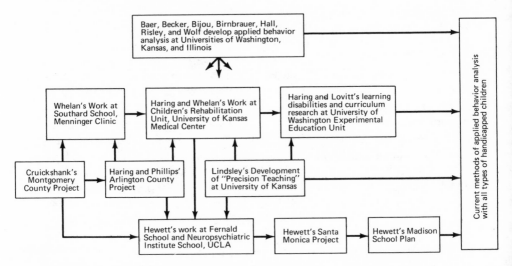

FIGURE 1.2.
*Several major developments in the behavioral approach to teaching emotionally disturbed and educationally handicapped children and the use of applied behavior analysis with exceptional children.**

* *This figure provides only a skeletal outline of some major developments and interrelationships. Numerous individuals and relationships have been omitted for the sake of clarity and simplicity.*

# Current Definitions
# and
# Prevalence

$2$

Taking into consideration the diversity of the services upon which the field of learning disabilities developed, it is not surprising that a number of "official" definitions have reached print. Two of the most frequently cited are those of the National Advisory Committee on Handicapped Children (1967) and Task Force II of the Minimal Brain Dysfunction National Project on Learning Disabilities in Children (1969). Both of these groups admirably performed the yeoman's task of compiling the points of view of numerous professionals and condensing them into concise statements.

According to the National Advisory Committee on Handicapped Children, learning disabilities may be defined in the following manner:

> Children with special learning disabilities exhibit a disorder in one or more of the basic psychological processes involved in understanding or in using spoken or written language. These may be manifested in disorders of listening, thinking, talking, reading, writing, spelling, or arithmetic. They include conditions which have been referred to as perceptual handicaps, brain injury, minimal brain dysfunction, dyslexia, developmental aphasia, etc. They do not include learning problems which are due primarily to visual, hearing, or motor handicaps, to mental retardation, emotional disturbance, or to environmental disadvantage.

In 1963, three task forces, supported by the collaborative sponsorship of several national agencies (Neurological and Sensory Disease

Control Program, Division of Regional Medical Programs, Health Services and Mental Health Administration, Department of Health, Education, and Welfare; Easter Seal Research Foundation, National Easter Seal Society for Crippled Children and Adults, Inc.; National Institute of Neurological Diseases and Stroke, National Institutes of Health; Bureau of Education for the Handicapped, U. S. Office of Education, Department of Health, Education, and Welfare) were formed to investigate a broad spectrum of issues germane to the new category of learning disabilities. These three task forces resulted in three documents—*Minimal Brain Dysfunction in Children: Terminology and Identification, Phase One of a Three-Phase Project* (1966), *Minimal Brain Dysfunction in Children: Educational, Medical and Health Related Services, Phase Two of a Three-Phase Project* (1969), and *Central Processing Dysfunctions in Children: A Review of Research* (1969). Task Force II proposed the following two definitions:

> Children with learning disabilities are those (1) who have educationally significant discrepancies among their sensory-motor, perceptual, cognitive, academic, or related developmental levels which interfere with the performance of educational tasks; (2) who may or may not show demonstrable deviation in central nervous system functioning; and (3) whose disabilities are not secondary to general mental retardation, sensory deprivation or serious emotional disturbance.
>
> Children with learning disabilities are those (1) who manifest an educationally significant discrepancy between estimated academic potential and actual level of academic functioning as related to dysfunctioning in the learning process; (2) may or may not show demonstrable deviation in central nervous system functioning; and (3) whose disabilities are not secondary to general mental retardation, cultural, sensory and/or educational deprivation or environmentally produced serious emotional disturbance.

Other definitions developed by various individuals in special education exist, but the above definitions proposed by national committees have done a remarkable job in including most of the major aspects of all of the definitions. The result has been that, while certain organizations and individuals may differ with regard to subtle nuances of the definition of learning disabilities, five major points are almost universally present in any definition. The learning disabled child: (a) has academic retardation, (b) has an uneven pattern of development, (c) may or may not have central nervous system dysfunctioning, (d) does not owe his learning problems to environmental disadvantage, and (e) does not owe his learning problems to mental retardation or emotional disturbance. Because of the importance of these five elements, a further look at each one is in order (see also Tarver & Hallahan, 1976).

## Academic Retardation

The most obvious characteristic assigned the learning disabled child is academic retardation. The term "retardation" here should not be confused with mental retardation. The adjective "academic" is crucial in that it indicates retardation of the child's ability to demonstrate knowledge of academic subject matter at a level commensurate with his intellectual ability.

There are basically two methods of determining if a child is achieving below his potential—informal and formal assessment procedures. Informal assessment involves spotting the discrepancy between the child's IQ score or scores and his standardized achievement test scores or in-class scores on academic subject tests. The fifth grader with an IQ of 100 and a third-grade reading ability might thus be considered academically retarded. Such a subjective method of determining the child's academic retardation is, of course, open to a substantial amount of error. What can be said of the fifth-grade child who has an IQ of 95 and is reading at the 4.3 grade level? In addition, though one might consider the second grader who is reading one year behind grade level to be academically retarded, would the eighth grader one year behind grade level be equally retarded academically?

Recognizing the problem of identifying learning disabled children on such a subjective basis, some individuals have suggested different methods of quantifying a child's achievement relative to his potential for achievement. The most commonly cited method of formal quantification of academic retardation has been proposed by Myklebust (1968). One first finds an expectancy age by using the following formula:

$$\frac{\text{Mental age} + \text{Life age} + \text{Grade age}}{3} = \text{Expectancy age}$$

Mental age is determined from an IQ test. The higher of the child's performance and verbal scores is used for the mental age component of the formula (Myklebust assumes the higher score gives a better reflection of the child's potential). The life age provides an indication of the child's physiological maturity based on chronological age. Grade age stands for the schooling experience of the child. Once obtained, the expectancy age provides an estimate of the child's potential for achievement. The grade level at which a child performs on a standardized achievement test then is divided by his expectancy age. This ratio between expectancy age and actual achievement age thus provides an index of a child's achievement relative to his potential. Myklebust has stated that an index of less than 90 is indicative of a learning disability.

Although they lend more objectivity to the specification of academic retardation than do informal methods based solely on subjective judgment, quantitative methods such as Myklebust's should not be used uncritically. In the first place, the values placed in the formula are dependent upon the reliability and validity of the intelligence and achievement test administered to the child. There are, also, certain unproven assumptions that must be made in using Myklebust's formula. First, one must assume that the higher of the two IQ scores (verbal and performance) gives the true indication of the individual's potential. Also, the formula assumes that the three components of mental age, life age, and grade age are of equal importance. Additionally, as Lerner (1971) has pointed out, the technique

> is not useful for the preschool youngster or the first-grade child who has not yet learned to read, since an achievement score is required by the formula. Such techniques have also been criticized because they neglect many important variables such as background, environment, language, motivation, and psychodynamics. Nevertheless, there are many times when such methods are helpful in making decisions. (p. 65)

It should be kept in mind that a particular strength of a method such as Myklebust's is that it is also applicable to individuals who have been classified as mentally retarded, or even gifted. The IQ level of the child is not a factor. As will be seen in the next chapter, a child can achieve below expectancy regardless of the level of his intelligence test score.

### Uneven Pattern of Development

Because learning disabled children are often purported to exhibit wide discrepancies among various areas of functioning, another common characteristic ascribed to them in most definitions is a large degree of variance in abilities. For example, a child may score very low in arithmetic ability and oral language skills in comparison to perceptual-motor development and reading ability.

One of the first individuals to point out this characteristic of uneven developmental patterns was Gallagher (1966). At a seminar called by Cruickshank (1966), Gallagher, in considering the concept of the brain-injured child, proposed the concept of "developmental imbalances" to replace the then popular term "brain injured." Arguing that a more behavioral definition was warranted, he noted that "developmental imbalances" would suggest the frequently described irregular development of brain-injured children. Noting the problem of using a definition that encompasses the wide range of manifested behavioral characteristics, Gallagher stated:

> One way out of this dilemma is to focus on a definition of ability patterns rather than of specific abilities.
>
> > *Children with Developmental Imbalances are those who reveal a developmental disparity in psychological processes related to education of such a degree (often four years or more) as to require the instructional programming of developmental tasks appropriate to the nature and level of the deviant developmental process. . . .*
>
> This present definition parts company with many that have previously been attempted for these unusual children. The emphasis here is on behavior and patterns of development, with fewer assumptions about the neurological etiology. (p. 28)

When the field of learning disabilities developed from work by individuals concerned with the education of brain-injured children, this concept of developmental imbalance was incorporated into the standard definitions (Gallagher, 1976).

A common way of looking at developmental imbalances involves the use of the Illinois Test of Psycholinguistic Abilities. Because it is divided into supposedly discrete areas of ability which can easily be placed on an ability profile, this test is frequently used to look at patterns of ability.

### May or May Not Have
### Central Nervous System Dysfunction

The "may or may not have" and "dysfunction" included in the wording of this characteristic are of crucial importance. Probably no other concern has caused more debate and controversy than has the issue of whether or not children with learning disabilities have suffered brain injury. As indicated in the discussion of the historical precursors to the development of the field of learning disabilities, some of the germinal work resulting in the emergence of this field was done with children known to have brain injury (e.g., Cruickshank et al., 1957) or presumed to have brain injury (e.g., Strauss & Lehtinen, 1947). Once it began to be recognized that some children of normal or near-normal intelligence also exhibited behavioral characteristics similar to those of brain-injured children, the concept of *minimal* brain damage (MBD) gained acceptance. Those children who exhibited the same abnormal behavioral characteristics, but to a lesser extent than children with a high probability of brain damage, were referred to as having *minimal* brain damage. Because the behavioral deviations were more subtle, the injury to the brain was considered to be of lesser severity.

The general popularity of the term "minimal brain damage," however, was of relatively short duration. Educators, psychologists, and many pediatric neurologists themselves (Birch, 1964) became uncomfortable because of the way in which MBD was diagnosed. The term "minimal" was reserved for the children in whom no definite diagnosis of brain injury could be ascertained but in whom there were a number of "soft" neurological signs. Soft neurological signs—subtle deviations in sensory and motor functioning—are, unfortunately, primarily behavioral in nature. In other words, MBD is described on the basis of a child's exhibiting slight deviations in behavior which, when grossly deviant, are the result of brain injury. When one is cognizant of the unreliability of even the more "hard" signs of brain damage (Werry, 1972), one recognizes a great gap in the inferential leap from the behavior of a child to brain damage as the cause of that behavior. (In fact, neurological procedures still remain so crude that autopsy affords the only fairly certain method of diagnosing brain injury.)

Besides the recognition of the fallibility of soft neurological signs, a substantial contribution to the demise of the acceptance of the concept of MBD was the increase in popularity of the behavioral school of thought. With their disdain for the usefulness of medical etiologies and their emphasis on the specific behaviors of children with learning problems, the behaviorists brought attention to the importance of behaviors over causes. Occurring almost simultaneously with the decline in popularity of the MBD label, the upsurge of interest in the behavioral orientation no doubt influenced the swift change in focus in the learning disabilities field to specific behaviors regardless of etiology.

The term "dysfunction," too, reflects a softening of the neurological position. "Dysfunction" does not specify whether there is actual tissue damage but that the brain is malfunctioning in some way. The problem, then, becomes one of whether one wishes to believe that the "dysfunctioning" causes the abnormal behavior or merely coincides with it or is really caused by it.

In considering the term "dysfunction," most authorities have given it causal status, as depicted in Figure 2.1. What this means is that because of some malfunctioning (which may or may not be the result of tissue damage) of the brain the child exhibits deviant instead of appropriate behavior. Also plausible, however, is the possibility that behavioral abnormalities caused by environmental stimulus events—for example, poor learning experiences—then result in brain dysfunctioning (See Figure 2.1b). There is no denying the fact that, when a child exhibits behavior, this behavior in *some* way is represented in activity in the brain. In this

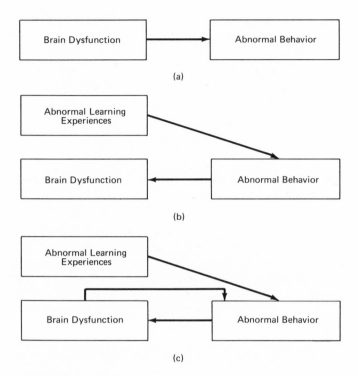

FIGURE 2.1.
Possible relationships among brain dysfunction, abnormal
behavior, and abnormal learning experiences.

sense, then, a child could behave abnormally due to the influence of an
environmental event, and the resultant activity of the brain therefore
would not be normal. That this hypothesized dysfunctioning due to abnormal behavior could then take on causal power of its own (See Figure
2.1c), while even more speculative, is still a possibility. The effects of
differential environmental events on brain chemistry and structure have
been demonstrated with rats. Rosenzweig (1966) found that rats placed
in stimulus "enriched" cages (e.g., numerous paraphernalia for exploratory activity), when compared with those in cages devoid of stimuli,
were found to have thicker cortexes and more acetylcholine, a chemical
intimately connected with the transformation of information in learning.
In other words, through manipulation of the physical environment of the
rats, changes were brought about in the tissue of the rats' brains. Although it is difficult to apply results on lower animals to humans, Rosenzweig's results are provocative.

    With regard to consideration of neurological insult, it is safe to say that former emphasis on the possible neurological aspects of learning disabilities is giving way to a more behavioral orientation. Teachers in particular have begun to recognize that, while etiological considerations due to possible brain injury are of critical research interest, day-to-day educational programming must rely upon the observable *behavioral* characteristics of their students.

### Not Due to Environmental Disadvantage

This exclusion clause, present in most definitions of learning disabilities, reflects an unfortunate situation that could deprive thousands of disadvantaged children of appropriate educational services. All available research data generally support the position that children from poor backgrounds are more likely than middle-class children to exhibit behaviors similar to those of learning disabled individuals. In particular, there is some evidence that the characteristics of poor attention, distractibility, impulsivity, and hyperactivity are displayed more frequently by economically disadvantaged children (Hallahan, 1970; Hess & Shipman, 1968; Klaus & Gray, 1968; Kohlberg, 1968; Schwebel, 1966; Zucker & Stricker, 1968). Too, some data suggest learning disabilities of the disadvantaged could be due to poor learning environments or to central nervous system dysfunctioning due to poor health care. Hallahan and Cruickshank (1973), for example, have reviewed the research literature on malnutrition and undernutrition and have concluded that either of these two variables could singly, or in interaction with a poor environment, cause learning disabilities.

Aside from the large data base pointing to the fact that learning disabled children can be found among the disadvantaged (and a considerable body of data can be used to argue that there are proportionately higher numbers of such children among the poor than among the nonpoor), the exclusion of disadvantaged children from the definition is illogical. The only statement with regard to etiology within the standard definitions of learning disabilities says that these children may or may not have central nervous system dysfunctioning. For those who do not have CNS dysfunctioning, what etiological alternatives remain? The most obvious, and the most frequently cited, posits that environmental circumstances are somehow responsible. If, when no organic cause can be specified, *environmental* circumstances are referred to as a causative agent in learning disabilities, then why cannot learning disabilities, in some instances, be caused by *environmental* deprivation? Anyone rejecting the latter possibility would have to defend the absurd position that environmental stimuli and events make a difference in terms of intellectual functioning for middle-class but not for lower-class children.

Not Due to Mental Retardation
or Emotional Disturbance

The exclusion of mentally retarded and emotionally disturbed children superficially appears to represent an appropriate distinction. It is, however, a major theme of this book that the similarities among the three areas of emotional disturbance, educable mental retardation, and learning disabilities far outweigh the differences. This chapter has referred to the influence of the first two fields upon the historical evolution of the third; the next chapter details the overlap of the three areas.

## DEFINITION OF LEARNING DISABILITIES
## BY THE PROJECT
## ON THE CLASSIFICATION OF CHILDREN

A newly formed definition which will undoubtedly have an impact is that which has emerged from the national Project on the Classification of Exceptional Children under the direction of Nicholas Hobbs. This project was funded by a number of national agencies in response to the growing concern over misdiagnosis and misclassification of various kinds of exceptional children. The committee concerned with the classification of learning disabilities has written a new definition which limits the number and types of children identified as learning disabled (Wepman, Cruickshank, Deutsch, Morency, & Strother, 1975). The definition they propose is the following:

> ᵥ Specific learning disability, as defined here, refers to those children of any age who demonstrate a substantial deficiency in a particular aspect of academic achievement because of perceptual or perceptual-motor handicaps, regardless of etiology or other contributing factors. The term perceptual as used here relates to those mental (neurological) processes through which the child acquires his basic alphabets of sounds and forms. (Wepman et al., 1975, p. 306)

The above definition places the emphasis upon *perceptual* functioning. The rationale behind this approach is that, as we discussed in Chapter 1, the forefathers of learning disabilities concentrated primarily on perceptual disturbances. While we see no problems whatsoever in using the description in the above definition in order to identify a category of exceptional children, it would be more direct to consider the above as a definition of *"perceptual* disabilities." Then perceptual disabilities could be considered as a subset, admittedly a large subset, of *learning* disabilities. If the term *learning* disability is to remain in use, we believe it accurate to refer to all instances of impaired learning whether they can be traced to perceptual problems or not. Most learning problems may be perceptual in nature, but there are theoretical difficulties in attempting to determine, for example, whether poor memory, hyperactivity, distractibility, and poor language production have a perceptual basis or not. They do, however, inhibit learning.

## THE DEFINITION OF LEARNING DISABILITIES
## USED IN THIS BOOK

The definition we have developed *for the purposes of this book* is broader than that proposed by the Wepman committee or any of the other officially recognized definitions. We do agree with the Wepman committee's position that a learning disability should be identified "regardless of etiology or other contributing factors." In the next chapter we present our rationale for the position that a child falling under the traditional classification of mild emotional disturbance or educable retardation can still be considered to have a learning disability.

In a paper presented to the International Federation of Learning Disabilities we have proposed the following definition:

> In attempting to formulate a definition of learning disabilities, it is our conviction that one must keep in mind the generic nature of this term. There are many different kinds of learning disabilities. For example, there are those which are primarily perceptual in nature taking in the various sensory modalities of vision, audition, and tactual and kinesthetic development. There are also learning disabilities related to attentional development. There are also learning disabilities related to language production. There are also learning disabilities related to social development. The list is endless. If this organization keeps the title of learning disabilities, then, it must recognize that it is dealing with a heterogeneous population of children. A group, which we *must* stress again, is not limited to children of normal intelligence. It is, thus, our suggestion that, *if the term learning disabilities is the one to be used, that it be used to refer to learning problems found in children who have traditionally been classified as mildly handicapped, whether it be emotionally disturbed, mildly retarded, or learning disabled.*
>
> Some may believe there is danger in so broad a definition as the one we propose. We do not believe there is if it is understood from the start that the term is broad. Where dangers arise in definitions in the field of special education is when people are led to believe that a definition has specificity when, indeed, it does not.
>
> Recognizing the breadth of this umbrella-like definition, then, it would behoove the teacher or researcher to specify further the particular child

or group of children with whom he is dealing. If he is referring to children who exhibit an across-the-board retardation in development, the term "general learning disability," as suggested by Dunn (1973) could meaningfully be applied. However, given what research indicates about the great variability of learning abilities even among students given the label "mildly mentally retarded," it is our considered opinion that this appellation will apply to relatively few children. If, on the other hand, one is referring to children with significant learning deficits only in specific areas, "specific learning disability" would be a more appropriate label. However, this term is totally meaningless unless a description of the specific learning disability is appended as, for example, "specific learning disability in remembering the spelling of words," or "specific learning disability in arithmetic." Obviously, many children could then acquire multiple labels, but with such a degree of behavioral specificity the labels would perhaps be less pejorative and facilitate communication among professionals and lay persons alike.

We, thus, hope that the field of learning disabilities will move toward adopting a definition that recognizes the heterogeneity of the population of children considered learning disabled. And we further, and most importantly, hope that under this broader definition there will be subsumed subgroups or subtypes of learning disabilities based upon specific behavioral deficits.

If we are going to group children, why *not* teach them grouped together because each one has, for example, an attention span of approximately 30 seconds for arithmetic problems of a certain type? Does this not make more sense than to place children together because they all have IQs somewhere over 71 and all have reading and arithmetic disabilities of some unspecified character?

It would, of course, be more difficult to group children according to specific behavioral deficits. It should be kept in mind, however, that leaders in the areas of precision teaching and operant conditioning are showing us that such precise measurement of specific behaviors can be done (see Kauffman, 1975a, for a review of behavior modification with learning disabled children). (Hallahan & Kauffman, 1975)

## THE PREVALENCE OF LEARNING DISABILITIES

Within all areas of special education, it is generally quite difficult to arrive at accurate prevalence estimates. Different sources come to different conclusions regarding the incidence of various categories of exceptional children. The single greatest problem in determining how many children, or what proportion of children, might have a particular behavioral exceptionality revolves around the difficulty involved in finding a common definition that everyone can agree to. The greater the amount of disagreement as to what constitutes a particular area of exceptionality the more varied will be the estimates of the numbers of children in that category. Because of the inordinate amount of confusion with regard to the criteria used to classify children as learning disabled, the prevalence estimates are the most diverse of all of the categories of special education. Consequently, it is not uncommon to hear or see estimates as low as 1 percent and as high as 30 percent of school-age children.

In two of the most "official" statements regarding prevalence, the National Advisory Committee on Handicapped Children (1968) estimated that 1 to 3 percent of schoolchildren are learning disabled and the United States Office of Education (1971) estimated that 1 percent of the school population evidenced learning disabilities. While less official but, perhaps, based more firmly on empirical data, Myklebust and Boshes (1969) screened a large population of public-school children. Using a cutoff score of 90 on Myklebust's Learning Quotient, they found that 15 percent of the children were learning disabled. When the cutoff score was lowered to 85 on any one test, the percentage fell to around 7. McIntosh and Dunn (1973) have reported a number of other studies pertinent to the prevalence issue.

> The Rocky Mountain Education Laboratory study (Meier, 1971) found approximately 15 percent of the children were two years or more below grade expectancy on various screening instruments; 6 percent were two years or more below using both screening and more precise educational diagnosis; and 4.7 percent were two years or more below using screening and medical diagnosis.
>
> . . . the U. S. Department of Health, Education and Welfare (1969) stated that 13.3 percent of the school population were underachieving in reading. Newbrough and Kelly (1962) cited a somewhat similar figure, namely, that 14 percent of a school population was achieving in reading two years below grade level. However, Bruinincks and Weatherman (1970) found only 5.8 percent of the school population to be two grades below expectancy in reading. (pp. 540–541)

It is obvious from the above that the professionals within learning disabilities are quite undecided regarding how many children should be identified as learning disabled. It should be kept in mind that the most accepted estimates are based on a definition of learning disabilities that excludes children who would also be classified as emotionally disturbed, educable mentally retarded, or economically disadvantaged. Without these exclusion clauses (and it is probably these exclusion clauses that make it so difficult to arrive at any kind of precise estimate of a purely learning disabled population), the prevalence estimates would increase greatly.

# Learning Disabilities versus Emotional Disturbance versus Educable Mental Retardation

# 3

The greatest amount of confusion with regard to the definition of learning disabilities involves the differentiation of children with learning disabilities from children categorized as emotionally disturbed or mentally retarded. The main reason for this difficulty should be clear by now. As indicated in Figure 1.1, children now identified as learning disabled display many psychological characteristics similar to those of children identified as mentally retarded and emotionally disturbed. Furthermore, ten years ago the children who now are educated in learning disabilities classes most likely would have been placed in classes for the emotionally disturbed and, less frequently, in classes for the educable mentally retarded. The two basic areas of concern with the greatest overlap among the three categories of learning disabilities (LD), emotional disturbance (ED), and educable mental retardation (EMR) are (a) etiological factors and (b) teaching methods.

## COMMUNALITY OF ETIOLOGICAL FACTORS

In terms of discovering causal factors, the state of the art is exceedingly similar for all three of these fields of special education. For the great majority of children identified as learning disabled, emotionally disturbed, and educable mentally retarded there is no known cause of the condition. It is generally estimated, for example, that around 80 percent of all educable retarded children fall into the "unknown causes" etiological category. Although no specific percentage figures have been advanced for the categories of emotional disturbance and learning disabilities, the literature generally supports the notion that no specific etiological agents can be identified in the vast majority of cases. Nevertheless, it makes little sense to adopt the nihilistic stance that there *are* no causes of these conditions. These high figures of cases of "unknown causes" no doubt reflect the current lack of sophistication in the measurement of neurological status, genetic transferral, and poor learning experiences. While in the large proportion of cases an etiological agent or agents cannot be *proven,* there are theorists in LD, ED, and EMR who hold particular points of view with regard to the etiology of children falling into the "unknown causes" category. The three most frequently espoused theories are that the cause is due to heredity, environment, or some combination of the two. No solid proof, however, has been forwarded for any of these three causal agents; and, therefore, the etiological factor or factors are considered unknown.

Among the so-called known causes of ED, LD, and EMR (it is actually more honest and accurate to refer to them as causal theories rather than assign them the status of "known" causes), the most frequently cited are those due to inadequate or pathological environmental experiences. With regard to etiology, all three conditions of exceptionality rely heavily upon this category. Among the most avid supporters of the position that the environmental history of the child is important in shaping his future behavior are the behaviorists, who ascribe the utmost importance to the opportunities the child has for appropriate learning and reinforcement experience during childhood (e.g., Bijou, 1971). Briefly stated, the behaviorist view posits that all behavior is learned and that learning takes place as the result of the consequent reinforcement or punishment of behaviors. Emotional disturbance (Ferster, 1961; Haring & Phillips, 1962), learning disabilities (Lovitt, 1967; Wallace & Kauffman, 1973), and mental retardation (Bijou, 1971) have all been considered by various authors within this behavioral framework. In other words, no one of the categories of ED, LD, and EMR is unique with regard to consideration of environmental events as causal agents of the condition. It is evident that environmental conditions can result in emotional disturbance, learning disabilities, or mental retardation.

Another etiological agent thought in some cases to be involved in producing ED, LD, or EMR is that of brain injury. There are, indeed, some children classified as ED, LD, or EMR who evidence strong indications of being brain injured. Insult to the central nervous system can and sometimes does result in emotional disturbance, learning disabilities, or educable mental retardation (it should be noted that brain injury is an even more frequent cause of retardation in the lower levels of retardation than it is in the educable range). Thus, no differentiation can be made among the three categories of ED, LD, or EMR based on the etiological agent of brain injury. Furthermore, there is as yet no evidence to suggest that different degrees of brain damage or damage to specific parts of the brain could be associated differentially with the resultant condition of ED, LD, or EMR. This fact, however, does not rule out the possibility that future research will find a relationship between specific kinds and loci of brain injury and the three conditions of exceptionality under discussion.

Genetic contributions to ED, LD, and EMR are also cited in the literature. Within the area of emotional disturbance, for example, there is increasing interest in the role of genetics in the development of behavior disorders (Bakwin & Bakwin, 1972). However, attempts to delineate precisely the function of hereditary mechanisms in emotional disturbance have not met with great success (cf. Kallman, 1956; Meehl, 1962). It is known that there is some relationship between heredity and the development of severe disorders such as schizophrenia or autism, but the nature and extent of that relationship are not clear. Genetic contributions to mild emotional disorders are even more obscure.

There has also been a renewed interest in a possible hereditary basis of mental retardation. Once almost totally ignored by those with an interest in mental retardation, the genetic study of mental retardation has recently begun to flourish. Much of this genetic research has been given its impetus from Arthur Jensen's controversial *Harvard Educational Review* article, "How Much Can We Boost IQ and Scholastic Achievement?" (Jensen, 1969), wherein the author contends that blacks do poorly on intelligence tests due to their particular genetic make-up. Although this paper caused a bona fide crisis in the behavioral sciences, because it generated an interest in the relationship between heredity and intelligence, it did serve to draw attention to the fact that much significant work is being done in the genetics of mental retardation. Certain varieties of mental retardation—phenylketonuria (PKU), Down's syndrome, Turner's syndrome, and Jacob's syndrome, for example—are now understood to occur through genetic transmission (Vandenberg, 1971). Even though most of the mentally retarded children in whom retardation is *known* to be genetic in origin are in the very lower ranges of intelligence, some of these individuals do score within the educable range—the level of intelligence with which we are concerned in our discussion here. With regard to children who generally fall within the educable mentally retarded range of intelligence, however, there is a much more tentative relationship established between heredity and lowered IQ.

Sporadic interest has grown over the years in the possible genetic basis of learning disabled children and children who would now be categorized as learning disabled. Orton (1937), an early authority in reading disabilities, postulated that mixed dominance (e.g., right-eyed and left-handed preference) was an inherited trait responsible for reading disabilities. Much of the theoretical justification for the causal role of mixed dominance came from the speculation that reading reversals (e.g., reading "was" for "saw," *b* for *d*) were the result of what was supposed to be the subdominant hemisphere of the brain (wherein the mirror image of the word was stored) dominating what was supposed to be the dominant hemisphere (wherein the true word was stored). Individuals with mixed dominance or unestablished dominance would thus experience reversals due to the occasional "take-over" of the subdominant hemisphere.

Little support has been generated for Orton's theory concerning mixed dominance, but his suggestion of a genetic basis for reading disabilities has prompted continued research efforts. Two such studies have used the behavioral scientist's classic technique of investigating hereditary factors—twin studies. By comparing the similarity of behaviors between monozygotic twins (identical, or twins from the same egg and hence with the same basic genetic material) and between dizygotic (fraternal, or two-egg twins), one then estimates the strength of genetic factors. For example, if there is more concordance on a psychological trait in monozygotic twins than in dizygotic twins, it is frequently inferred that heredity influences the particular psychological trait. Owen, Adams, Forrest, Stolz, and Fisher (1971) have reviewed two available twin studies on reading disabled children:

> A different approach to the study of genetic etiology is available through twin studies that compare frequencies of disorders in monozygotic and dizygotic twins. Hallgren (1950) . . . and Norrie (1959) have both published such data . . . [I]n the three pairs of Hallgren's identical twins there was concordance; but there was concordance in only one of his three pairs of fraternal twins. Norrie reported concordance in all nine identical twin pairs but in only 10 of the 30 fraternal twins. Since all of the monozygotic twins in these studies showed concordance, we may speculate that heredity is a critical etiological factor in certain types of learning disorders. (Owen et al., 1971, p. 2)

It should be emphasized that, as Owen and his colleagues stated, the foregoing hypothesis is merely speculation. As numerous authorities have stated (Bijou, 1971; Ginsberg & Laughlin, 1971; Gordon, 1971; Vandenberg, 1971), it is difficult to draw definitive conclusions from twin studies. One of the problems, for example, is that parents, peers, teachers, and other significant people in the child's environment, and the identical twins, themselves, may create more similar environments for the

identical twins than for the fraternal twins. Hence, environmental variables cannot be ruled out as causal factors. Evidence is accumulating,
however, that learning disorders do tend "to run" in families (Owen et
al., 1971; Walker & Cole, 1965). How much this tendency is due to
genetics or to environmental influence awaits further research. The possibility of a hereditary influence certainly cannot be ruled out.

## COMMUNALITY OF TEACHING METHODS

As demonstrated in the historical flow charts of Chapter 1, many of the
teaching methods used today with the learning disabled have been, and
continue to be, used with the mentally retarded and the emotionally
disturbed. While many of the advertisements for methods books and
educational materials would have us believe that the emotionally disturbed, the learning disabled, and the mentally retarded require very
different materials, the fact of the matter is that close scrutiny will reveal
a great deal of concordance among the needs of the three groups. Furthermore, the competent teacher soon finds out that what worked for his
class of educable mentally retarded last year in New York City is also
working this year for his learning disabled students in Steubenville. Too,
if he decides next year to take that Punxsutawney teaching position with
the emotionally disturbed, he will be wise to approach his class within
the same general educational frame of reference. School administrators,
also, should soon discover that in filling a position for the learning
disabilities class, the best choice would be a former successful teacher
of the educable mentally retarded or emotionally disturbed rather than
a former mediocre teacher of the learning disabled.

The strongest case for the communality of effective instruction for
the emotionally disturbed, learning disabled, and mentally retarded can
be found within the behaviorist position. The advocate of behavior modification is not concerned with the diagnostic label of the child but, instead, is concerned with the behavioral characteristics of the child.
Everything else being equal, the ED hyperactive child with a figure-
ground reversal problem, the LD hyperactive child with a figure-ground
reversal problem, and the EMR hyperactive child with a figure-ground
reversal problem will all be taught in the same manner. The behaviors
exhibited, and not the diagnostic category in which the child has been
placed, are the crucial variables on which the teaching strategy should
hinge. The behavioral position is discussed further in Chapter 5.

## POINTS OF DIFFERENCE AMONG
## LEARNING DISABILITIES, EMOTIONAL DISTURBANCE,
## AND EDUCABLE MENTAL RETARDATION

At this point the reader may be wondering if there are *any* differences among the ED, LD, and EMR. As discussed above, existing research supports the position that these groups cannot be differentiated on the basis of etiological agents. In addition, the teaching methods employed for all three groups overlap extensively. Since the teaching methods are (or should be) primarily based upon the particular behavioral character-istics of each child, it therefore follows that many of the same behavioral characteristics are evidenced within all three categories of exceptionality under consideration. It can safely be stated, for example, that, with the exception of the lower IQ of the EMRs, no behaviors are specific to any of the three conditions. If one considers that mental age more than the IQ of the child is what should determine the teaching strategy, then even the IQ difference between the EMRs and the ED and LD children can be viewed as of trivial importance. In other words, *everything else being equal,* * two children with mental ages of ten would be taught very similarly even if one had a chronological age of ten (hence, an IQ of 100) and the other had a chronological age of fourteen (therefore, an IQ of 71). This is true even if one assumes that a faster rate of learning can be expected for the child of higher IQ.

Some subtle differences do arise in the *frequency* with which certain behaviors are exhibited in ED, LD, and EMR populations. In other words, though there is a great deal of overlap in the behavioral characteristics of ED, LD, and EMR children, certain behaviors or aspects of behavior are displayed *more often* in one area than in the other.

The Venn diagrams in Figure 3.1 serve to illustrate hypothesized relationships among the three classifications of exceptionality in terms of etiology, teaching methods, and behavioral characteristics. The particular areas within the circles should not be taken literally, but should be construed to indicate the *approximate* relationships among the classifica-tions and to provide a frame of reference within which to consider the differentiation of ED, LD, and EMR.

What Figure 3.1 shows is that within the domain of kinds of etiologies (Figure 3.1a), kinds of teaching methods (Figure 3.1b), and kinds of behavioral characteristics (Figure 3.1c) there are little, if any, differences among ED, LD, and EMR children (especially when the

---

* A viewpoint—the developmental orientation—becoming popular within the area of mental retardation, is that, in fact, everything else *is* equal between the educable mentally retarded and normal children when the two are of equal mental age (Zigler, 1969).

EMR are equated with the other two on mental age). With regard to the frequency of certain behaviors, there are some differences (Figure 3.1d). These differences, however, have to be regarded within the framework of the extensive overlap of these three classifications. This latter statement is illustrated by the fact that the area within 3.1d-7, wherein ED, LD, and EMR overlap, is greater than each of the areas, 3.1d-2, 3.1d-4, and 3.1d-6, wherein ED overlaps with EMR, LD overlaps with EMR, and

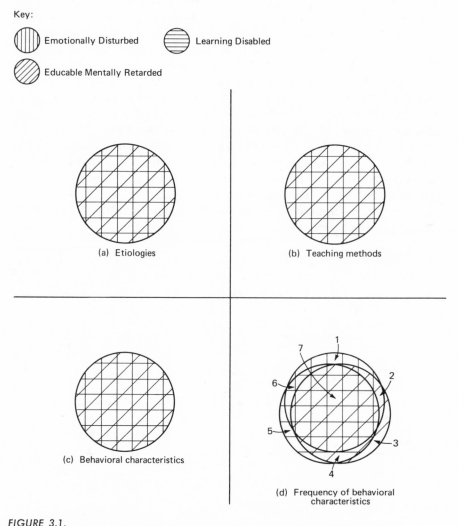

Key:

Emotionally Disturbed    Learning Disabled

Educable Mentally Retarded

(a) Etiologies

(b) Teaching methods

(c) Behavioral characteristics

(d) Frequency of behavioral characteristics

*FIGURE 3.1.*

*Venn diagrams illustrating the similarities and differences among the conditions of emotional disturbance, learning disabilities, and educable mental retardation.*

ED overlaps with LD. In turn, each one of these areas of concordance is greater than any one of the areas that represents behavioral characteristics unique to that particular exceptionality, 3.1d-1 for ED, 3.1d-3 for EMR, and 3.1d-5 for LD.

Figures 3.2 through 3.5, which delineate further the relationships represented in Figure 3.1d, depict the current thinking on the differentiation of ED, LD, and EMR children with regard to the frequency with which certain behavioral characteristics can be attributed to each of the populations. (The hypothetical means and ranges for these figures are represented by circles and lines respectively.) The four major areas of behavior in Figures 3.2 through 3.5—IQ, pattern of development, adaptability of social-emotional behavior, and academic retardation—have been considered on a continuum. Figure 3.2, for example, shows the relationship of each of the three conditions of exceptionality with measured IQ. As stated previously, IQ is one variable that, *by definition*, separates the EMR group from the other two groups. There is, however, total overlap on this variable between the ED and LD areas. Even the differentiation of the EMR group on IQ should be looked at in terms of the utility of such a differentiation. It can be seriously questioned what educational and psychological relevance exists when one child has an IQ of 90 and the other one of 70 if in all other ways the two children are essentially equal. The distinction becomes even more questionable if the child with the IQ of 70 has a higher chronological age and hence represents approximately the same mental age.

Figure 3.3 does indicate, however, one way in which mental retardation is frequently distinguished from emotional disturbance and learning disabilities. Descriptive and clinical literature often states that

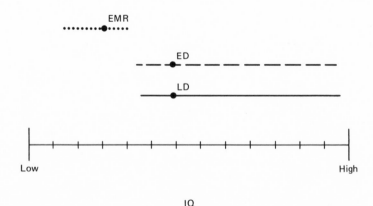

*FIGURE 3.2.*

Comparison of IQ among educable mentally retarded, emotionally disturbed, and learning disabled populations.

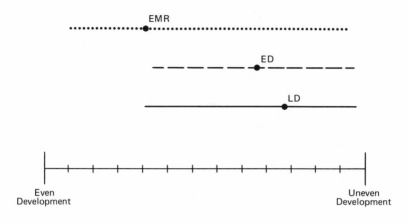

Patterns of Ability

*FIGURE 3.3.*
*Comparison of patterns of ability among educable mentally retarded,*
*emotionally disturbed, and learning disabled populations.*

mentally retarded children are uniformly low in almost all aspects of development. Emotionally disturbed, and especially learning disabled children, on the other hand, frequently are considered to be low in some types of ability but high in others. It should be noted that these assumptions about differences in patterns of ability have been forwarded with very little research evidence to back them up. It may actually be that there is even more overlap among the three categories on this behavioral characteristic. In other words, ED and EMR children may also demonstrate an extremely varied pattern of development. Hence, Figure 3.3 represents only the current popular thinking on the subject. A study by O'Grady (1974) comparing ED, LD, and normals on the ITPA found the EDs and LDs not to differ. Furthermore, there was no pattern specific to either area.

Another popular way of distinguishing the three groups involves behaviors indicative of social-emotional adjustment (Figure 3.4). Emotionally disturbed children are defined by the degree of maladjustment they exhibit. The literature, however, also supports the notion that learning disabled and mentally retarded children exhibit poor interpersonal relationships. Thus, the distinction among the groups, particularly between ED and LD children, is a fuzzy one.

Figure 3.5 shows the final category of behavior under consideration —academic retardation—and the degree to which children in each of the three classifications are reported to exhibit this characteristic. Learning disabled children are, by definition, achieving below their expected potential. Evidence indicates that the mentally retarded and emotionally

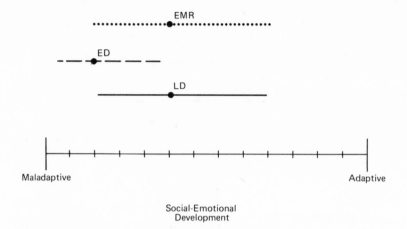

FIGURE 3.4.
Comparison of social-emotional development among educable mentally retarded, emotionally disturbed, and learning disabled populations.

disturbed also do not achieve in school subjects at a level comparable with their measured intelligence (Kirk, 1964). In the classic study of Morse, Cutler, and Fink (1964) of public school classes for the emotionally disturbed, they found that the single most distinguishing characteristic of emotionally disturbed children was underachievement. In addition, there is a substantial amount of evidence to indicate that

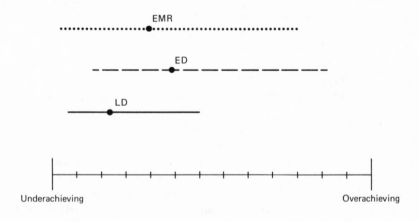

FIGURE 3.5.
Comparison of academic achievement among educable mentally retarded, emotionally disturbed, and learning disabled populations.

educable retardates are underachievers (Blake, Aaron, & Westbrook, 1969; Meyen & Hieronymous, 1970; Schwarz, 1969; Schwarz & Cook, 1971). Figure 3.5 thus reflects the position that there is extensive overlap among the EDs, LDs, and EMRs with regard to academic achievement.

As illustrated by Figure 3.1d, the continua of Figures 3.2 through 3.5 further emphasize the fact that the degree of overlap is substantially greater than the degree of behavioral uniqueness. Another, more concrete, way of stating this is that, in general, most ED children behave similarly to LD and EMR children, most LD children behave similarly to ED and EMR children, and most EMR children behave similarly to ED and LD children. These children, therefore, cannot be neatly categorized into discrete groups, a fact which has obvious ramifications in terms of special class placement. The presently fashionable practice of placing children on the basis of their diagnostic category does not have the logical appeal possessed by grouping in terms of behavioral characteristics.

## LEARNING DISABILITIES
## AS A BEHAVIORAL CONCEPT

Is there, then, any justification for the establishment of special classes specifically for the learning disabled, specifically for the emotionally disturbed, and specifically for the educably mentally retarded? The answer to that question must be negative if one strives to operate an efficient and pedagogically sound educational program for exceptional children.

Of what use, it may be asked, is the term "learning disabilities"? It is, we believe, of the *utmost* utility if used as a concept rather than as a category. Literally, "learning disabilities" is a term indicating *learning problems in one or more areas of development or ability,* and this definition is common to ED, LD, and EMR alike. Because children placed in each of these categories all have learning problems, "learning disabilities" can provide a much needed unifying theme whose emphasis is upon the specific behavior, abilities, and disabilities of the child. Overworked verbally, though underworked in practice, is the established maxim that it behooves the teacher to be aware of *individual differences.* Children have different abilities, disabilities, and patterns of these abilities and disabilities. Not really until the advent of the "learning disabilities specialist" was anything but lip service paid to the concept of individual differences. What must now be achieved is the application of this concept in its purest form to all children with learning problems, regardless of the diagnostic classification of those children.

The concept of "learning disabilities," and the professionals currently in this field, should also be followed in yet another way. By emphasizing and focusing on differential abilities, the educators in learning disabilities, much more than most professionals in emotional disturbance and mental retardation, have directed a major portion of their efforts toward *teaching* the children in their charge. ED and EMR educators have been distracted far too much by the problem behaviors specific to their fields (the areas of the Venn diagram of Figure 3.1d-1, 3, and 5). Some critics have contended, in fact, that many teachers of the emotionally disturbed and the educable mentally retarded too often have used the unique aspects of their field as excuses for shirking their teaching responsibilities. To concentrate all of one's energies on the maladaptive social-emotional behaviors of one's children is to slight simultaneously the fact that ED children also need to be taught academic skills. The point to be remembered (refer again to Figure 3.2c) is that ED children are not particularly unique with regard to social-emotional problems, so that a total concern for social-emotional as opposed to cognitive learning tasks is not justified. This attention to particulars of the population has prohibited EMR teachers, for the most part, from attempting to teach; the emphasis on the uniformly low ability of EMR children has often resulted in an unforgivably "watered down" curriculum. While the tendency may be for EMR children to present an even and low profile of abilities, some EMR children do have specific abilities in greater need of training than others. Even a uniformly low profile should not discourage the teacher from teaching the child in each of his disabilities.

### Learning Disabilities and Learning Principles

Given the great overlap in behavioral characteristics of ED, LD, and EMR children, the similarities in appropriate educational methods for them, and the utility of the concept of learning disabilities, educators need a set of principles and procedures to guide them in meeting the needs of individual children. In attempting to provide for individual differences in a manner consistent with the concept of learning disabilities, teachers are beginning to rely heavily on modern learning principles (sometimes called "learning theory"). The principles of learning apply to *all* children, regardless of their category or handicap. When it comes to an explanation of the basic processes by which he acquires information and skills, it makes no difference whether a child is considered ED, LD, or EMR. There are individual differences in the *specific conditions* under which children learn, of course, and modern learning principles suggest adjustments in methodology to match these differences. In short, learning principles are totally consistent with the concept of learning disabilities in that they provide a coherent conceptual framework for analyzing children's problems and demand modification of teaching methodology to fit the unique requirements of the individual.

Learning principles and their application have commonly been referred to as "behavior modification" or "applied behavior analysis." Behavior modification is the systematic arrangement of the environment to bring about specific changes in observable behavior. Applied behavior analysis involves "applying sometimes tentative principles of behavior to the improvement of specific behaviors, and simultaneously evaluating whether or not any changes noted are indeed attributable to the process of application—and if so, to what parts of that process" (Baer, Wolf, & Risley, 1968, p. 91). In essence, the application of learning principles to the difficulties of children requires careful assessment of the individual child and his environment, precise modification of the environment, and empirical assessment of progress or change. This approach, with its emphasis on precision, individualization, and empirical evaluation, is a natural complement of the learning disabilities concept, and it applies equally well to ED, LD, and EMR children.

# Diagnostic-Prescriptive Teaching

## 4

The use of formal, standardized tests has a long history within the field field of special education. The first formalized attempt at constructing a test of intelligence, in fact, was made by Alfred Binet in an effort to predict those pupils likely to fail in school. Through the work of Binet, and after much field testing and revising, the Stanford-Binet, along with the Weschler Intelligence Scale for Children (WISC),* have become the standbys in the realm of individual intelligence testing. Because the wide use of the Stanford-Binet and WISC has such a long history, many of the tests concerned with other aspects of an individual's function—for example, achievement and personality—have been constructed within the same general orientation of these two tests. Specifically, the most frequently used tests employed in decision-making situations in schools are of a formal, standardized nature. Thus, standardized tests are usually used in order to determine whether a child should be placed in a special education class.

It has been assumed that by evaluating a child with a test that has standardized norms based on a large number of children, one can separate children into homogeneous diagnostic categories or groups. The children so categorized are presumed to share essential characteristics that are relevant to their education. Unfortunately, attempting to differentiate groups of children with educationally relevant characteristics via standardized tests alone has been a dismal failure.

The three fields of learning disabilities, emotional disturbance, and educable mental retardation all rely upon standardized tests for educa-

---

* A new, revised edition of the WISC, referred to as the WISC-R, has been recently published.

tional placement. In the area of mental retardation, the intelligence test has dominated traditional assessment procedures. A child's score on a standardized IQ test has been the primary criterion for a diagnosis of mental retardation, for classification of the child in special education programs, and for prediction of the child's behavior as an adult. Individually administered IQ tests, such as the Stanford-Binet and the WISC, are the instruments that have been relied upon most. These two tests purportedly sample a wide range of cognitive abilities, and they require considerable time and expertise for proper administration. Recently, tests that are simpler to administer and that sample a narrower range of abilities, such as the Peabody Picture Vocabulary Test (PPVT) and the Slosson Intelligence Test (SIT), have become popular as either screening instruments or supplementary tests, or both, with certain populations (e.g., the PPVT is commonly used with nonverbal children).

Currently, there is widespread disenchantment with intelligence testing in general because ($a$) it is thought that all IQ tests are, at least to some degree, culturally biased and are not, therefore, suitable for use with members of minority groups; and ($b$) it is recognized that the child's overall pattern of development and adaptive behavior are equally as significant as his tested IQ in terms of the diagnosis of mental retardation. In other words, psychologists and special educators have come to two conclusions: that a score two standard deviations below the mean on an IQ test (i.e., an IQ of about 70) does not, by itself, mean that a child is mentally retarded and that scores per se on IQ tests are neither extremely accurate predictors of educationally relevant behavior nor sensitive guides to the development of educational programs.

Emotionally disturbed children have traditionally been evaluated by tests of personality or intrapsychic functioning. Most of these tests are "projective" in that the child's responses are said to project significant aspects of his emotions or thoughts that cannot be observed directly. The Rorschach, the Thematic Apperception Test (TAT), the Family Kinetic Drawing Test, sentence completion tests, doll play, and so forth, are common methods of assessing the "inner life." Projective testing as a means of personality assessment is decreasing in popularity because it is of limited value in designing a treatment program for the child.

More recently, ED children have been assessed through the use of nonprojective behavior rating scales or behavior checklists (e.g., Bower, 1969; Burks, 1969; Spivack & Spotts, 1966; Walker, 1969). However, many teachers and researchers are finding that rating scales and checklists also have limitations, and they are looking for more precise, functional assessment methods.

Assessment of children with learning disabilities has focused on academic achievement and abilities in specific areas, such as auditory and visual discrimination, receptive and expressive oral language, reading, and perceptual-motor performance. Standardized academic achievement tests are one means of estimating the discrepancy between a child's educational progress and his apparent intellectual ability, and tests such as the California Achievement Test (CAT), the Peabody Individual Achievement Test (PIAT), and the Wide Range Achievement Test (WRAT) have commonly been used with LD children. Too, the determination of learning disabilities usually depends to some extent on the administration of an IQ test. Because the common definitions of learning disabilities exclude individuals scoring in the retarded range and include individuals who are scoring below *intellectual* potential, an IQ test is commonly employed to diagnose learning disabilities.

In summary, the traditional approach to assessment of ED, LD, and EMR children has stressed the use of formal, standardized tests. Although certain types of tests tend to be used most frequently with children falling into one of these categories (e.g., IQ tests with EMR children), most exceptional children are assessed with more than one type of test. ED and LD children, for example, typically are given IQ as well as personality and achievement tests. In each of the three spheres of special education, ED, LD, and EMR, professionals are cognizant of the need for better tools for determining both the problems of children and the intervention programs to ameliorate these problems.

## DIAGNOSIS FOR IDENTIFICATION
## VERSUS DIAGNOSIS FOR TEACHING

### Diagnosis for Identification

Many of the problems concerned with standardized tests are due to the *use* to which these instruments have usually been put. It has been fashionable for many years to use standardized tests in order to classify or place children into one kind of a class or another. The use of tests solely to identify children as problem learners does not go far enough to be useful in the educational setting.

The use of tests for the sole purpose of identification and classification may serve the administrative needs of a school system. Administering standardized tests is a convenient way of assessing large numbers of children in a relatively short period of time. The fact that the testers and tests purport to be able to differentiate the "problem" children into homogeneous subgroups makes traditional psychological and educational testing appear all the more administratively expedient. The decision of whether and where to place a child with learning problems is made easier by simply referring to his test scores. However, it is a fact that what suits the needs of the administrator is not always conducive to the education of the child. Placement based upon the single test score or a group of test scores, with no further analysis of the scores, serves the function of placing children with myriad behavioral characteristics into the same classroom. Though this placement of certain children into classes for the learning disabled, emotionally disturbed, or educable mentally retarded is under the guise of differential diagnosis, as was pointed out in Chapter 3, merely identifying them as LD, ED, or EMR is insufficient for educational purposes.

A matter related to the employment of tests for identification involves the problems inherent in the process of labeling. By labeling children as LD, ED, or EMR, professionals frequently feel that they have accomplished their obligation. Unfortunately, the labels of LD, ED, and EMR are little more than gross indicators of a child's functioning. Labels are only helpful when they convey useful knowledge about the individual so labeled. Saying that a child is "learning disabled" offers but a mere fraction of the information needed to *teach* that child. What often occurs in the usual labeling process is that the label takes on causal status. For instance, we frequently hear individuals say, "He can't learn in school *because* he's learning disabled." With the wide variety of behaviors subsumed within the category of learning disabilities, this is about as helpful as saying, "He can't learn in school because he can't learn in school."

### Diagnosis for Teaching

In using labels, then, the real danger occurs when one uses labels that are vague. The overlap in characteristics among LD, ED, and EMR children makes the use of such terms as "learning disabled," "emotionally disturbed," or "educable mentally retarded" relatively meaningless. The teacher is in need of descriptive terms that define the specific attributes of the child in his class. If a child is labeled an "auditory learner," for example, we are a step beyond the indication that he is learning disabled. If the teacher knows that the child has figure-background disturbances in the visual sphere and has a problem in remembering material presented visually but not auditorially, then, he has even more data upon which to base his curricula and methods. Using tests for the purpose of looking for educationally meaningful data on children is warranted and should be the *primary* justification for doing any testing at all. This use of testing is at the very core of the differentiation between diagnosis for identification versus diagnosis for teaching. The latter purpose is *necessary* for good teaching; the former is a potential hindrance to the teacher in that it purports to provide meaningful information when in fact it does not.

FUNCTIONAL ANALYSIS.* Standardized tests, then, *can* be put to good use. The advent of the field of learning disabilities has led to a more beneficial use of standardized tests. Though it was not until the recent upsurge of interest in the field of learning disabilities that testing has been used as an instrument for educational recommendations, Werner and Strauss in the late 1930s were advocates of just such an approach to testing (Werner, 1937; Werner & Strauss, 1939a). Together they proposed functional analysis: "the examination of an individual in critical situations which elicit impaired functions" (Werner & Strauss, 1939a, p. 61). Werner and Strauss stated that, in testing, what is important is not the final score, but how the child went about obtaining that score. In other words, there are a variety of reasons why a child might score below grade level on a standardized achievement test. A useful functional analysis would be concerned with an interpretation of the low test score.

There is, to be sure, a great deal of subjectivity involved in the interpretation of test scores. It takes an experienced school psychologist or teacher to make inferences regarding behaviors sampled by tests. The tester needs to be aware of and on the alert for a number of factors which could result in a child's missing an answer. To name a few, the child might have problems in attention, visual or auditory discrimination, visual or auditory memory, vocabulary, and so forth. The tester needs to be able to comprehend all of the elements of behavior that are required of individual items of the test he is administering.

INTRA- VERSUS INTER-INDIVIDUAL TESTS. Related to the above concern for appreciation of how a child misses or passes individual items is the dichotomy between intra- and inter-individual tests. In the quest to determine what specific abilities and disabilities a particular child has, the tester is concerned with the differences in abilities a child possesses *within* himself, that is, the tester is attempting to discover the *intra*-individual differences of a child. This intra-individual testing approach, while it has its roots in the functional analysis method of Werner and Strauss and has been practiced on a limited scale for years by many clinicians, has been given its greatest impetus by the learning disabilities profession.

Educational and psychological testing have traditionally been concerned with comparing a child to how others have performed on the test.

---

* Functional analysis, as the term is used here, should not be confused with the functional analysis of behavior suggested by B. F. Skinner and his fellow behaviorists.

The emphasis has been on *inter*-individual differences. The
question being answered by an inter-individual test is if a p₁
child differs on the test from other children of his same age. W.
expansion of the field of learning disabilities, however, has com. the
realization that educational purposes are much better served by looking
at the intra-individual variation of a child. It is much more valuable for
the teacher to know a child's *particular* strengths and weaknesses before
proceeding to construct a remediational program.

The dominant position of inter-individual relative to intra-individual testing has gradually eroded over the years. The model of intelligence
upon which the "grandfather" test—the Stanford-Binet—was built was one
of general intelligence. As Hallahan and Cruickshank (1973) have stated:

> Relative to mental measurement, there has been an historical shift
> in the popularity of theories pertaining to the structure of the intellect.
> The primary figure in the initial stages of intelligence testing was Binet.
> Although theoretically conceiving of factors in intelligence, he promoted
> with his test a concept of general intelligence. Spearman (1904, 1927),
> through correlational and other statistical techniques, adopted a two-
> factor theory with "g" (general intelligence) as the dominant factor.
> In the 1930s Spearman revised his formulations to include group factors.
> Thurstone (1938) in the late 1930s posited 13 factors comprising intel-
> ligence. In keeping with the trend, Guilford (1956) constructed a three-
> dimensional model of the intellect, allowing room for an even greater
> number of factors. Thus a change has been initiated among some theorists
> (most notably Spearman, Thurstone, and Guilford) from a theory of a
> unified general intelligence factor, "g," to more refined group factors,
> and finally to specific ability theories. The culmination of this theoretical
> evolution, occurring in the late 1950s with Guilford's formulations, but
> evident at least since the work of Spearman two decades earlier, helped
> to provide a ripe climate for the development of learning disability
> theory. Since the concept of specific abilities and disabilities can be con-
> sidered a sine qua non of learning disability theory, the historical trend
> within mental measurement theory to concern for identification of spe-
> cific abilities assumes tremendous importance.* (p. 88)

Within this framework of an emerging recognition of specific
abilities, the first major attempt at constructing a test of various facets
of intelligence was the WISC. It is composed of two sets of subtests—
verbal and performance. The verbal tests are:

  1.  General Information—This subtest assesses the child's general knowl-

* D. P. Hallahan & W. M. Cruickshank, *Psychoeducational Foundations of
Learning Disabilities*, Englewood Cliffs, N.J.: Prentice-Hall, 1973, p. 88. Reprinted
by permission.

edge about his environment. The child's breadth of reading and learning experiences would be important.

2. General Comprehension—The child is required to show that he has good judgment.
3. Arithmetic—The child must manipulate arithmetical operations "in his head."
4. Similarities—This subtest measures the child's ability to form verbal concepts. He is asked in what way two different objects are alike.
5. Vocabulary—The child is required to define various words.
6. Digit Span—The child is presented verbally with a series of digits and must repeat them. He is then given some which he must repeat backwards.

The performance tests are:

1. Picture Completion—Given pictures with missing parts, the child is to determine what is missing.
2. Picture Arrangement—This test determines the child's ability to plan and organize a sequence of picture cards in order to tell a story.
3. Block Design—This visual-motor subtest requires the child to reproduce with blocks a geometric design.
4. Object Assembly—Given puzzle-like pieces of a familiar object, the child is to assemble them.
5. Coding—This subtest requires the child to associate two different aspects of a number of figures by supplying the second part when given just one aspect.
6. Mazes—This subtest requires the child to exhibit visual-motor and planning skills in drawing his way out of mazes.

The WISC is thus constructed in order to enable a psychologist to determine specifically in what aspects of intelligence a child may be low and high. This approach is in contrast with that of the Stanford-Binet which is not broken down into subtests purporting to measure discrete kinds of ability. The Binet, itself, however, if given by an astute clinician can also be used to assess specific abilities and disabilities. By observing responses on individual items a skilled clinician can arrive at some conclusions regarding a child's specific disabilities. The WISC, however, because it is organized into different ability subtests, has become more appealing to many school psychologists who assess children with suspected learning disabilities.

The primary danger in using the WISC for assessing intra-individual abilities is that the clinician may have a tendency to place too much faith in the names of the subtests. As Rapaport, Gill, and Shafer (1968) have noted, the proper approach to intelligence testing has certain requirements. One of these requirements "is not limited to the individual tester, but is pertinent as a warning to clinical psychology in general: reports stating, for instance, that 'The subject has good Information but his Digit Span, especially Digit Span backwards, is very poor' are psychologically meaningless . . ." (p. 68). Simply stating that a child has poor Digit Span ability, or poor Block Design ability, or poor coding ability, and so forth adds only a gross degree of information about the child. The subtest names cannot be used as refined descriptors of behavior. There are, for example, any number of reasons why a child might score poorly on the Digit Span (backwards) subtest. As Rapaport and his co-authors (1968) have stated, "we found that one must consider not only every subtest score, but every single response and every part of every response, as significant and representative of the subject" (p. 67).

Another test, which even more than the WISC is aligned with the field of learning disabilities, is the Illinois Test of Psycholinguistic Abilities (ITPA). This test is discussed in more detail in Chapter 9, but suffice it to say here that it has provided the greatest impetus toward assessing intra-individual differences. In accord with the concept of diagnosis for teaching, books have been published that provide educational recommendations for children scoring low on each of the subtests. Designed to measure different communication abilities, the use of the ITPA is open to the same pitfalls as the WISC.

Specific abilities or disabilities have been assessed with instruments such as the Detroit Test of Learning Aptitude, the Purdue Perceptual-Motor Survey, the Wepman Auditory Discrimination Test, the Frostig Developmental Test of Visual Perception, the Parson's Language Sample, the Gates-McKillop Reading Diagnostic Tests, among others. Attempts have been made to obtain a diagnosis by comparing the child's scores on these tests with age and grade norms, as well as by comparing his scores across subtests and instruments, and then developing a prescription for the child's instruction based on these test data.

PRESCRIPTIVE TEACHING. The concerns expressed in the above discussion regarding diagnosis for teaching, functional analysis, and intra-individual assessment can be subsumed under what has come to be known as "prescriptive teaching" or "diagnostic-prescriptive teaching." This method of teaching, popularized within the field of learning disabilities but applicable for all exceptional children, emphasizes that good teaching relies upon good, educationally meaningful diagnosis. As a medical doctor diagnoses a patient's symptoms and then *prescribes* treatment based on these symptoms, so the teacher or school psychologist diagnoses the behaviors or learning symptoms of the child and, then, *prescribes* an appropriate educational treatment (Kauffman & Hallahan, 1974).

Laurence J. Peter (1965) in a now classic book entitled *Prescriptive Teaching* has made a major impact on how one views the function of psychological and educational testing. In this book, Peter was the first to present a systematic approach to diagnosis for the sake of teaching. Figure 4.1 is Peter's model for prescriptive teaching. The model specifies that in order to translate diagnostic data into a teaching strategy, the teacher and other members of an interdisciplinary team must consider

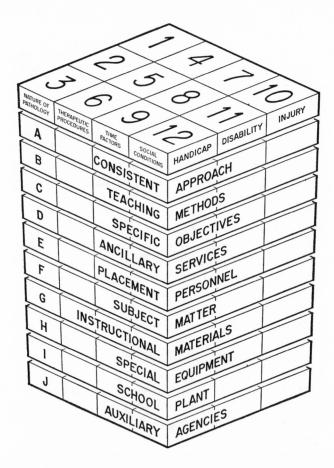

FIGURE 4.1.
Model for translating diagnostic findings into a prescription for teaching.

Source: L. J. Peter, Prescriptive Teaching (New York: McGraw-Hill 1965). Reprinted by permission.

three main dimensions of (1) problem, (2) situational, and (3) school variables. The twelve numbered cells across the top of the model represent the diagnostic considerations.

The problem variables are those of handicap, disability, and injury. While an injury indicates actual physical damage, disability describes functional problems. A handicap, as defined by Peter refers to something that hinders one in a specific activity.

The situational variables—social conditions, time factors, therapeutic procedures, and nature of pathology—define various aspects of the environment in which the child is situated. The various environments in which the child functions must be considered in the educational prescription.

The school variables focus on those environmental factors that are specific to the school situation. A number of changes in the school situation are frequently necessary in order to provide the best possible education for a problem learner. Peter believes, for example, that a consistent approach is an important component of an educational prescription for many exceptional children. In addition, other aspects of a child's school environment will need to be changed based on diagnostic information—teaching methods, specific objectives, ancillary services, placement personnel, subject matter, instructional materials, special equipment, school plant, and auxiliary agencies.

In terms of ease of modifiability, the 132 cells are arranged from the most to least modifiable from the front to the back and from the top to the bottom. Thus, the most easily changed aspect of a child's educational program would include providing a consistent approach while changing the social conditions for a child with a handicap.

The complexity of Peter's model makes it a thorough one. The broadness of the range of children and situations that it covers makes it useful for interdisciplinary teams. An interdisciplinary effort based on the general framework and spirit of this model could be brought to bear on the education of exceptional children. However, the broad scope of the model provides only a gross set of guidelines for a *teacher* to follow with an individual child. The teacher is in need of an additional, more specific model for translating diagnostic information into educational strategies.

CRITERION REFERENCED TESTING. A much more specific approach to diagnostic testing which falls within the realm of diagnosis for teaching is that of criterion referenced testing. All the tests mentioned so far in this chapter are what are known as normative referenced tests, that is, individual scores are compared with normative group scores. The vast majority of tests used in education and psychology are normative in orientation. The normative referenced test is one in which standardized norms have been established by giving the test to large numbers of children. With these established norms, the score an individual child obtains is compared with a reference group appropriate to that child's age. Even the intra-individual tests such as the ITPA are normative referenced in that each subtest has its own set of norms and the subtest scores that are compared within an individual are first converted to scores that reflect the child's score relative to his peers.

Within the educational arena, a radically different approach from comparing children to norms has begun to be used: criterion referenced testing. In this method of assessment, each child's score is measured against a criterion that the teacher has set for the child. For example, the teacher may set a criterion of having the child compute twenty out of twenty-five long-division problems correctly in twenty minutes. If the child does not achieve the criterion, then the teacher must consider that either the criterion is not appropriate or the child needs more skill-building to complete the required task.

The particular advantage of criterion referenced testing is that it suits quite well the particular assessment needs relative to children with learning problems. Normative referenced tests usually have not been standardized on populations containing children with deviant learning styles; therefore, it is difficult to obtain educationally meaningful information from these tests. Criterion referenced testing, on the other hand, allows the teacher to set *specifically* the kinds of educational goals for *each* child that he has in class. The primary danger in the criterion referenced approach is that the teacher must be able to set accurate criteria and recognize when he has established an inappropriate criterion. A criterion of twenty out of twenty-five correct might, for instance, be either too easy or too difficult. If too easy, it is a waste of the child's time to engage in the activity. If too difficult, the teacher might spend an inordinate amount of time training the child to conquer the last two or three problems when time could be better spent extending the child's skills in another activity.

Drew, Freston, and Logan (1972) have noted the utility of the criterion referenced approach but have also maintained that some reference to a child's peers must be made. Without any consideration of norms, the teacher would be at a loss in terms of developing appropriate criteria. Drew and his colleagues have consequently forwarded an evaluation model that combines normative and criterion referenced procedures. Figure 4.2 presents their evaluation of a hypothetical child. The evaluation at this stage is primarily normative referenced. From Figure 4.2 it can be seen that this particular child's disability lies in the area of reading. It is then the teacher's task to determine what *specific* behaviors are

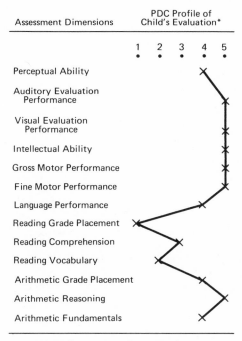

|                              | PDC Profile of |
|------------------------------|----------------|
| Assessment Dimensions        | Child's Evaluation* |

*Likert Scale (1=very low, 5=very high)
in terms of child's measured performance
relative to expectations.

*FIGURE 4.2.*
*Hypothetical primary distinguishing*
*characteristics (PDC) profile resulting from*
*teacher identification and formal diagnosis.*

Source: C. J. Drew, C. W. Freston, & D. R.
Logan, "Criteria and Reference in Evaluation," Focus on Exceptional Children, March,
1972, p. 5. Reprinted by permission.

deficient in this child to such an extent that he does poorly in reading. To
put it another way, the teacher does a task analysis in order to decide
what behaviors are necessary for a child to read successfully. Figure 4.3
demonstrates how this hypothetical child scored on a number of behaviors specified by the teacher as being components of reading. In this
stage of evaluation, the assessment approach is primarily on a criterion
referenced basis. From Figure 4.3 it is evident that this child is particularly deficient in formulating letter sounds, in reproducing vowels,
and in blending sounds. The educational program for this child would be
to improve these particular learning disabilities.

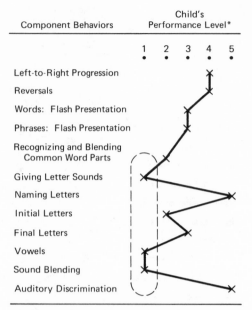

*Likert Scale (1=very low, 5=very high)
in terms of the child's performance assessed
on an intra-individual basis.

*FIGURE 4.3.*

*Formative evaluation primary distinguishing
characteristics (PDC) profile representing
criterion behavior performance.*

*Source: C. J. Drew, C. W. Freston, & D. R.
Logan, "Criteria and Reference in Evaluation,"* Focus on Exceptional Children, *March,
1972, p. 6. Reprinted by permission.*

# Applied
# Behavior Analysis

# 5

The specification of discrete behaviors advocated by Drew, Freston, and Logan (1972) is quite different from the traditional mode of academic assessment in which standardized achievement and intelligence tests are the only tests administered to a child. The use of intra-individual tests and criterion referenced tests within a prescriptive teaching framework provides the teacher with tools that have educational utility.

There is an approach to teaching, however, that is even more oriented toward the specification and analysis of molecular units of behavior that are important for learning in school. Those who espouse a behavior modification approach are among the strongest proponents of behavioral assessment or analysis. Interested in the teaching of specific skills to children with specific learning problems, the advocates of behavior modification or applied behavior analysis seek to improve specific behaviors and to determine precisely the teaching procedures that are responsible for the improvement. As Baer, Wolf, and Risley (1968) have summarized:

> An *applied* behavior analysis will make obvious the importance of the behavior changed, its quantitative characteristics, the experimental manipulations which analyze with clarity what was responsible for the change, the technologically exact description of all procedures contributing to that change, the effectiveness of those procedures in making sufficient change for value, and the generality of that change. (p. 97)

Applied behavior analysis, with its emphasis on specific behaviors exhibited by the individual child and on learning principles, has several characteristics that make it particularly useful in the education of ED, LD, and EMR children:

1. It allows great precision in measurement.
2. It is based on empirical data obtained directly from the child's performance.
3. It suggests specific remedial teaching methods.
4. It facilitates individualization of instruction.
5. It provides continuous evaluation of teaching procedures.

Throughout the rest of this book, we will include an applied behavior analysis perspective. At the end of each succeeding chapter examples are provided of how behavioral assessment and learning principles can be used in teaching children with the specific learning and behavioral characteristics discussed in that chapter. Several basic features of applied behavior analysis are outlined here to provide an orientation to our discussion of specific educational problems and methods in the chapters that follow. (For more detailed discussion of behavioral assessment and learning principles, see Baer, Wolf, & Risley, 1968; Haring, 1974a, 1974b; Haring & Lovitt, 1967; Haring & Phillips, 1972; Kauffman, 1975; and Lovitt, 1967.)

## DIRECT, CONTINUOUS, AND PRECISE MEASUREMENT

One of the most important features of applied behavior analysis, and possibly its greatest contribution to education, is direct, continuous, and precise measurement of behavior. Excellent teachers have for many years known and used effective instructional techniques with exceptional children. It is only recently, however, that children's behavior and the effects of teaching methods have been measured in such a way that truly adequate evaluation of educational methodology is possible.

*Direct* measurement implies that the child's behavior can be observed and counted or recorded meaningfully as it occurs. Behavior is defined as an overt movement of the child rather than as a covert process or an internal state. Behavior analysts speak of tasks or responses which children can be observed to perform. Thus, the child's specific academic or social behaviors themselves, not abilities or attitudes supposedly revealed by a sampling of related test performances, are the central concern. For example, "if the target behavior is reading, direct measurement on various reading components would be obtained instead of using a standardized reading or achievement test to determine skills" (Lovitt, 1970, p. 88). The reading behavior to be measured may be defined as answering comprehension questions, reading specific sight words, oral reading rate, and so on. Arithmetic behavior may be defined as counting, performing specific operations, making specified computational errors, solving certain equations, and so forth. In the area of social behavior, responses may be defined as hitting other children, crying, getting out of seat without permission, saying "Thank you," or any other directly measurable activity.

Direct measurement necessitates an answer to the question, "Exactly what is it that the child does (or should do) that can be observed directly and quantified?" When behavior is adequately defined for purposes of direct measurement, it can be stated with little or no equivocation that it did or did not occur in any given instance. Thus, the child's particular behavioral deficits or excesses can be pinpointed. Direct behavioral measurement provides, obviously, a distinct advantage over other methods in prescribing remedial training and in quantifying progress.

*Continuous* measurement requires that a behavior be recorded repeatedly (usually daily) over a period of time. A child's reading rate or subtraction performance, for example, might be recorded each day over a period of weeks. Such continuous measurement has clear advantages over other methods, such as standardized testing in which the child's performance is sampled infrequently or only once. With direct daily measurement, day-to-day variation in performance can be seen; a more reliable estimate of the child's true capabilities can be obtained; the effects of specific teaching techniques on the child's performance can be immediately and directly assessed; and the child's performance can be easily and precisely communicated to others.

When measurement of the child's behavior is direct and continuous, the data from the child's performance can be displayed most intelligibly on a graph. Consequently, nearly every behavior modification or applied behavior analysis project includes a graph of the child's performance. Time, usually days or instructional sessions, is typically plotted on the abscissa and the quantitative level of the child's behavior, variously graphed as rate, frequency, or percent, is usually plotted on the ordinate. The illustrations included in this chapter provide examples of the graphic display of data obtained by direct daily measurement.

*Precise* measurement demands that observation and recording techniques be reliable. Unreliable measurement will invalidate the evaluation of behavioral data. Therefore, applied behavior analysis is characterized by reliability checks or estimates. The reliability of observational data is most often estimated in applied behavior analysis by comparing the records of two or more independent observers who have recorded the same behavior of the same individual at the same time. The closer the agreement among observers, the greater the presumed reliability.

Discussion of specific measurement techniques and issues in the measurement of behavior is beyond the scope of this chapter. Nevertheless, it is of crucial importance to recognize the measurement characteristics that distinguish applied behavior analysis from other methods and to grasp the importance of these characteristics for the assessment and modification of children's behavior. (For further discussion of measurement see Bijou, Peterson, Harris, Allen, & Johnston, 1969; Cooper, 1975; Hall, 1971; and Kauffman, 1975.)

## ENVIRONMENTAL MANIPULATIONS

Learning principles suggest that children learn because of environmental events, mainly those that occur immediately after the child performs a behavior. The way to modify a child's behavior, therefore, is to change what happens to him—specifically, to change the events surrounding the behavior that has been defined and recorded. Applied behavior analysis may involve both the manipulation of events that precede the child's behavior (antecedent events or stimuli) and the manipulation of events that follow the child's behavior (subsequent events or consequences). Antecedent events include instructions, cues, prompts, examples (or models), or other signals that set the occasion for a specific response. Consequences include positive reinforcers (such as food, praise, tokens, privileges, etc.) and negative reinforcers (such as pain, reprimands, loss of privileges, or other aversive events) that can be presented or withdrawn immediately following a behavior and can be used to increase or decrease the strength of the behavior they follow. When consequences are applied if and only if a certain behavior occurs, they are said to be *contingent* on that behavior. The arrangement then specifies the contingency of reinforcement. For example, if a child receives food as a consequence if and only if he walks, then food is contingent on walking.

Consequent environmental events or stimuli are classified according to their effects on the behavior they follow. When a stimulus or event is contingently presented (i.e., added to the environment) following a behavior, and that behavior takes place more frequently than during baseline (no consequence) conditions, then the event is by definition a *positive reinforcer*. For example, under baseline conditions a child completes an average of ten arithmetic problems a day. However, when he averages thirty problems a day because he receives one minute of extra playtime for each ten problems completed, then extra playtime would be considered a positive reinforcer for that child. When an event is contingently presented following a behavior and that behavior occurs less frequently than during baseline conditions, then the event is defined as a *punishing stimulus* (*punisher* and *negative reinforcer* are for practical purposes synonomous with punishing stimulus).

It is important to keep in mind that any environmental event may be a potential positive reinforcer or punishing stimulus in a given case, but it is always the individual's response to the event that defines its function. If an event is not shown to strengthen a behavior when it is contingently presented, then it simply is not a positive reinforcer for that individual. An event cannot be considered a punishing stimulus unless it is demonstrated to weaken or suppress the behavior it follows when it is contingently presented.

Within a behavior modification framework there are several means of changing behavior by using consequent environmental events. The description of these procedures must be precise, for the differences among them are not irrelevant technicalities. As Baer, Wolf, and Risley (1968) have mentioned, applied behavior analysis includes an exact description of the procedures used to change behavior. Without knowledge of the types of interventions that can be used and adequate description of the specific procedures involved in a given case, it is impossible to evaluate adequately the behavior change that may have been produced or to replicate the instructional procedures.

### Extinction

When a behavior persists over a period of time, it is safe to assume that it is being followed by reinforcement, that is, that it is being reinforced. Learning principles lead to the conclusion that were this not so, the behavior would weaken in strength and eventually die out or be extinguished altogether. It is possible to use this phenomenon, called extinction, to eliminate some inappropriate or undesirable behaviors. If the reinforcer that is maintaining the behavior can be identified and terminated, the response will cease. A case in point was presented by Harris, Wolf, and Baer (1967). They found that when the solicitous concern and attention of a preschool teacher no longer followed the crying and whining behavior of a four-year-old boy, he stopped crying. Apparently, such adult attention for crying served as a reinforcer for the behavior, and when this reinforcer was no longer forthcoming, extinction occurred.

### Reinforcement

Reinforcement means manipulating the consequences of a behavior in such a way that the behavior is increased in frequency or strength (or, one might say, in future probability). There are two reinforcement procedures—positive reinforcement and negative reinforcement—both of which strengthen the response which is reinforced. Positive reinforcement is the result when a positive reinforcer is added to the environment or applied following a behavior. If teacher attention is a positive reinforcer (rewarding consequence) for a child and he receives such attention following the response of talking out (which strengthens that response), then talking out behavior has been strengthened by positive reinforcement. Negative reinforcement results from subtracting from the environment or withdrawing a negative reinforcer following a behavior. For example, if arithmetic is a negative reinforcer (unpleasant event or punishing stimulus) for a child, and arithmetic tasks are withdrawn following his response of crying (which strengthens the likelihood of that response in future similar circumstances), then crying has been strengthened by negative reinforcement. Negative reinforcement strengthens escape and avoidance behaviors—those behaviors that allow an individual to terminate or avoid contact with negative reinforcers. It is important not to confuse negative reinforcement with punishment or with extinction.

Table 5.1 summarizes the essential differences among these procedures. Extinction occurs in a setting in which the response in question has previously resulted in reinforcement (either positive or negative). When an extinction procedure is in effect, however, reinforcers are not available for that response, that is, reinforcement is not forthcoming and

TABLE 5.1    Use of Consequences to Change Behavior

| Method | Antecedent Condition or Setting | Consequence of Response | Effect |
|---|---|---|---|
| Extinction | Reinforcers were previously available for response | Reinforcers not available | Response weakened |
| Positive reinforcement | Positive reinforcers not available without response | Positive reinforcers made available | Response strengthened |
| Negative reinforcement | Negative reinforcers present without response | Negative reinforcers withdrawn | Response strengthened |
| Punishment 1 (aversive conditioning) | Punishing stimuli not present without response | Punishing stimuli applied | Response weakened |
| Punishment 2 (response cost) | Positive reinforcers present without response | Positive reinforcers withdrawn | Response weakened |

the response is weakened. In contrast, negative reinforcement occurs in a setting in which negative reinforcers are present unless a response is made. The consequence of the response in question is that the aversive condition is terminated, and the "relief" of escaping or avoiding the unpleasantness strengthens the response. Negative reinforcement differs from punishment in two fundamental respects: negative reinforcement strengthens a behavior (specifically escape and avoidance behavior), whereas punishment weakens the response; and negative reinforcement is associated with relief from aversive conditions, whereas punishment is associated with the onset of punishing stimuli or the loss of positive reinforcers.

Extinction (i.e., nonreinforcement of a particular behavior) is a useful procedure for eliminating inappropriate responses in many educational situations, but it is most effective only when positive reinforcement is applied to other appropriate behaviors. To be most effective, a teacher should not only stop reinforcing inappropriate out-of-seat behavior but also should make a point of reinforcing appropriate in-seat behavior. In the study by Harris, Wolf, and Baer (1967), it is very important to note that not only was crying ignored, but noncrying behavior was reinforced. Without reinforcement for appropriate responses, extinction of inappropriate responses will be of little or no value in improving the child's condition.

Negative reinforcement is characteristic of undesirable educational situations in which escape and avoidance are the primary motivational factors. Positive reinforcement, on the other hand, characterizes education in which the consequences of learning and responding are appropriately rewarded. The key to the solution of many educational problems, though by no means all, is to find ways to arrange positive reinforcement for appropriate behavior.

### Punishment

While it is relatively seldom that punishment is needed in education, there are circumstances under which its use is warranted (MacMillan, Forness, & Trumbull, 1973). Furthermore, while punishment may involve inflicting pain, pain and suffering are *not* necessary for effective punishment (Hall, Axelrod, Foundopulos, Shellman, Campbell, & Cranston, 1971).

Punishment means applying or withdrawing reinforcers in order to weaken the strength of a response. As Table 5.1 shows, there are two ways to arrange punishment. A response may be punished by following it with the presentation of a punishing stimulus or negative reinforcer. For example, Hall and his co-workers (1971) found that when the teacher pointed at a child and shouted "No!" contingent on a specific inappropriate behavior, that behavior was weakened—it decreased in frequency. A response may also be punished by taking away a positive reinforcer (response cost) when a behavior occurs. Hall and his colleagues also found that the teacher could give a young child several positive reinforcers (in this case nothing more than colored strips of paper with the child's name written on them) and punish a specific response by taking away one of the slips whenever the child performed the undesirable behavior. Using a similar response cost procedure, Sulzbacher and Houser (1968) were able to punish "naughty finger" behavior in a class of EMR children. The children were given a special ten-minute recess which could be lost only for "naughty finger" responses. Any time the teacher observed someone showing the middle finger extended or heard any reference to this gesture, the class lost one minute of the special recess. The inappropriate behavior was effectively suppressed using this response cost contingency.

A frequently used technique for reducing the strength of undesirable behavior is "timeout." The term connotes "time out from positive reinforcement," or the lack of opportunity to respond and be reinforced for an interval of time. In its usual classroom application, timeout combines features of both types of punishment—aversive conditioning and response cost. Because the child is removed from the situation in which he is receiving reinforcement, timeout includes a response cost feature. The child is ordinarily placed in an unstimulating environment, such as an isolation booth or a screened-off part of the classroom; timeout, therefore, usually includes the presentation of a punisher (the unstimulating environment, which is aversive for most children).

Care must be taken in the use of punishment so that unpleasantness does not dominate the child's educational experience and unwanted side effects do not occur. With proper guidelines, punishment can be a humane and valuable tool in the teacher's armamentarium (MacMillan, Forness, & Trumbull, 1973; O'Leary & O'Leary, 1972).

### Instructions

It has often been observed that instructions effective with most children have little effect on ED, LD, and EMR children. Consequently, instructions have been overshadowed by consequences in behavior modification methodology. It is unfortunate but understandable that this has occurred. Instructions will be effective only if the child is reinforced for following them, and many ED, LD, and EMR children have not been appropriately reinforced. Also, instructions must be particularly explicit and clear if they are to be effective with the ED, LD, or EMR child. Only recently have special educators begun to call for the careful assessment and appropriate use of instructions in modifying such children's behavior (Berman, 1973; Kauffman, 1975; Lovitt & Smith, 1972).

Based on an experiment with a nine-year-old learning disabled boy, Lovitt and Smith (1972) speculated that some children in school may exhibit apparent academic disabilities because they are uncertain of what is expected of them—they are never told *explicitly* what to do. In their study, the child produced specific language responses when he was merely told exactly what types of changes to make in his descriptions of pictures. No reinforcement was given, and yet he produced responses he did not appear to be capable of making without the instructions. Because instructions may often be the simplest and most efficient means of obtaining the desired behavior from children, teachers should not overlook them as a potentially powerful environmental manipulation.

### Imitative Stimuli and Vicarious Consequences

A great body of theory and research has accumulated in recent years regarding how children learn by observing the behavior of others and the consequences they receive. Much of this research on observational learning has definite implications for special education (Cullinan, Kauffman, & LaFleur, 1975). In their natural environment, children are constantly exposed to peer and adult examples, and much of children's learning appears to involve imitation of the behavior of these models. Moreover, it is known that children may be either more or less inclined to perform a given response depending on their vicarious experience of the consequences they observe others receiving for that response (cf. Bandura, 1969) or on the imitation of their behavior by others (Kauffman, Kneedler, Gamache, & Hallahan, 1975; Kauffman, LaFleur, Hallahan, & Chanes, 1975).

It is not surprising, then, that imitative stimuli (i.e., models, examples, or demonstrations) and vicarious consequences have been manipulated purposefully by special educators to obtain certain performances. When teachers show children what they want them to do, have other children provide an appropriate model of a behavior, or demonstrate the correct response, they are manipulating antecedent environmental events called imitative stimuli which they hope will induce the child's imitative response. When teachers praise or otherwise reinforce children who are behaving well in the presence of another child who is misbehaving, they are attempting to use vicarious reinforcement to induce good behavior in the miscreant.

## EVALUATION OF ENVIRONMENTAL MANIPULATIONS

It is of utmost importance for teachers to apprise themselves of the most effective teaching methods. A trustworthy apprisal demands sound empirical evaluation of instructional and behavior management techniques rather than folk wisdom, superstition, and unreliable assays. In other words, the teacher must be to some degree a scientist and researcher as well as a practitioner. The traditional methods of evaluating the effects of remedial instruction or behavioral interventions have been the non-experimental case study or a group experimental design, in which averages for groups of children are compared statistically. The limitations of these methods for teachers are profound. The data evaluated using these methods usually are anecdotal reports, ratings, or test scores—data that do not represent direct observation of the target behavior itself and that are obtained on only one or a very few occasions (e.g., a pretest and a posttest). Additionally, when group experimental designs are used, nothing can be said of a single individual's performance—only *averages* are analyzed for significant differences. Thus, the teacher is left with information that may not accurately reflect the child's performance and evaluation techniques that are either nonexperimental (and, therefore, do not allow one to determine cause-effect relationships) or offer no help in determining whether the desired effect was achieved for a specific individual. This is not to say that traditional experimental control group methods and nonexperimental case reports are never of value, only that for teachers, and for many others who work in applied fields, they are of *limited* value.

Applied behavior analysis offers alternative methods for evaluating behavioral change in pupils. These alternative techniques *do* allow the teacher to make statements regarding cause-effect relationships between teaching methods and children's learning based on experimental evidence. Furthermore, the teacher can examine effects for individual children or treat a classroom group as a unit whose behavior can be modified. (For additional discussion of single subject research design see Kazdin, 1973, and Leitenberg, 1973.)

In all experimental education, whether using traditional group statistical designs or single subject applied behavior analysis designs, the purpose of the experimental method is to answer the question, "How can I eliminate reasonable doubt that the experimental teaching method I used, rather than other factors I did not control, was responsible for the child's learning?" Group statistical designs rely on randomization and mathematical probability statements to answer the question. Applied behavior analysis designs, on the other hand, for the most part depend on objective data obtained from direct daily measurement of pupils' behavior during various experimental conditions. A teacher using applied behavior analysis seeks to show what teaching behaviors control learning by demonstrating that he is able to produce learning:

> The analysis of a behavior . . . requires a believable demonstration of events that can be responsible for the occurrence or nonoccurrence of that behavior. An experimenter has achieved an analysis of a behavior when he can exercise control over it. By common laboratory standards, that has meant the ability of the experimenter to turn the behavior on or off, or up and down, at will. (Baer, Wolf, & Risley, 1968, pp. 93–94)

Applied analysis of behavior always requires that one first establish a baseline level of the behavior (i.e., the quantitative level of the behavior *before* any environmental manipulation). The effects of teaching procedures or other interventions can then be evaluated by comparing the baseline data with the quantitative characteristics of the behavior on days when the interventions were in effect. Obviously, one can note trends in the child's performance when data are recorded daily, and changes in performance can be observed when an instructional procedure is initiated. However, if one is interested in scientific evidence that the instructional procedure *caused* the change in the child's behavior, further manipulations ordinarily are required. These manipulations constitute applied behavior analysis research designs, several of which will be described briefly.

In the *reversal or withdrawal design,* a teaching method or behavior management technique is alternately introduced and reversed or withdrawn.

> Here a behavior is measured, and the measure is examined over time until its stability is clear. Then, the experimental variable is applied. The behavior continues to be measured, to see if the variable will produce a behavioral change. If it does, the experimental variable is discontinued or altered, to see if the behavioral change just brought about depends on it. If so, the behavioral change should be lost or diminished (thus the term "reversal"). The experimental variable then is applied again, to see if the behavioral change can be recovered. If it can, it is pursued further, since this is applied research and the behavioral change sought is an important one. It may be reversed briefly again, and yet again, if the setting in which the behavior takes place allows further reversals. (Baer, Wolf, & Risley, 1968, p. 94)

Lahey, McNees, and Brown (1973) used a withdrawal design to evaluate the effects of reinforcement on children's comprehension of oral reading. After collecting baseline data on children's comprehension of oral reading, they began reinforcing correct comprehension responses with praise and pennies. After fifteen days of reinforcement, they withdrew the reinforcement procedure (i.e., returned to baseline conditions) and, finally, reinstated the reinforcement condition. As can be seen in Figure 5.1, systematic changes in percent of comprehension questions answered correctly were produced by reinforcement; comprehension increased under both reinforcement phases and decreased to a level close to that of the initial baseline during the second baseline phase. Such systematic changes strongly infer that the reinforcement procedure was *causally* related to reading comprehension for these children.

Goetz and Baer (1973) investigated the effects of reinforcement on children's block building by using a reversal design. First, they collected baseline data on form diversity; second, they provided social reinforcement (teacher attention and praise) for diversity of form; third, they reversed the reinforcement contingency (i.e., provided reinforce-

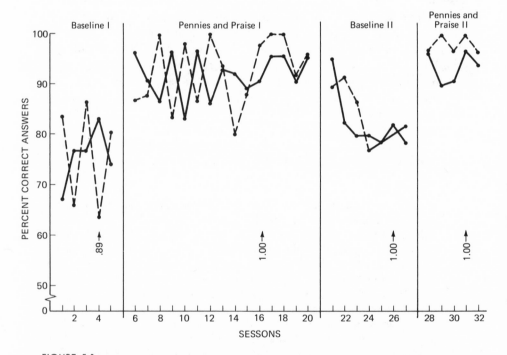

FIGURE 5.1.

Per cent of questions answered correctly by Subjects A and B, whose oral reading was tested to be on grade level and whose reading for comprehension was tested to be below grade level. Subject A drawn in dotted line, Subject B in solid line.

Source: B. B. Lahey, M. P. McNees, & C. C. Brown, "Modification of Deficits in Reading for Comprehension," Journal of Applied Behavior Analysis, 1973, 6, p. 478. Reprinted by permission.

ment only when children produced the same forms); and, finally, they again reinforced diversity of form in the children's constructions. Figure 5.2 is a graph of the children's block-building performance. The orderly

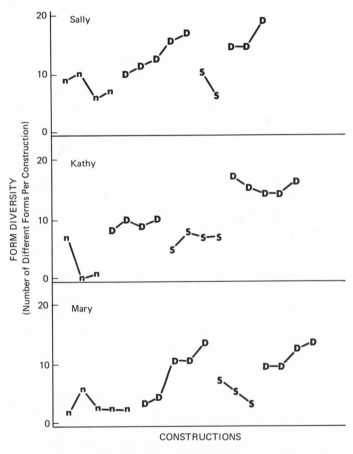

FIGURE 5.2.
Form diversity scores of three children in the course of block-building training. Initial points, labeled as n's, represent scores produced when no reinforcement was programmed; points labeled as D's represent scores produced when reinforcement was programmed only for different (non-repetitive) forms; and points labeled as S's represent scores produced when reinforcement was programmed only for repetition of the same forms used previously that session.

Source: E. M. Goetz & D. M. Baer, "Social Control of Form Diversity and the Emergence of New Forms in Children's Blockbuilding," Journal of Applied Behavior Analysis, 1973, 6, p. 213. Reprinted by permission.

changes in block building associated with reinforcement indicate that form diversity was increased by social reinforcement.

Reversal and withdrawal designs are not the only options in applied behavior analysis. An alternative is a technique called the *multiple baseline design*.

> This alternative may be of particular value when a behavior appears to be irreversible or when reversing the behavior is undesirable. In the multiple-baseline technique, a number of responses are identified and measured over time to provide baselines against which changes can be evaluated. With these baselines established, the experimenter then applies an experimental variable to one of the behaviors, produces a change in it, and perhaps notes little or no change in the other baselines. If so, rather than reversing the just-produced change, he instead applies the experimental variable to one of the other, as yet unchanged, responses. If it changes at that point, evidence is accruing that the experimental variable is indeed effective, and that the prior change was not simply a matter of coincidence. The variable then may be applied to still another response, and so on. The experimenter is attempting to show that he has a reliable experimental variable, in that each behavior changes maximally only when the experimental variable is applied to it. (Baer, Wolf, & Risley, 1968, p. 94)

Multiple baseline designs may involve: (*a*) multiple schedules, in which the same behavior of an individual or group is recorded in several different settings or under different stimulus conditions; (*b*) multiple responses, in which several different behaviors of the same individual or group are recorded under the same conditions; or (*c*) multiple subjects, in which the same behavior of several different individuals or groups is recorded under the same conditions and modified using the same procedure. Examples of all three types of multiple baselines have been provided by Hall, Cristler, Cranston, and Tucker (1970). Figure 5.3 shows their use of a multiple schedule design. (Note that a withdrawal design is also included in this study.) The number of children returning late to their classroom after the morning, noon, and afternoon recesses was recorded. The teacher was able to reduce the number of pupils returning late from each recess by posting the names of children who were on time on a "Patriots Chart." Because the behavior of the children changed systematically for each recess independently and at the time the intervention was begun, the study offers strong experimental evidence of the efficacy of the chart with these children.

In a second study, Hall and his co-workers recorded and successively applied consequences to three different behaviors—clarinet practice, campfire project, and reading—of a ten-year-old girl, demonstrating

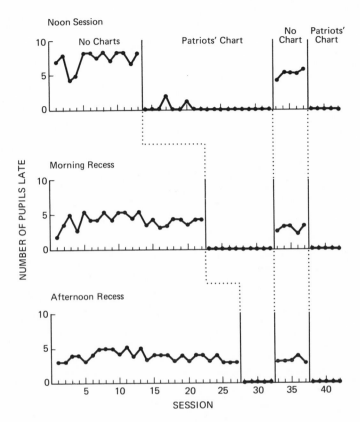

*FIGURE 5.3.*

*Record of the number of pupils late in returning to their fifth-grade classroom after noon, morning, and afternoon recesses. No Charts— baseline, before experimental procedures. Patriots' Chart—posting of pupil names on "Today's Patriots" chart contingent on entering class on time after recess. No Chart—posting of names discontinued. Patriots' Chart—return to Patriots' Chart conditions.*

*Source: R. V. Hall, C. Cristler, S. S. Cranston, & B. Tucker, "Teachers and Parents as Researchers Using Multiple Baseline Designs," Journal of Applied Behavior Analysis, 1970, 3, p. 249. Reprinted by permission.*

a multiple response design. Figure 5.4 shows the results of their intervention in each of the three baselines. When the girl was required to go to bed one minute early for each minute less than 30 that she spent on an activity, she spent more time engaged in that activity than she had spent during baseline conditions. Because the time she spent on each activity increased when and only when the contingency was in effect, the inference is strong that the contingency was the causal factor.

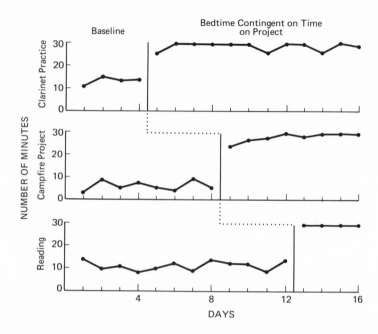

FIGURE 5.4.

*Record of time spent in clarinet practice, campfire honors project work, and reading for book reports by a 10-year-old girl. Baseline—before experimental procedures. Early Bedtime Contingent on Less Than 30 Minutes of Behavior—1 minute earlier bedtime for each minute less than 30 engaged in an activity.*

Source: R. V. Hall, C. Cristler, S. S. Cranston, & B. Tucker, "Teachers and Parents as Researchers Using Multiple Baseline Designs," Journal of Applied Behavior Analysis, 1970, 3, p. 251. Reprinted by permission.

Hall and his colleagues also recorded and changed in succession the French quiz grades of three high-school students, demonstrating the use of a multiple subject design. Figure 5.5 relates the results of this project. The contingency stated that if the pupil earned a D or F grade on his French quiz he would have to stay after school for tutoring until he had mastered the material. When this contingency was put into effect, it resulted in higher grades on the quizzes, and this effect was observed for each pupil. Evidently, the contingency was the variable affecting the pupils' performances.

Yet another alternative type of design, a *changing criterion design,* has been suggested by Hall (1971). This design consists of setting a succession of behavioral criteria for obtaining a consequence and observing whether the behavior changes to meet those criteria in a systematic

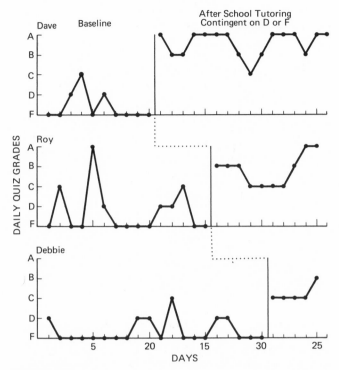

FIGURE 5.5.
Record of quiz score grades for three high-school French-class students. Baseline—before experimental procedures. After School Tutoring Contingent on D and F Grades—pupils required to stay after school for tutoring if they score D or F on daily quizzes.

Source: R. V. Hall, C. Cristler, S. S. Cranston, & B. Tucker, "Teachers and Parents as Researchers Using Multiple Baseline Designs," Journal of Applied Behavior Analysis, 1970, 3, p. 252. Reprinted by permission.

manner. If the level of the behavior closely and consistently parallels the criteria, there is evidence that the contingencies were responsible for those changes. Deitz and Repp (1973) recently reported an experiment in which they established a series of behavioral criteria for reinforcement that resulted in a parallel decline in inappropriate behavior. The results of their study are illustrated in Figure 5.6. The students were fifteen girls in a high-school business class who had a tendency to change the subject of class discussions away from academic topics, hence "subject-changes" per minute are plotted on the ordinate. If the girls changed the subject fewer than a specified number of times per period for the first four days of the week they earned a "free" Friday, a day to spend the 50-minute

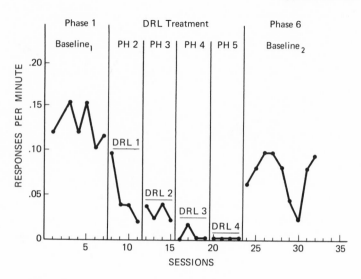

FIGURE 5.6.

*The rate of subject-changes for a class of high-school senior girls during Baseline 1, treatment, and Baseline 2 phases. "Free" Fridays could be earned by the group if they made fewer than the specified number of subject-changes for each of the first four days of the week. The limit for the first treatment week was five or fewer subject-changes during the 50-minute sessions (DRL 1). DRL 2 required three or fewer subject-changes. DRL 3 required one or fewer and DRL 4 required zero subject-changes.*

Source: S. M. Deitz, & A. C. Repp, "Decreasing Classroom Misbehavior through the Use of DRL Schedules of Reinforcement," Journal of Applied Behavior Analysis, 1973, 6, P. 459. Reprinted by permission.

period as they wished. (The letters DRL stand for "Differential Reinforcement of Low Rate," a technical designation for the type of reinforcement schedule employed here.) As the criterion for reinforcement was lowered, the subject-changing behavior declined to meet the criterion, strongly suggesting that the criterion was causally related to the behavior.

Applied behavior analysis offers powerful tools for use in measuring and changing pupil performance and for evaluating instructional methods. While it is not a panacea for educational ills, it does offer many suggestions for remedial techniques. The competent teacher of exceptional children will seek more information about applied behavior analysis than is offered in this chapter and will attempt to stay abreast of new developments in this young and rapidly growing technology.

# Visual
# Perceptual Disabilities

# 6

Not all children identified as learning disabled evidence visual perceptual problems. To the reader for whom this text is his very first exposure to the field of learning disabilities the above statement will probably seem so logical as to be a trifle trivial. We have chosen to begin this chapter with such an assertion, however, in order to alert the introductory student to one of the most common misconceptions in the area of learning disabilities. Though it should be obvious that children can have learning problems for a variety of reasons, in some circles the term "learning disabilities" is synonomous with the term "visual perceptual disabilities." As has been pointed out in Chapter 1, the fact that the field of learning disabilities evolved from the pioneering work of Werner and Strauss, whose primary interests were in visual processes, has undoubtedly led to the present emphasis on visual perceptual problems. The most frequently occurring mode of educational programming for learning disabled children focuses upon visual perceptual training activities (Hallahan & Cruickshank, 1973).

In reaction to this strong emphasis on visual perceptual training, there is a growing movement to discount the existence of visual problems in favor of the consideration of disabilities in other spheres of development—language, cognition, audition, for example. As will be discussed later in the next chapter, it is undeniably true that visual perceptual training programs as they are usually employed are of questionable benefit. Unfortunately, in their vociferous attack upon the efficacy of visual training, critics have implied that one should not be concerned about whether or not a child has a visual problem (e.g., Cohen 1969a, b). On the other hand, in defense of their positions, advocates of visual training often sound *as if* they believe that all learning disabled children have visual deficits.

The common-sense point of view holds that ( *a* ) not all children with learning problems have visual deficits, ( *b* ) some children with learning problems have visual deficits, and ( *c* ) the remediation of visual perceptual disabilities may *help* in the remediation of the child's learning problems (we will return to point ( *c* ) later in the chapter). The question of the efficacy of the various visual training programs is an empirical one and should not be confused with the fact that some children find it difficult to learn because of visual perceptual disturbances. Given that some children who perform poorly on educational tasks do so for reasons *other* than visual perceptual deficits, it is no wonder that research in which such children are not carefully eliminated from the study may show visual perceptual training to be of little value.

The kinds of visual perceptual disabilities with which we are concerned in this chapter should be distinguished from the types of visual deficits that are most commonly associated with the blind and partially sighted, that is, deficits in visual acuity. The latter defects are caused by improper functioning of the sensory organ itself—the eye—due to malformation, injury, or disease (DeMott, 1974). Examples of such visual deficits are myopia (nearsightedness), caused by the projection of visual stimuli on a point too far in front of the retina, and hyperopia (farsightedness), caused by the focal point of the visual stimuli falling behind the retina. Strabismus (cross-eyed) and nystagmus (jerking eye movements) are yet further examples of problems that may be due to a functional problem of the eye. The visual perceptual problems addressed within the field of learning disabilities, however, are concerned with disabilities that occur in a child despite the fact that he has structurally sound eyes and adequate muscular control over them. Getman (1965) draws the distinction between problems associated with a defect in the sensory organ and a problem due to a *perceptual* disability when he distinguishes between "sight" and "vision."

> Neither can vision and sight be equated. In the hope that this confusion can be terminated once and for all, time and space will be taken to define vision so all phrases in which it is used will be more meaningful and productive. Certainly, vision is usually related to the actions of the eye, and to the impact of light upon a retina. We must constantly remember that vision will not, and cannot, occur JUST BECAUSE light patterns are distributed across the retina. The eye is not a camera that takes pretty pictures which are then sent on to the brain for storage in a film locker. When light strikes the eye, there is *sight* response in the eye itself, but if the organism is to profit from this sight action, there must be an integration of this information with all other information systems

before any interpretation of the light pattern is achieved. Vision is a very complex result of a very simple action in the light receptor end-organ. (p. 51)

Thus, a child may have 20/20 visual acuity and still have a visual perceptual problem. It is not enough simply to administer a standard test of visual acuity such as a Snellen chart to a child experiencing learning problems in school. The child's ability to make perceptual judgments must also be assessed.

## ANALYSIS OF DISTINCTIVE FEATURES

Visual perception has been a topic under investigation by psychologists for many years, but it has not been until relatively recently that any systematic theoretical construction has occurred. This is particularly true with regard to the study of visual perceptual development in children. With an increase in methodological sophistication and mechanical recording techniques, investigators have begun to make advances in understanding the perceptual development of infants and young children. The experimental work and theory of Eleanor Gibson, in particular, is seen as a viable way of viewing perceptual development (Pick & Pick, 1970; Reese & Lipsitt, 1970).

Gibson's (1969) theory of perceptual learning posits that as children develop perceptually they learn to discriminate among stimuli on the basis of what have been termed "distinctive features." The child learns to distinguish objects by noting those particular features that are most salient in terms of defining the particular object being perceived. The child learns, for example, that a square is different from a circle because one has corners and the other has no corners at all. The feature that distinguishes a square from a circle is the existence of corners. The discrimination between a square and a rectangle, however, is based upon the further distinctive feature of the relationship between the lengths of the four sides of the square and the lengths of the four sides of the rectangle.

How children come to develop visual discrimination ability is similar to how adults come to discriminate between birds. The adult who takes up the hobby of bird watching is, at first, overwhelmed with the myriad sizes, shapes, and colors of birds. After repeated exposure to the same birds, however, the experienced bird watcher is able to pick out species at a glance. He learns, for instance, that a great many varieties can be distinguished by coloring, shape of head, and shape of tail. On the other hand, from a distance he learns that birds cannot be readily distinguished on the basis of their feet and legs. The features of coloring and head and tail shape, then, become the ones to which he attends when he first catches a glimpse of a bird in the woods. Gibson reports a concrete example of how adults use distinctive features when confronted with difficult perceptual problems. She notes that the first use of distinctive features under experimental conditions was conducted by Gagne and Gibson (1947) with Air Force trainees. In times of combat it is important that pilots be capable of identifying various kinds of aircraft. Gagne and Gibson tested two different methods of training pilots to identify numerous planes. One group was provided a standard set of distinctive features to distinguish planes while the other group was trained to focus on the whole form of the planes. The group receiving distinctive feature training was clearly superior.

We have briefly outlined Gibson's theory of distinctive features because much of what can be said about visual perceptual disabilities can be stated within its framework. The kinds of disabilities children display in the visual realm can be understood within the context of Gibson's differentiation theory. This is not to say that it can account for every detail concerning the whys and wherefores of visual deficits, but that it is important to attempt to relate visual disabilities to what is currently known about the normal development of visual perception.

## VISUAL PERCEPTION DISABILITIES

Children with learning problems manifest numerous kinds of visual perceptual disabilities. Three of the most common will be discussed in this chapter: problems in form, position in space, and visual closure. These particular disabilities have been chosen because they are among the most frequently cited visual problems and are deemed influential in contributing to academic disabilities. One other disability—figure-background (the difficulty in differentiating between figure and background) —could be included here, but we have elected to include that disability within the chapter on distractibility.

### Form Perception

Perhaps the most basic visual discrimination that the child makes is that of the perception of the property of form. Whether it be the differentiation of the letter $B$ from $P$ or the shape of a ball from a block, the ability to perceive the shape of objects and pictures is an important skill for the developing child to obtain.

Apparently one of the first forms to be perceived by the infant is that of the human face. In a number of now classic studies, Fantz and his colleagues (Fantz, 1958; 1961; 1963; 1966; Fantz, Ordy, & Udelf, 1962) have investigated infants' responses to various kinds of facial patterns. They have found that infants less than a week old exhibit preferences for looking at patterned rather than unpatterned circles and particularly at circles containing a schematic of a face. The research on infant perception of faces reviewed by Gibson (1969) indicates that by about six months the infant is capable of perceiving the human face. The baby is able to differentiate it from other patterns (Kagan & Lewis, 1965) and from scrambled line drawings of faces and faces with only one eye (Lewis, 1965). Besides using the frequency and amount of time infants fixate on patterns, some investigators have relied on the smiling response of infants to indicate the ability to perceive form. Gibson notes, for instance, that Ahrens (1954) has found by eight months the infant is capable of making quite refined discriminations—a smile was elicited for familiar adults and not for strangers, and in response to a smiling adult and not to an unsmiling adult.

Thus, at a very early age the human infant is capable of perceiving some rather complex forms based upon quite subtle distinctive features. While faces are certainly not the only forms the baby perceives within the first half year of life, they are a universal figure that most children come in contact with frequently. That the human adult face can also be associated with reinforcement (e.g., the child looks at the face and the adult picks the child up or fondles him in some way) is no doubt a factor in establishing the child's perceptual discrimination of facial features, at first, and later of familiar faces.

Although the ability to perceive facial forms has not yet been studied in children who have visual perceptual disabilities, it is of interest to consider the effect of a visual perceptual disability on the capacity to distinguish faces. For the child who has a perceptual disability manifest within the first year of life due to brain dysfunction, maturational slowness, or some other cause, we could expect that he would have difficulty in discriminating the facial form. Besides depriving the infant of the opportunity to build appropriate percepts of faces, human figures, and other objects, such a perceptual disability might create an unhealthy relationship between the parents and child. We will discuss the problem of parent-child social interaction in Chapter 10; suffice it to say here that a child who is unable to discriminate the facial form of his parents may lead his parents to reject him or at least to withhold reinforcement for perceptual responses.

In addition to considering the effect an already existent perceptual disability could have on discriminating the facial form, it is also worthwhile to speculate that one environmental determinant of form perception problems might originate at the time when the infant should be discerning the distinctive features of the face. If, for example, the parent seldom places his or her face in close proximity to the child's, there would be little opportunity for the child to recognize the facial form. A child who sees numerous faces (e.g., the institutionalized child) but no one face consistently may also have problems. Also, if the adult does not reinforce the looking and smiling responses of the child, it can be speculated that this might lead to a child's inability to perceive the facial form. Obviously, it will be a number of years before the infant will be required to perceive various forms in an academic situation, but the notion of "critical periods"* for development alerts one to consider the possibility that the infant who is thwarted in his efforts to perceive facial features may be hindered in perceiving various forms as he develops.

FORM PERCEPTION AND ITS RELATIONSHIP TO ACHIEVEMENT. The child with poor form perception is at a distinct disadvantage when confronted with school-related activities. The printed materials the teacher presents to the child require him to be able to discriminate among a variety of forms. The classroom and many of the activities and materials that take place within it are extremely visual in nature. Visual stimuli are constantly being presented to the child, and he must be an efficient perceiver of a variety of shapes. The inability to discriminate form can produce a chaotic and frustrating world for the child.

There is hardly an academic activity that does not require the child to engage in form perception. Consider, for example, the typical math problems presented. In the early stages, the proverbial concrete aid of the pictures of three apples and two apples shown to the child with the statement, "If we have three apples and add two more apples, how many will we have?" will be of little benefit to the student unable to perceive the apples as individuals and groups. During the later stages of math a child will be able to perform computations in "his head"; if he has a visual perceptual problem, however, he will likely have difficulty with problems in written form. The child who has difficulty in discriminating between a + and a — or a 7 and a 1 will have problems on his math worksheets.

The most obvious classroom activity requiring the child to discriminate forms is that of reading. The learning of the letters of the alphabet, syllables, and words will undoubtedly be impeded if there is difficulty in perceiving the form of the letters, syllables, and words. That

* There is a body of literature (see Hunt, 1961) to suggest that lower animals and humans who miss the chance to engage in certain activities at certain times in their development will have difficulty later in obtaining the skills involved in those activities.

the discrimination of letters is a crucial skill in the early stages of reading is evidenced by an extensive literature review conducted by Chall (1967). She concluded that the letter knowledge of young children is a better predictor of early reading ability than the various tests of intelligence and language ability. The work of Staats (Staats, Brewer, & Gross, 1970; Staats & Butterfield, 1965; Staats, Finley, Minke, & Wolf, 1964; Staats, Minke, Goodwin, & Landeen, 1967) also stresses the importance of letter discrimination, and his reading program (which will be discussed later in this chapter) emphasizes the training of letter discrimination. As Staats, Brewer, and Gross (1970) state:

> However, in the area of reading learning, one very basic skill is the discrimination of letters. That is, the stimuli involved in reading letters are in the child's world of stimuli quite similar, even when generally considered (Staats, 1968). For example, if one trained a child to read the letter A mixed in with a group of pictures, it would be found that the child would also give the response A to *any* other letter presented. Some letters are even more similar and difficult to learn to discriminate. (p. 10)

Gibson (1969) has conducted a series of investigations that have determined which letters are more difficult to discriminate than others. She has found that discrimination difficulty relates directly to the kinds and numbers of distinctive features of the letters. The chart in Figure 6.1 presents the distinctive-feature analysis for the capital letters of the alphabet. For example, the letter W is composed of two diagonal lines. It also possesses cyclic redundancy in that it is composed of the two forms V and V. It also has the property of symmetry. Letters that possess similar features are the most difficult to distinguish from one another. One would expect, for instance, that children would have a relatively harder time discriminating an M from an N and an M from a W than an O from an N or an R from an M. Gibson has also found that letters containing diagonals were quite difficult. Letters differing only on the feature of curved versus straight (e.g., P and F), however, were easily differentiated.

Armed with the knowledge of the distinctive features of letters, the classroom teacher can be more aware of the specific task demands he makes of his pupils. For example, the teacher should not be alarmed if in the early stages of learning letters a child has some initial difficulty in distinguishing those that are composed of diagonal lines. Occasional mistakes with difficult letters should also be expected. It is the child who continues to have difficulty and who even makes frequent errors on easily discriminable letters who should be given extra attention. In the

| Features | A | E | F | H | I | L | T | K | M | N | V | W | X | Y | Z | B | C | D | G | J | O | P | R | Q | S | U |
|---|---|---|---|---|---|---|---|---|---|---|---|---|---|---|---|---|---|---|---|---|---|---|---|---|---|---|
| **Straight** | | | | | | | | | | | | | | | | | | | | | | | | | | |
| horizontal | + | + | + | + | | + | + | | | | | | | + | | | | + | | | | | | | | |
| vertical | | + | + | + | + | + | + | + | + | + | | | | + | | + | | + | | | | + | + | | | |
| diagonal / | + | | | | | | | + | + | | + | + | + | + | + | | | | | | | | | | | |
| diagonal \ | + | | | | | | | + | + | + | + | + | + | + | | | | | | | | + | + | | | |
| | | | | | | | | | | | | | | | | | | | | | | | | | | |
| **Curve** | | | | | | | | | | | | | | | | | | | | | | | | | | |
| closed | | | | | | | | | | | | | | | | + | | + | | | + | + | + | + | | |
| open V | | | | | | | | | | | | | | | | | | | + | | | | | | | + |
| open H | | | | | | | | | | | | | | | | | + | | + | | | | | | + | |
| Intersection | + | + | + | + | | | | | | | | | + | | | + | | | | | | + | + | + | | |
| | | | | | | | | | | | | | | | | | | | | | | | | | | |
| **Redundancy** | | | | | | | | | | | | | | | | | | | | | | | | | | |
| cyclic change | | + | | | | | | | | | | + | | | | + | | | | | | | | + | | |
| symmetry | + | + | | + | + | + | + | + | | | + | + | + | + | | + | + | + | | | + | | | | | + |
| | | | | | | | | | | | | | | | | | | | | | | | | | | |
| **Discontinuity** | | | | | | | | | | | | | | | | | | | | | | | | | | |
| vertical | + | + | + | + | | + | + | + | + | | | | | + | | | | | | | | + | + | | | |
| horizontal | | + | + | | | + | + | | | | | | | | + | | | | | | | | | | | |

FIGURE 6.1.
*Chart of distinctive features for a set of graphemes.*

*Source: E. J. Gibson,* Principles of Perceptual Learning and Development, © 1969, *p. 88. Reprinted by permission of Prentice-Hall, Inc.*

teaching process itself, awareness of the distinctive features of letters will enable the teacher to focus his efforts on the most probable cause(s) for error. The child making errors in differentiating an *R* from a *P* can be instructed that the difference between the two letters is the addition of a diagonal line on the letter *R*. The child's attention can also be drawn to the crucial distinctive feature by highlighting the diagonal line with a bright color cue.*

### Position in Space

The ability to perceive the particular spatial orientation of stimuli in the environment has come to be known as "position in space" ability. Position in space ability can be thought of as a more refined or particular kind of form perception ability. The child with this disability has problems with the relative position of stimuli.

The classic example of a position in space disability is that of the

---

* The use of color cues is especially recommended for children who have attentional problems.

child who has a strong tendency to reverse letters or whole words while reading. For example, he might read "ben" instead of "den" or "was" instead of "saw." At one time the reading disability literature contained many references to "reversal" problems and numerous case studies were discussed. There is no solid empirical basis for establishing the proportion of poor readers who exhibit reversals. Nonetheless, the general notion espoused today is that reversal problems occur in fewer children than was previously thought.

Some children do, of course, make reversals in reading, and a few of them make enough such errors to be considered to have position in space problems. Every teacher of the early elementary grades can attest to the fact that some children exhibit an inclination to reverse letters and words. It is the *severity* of the reversal problem that must be considered.

If it is a relatively normal phenomenon, and the experienced teacher can verify this, for normal children to confuse letters that may be reversed —*b* and *d, g* and *d, p* and *g*, and so forth—then when should the teacher become concerned? Gibson and her colleagues have performed experiments that provide the teacher with general guidelines regarding the relative frequency of reversals. Gibson, Gibson, Pick, and Osser (1962) conducted a classic study in which twelve variants were drawn for a number of artificial graphic forms. The letterlike forms were made to correspond closely to the distinctive features of actual letters. The standards (S column) along with their variants are presented in Figure 6.2 taken from Gibson (1963). There were four kinds of variations used. The lines of a form could be changed to curves or vice versa. The forms could be rotated to various degrees or reversed. The forms could be changed with regard to perspective, and they could undergo a topological change with regard to a break or close in lines.

Children aged four to eight years were presented with a matching task. Given a standard figure, the child was required to find from among the variants at least one identical form among the figures that was the same as the standard. The results are shown in Figure 6.3. Relevant to our discussion here, the graph indicates that at early ages the reversal transformation is a difficult one. However, children's reversal errors drop markedly until by age seven or eight they are few in number. This study should, therefore, provide an *indication* to the teacher that in the very early grades children may have some initial reversal problems. By second or third grade, however, reversal errors should occur infrequently, if at all.

Gibson's rationale for why there is such a sudden drop in errors from ages five to seven years is, in fact, related to the child's experiences in school. Up until the time the child is exposed to letters in school, he does not have to use the distinctive feature of orientation to distinguish

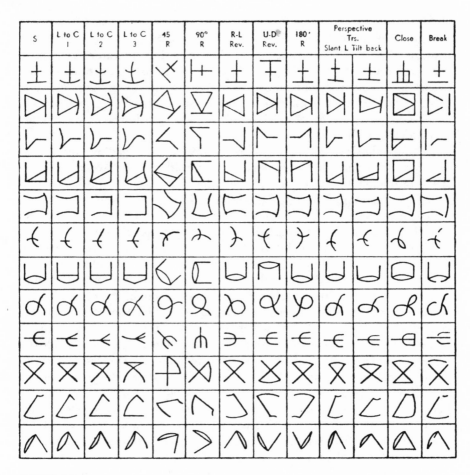

FIGURE 6.2.

Artificial graphic forms and twelve variants. [Note: S is the standard. The four variations are: lines to curves (L to C); rotation (45°, 90°, 180°), or reversal (right to left, up and down); perspective changes; and break or close in lines]

Source: E. J. Gibson, "Development of Perception: Discrimination of Depth Compared with Discrimination of Graphic Symbols," in J. C. Wright and J. Kagan (Eds.), Basic Cognitive Processes in Children, Monographs of the Society for Research in Child Development, 1963, Ser. No. 86, Vol. 28, No. 2, p. 17. Reprinted by permission.

objects.* An object in the child's environment remains the same object even when rotated. Some letters, however, are different *solely* because

---

* That analysis of distinctive features can be learned at a much earlier age than is usual for school children when appropriate instruction is provided is suggested by the work of A. W. Staats and others who have taught reading skills successfully to preschoolers (cf. Staats, 1973).

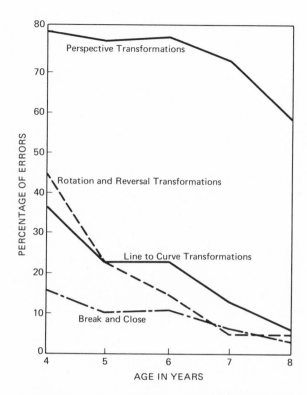

FIGURE 6.3.

*Errors in matching variants with standard graphic forms by type of variant and age of S.*

Source: E. J. Gibson, "Development of Perception: Discrimination of Depth Compared with Discrimination of Graphic Symbols," in J. C. Wright and J. Kagan (Eds.), Basic Cognitive Processes in Children, Monographs of the Society for Research in Child Development, 1963, Ser. No. 86, Vol. 28, No. 2, p. 19. Reprinted by permission.

they differ in orientation, like *b* and *d*. Consequently the normal child learns through schooling to pay attention to the feature of orientation.

Gibson states that the previous use of a transformation for distinguishing objects also explains why certain other transformations in the above experiment were either easy or difficult. Because perspective transformations are not important for the identification of objects nor for the discrimination of letters in school, errors remained high for forms that varied in slant and tilt in the experiment. On the other hand, Gibson states that because the break versus close feature is crucial for discrimination of both objects and letters there is logic to the finding that all of the subjects, even the youngest, had little trouble distinguishing open from closed forms. This analysis of the previous use of the distinctive features required for differentiating letters can explain why it is that children with reading disabilities are described more often as having problems in confusing letters such as *b* and *d* (reversal transformation) compared with letters such as *P* and *F* (closed versus break transformation).

With regard to the orientation of letters, the examples we have used thus far have been those in which the letters were left-right reversals of each other: *b* and *d*. It is usually reported by teachers that the left-right reversals are the more frequent; however, there are also instances when children will confuse up-down reversals, for example, *p* and *b*. The research on normal children also supports the teachers' observations that left-right reversals are more frequent in the process of reading. Sekuler and Rosenblith (1964) and Huttenlocher (1967) found that whether the letters to be discriminated are aligned vertically or horizontally will make a difference in whether the left-right or up-down reversal is more confusing. When the letters are presented horizontally (as they are in reading), the left-right reversal (e.g., *b* and *d*) is more difficult than when the letters are presented vertically. Just the opposite is true for up-down reversible letters. Table 6.1 summarizes the results of the two studies. Pick and Pick (1970) speculate that the reason for the interaction between mode of presentation and difficulty of discrimination may be due to the scanning strategies of children:

> Why should there be an interaction of this type? A scanning hypothesis might be invoked. Suppose S scanned repeatedly across a pair of stimuli in the direction of their alignment, as in a TV scanner, registering only the number of elements present on each scan. Then left-right mirror images would register identically in horizontal alignment, and up-down mirror images would register identically in vertical alignment. (p. 801)

Whatever the exact reason, the results of these studies corroborate the reports of teachers that left-right reversals are more frequent than

TABLE 6.1     Reversible Letters Presented Horizontally or Vertically

| *Letters to be Discriminated* | *Mode of Presentation* | |
|---|---|---|
| | *Resulting in More Errors* | *Resulting in Fewer Errors* |
| b and d | b  d | b<br>d |
| b and p | b<br>p | b  p |

up-down reversals. Inasmuch as reading is a left-to-right activity rather than an up and down process, we would expect the left-right reversible letters to be harder to discriminate than the up-down reversibles.

Given the evidence that left-right reversals are more difficult to discriminate in reading from left to right than when they are presented one above the other, the teacher may wish to incorporate this knowledge in his teaching techniques. The child who exhibits problems in differentiating $b$ from $d$ may be given a series of teacher-made training exercises in which the $b$ and $d$ are presented vertically on flash cards. After a number of successful discriminations with these presentations, the teacher could gradually align the $b$ and $d$ closer and closer to the horizontal on the flash card. After a series of exercises the $b$ and $d$ would be aligned vertically.

### Visual Closure

Another disability of visual perception frequently attributed to children with learning disabilities is visual closure ability. Concern for visual closure originated with the work of the Gestalt psychologists who were interested in how individuals formed visual "wholes" or Gestalts of forms. Visual perceptual psychologists working within the Gestalt tradition have conducted a number of experiments in which stimuli are presented with parts missing. The subjects are then asked to identify the object. The reader can grasp the general idea of what is involved by writing a few words or drawing a picture in pencil on a paper and then running his eraser through it a couple of times. If shown just the final product (see, for example, Figure 6.4), an individual must provide the missing information himself in order to recognize the picture or words.

Relating to visual closure ability, there are theories of perceptual development which hold that as children develop they are better able to recognize objects when provided with only partial perceptual cues. Wohlwill (1970), for example, notes that redundancy of stimulus information is necessary for young children, but with age children require fewer and fewer visual cues. Experimental evidence on this subject has been

FIGURE 6.4.
Example of some words that require visual closure ability for recognition.

obtained by Gollin (1956; 1960) who has presented children with pictures of incomplete objects. Older children require less complete pictures in order to make accurate identifications.

Studies on eye movements of children also support the contention that children develop the ability to perceive accurately without attending to all of the visual information provided them. As Wohlwill (1970) has noted:

> For the older child and adult, particularly when dealing with familiar stimuli or stimuli that can be readily assimilated to relevant schemata, perception probably takes on a more economical character, with briefer glances from a fixation point within the periphery of the object sufficing for identification or even discrimination (e.g., Piaget and Vinh-Bang, 1961). Indeed, it has been found that adults do not need to explore a visual shape through eye movements in order to recognize it (Mooney, 1958) or to make judgements of qualities such as symmetry (Zusne and Michels, 1964); this holds true even for fairly complex and unfamiliar stimuli.* (p. 399)

The ability to make perceptual judgments based on only partial stimulus information is crucial for the academic activity of reading. Research evidence indicates that efficient readers do not focus with their eyes on all of the letters of all of the words that they read. As a child matures he is able to take in more and more words or phrases at a glance (Gibson, 1969). Experiments have determined that the eye "gets ahead" of what is being read and thus provides the reader with perceptual information before it is actually "read" by the reader (see Chapter 9 for further discussion of this matter). In order to become an efficient reader, then, we can assume that a child must be able to recognize words and even groups of words even though his eyes do not orient to every individual letter. The basis for the commercial programs designed to increase people's reading speed (the technique of "speed reading"), in fact, relies upon the training of the ability to recognize phrases without focusing specifically on each word. The child who manifests difficulty in visual closure would thus be hampered in his reading efficiency. To have to focus on each and every letter would certainly slow down the child's rate of reading. The reader of this text can obtain an idea of what a slow and painful process this would be by taking an index card and cutting a small hole in it so that only one letter at a time can be seen through it. Covering a line of print with the card and slowly moving it across the page would provide an indication of how difficult it is to read when one needs to orient to every

* J. S. Wohlwill, Perceptual development, in H. W. Reese & L. P. Lipsitt, (Eds.), *Experimental Child Psychology* (New York: Academic Press, 1970), p. 399. Reprinted by permission.

letter on the line of print. Not only is speed drastically reduced, but one also finds that there is an increased burden on one's memory. By the time the end of a relatively long word is reached, the memory for the beginning letters is taxed. While it is admittedly speculative to attempt to "get inside" the mind of a child with a learning problem, the above is a plausible description of how a visual closure disability hinders the child in his ability to read.

## STANDARDIZED ASSESSMENT
## OF VISUAL PERCEPTUAL ABILITY

When a child is referred to a school psychologist because he is exhibiting a reading disability, one of the first areas to be assessed is usually that of visual perception. The school psychologist may choose to administer tests designed to look at the visual abilities of the child—for instance, Frostig's Developmental Test of Visual Perception—or he may select tests that include certain items or subtests constructed to require the child to use his visual perceptual abilities—the Stanford-Binet or WISC tests, for example. It is, of course, essential that a number of measures be taken.

Many of the visual tests (such as Bender-Gestalt) or visual items on more general tests require the child to copy a figure or in some other way to use both his motor and visual skills at the same time. We will deal more specifically with visual-motor abilities and their assessment in the next chapter; nevertheless, a word needs to be said here regarding the difference between visual perceptual and visual-motor problems. If a child copies a figure incorrectly, the teacher or psychologist cannot assume that he has a visual perceptual difficulty *or* a visual-motor problem. More information is needed. One technique that can be used was employed by Bortner and Birch (1962) in an experimental study. If a child copies a number of figures incorrectly, he can later be shown the correct figure as a standard to which he is to choose a match from choices including a correct one plus his incorrect copy. If he can match correctly, then there is an indication that his problem is a visual-motor one. If he chooses his incorrect copy as being identical to the standard, then there is evidence that he has a visual perceptual difficulty.

### Assessment of Form Perception

With the above caution regarding the difference between visual perceptual and visual-motor problems in mind, many of the tests that require the child to draw or copy a figure can be indicative of form perception problems. The tester must be sure to ascertain that the problem is not a motor or visual-motor one. Examples of tests and subtests that require the child to draw a figure are the Bender-Gestalt, the Visual-Motor Coordination subtest from Frostig's Developmental Test of Visual Perception, the Draw-a-Design and Draw-a-Child subtests from the McCarthy Scales of Children's Abilities, and the Visual Achievement Forms from the Purdue Perceptual-Motor Survey.

Another way of looking at a child's visual discrimination ability, without involving any drawing by the child, is to analyze carefully how the child responds to items or subtests that require a response to visually-presented material. For example, at the four-year-old level there is a test on the Stanford-Binet entitled Picture Vocabulary. The child is required to identify by name fourteen out of eighteen line drawings of familiar objects: airplane, telephone, horse, et cetera. If a child does poorly on this test, any number of reasons still obtain as to why he does so. There are some ways, however, in which one can attempt to find out what the chances are that the poor performance is due to poor visual discrimination. Let us consider the following hypothetical example. Note in this case how the psychologist uses a standardized test in a rather unorthodox manner in order to obtain a clearer picture of what the specific disability of the child is.

Freddy, aged seven years, has been referred by his second-grade teacher to the school psychologist for evaluation. The teacher has observed that though Freddy seems to have a more than adequate vocabulary, he has a great deal of difficulty in reading. The school psychologist administers the Stanford-Binet IQ test and obtains an overall IQ of 110. He is curious about Freddy's visual perceptual functioning, however, so he goes back and administers the Picture Vocabulary subtest of the Stanford-Binet. This would not normally be done because Freddy had generally passed all of the tests well-beyond the four-year level. The psychologist, however, finds that Freddy has a very difficult time with the Picture Vocabulary, identifying only six of the eighteen pictured objects (fourteen are required in order to pass at the four-year-old level). On the other hand, Freddy was quite capable of defining words on the Vocabulary test (orally administered) at the eight-year-old level; he did well enough, in fact, to get credit for the eight-year level even though he was only seven years old. Before concluding that Freddy might have a visual perceptual disability that caused him to do quite poorly on Picture Vocabulary compared with Vocabulary, the school psychologist did one more thing. To determine if Freddy might have a problem in recalling names of objects, the examiner *read* a definition of the objects from the Picture Vocabulary test without showing the pictures. On this kind of administration, Freddy was able to identify sixteen of the eighteen objects, indicating that he was able to recall their names. The school psychologist therefore concluded that it was *quite possibly* the fact that Freddy had difficulty in visually discriminating objects that caused him to do poorly in naming pictures of objects.

The words *"quite possibly"* are italicized in the preceding sentence because it is never wise to come to firm conclusions based upon a few instances of test behavior. In the above example, further indications would need to be looked for on the Stanford-Binet and other tests. For example, the examiner might wish to administer another test—Discrimination of Forms—from the Stanford-Binet. Again, this test is from the four-year level, but because there is already some information to suggest that Freddy is well below his chronological age level of seven, it would be quite appropriate to administer it to him. The test requires the child to match a geometric figure—e.g., a circle, a square—with an identical one from among a number of alternatives. If Freddy were to do poorly on this four-year-old-level test, then there would be an even stronger case that his problem was a visual perceptual disability.

The Visual Reception subtest of the ITPA is yet another device that is often used to indicate the visual discrimination ability of children. Here the child is shown a picture of a familiar object (e.g., a dog) for three seconds. A card containing another dog and a number of other figures is shown to the child and he is asked to find an object in it like the one in the original picture. The correct answer, of course, is the dog on the new card. On the early cards, the child must find choices that are of the same specific category, e.g., dogs, wagons, balls. On later cards, however, the matching becomes more difficult in that the child must match on the basis of the function of the object, even though there is no similarity in what the two objects look like. In fact, "look alikes" are included as distracters among the alternatives. A stoplight is to be paired with a stop sign and one of the alternatives is a picture of three pie plates attached to a stick which looks like a stoplight in a gross way. The child is thus required to obtain visual meaning from the pictures. Form perception problems would prohibit a child from performing well on the Visual Reception subtest. However, if a child were to do poorly only on this subtest and appropriately on other tests of visual perception (e.g., Bender-Gestalt, Discrimination of Forms test on the Stanford-Binet), one would *suspect* that form discrimination was adequate in the child but that the child had problems in deciphering the conceptual meaning of visual pictures.

### Assessment of Position
### in Space Ability

In many of the above examples of potential perception of form disabilities, the possibility of an even more specific disability cannot be ruled out. The child, for instance, may be unable to match two squares on the Discrimination of Forms test of the Stanford-Binet because he cannot perceive the spatial orientation of the figures. For him, the square may be perceived in a state of rotation.

There is one subtest in particular that has been designed to test the ability to appreciate the perceptual characteristic of position in space —the Position in Space subtest of Marianne Frostig's Developmental Test of Visual Perception. On this subtest the child is shown an object in a particular position. He is to choose the same object in the same position from among a number of choices of the same object in a variety of positions. Figure 6.5 is an example of one of the items from the Position in Space subtest.

Another test that could cause problems for the child with a position in space disability is the Patience: Rectangles test from the fifth year of the Stanford-Binet. The tester presents two pieces of cardboard like those pictured in Figure 6.6. The child is then instructed to put the two pieces together in order to make a rectangle. It is easy to see from Figure 6.6 that a child with an orientation problem could have difficulty on this task.

As with form perception, position in space ability should be assessed by looking for a number of different instances in which position in space perception is required for appropriate performance. Final diagnosis based on a single item is not appropriate. In the case of position in

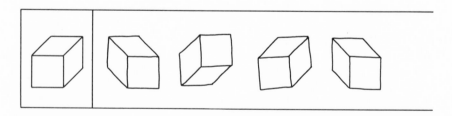

FIGURE 6.5.

Example of one of the items from the Position in Space subtest of the Marianne Frostig Developmental Test of Visual Perception.

Source: Reproduced by special permission from Marianne Frostig Developmental Test of Visual Perception by Marianne Frostig in collaboration with Welty Lefever, Ph.D. and John R. B. Whittlesey, M.S., Copyright 1961, published by Consulting Psychologists Press Inc.

Child is required to make a rectangle

from two triangles placed before him.

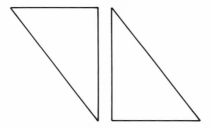

FIGURE 6.6.
The Patience: Rectangles test from the
Stanford-Binet.

Source: Stanford-Binet Intelligence Scale,
Revised, 3rd edition (Boston: Houghton
Mifflin, 1973). Reprinted by permission.

space ability, the teacher's observation that the child frequently reverses letters while reading is a cue that he, or the school psychologist, should look carefully to determine whether the child possesses a disability in visual perception of position in space.

### Assessment of Visual Closure Ability

There are fewer devices to use to test children's ability to close visually than instruments for the assessment of form perception or spatial position. The ITPA has a subtest named Visual Closure. On an item from this subtest, the child is presented with a strip of paper containing pictures of several objects—for example, bottles—in various positions partially hidden among a number of other distracting objects. The tester asks the child to find as many of the bottles as he can within a specified time period. The assumption is that the child must be able to supply the missing portions of the bottles in order to find them. Another way of looking at it, is that there is an assumption that the child must be capable of identifying objects based upon limited stimulus information. It should also be pointed out, however, that a highly distractible child could have difficulty on this subtest due to the fact that the objects to be found are embedded and surrounded by other objects. The child must be able to ignore the irrelevant objects in order to find the relevant ones quickly.

Two other tests that can be considered as indicators of a child's visual closure ability are the Picture Completion subtest of the WISC and the Mutilated Pictures test from the Stanford-Binet. In both of these the child is shown a number of pictures of objects that have missing parts— a comb, for instance, with some teeth missing. The child is required to identify what is missing.


## REMEDIAL PROGRAMS FOR
## VISUAL PERCEPTUAL DISABILITIES

Given that a child, or group of children, has a visual perceptual disability, what can the teacher do about it? There have been several remedial programs developed specifically for aiding children who have visual perceptual deficits. We will briefly outline two such programs here—the Getman, Kane, Halgren, and McKee (1964) and the Frostig and Horne (1964). It will become apparent from the description that both of these approaches contain activities designed for more than only visual deficits. In particular, visual-motor problems, which will be the topic of the next chapter, are dealt with by the Getman and the Frostig-Horne programs. The two approaches are presented in this chapter for the sake of cohesiveness and clarity. The reader should keep in mind, however, the idea that many aspects of the remedial programs presented in this chapter for visual deficits are also designed for visual-motor problems and vice versa.

### Getman, Kane, Halgren, and McKee's
### "The Physiology of Readiness"

In 1964 Getman and his colleagues published a manual of practical training activities for children with visual disabilities—*The Physiology of Readiness: An Action Program for the Development of Perception in Children.* This booklet includes activities that Getman had found successful in his many years of clinical work as an optometrist. Getman's program is based to a large extent upon the work of A. M. Skeffington, another optometrist (see Getman, 1976). Skeffington contributed almost forty years of papers through what is known as the Optometric Extension Program.

The program of Getman and his associates is based upon the following assumptions:

1. Academic performance in today's schools depends heavily upon form and symbol recognition and interpretation.

2. There are perceptual skills which can be developed and trained.

3. The development of perceptual skills is related to the levels of coordinations of the body systems, i.e., the better the coordinations of the body parts and body systems, the better the prospects are for developing perception of forms and symbols.

4. The child whose perceptual skills have been developed and extended is the child who is free to profit from instruction and to learn independently. The greater the development of the perceptual skills, the greater the capacity for making learning more effective. (p. iii)

The program of Getman and his co-workers is composed of activities subsumed under six general divisions:

1. General Coordination
2. Balance
3. Eye-Hand Coordination
4. Eye Movements
5. Form Perception
6. Visual Memory (Imagery)

PRACTICE IN GENERAL COORDINATION. This aspect of the program is designed to provide children with practice in total body movement. The exercises here deal mostly with movements of the head, arms, and legs. *Some** examples of such activities are:

1. The teacher requires the child to turn his head from side to side while he is lying on the floor. He is encouraged to turn his head until his ear touches the floor.

2. While lying on the floor, the child is asked to move his arms, with elbows straight, over his head until his hands touch.

3. While on his back, the child moves his legs, with knees straight, in scissors fashion.

4. The child is asked to make "Angels in the Snow" movements. He moves his arms up over his head and spreads his legs out and then brings his arms back to his side while moving his legs back together. The child repeats this procedure several times.

---

* These examples are described in order that the reader will be generally aware of the Getman program. For *proper* use of the program and others we describe, the reader should obtain a copy of the program itself.

5.   The child is to jump, hop, and skip.

PRACTICE IN BALANCE.   These activities involve the use of visual perception for the acquisition of better balance. Most of the activities include the use of a balance beam—a two-inch by four-inch board of about eight feet in length that is raised a couple of inches off the ground on supports. The child is involved in a number of exercises in which he is to walk on the four-inch width of the balance beam. For example, the child may be asked to:

1.   Walk heel-to-toe along the beam.
2.   Walk backwards toe-to-heel on the beam.

PRACTICE IN EYE-HAND COORDINATION.   For this part of the program the child is engaged in numerous chalkboard exercises. These activities are designed for the purpose of increasing the child's ability to coordinate his eyes and hands. Some of the chalkboard activities include having the child with both hands draw circles, horizontal lines, and vertical lines on the chalkboard. An exercise involving two children has one child place Xs on the board while the other one draws lines from one X to the next without taking the chalk off the board.

PRACTICE IN EYE MOVEMENTS.   Activities in this part of the program attempt to increase the child's ability to move his eyes quickly and accurately from one object to another. In one exercise, for example, the child is asked to alternate his fixation from his thumbs on his hands held in front of him to the teacher who is standing farther away. This training is for the development of near and far smooth eye movements.

PRACTICE IN FORM PERCEPTION.   Here there are two kinds of templates used—chalkboard and desk templates. The child uses templates of various figures—circle, square, triangle—in order to trace them first on the chalkboard and then on paper at his desk. Once he has mastered this skill, he is encouraged to draw the figures without the aid of templates.

PRACTICE IN VISUAL MEMORY.   These exercises are for the purpose of developing the child's imagery ability. A tachistoscope is needed so that the teacher can flash slides on the board. The Getman team indicates that if a tachistoscope is not available, one can manually move a piece of cardboard in front of and to the side of the projector lens. The child is shown various figures via the slide projector for very brief exposure periods. After a slide is shown, he is asked to respond to one of the figures in a variety of ways: name it, trace it in the air, circle it on a worksheet, trace it on a worksheet, draw a replica of it. Other slides are presented that show more complex figures and require the child to do different activities with them. The teacher can vary the exposure times, decreasing them as the child becomes more proficient.

### The Frostig-Horne
### Visual Perception Training Program

Frostig and Horne (1964) have written a commercially available program designed for remediation purposes or for readiness training. Like Getman, Marianne Frostig has been a pioneer in the field of learning disabilities. She is the founder of the Marianne Frostig Center of Educational Therapy in Los Angeles where many aspects of the Frostig-Horne program are implemented (see Frostig, 1976). The Frostig-Horne program follows closely the areas assessed in the *Marianne Frostig Developmental Test of Visual Perception* (Frostig, Lefever, & Whittlesey, 1964).

EYE-MOTOR COORDINATION EXERCISES. Worksheets are provided in the program for the teacher to give to the child. Activities for the child consist of a number of exercises that offer the child an opportunity to coordinate his eyes and hands. Boundaries are provided on the worksheets for the child to draw within. The boundaries vary in their direction and shape, curved or straight. The difficulty of the exercises is also controlled by the width of the boundary lines.

FIGURE-GROUND EXERCISES. These worksheets require the child to find and trace figures embedded within other lines and figures. The worksheets are sequenced so that the figures to be found and the background become more complex.

PERCEPTUAL CONSTANCY EXERCISES. The ability trained in this section of the Frostig-Horne program is that of perceptual generalization. The child is trained in recognizing that an object remains the same object even though it may be presented in a different form, color, size, or context. For example, a child must learn that two objects are both chairs even though one is smaller and softer than the other.

POSITION IN SPACE EXERCISES. This aspect of the program was included by Frostig and Horne for helping the child who exhibits reversals. The child is required to place himself in various positions in relation to objects in the classroom. He is to appreciate, for example, the position of being under or over a table. Worksheets are given that require the child to discriminate figures in various positions.

SPATIAL RELATIONS EXERCISES. The exercises included here are designed to provide a child with an appreciation of the spatial relationships among objects. Worksheets involve a number of activities where the child is required to observe spatial relationships.

### Kirk and Kirk's
### Visual Perceptual Training Suggestions

Kirk and Kirk (1971) have also made suggestions for training in visual perception. Their remediation techniques are outlined in *Psycholinguistic Learning Disabilities: Diagnosis and Remediation*. They present teaching activities based upon how a child scores on their test—the ITPA. While their activities are not as detailed as Getman's or Frostig's, they do list a number of general teaching strategies. Within the sphere of visual reception—the ability to obtain meaning from visually presented stimuli—Kirk and Kirk believe that there may be at least five different reasons for failure. The child may:

1. Lack prerequisite skills of visual-motor perception.
2. Not have the appropriate knowledge and experience.
3. Not observe stimuli within his visual field.
4. Not be able to associate meaning with visual symbols.
5. Not be able to use visual imagery.

For each of these five potential visual reception problems, Kirk and Kirk have devised teaching activities. To provide the child with visual-motor perception, for example, the teacher can use many of the same activities recommended by Getman and Frostig. If the child lacks visual experience, he is encouraged to explore his environment and the teacher discusses the things the child sees. For the child who is not observant of objects in his visual field, some suggested approaches are to instruct the child to pay attention to his visual environment. One recommended game is to bring the child into a room and then remove him and ask him to name what was in it. The child who has difficulty associating meaning with visual symbols is encouraged to do so by performing such activities as discriminating objects on the basis of color, size, shape, and so forth. Visual imagery is trained, for example, by asking the child to recall and describe pictorially past events.

Kirk and Kirk also have described activities for children with visual closure difficulties. Some activities they recommend include:

1. Asking the child to identify pictures that have missing parts.
2. The same procedure as above except with words.
3. Asking the child to identify silhouettes and dotted outlines.

There is an assortment of activities that have been recommended by individuals for the training of visual perceptual skills. Many of them are not included within any one program, but are contained in various sources (books, pamphlets, kits, movies). Many are also included within formal programs such as those of Getman and Frostig-Horne. Some activities have been used in different settings and have been included in such a wide variety of sources that it is impossible to tell who it was who first used the technique. In the field of learning disabilities, considerable overlap exists among commercial programs and books in recommended teaching strategies (see Wallace & Kauffman, 1973).

With regard to the utility and effectiveness of visual perceptual training, considerable controversy also exists. In the next chapter, we will discuss the efficacy of visual perceptual and visual-motor training.


## APPLIED ANALYSIS OF VISUAL PERCEPTION

From an applied behavior analysis standpoint, teaching children to make necessary visual discriminations is the essential element in teaching beginning reading and arithmetic skills. Children who evidence deficits in form perception, perception of position in space, or visual closure have failed to learn appropriate discriminations among visual stimuli. The remedial teacher's task, therefore, is to teach the visual discriminations that will allow the child to make correct academic responses.

An individual has learned a discrimination when he reliably responds to a given stimulus. A child has learned to discriminate $d$ from $b$ when he reliably responds by saying "dee" when shown the letter $d$ and by saying "bee" when shown the letter $b$. If a child reliably calls the correct word when shown the stimulus $dog$, but does not respond "dog" when presented with any other configuration of letters, then he has learned a word discrimination. Discrimination may involve auditory, visual, tactile, or other types of stimuli or complex combinations of stimuli. Furthermore, certain properties of stimuli, such as size, color, shape, intensity, may be discriminated. The crucial factor to be considered in children's visual perceptual difficulties is how to teach them to discriminate the relevant visual stimuli that are a part of academic tasks.

Children's discrimination learning has been studied extensively in the laboratory as well as in the classroom (cf., Bijou & Baer, 1966; Stevenson, 1972). It ordinarily consists of presenting the training stimulus and reinforcing the desired response. In the case of a laboratory experiment, the discrimination training may involve a comparatively simple stimulus, such as a small light mounted on a box, and a relatively simple response, such as pushing a lever protruding from a box. The experimenter may then train children to push the lever when the light is on and not to push when the light is off. He does this by giving the children reinforcers—tokens, trinkets, candies—for pushing the lever when the light is on and withholding the reinforcers for pushing the lever when the light is off. When a child consistently pushes the lever and obtains reinforcement in the "light on" condition but seldom or never pushes the lever in the "light off" condition, he has learned a simple visual discrimination. The experimenter may then be interested in studying certain aspects of discrimination by varying the reinforcement procedure, the color or intensity of the light, other stimuli that are paired with the light, and so on. In this way, significant information may be obtained about what discriminations a child can learn and how best to teach certain discriminations.

In the classroom, discrimination training makes use of the same basic principles and procedures used in the laboratory. If a teacher wishes to teach a child to discriminate his name from other words, he must present the child's name, perhaps printed on a card, and provide reinforcement only for the appropriate response, that is, saying his name. The teacher must withhold reinforcement for the child's incorrect responses, such as saying his name when another child's name is shown, saying his name before any card is shown, or saying another child's name when his own name card is shown. Whether or not the teacher is successful in teaching a child to discriminate his name, or to make any other discrimination, may depend on precisely how the name and other stimuli are presented, how the teaching trials are timed, how incorrect responses are handled, how reinforcement is given, and so forth.

The remainder of this chapter will be a discussion of how basic visual discriminations necessary for academic learning, especially reading, can be taught using applied behavior analysis methodology.

### Acquisition of
### Initial Visual Discriminations

Much of our knowledge about how children learn beginning reading, writing, and arithmetic skills has been contributed by Arthur W. Staats (Staats, 1973; Staats, Brewer, & Gross, 1970; Staats & Staats, 1963). After more than a decade of careful research, Staats has outlined a theory of reading that has as a basic tenet: learning to read involves the sequential acquisition of a hierarchy of visual discrimination skills. The child must first learn to attend to relevant stimuli (we will discuss the acquisition of attention skills in a later chapter). Next, he must learn to discriminate simple forms.

> These basic behavioral skills form the basis for learning the alphabet discriminations; these form the basis for learning the elementary reading units (grapheme-phoneme, i.e., letter-sound correspondences); these form the basis for acquiring a large repertoire of word-reading responses; and so on. (Staats, Brewer, & Gross, 1970, p. 76)

Reading, as well as other basic academic skills, requires learning that is cumulative and hierarchical. Learning new skills depends on having acquired more fundamental abilities, and learning proceeds from simpler to more complex tasks in an orderly fashion. Thus, if a child is experiencing learning difficulties or is not performing as expected for his age, one must analyze precisely the skills in this hierarchy that the child has acquired and teach those skills in which he is deficient. If a child is retarded in reading ability, it is essential to determine whether he has acquired certain component skills. If he can discriminate the letters of the alphabet but has not learned letter-sound (grapheme-phoneme) correspondences, then he must be instructed on letter-sound tasks.

Some theories of learning attribute much to a biological unfolding or "readiness" that develops from a mechanism within the child. A behavioral analysis, on the other hand, suggests that learning is acquired through explicit training. One need not (indeed *should* not) merely wait for the child to mature to the point of "readiness" when learning difficulties are encountered, for "it is *learning that makes the child ready!*" (Staats, 1973, p. 213). A child can be made ready to learn a specific skill by teaching him the more fundamental or prerequisite skills—those lower on the hierarchy. Included in the studies of Staats and his associates were children with severe learning problems, but these children were found to learn well when proper teaching procedures were employed. This finding suggested to Staats, Brewer, and Gross (1970) that appropriate teaching may be a preventative measure for learning difficulties:

> These . . . findings encourage the wider employment of [our] approach in treating children with problems *at an early age*. This should be done so that children do not develop deficits in behavior that will make appropriate later adjustment difficult or impossible. (p. 79)

Another prominent feature of Staats's theory is that because learning oral language and learning to read involve essentially the same principles, the child who learns oral language can learn to read *if appropriate con-*

*ditions are arranged* (Staats, 1973; Staats & Staats, 1962, 1963). It may be inappropriate and unproductive to attribute a child's reading problems to biological or central nervous system deficits *as long as the child has normal language.* Staats has observed that children usually are given many learning trials in the acquisition of oral language. In the acquisition of reading, on the other hand, children typically are provided with far fewer and more poorly arranged opportunities to learn. In teaching their child to talk, parents speak to him many thousands of times, giving him many thousands of explicit opportunities to respond and giving him clear, immediate reinforcement or feedback on his performance. But in learning to read the child typically is faced with a very different situation. He may be in a class with 25 other children, be given only a few opportunities to respond each day, and be given delayed reinforcement or ambiguous feedback on his performance. Therefore, it is helpful to design an instructional procedure that includes a very high frequency of opportunity to respond to explicit tasks and very frequent reinforcement for correct responses.

In order to arrange the optimum conditions for learning the visual discriminations required for reading, Staats devised the apparatus shown in Figure 6.7. The child sat facing the small window in the partition. The teacher sat in the other chair to the side of the partition and placed five-by-eight-inch cards with stimuli to be read (e.g., letters or words) in the window. Marbles could be dropped down the chute by the teacher. When a marble dropped into the box at the end of the chute, the teacher could instruct the child to put the marble in the hole at the upper right corner of the partition (returning it to the container on the teacher's side and receiving a trinket or other reinforcer) or to drop it in one of the tubes on the child's left, where accumulation of marbles could earn the toy displayed above the tube.

> The apparatus and reinforcement procedure, with adaptations in terms of type and kind of stimulus presentation and recording and type and kind of behaviors and recording, appears to enable the collection of objective data over long periods of time dealing with repertoires of varying degrees of complexity. It has the same advantages for children, and the study of complex learning, as the Skinner box has for animals and the study of simple learning. (Staats, 1968b, p. 50)

In his early research with preschoolers, Staats used marbles as token reinforcers that could be exchanged for trinkets, candies, or toys (Staats, Brewer, & Gross, 1970). At first, the children were asked to name pictures. Then, gradually, letters were introduced. The letter *A* was shown and the child was told its name and asked to say it. Letter naming trials

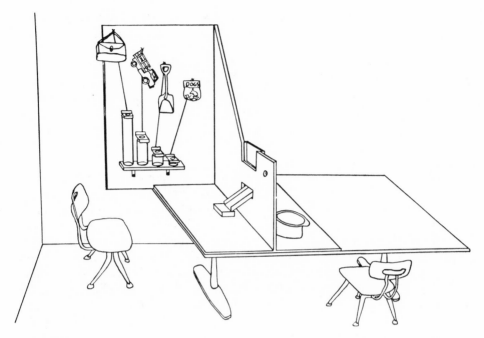

FIGURE 6.7.
*The child learning apparatus.*

*Source: A. W. Staats, "A General Apparatus for the Investigation of Complex Learning in Children,"* Behaviour Research and Therapy, *1968, 6, 47. Reprinted by permission.*

were interspersed with picture naming trials, and new letters were introduced only when the child had mastered those previously shown. Prompts (i.e., telling the child the letter name if he did not know it) and picture naming were gradually removed from the trials as the child mastered the tasks. Reinforcement was given very frequently for correct answers, and the teacher was careful to prevent the child from making errors at each stage. Teaching sessions were kept very short (average length 3.2 minutes) and the sessions were stopped at the first sign of inattention. Careful records were kept of the stimuli presented, the child's responses, the length of the sessions, and the reinforcers given. Staats and his associates (1970) found that as children learned more letters they became more efficient learners—fewer trials, less time, and fewer reinforcers were required to learn successive groups of letters (e.g., $A$ to $D$ as compared with $Q$ to $T$).

After the children had learned the letters of the alphabet, they were taught word discrimination tasks. Using essentially the same approach that had been applied in the teaching of letters, they taught the children phonetic sets of words (cad, mad, pad, rad, sad, tad, or cat, mat, pat, rat, sat, tat). The children learned phonetic reading skills, and they became more efficient learners as their training progressed. It is important to note that the training in alphabet and word reading was done in about 120 brief sessions and that the children were given thousands of learning trials and earned hundreds of reinforcers.

### Reinforcement of Reading Behavior

The work of Staats, Brewer, and Gross showed that very young children (age three and a half to four and a half years) could be taught the visual discrimination and cognitive skills necessary for beginning reading when appropriate motivation (reinforcement) was provided and tasks were appropriately sequenced. These results suggested to Staats that older children with learning difficulties also could be taught to read if the necessary motivational and instructional techniques were used. Consequently, he devised a token reinforcer system, in which the child was given plastic disks as tokens (which could be exchanged for a wide variety of toys or other items) for correct responses, and a simple, highly structured teaching method. His token reinforcement system was the first use of such procedures in educational behavior modification.

> This reinforcer system was first tried on several children who were considered to be difficult problems in the traditional classroom and to be retarded in reading. The learning materials concerned reading and were designed to be simple to administer and to facilitate the recording of the child's progress. That is, the child first learned the new words to be presented in the story: the word was presented singly and the child was told its name and was reinforced for looking at the word and saying its name. When the child could spontaneously read all the words, they were presented in the paragraphs of the story and then the whole story. Better performance was reinforced with a higher value plastic disk (there were three values). The important result was the immediate change in the children's behavior. They became vigorous, attentive workers and they learned well. (Staats, 1973, p. 201)

Similar teaching and reinforcement procedures have been used with a wide variety of children and instructors in a large number of studies (e.g., Ryback & Staats, 1970; Staats & Butterfield, 1965; Staats, Finley, Minke, & Wolf, 1964; Staats, Minke, & Butts, 1970; Staats, Minke, Finley, Wolf, & Brooks, 1964; Staats, Minke, Goodwin, & Landeen, 1967). In some of these studies, the children were taught by parents, volunteer housewives, high-school seniors, or other nonprofessionals. The results of using the Staats techniques have been consistently impressive.

The study by Ryback and Staats (1970) provides another example of the type of research done by Staats and his colleagues. The teachers were four high-school-educated mothers who were trained to use the Staats Motivation-Activating Reading Technique (SMART) to teach their own children. The four children were eight and one-half to thirteen years old: The first was mentally retarded, the second had reading difficulties and emotional problems, the third had learning disabilities and "minimal cerebral dysfunction," and the fourth had learning disabilities and a heart ailment. The instructional materials were stories chosen from one of the Science Research Associates Reading Laboratories. The new words for each story (i.e., words the child did not know but which appeared in the story) were printed on five-by-eight-inch cards. Each of the new words was presented as a stimulus. If the child could not call the word he was prompted (i.e., told the word). After the child had read all the new words for the story correctly on one unprompted trial (words read correctly were deleted from the list), he read orally the paragraphs of the story. The paragraphs were typed on 8½-by-11-inch paper. If the child could not read a word in the context of the paragraph, he was prompted. Each paragraph was reread by the child until he made no errors. After reading the paragraphs orally, the child read them silently, and subsequently answered the comprehension questions that accompanied the story. If he made an error in answering a question, the child reread the relevant paragraph and corrected his error. No criticism or punishment was given if the child made an error. All the child's efforts at reading were reinforced with praise, and many responses were reinforced with tokens that could be exchanged for a variety of back-up reinforcers. The more crucial behaviors (e.g., reading a word correctly on the *first* trial) earned tokens of greater value. The parents who served as tutors kept detailed records of the reading tasks they presented, their children's responses, and token reinforcers given.

The results of the Ryback and Staats study are very encouraging. All four of the children made significant gains on standardized tests as well as on vocabulary tests constructed from the reading materials by the authors. Initial training of each parent took only one hour, and subsequent supervisory sessions required only about five hours per parent. The children were tutored for an average of 51.25 hours, made an average of 74,730 single-word reading responses, and received tokens to purchase back-up reinforcers worth an average of $18.34 per child. The ratio of the monetary value of the tokens given to the number of reading responses made by the child *decreased* over time. Two of the tutored children's untutored siblings who had reading difficulties did not make gains comparable to those of tutored children, although one of them was receiving special tutoring by a remedial reading specialist. Follow-up measures of the children's reading skills indicated that they retained a good proportion of what they learned during the tutoring.

In short, the work of Staats and numerous other researchers (see Kauffman, 1975, for a review of this research) has shown that when specific reading tasks appropriate to the child's level of previous learning are presented and the child's correct responses are reinforced, children with a wide range of behavioral and academic deficits can learn to read. Neither the child's diagnostic label nor the formal education of the teacher are of real importance. What is important is that the child's teacher be trained to teach and reinforce specific reading skills.

### Visual Discrimination in Arithmetic, Writing, and Spelling

As will be discussed in other chapters, writing and spelling require the acquisition of specific motor or visual-motor skills. Initial arithmetic learning also involves visual-motor behaviors. However, it is clear too that an essential component of these academic tasks is visual discrimination. A child must be able to discriminate number (i.e., numerosity) and numerals to perform many counting and computing tasks. Writing and spelling require not only the motor responses that produce letters and words but visual discrimination of the models that are copied and the configurations that are produced. Because visual discrimination is not the *primary* consideration in the acquisition of arithmetic, spelling, and writing, detailed discussion of these academic areas will be found in other chapters. Nonetheless, it may be instructive here to consider the way in which applied behavior analysis was used to discover the controlling factors in a case of apparent visual discrimination or visual-motor disability involving arithmetic.

Hasazi and Hasazi (1972) reported an interesting case in which behavior modification was used to reduce incorrect arithmetic responses. The subject of their study was an eight-year-old boy who almost invariably reversed the digits in two-digit sums. Otherwise, this child was a very capable student. Because his reversal behavior had persisted for nearly a year, he had been referred for several neurological and visual examinations. His teachers had been giving him "extra help" because of his apparent neurological or perceptual deficits. Careful observation of his behavior, however, revealed that his reversals were likely a function of the teacher's attention (i.e., reinforcement) rather than true perceptual problems:

First, Bob was able to discriminate easily between numbers containing the same but reversely ordered digits, such as 12 and 21. Second, he often pointed out reversals on his own paper to the teacher when she failed to notice them. Finally, he was observed on several occasions erasing correctly ordered sums and reversing the order of the digits contained. (Hasazi & Hasazi, 1972, p. 158)

When the teacher withdrew "extra help" (i.e., marked all sums "correct" whether reversed or not) and reinforced correct digit order with attention, Bob's digit reversals decreased to near zero, as shown in the Experimental 1 phase of Figure 6.8. Because Hasazi and Hasazi wanted to make sure that teacher attention was in fact the reinforcer maintaining reversed digits, they instituted a reversal of the contingency: the teacher again attended with "extra help" to Bob's reversals (Baseline 2 in Figure 6.8). After Bob began to write reversed digit sums, just as he had during the first baseline condition, the teacher once more began to ignore reversed digits (Experimental 2). The results shown in Figure 6.8 are convincing evidence that Bob's problem was not primarily neurological or percep-

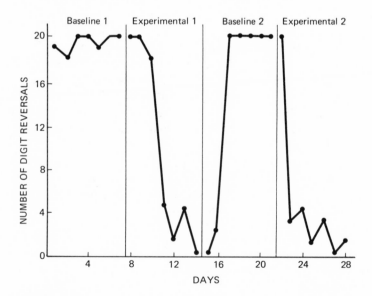

FIGURE 6.8.
Number of digit reversals per day under baseline and experimental conditions.

Source: J. E. Hasazi & S. E. Hasazi, "Effects of Teacher Attention on Digit-Reversal Behavior in an Elementary School Child," Journal of Applied Behavior Analysis, 1972, 5, p. 160. Reprinted by permission.

tual. The problem was with the teacher's correction (and inadvertent reinforcement) of digit reversals.

### Reinforcement and
### Distinctive Feature Analysis

Given the powerful effect of reinforcement on discrimination learning and on pupils' performance once discriminations have been acquired (as in Bob's case), it is important to know how best to use reinforcement in teaching. As we mentioned earlier in this chapter, the analysis of distinctive features of stimuli is an important aspect of visual perception. One might reasonably ask whether reinforcing children for attending to certain distinctive features of visual stimuli will facilitate their discrimination of letters. Tawney (1972) has conducted a teaching experiment to answer this question. With four-year-olds from a Head Start program as pupils, he designed a program for teaching children to discriminate letter-like forms. He also carefully assessed the ability of the children to discriminate letters before and after their training in discrimination of the letter-like forms. During training, the pupils received token reinforcers which they could later exchange for various "prizes," similar to the Staats procedures. Some of the children were reinforced for discriminating among forms on the basis of distinctive features that are thought to be critical for discriminating letters; others were reinforced for discriminating among forms on the basis of noncritical features. The results showed that reinforcing children for discriminations based on critical features increased their performance on letter discrimination tasks more than reinforcing children for responding to noncritical features.

> This experiment confirmed the utility of a behavioral approach to the problem of letter (visual/perceptual) confusion. When a task is analyzed, critical features identified, and immediate reinforcement provided, young children can be trained to discriminate among stimuli that they had previously confused. Further, this approach proved more successful than reinforcing responses to features of stimuli that are "simple" but not critical to letter discrimination. (Tawney, 1972, p. 464)

The results have important implications for teachers. Not only must reinforcement be given for specific visual discriminations or reading responses, but the selection of the responses to be reinforced is of crucial importance. Learning will be maximized only when reinforcement is provided for attention and response to the most relevant, distinctive, or critical elements of visual stimuli.

## Stimulus Fading
## in Discrimination Training

We have stated previously that discriminations can be taught by reinforcing an appropriate response to a given stimulus and withholding reinforcement for that response to other stimuli (e.g., reinforcing the response "dog" to the letters d-o-g and withholding reinforcement for the response "dog" to any other combination of letters). However, children who are considered ED, LD, or EMR (as well as other handicapped children) often are unable to learn the relatively difficult discriminations required for academic learning unless special teaching procedures are used in addition to reinforcement. If a child is presented with a very complex or difficult (for him) discrimination problem—one in which he cannot attend to and perceive the relevant or distinctive features—reinforcement will be of little value.

One must begin with stimuli that are perceptibly different to the child in order to teach him a new or more complex discrimination. Discrimination is then "transferred" from the features already known or perceived to the new features being learned. In the case of a bright normal who is being taught a new sight word, the word ordinarily is presented along with a verbal prompt by the teacher (i.e., the teacher shows the word *and* says it). After one or more paired presentations of this kind, the teacher drops the prompt. In the beginning, the child may depend on the verbal prompt in order to make the correct response —if the teacher does not say the word but only shows it, the child may not be able to respond correctly. After one or more trials, however, the child makes the discrimination on the basis of the configuration of the word alone. Sometimes teachers find it helpful to "fade out" a verbal prompt. The child no longer needs to be told the whole word ("dog"); he now can make the discrimination with a "partial" prompt, such as "duh." Eventually, the prompt can be dropped entirely, but sometimes this must be done in successive stages.

For children who have special difficulty in learning discrimination, the fading procedure may need to be more elaborate or more carefully arranged. In devising a fading procedure, special attention must be given to relevant stimulus "dimensions." If there are ways in which two stimuli can be said to be similar or to differ, these similarities or differences may be considered dimensions of the stimulus. Stimuli may vary, for example, along the dimension of size, shape, color, texture, or some combination of these dimensions. When the fading technique is used, the stimuli to be discriminated must in the beginning differ along *two or more* dimensions. Inasmuch as the objective of the fading procedure is to teach a discrimination that otherwise could not be learned (or could only be learned very slowly), at least one of the dimensions along which the stimuli at first are different must be a dimension that represents an already learned discrimination. This "fading dimension" is then gradually changed or eliminated so that the only dimension that differentiates the stimuli is now the one that the child initially could not discriminate. If a child cannot discriminate "was" from "saw," but he can discriminate black from red, a color-fading procedure might be employed. "Was" might be written in black ink and "saw" in red ink. The stimuli would then differ along two dimensions, letter configuration or form and color. The child will at first discriminate between the words only on the basis of the color dimension. Over many reading trials the red ink for "saw" could be gradually darkened until, in the final trials, "saw" is black and the words differ only along the dimension of letter configuration. Color, in this example, is the fading dimension, and the child's discrimination is transferred from the color to the configuration dimension.

It is possible to fade multiple dimensions of stimuli and to fade dimensions "in" as well as "out" in order to teach a new discrimination. The essential nature of the fading technique, however, is that the child learns to respond (and, apparently, to attend) to dimensions of stimuli that previously were of no functional significance to him. Furthermore, fading makes it possible to teach a discrimination with very few errors, because training begins with a discrimination the child has already learned and the fading stimulus is attenuated or introduced as gradually as necessary in order to avoid most errors. The high ratio of successful responses that fading makes possible is particularly relevant in teaching emotionally disturbed, learning disabled, and educable mentally retarded children, who typically have experienced chronic failure.

Many laboratory studies have shown that stimulus fading is an effective technique in teaching visual discriminations to retardates (cf., Bijou, 1968; Estes, 1970; Stevenson, 1972). With fading, even severely retarded children have been taught discriminations which previously seemed impossible for them to learn. Less severely handicapped and normal children also have profited from the use of fading techniques. Corey and Shamow (1972), for example, found that normal nursery school children acquired and retained oral reading behaviors better when pictures representing the words were superimposed over the words and then gradually faded out. The use of fading techniques in teaching any discrimination is limited primarily by the teacher's ability to identify and attenuate stimulus dimensions that will help children learn. Many simple fading techniques are known to experienced teachers and can be devised using materials that are readily available. For instance, color cues can be used for letters or words and the cues can be faded. The color may be a part of the word itself (e.g., the ink or other medium in which it is written or part of a letter) or the background color on which it is written. The configuration of a letter or word or a second stimulus associated with it, such as a dot or an underline or an arrow, can also be faded. Pictures, dots, underlines, arrows, and other stimuli may be associated with a letter or word and gradually faded in size, as shown in Figure 6.9. The creative and resourceful teacher will be able to devise simple but effective fading procedures. It must be kept in mind, however, that the child's responses are the best guide to instructional effectiveness. A fading procedure is of no value whatever, no matter how clever it appears to others, if the child can learn the discrimination without it or, on the other hand, if it does not result in the child's learning to discriminate.

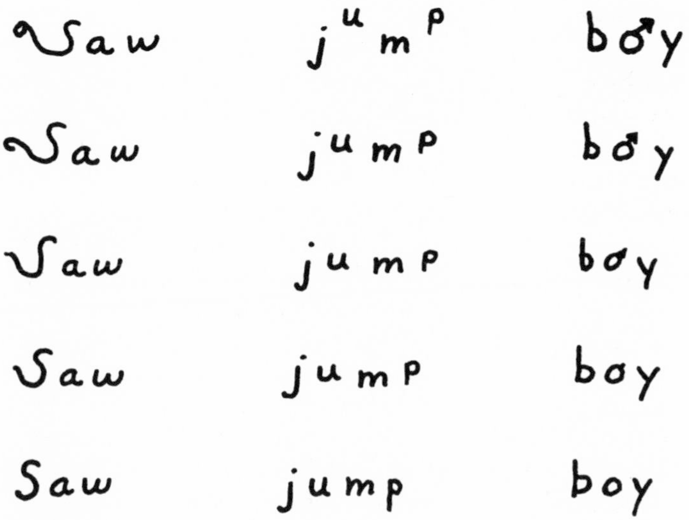

FIGURE 6.9.
Possible techniques of fading in teaching word discrimination.

# Visual-Motor, Motor, Tactual, and Kinesthetic Disabilities

# 7

Of all the sensory modalities—auditory, tactual, olfactory, gustatory, visual—the visual has been the one of most concern to the field of learning disabilities. Associated with this interest in visual perception has been the great effort put forth toward the remediation of visual-motor deficits by professionals in the field of learning disabilities. The frequency with which we must coordinate our visual and motor systems in day-to-day activities no doubt accounts for the extensive interest in problems of a visual-motor nature. In terms of the school-age child, for example, visual-motor skill can be considered to be intimately connected with a wide gamut of everyday experiences—from using a pencil and paper to navigating one's way through a doorway.

The last chapter was primarily concerned with problems of visual perception; this one deals with disabilities relating to the integration of the visual and motor systems. Because of its obvious close connection with visual-motor development, motor activity per se is also discussed in this chapter. And because of their link with motor development, the sensory development of touch (tactual) and body movement (kinesthetic) are also included. The kinesthetic process is defined as the sensations gained from moving one's body or a portion of one's body (e.g., an arm).

As with visual perception, interest in visual-motor, motor, tactual, and kinesthetic development can be traced back to the early work of Werner and Strauss, who studied the visual perceptual and visual-motor problems of mentally retarded children. They believed that one of the behavioral symptoms of brain damage was faulty visual-motor coordination. They popularized the position that adequate conceptual development is dependent upon appropriate perceptual development. Among the most frequently recommended educational activities were those relating to the integration of visual and motor processes. Numerous suggestions were made for training visual-motor skills, not only for their own sake but also for the betterment of visual perceptual abilities and ultimately higher-order, conceptual abilities.

The myriad visual-motor activities recommended in programs and commercial materials (some of which we will describe in this chapter) for learning disabled children today have their origins in the work of Werner and Strauss with the retarded. Newell Kephart, who can be most strongly associated with the use of visual-motor training activities (and whose approach we will describe in greater detail later in this chapter), was a colleague of Werner and Strauss at the Wayne County Training School in the 1940s. Kephart's educational procedures were thus strongly flavored by the ideas of Werner and Strauss. Kephart, in fact, was a co-author with Strauss on the second volume of *Psychopathology and Education of the Brain-Injured Child* (Strauss & Kephart, 1955). Critical for the eventual evolution of the field of learning disabilities, this book included a section on the brain-injured child of normal intelligence.

## VISUAL-MOTOR PROBLEMS

### The Perceptual-Motor Match

Kephart's own theoretical formulations and educational program are contained in *The Slow Learner in the Classroom* (Kephart, 1960). The major theoretical construct Kephart espoused was that of the *perceptual-motor match*. Basically, the perceptual-motor match is concerned with the coordination of the eyes and the hands. The perceptual-motor match was considered by Kephart to be the foundation upon which higher conceptual thinking is built.

There are two essential aspects of the perceptual-motor match: (1) motor development precedes visual development, and (2) kinesthetic sensation obtained from motor functioning acts as a feedback device for the monitoring of visual-motor activities. The following summarizes Kephart's conception of the perceptual-motor match:

> This process of establishing a perceptual-motor correspondence has been called the perceptual-motor match. It normally occurs in three stages best illustrated by the development of eye-hand coordination. In the first stage, the hand leads and generates most of the information. In this stage, the process is hand-eye, the hand leading and the visual information being matched to it. As this matching becomes more com-

plete, the rapid, extensive nature of the visual data becomes apparent and the child learns to monitor and let kinesthesis control the response while he uses the visual data for more remote predictions. He has entered the second stage: eye-hand. Here the greatest reliance is upon vision, the hand being used only to confirm or to solve complex or confusing situations. Finally, the match is close enough that he can depend upon vision alone. He can explore with his eyes in the same way and get the same information as he originally did with his hand. This shift is possible because of a firm, accurate perceptual-motor match. The child has entered the third stage and become perceptual. (Kephart, 1975, pp. 65–66)

The most important element, the one Kephart emphasized over and over again, of Kephart's perceptual-motor match was his strong conviction that motor development precedes visual development. Because of this supposedly invariant ordering, Kephart maintained that meaning is gained from visual activity only if it can be matched with previously acquired motor experiences. If these prior motor learnings are deficient, then, the child will be unable to achieve a perceptual-motor match. Such a child would be referred to as one who has a perceptual-motor disability. Kephart postulated that the education of the perceptual-motor disabled child must proceed with the training of motoric development prior to the training of visual skills. In other words, the order of remediation is to correspond with the order of development—from motor to visual.

### Visual Versus Motor Development

Kephart's postulation that motor precedes visual development is by no means the only point of view within child development, nor could one say that it is presently the dominant viewpoint. Eleanor Gibson (1969), for example, maintains a different hierarchy of development. She posits that first the child learns that there are distinguishing features of a visual nature that differentiate objects from one another (refer again to Chapter 6). With these distinctive features in his mind, the child proceeds through three stages: (1) discrimination, (2) recognition, and (3) production. The first two stages are concerned with the visual modality whereas the third, the combining of visual and motor processes, corresponds to Kephart's perceptual-motor match. Gibson's match, however, is in the opposite direction: visual development is prior to visual-motor coordination.

Gibson also presents several research studies that support her contention that visual perception precedes motor and tactual development. The classic longitudinal study of White, Castle, and Held (1964) on visual-motor development, for example, found that at about one month of age the infant begins following moving objects with his head and eyes. Between the ages of six weeks and two months, the infant's tracking becomes more precise. When presented with an object at about two months of age, the infant first fixates the object and *then* hits it with his closed fist. The infant then enters a period of trial and error in which he attempts to reach for objects while glancing back and forth between the object and his hand until he attains what Gibson refers to as "top level reaching" at about five months. The infant's first graspings of objects at about four months, it should be noted, are of a very gross nature. The study of White and his colleagues thus indicates that the first systematic exploration of the environment is made with the eyes and not the hands. Only after a period of some months does the infant's motor activity of reaching catch up with his visual tracking ability. Furthermore, the initial tactual contacts with objects are quite undifferentiated, and it is some time before the infant is capable of manipulating objects with his fingers and hands.

Gibson herself has conducted some infant studies that tend to support her contention. Along with R. D. Walk, Gibson investigated the development of depth perception in infants (see Gibson, 1963). Their studies involved the ingenious use of a "visual cliff" apparatus (Figure 7.1). The infant is placed on top of a table covered by glass. On the portion where he is placed there is a checkerboard pattern immediately below the surface of the glass; however, on the opposite side of the table the pattern can be seen on the floor. While there is still glass over the portion of the table that has the pattern on the floor, the clarity and non-reflective nature of the glass gives the visual impression that there is a sharp drop-off, or visual cliff. The question posed by this apparatus is whether the infant will crawl out over the "deep" side. Gibson and Walk have found that as soon as infants are testable (have crawling skills, that is—around six months of age) they evidence depth perception in that they will not cross over onto the "deep" side even though their mothers coax them to do so. As Gibson (1963) has concluded:

> We are ready to assert, therefore, that perception of depth has developed as soon as locomotion is possible in this young organism. The same assertion applies to other slow-maturing organisms, such as kittens. *Development of this discrimination, therefore, is not dependent on stepping down, climbing up, or walking into things.* (p. 12; italics added)

The italics underscore the point that motoric experience with depth was evidently not necessary for the visual discrimination of depth.

Gibson, as well as Pick and Pick (1970), has reviewed numerous Soviet studies (Lavrent'eva & Ruzskaya, 1960; Tarakanov & Zinchenko, 1960; Zaporozhets, 1965; Zinchenko, 1957; 1960; Zinchenko, Chzhi-tsin,

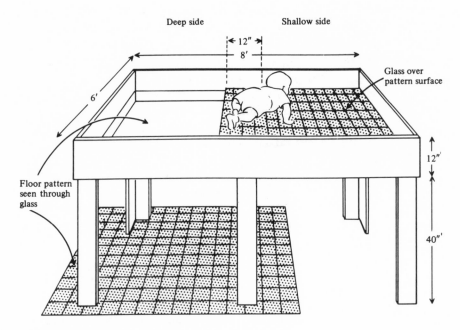

**FIGURE 7.1.**
Visual cliff for human infants.

*Source: E. J. Gibson, "Development of Perception: Discrimination of Depth Compared with Discrimination of Graphic Symbols," in J. C. Wright and J. Kagan (Eds.),* Basic Cognitive Processes in Children, *Monographs of the Society for Research in Child Development, 1963, Ser. No. 86, Vol. 28, No. 2, p. 11. Reprinted by permission.*

& Tarakanov, 1962; Zinchenko, Lomov, & Ruzskaya, 1959; Zinchenko & Ruzskaya, 1960a, 1960b) with children of early childhood age that confirm the position that visual development advances more rapidly than tactual-motor ability. An example of the format of these experiments is that children are given wooden forms of various shapes to explore either tactually or visually and then are required to recognize the same shape from among a number of choices presented either visually or tactually. The findings consistently reveal that visual-visual matching is the easiest and tactual-tactual the most difficult. The results of these studies are strongly against the position of Kephart that motor development precedes visual development. The findings, in fact, are in the opposite direction of what the Soviet psychologists had expected: "It also is interesting to note that these investigators started with the Berkleyian idea that touch teaches vision but were forced by their data (precise identifications earlier by vision than by touch) to reject this hypothesis" (Pick & Pick, 1970, p. 784).

### The Interaction of
### Visual and Motor Abilities

Although the research evidence does not support Kephart's notion of motor precedence over vision, his strategy of combining motor and visual skills whenever possible can be substantiated in the literature. There are a number of sources that can be used to justify the educational procedure of attempting to link the visual and motor domains. Kephart's postulation of the importance of motor learning for visual development has a research foundation.

The classic study of Held and Hein (1963) emphasizes the importance of motor movement for the development of visual-motor skills. Held and Hein placed two kittens in an apparatus pictured in Figure 7.2. The two animals were yoked so that whenever the one cat walked around in a circle the other cat was passively moved around in a gondola without the opportunity of locomotion. Thus, the one kitten saw the environment and walked in it while the other one saw the very same

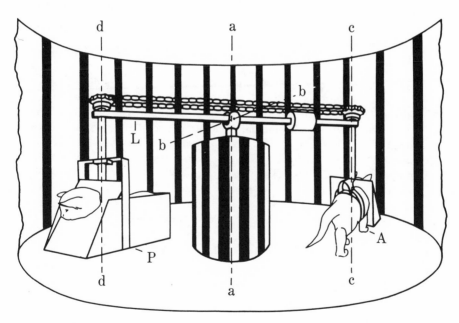

FIGURE 7.2.
The kitten carrousel.

Source: R. Held & A. Hein, "Movement Produced Stimulation in the Development of Visually Guided Behavior," Journal of Comparative and Physiological Psychology, 1963, 56, 873. Copyright 1963 by the American Psychological Association. Reprinted by permission.

environment but did *not* walk. On subsequent tests of a visual and visual-motor nature, the walking kitten was distinctly superior to the kitten who had been deprived of motoric experiences.

That motor feedback is a significant factor in terms of the visual development of humans is also supported by a review of research by Wohlwill (1970). Their conclusions are that motoric and haptic (tactual) responses of the child serve a monitoring function in that they enable him to compare visual and motor input, and based upon this match (similar to the perceptual-motor match of Kephart) visual judgments can be altered. As Wohlwill states:

> Thus, the early development of perception (e.g., through the pre-school years) can be conceptualized in terms of the improved ability to utilize feedback from self-produced activity. In the early years of life such activity is almost absent, apart from orienting movements that keep the individual in touch with the stimulus in a gross sense for increasingly longer periods of time (as in the study by Smith et al., 1963). Subsequently, a variety of motor actions, involving not only haptic exploration, but also active manipulation of objects in a "practical" context (inserting pegs into holes, building with blocks, handling tools in a variety of ways, as in a child's "carpentering" activities, and the like), have the effect of providing continual feedback as to the shapes and sizes of things—as brought out nicely in some of the Soviet research summarized by Zaporozhets (1965). The information involved in such feedback becomes increasingly subtle, depending on more highly organized and more finely coordinated activities. Compare, for instance, the gross motor responses involved in a child's play with a peg board, with the responses involved in his tactual exploration of the outline of a form, and finally with the highly coordinated movements demanded for the scanning of the visual stimulus. Lastly, internalized schemata take over to guide the direct visual exploration, supplanting the role of movement-produced feedback.* (p. 402)

In terms of direct classroom application Reese and Lipsitt also report the results of a study that indicate the usefulness of engendering motor responses in children. Hendrickson and Muehl (1962) trained kindergarteners to push a lever in the opposite direction for the presentation of a *b* or *d* while also labeling them. The exposure to the simple motor training facilitated the discrimination of these two potentially reversible letters.

While Kephart's contention that motor development precedes visual development is suspect, the position that visual and motor development

---

* J. S. Wohlwill, Perceptual development, in H. W. Reese & L. P. Lipsitt, (Eds.), *Experimental Child Psychology* (New York: Academic Press, 1970), p. 402. Reprinted by permission.

can interact to aid one another is generally supported. The teacher who has a child with either a visual or a motor problem should thus attempt to train the child to combine the two sources of information (visual and motor).

### Copying

There are certainly occasions when a child is required to exhibit the skill of drawing something from memory (later stages of printing and handwriting), but the most frequent concern of the early elementary teacher is the child's ability to copy. The kindergarten child who is unable to use a pencil and paper or crayon and paper in order to reproduce simple lines and geometric figures may be exhibiting a visual-motor deficit. Likewise, the child in the early elementary grades who cannot copy geometric forms or the letters of the alphabet, but who can visually discriminate among them, may have a visual-motor disability.

Figure 7.3 presents the productions of a girl, six years, seven months of age who had visual-motor skills equivalent to that of a child of five years, eight months.* Even though her IQ was 123 as assessed by the Peabody Picture Vocabulary Test, she was extremely deficient in her copying ability. The two items taken from the Developmental Test of Visual-Motor Integration (Beery & Buktenica, 1967) indicate the primitive nature of her visual-motor coordination. She evidences a great deal of difficulty in drawing intersecting lines in the figure on the left. Some investigators might see this response as representative of a problem associated with the ability to cross the mid-line. The attempted copying of the circles is noteworthy in at least two ways. The positioning of the circles is poor (possibly indicative of a position in space visual problem). In addition, her rendering of the forms of the circles themselves is quite immature in relation to her chronological age.

COPYING AS A CONCEPTUAL ACT. The ability to copy is a more complex activity than is at first apparent. Not only does the child have to perceive the to-be-copied figure accurately and then coordinate his hand and his eyes (an extremely complex phenomenon in itself, as noted by our previous reference to the study of White, Castle, and Held [1964]), but he must also spatially organize and plan his drawing movements. This latter activity of building a spatial "layout" of the pattern before and during the construction of the figure is what differentiates copying from tracing. In the former task, the child is much more on his own to

* Thanks are extended to Dr. Eleanore C. Westhead for the use of this child's responses.

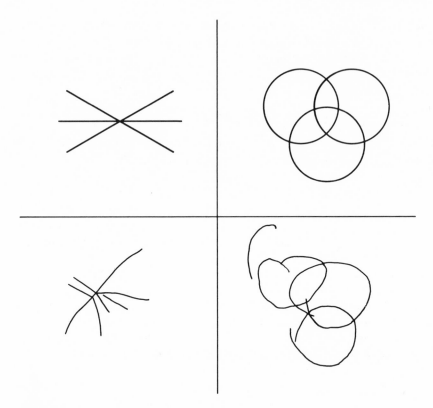

FIGURE 7.3.
Models and sample responses on the Beery-Buktenica Developmental Test of Visual-Motor Integration.

*Source:* Developmental Test of Visual-Motor Integration *by Keith E. Beery and Norman A. Buktenica. Copyright © 1967 by Keith E. Beery and Norman A. Buktenica. Used by permission of Follett Publishing Company.*

decide how to organize the strokes of his pencil in order to obtain the final product of an accurate representation. In tracing, the child must merely coordinate his eyes and hand to follow a prescribed path: the child is less concerned with how to organize his movements to reach an end product. Copying requires the child to be aware of the relationships of the component movements necessary to complete the drawing of the figure.

In copying an equilateral triangle whose sides are all two inches long, for example, the child must consider a number of factors *both before and while he is drawing.* He will be greatly aided if he notes that: (*a*) the figure is composed basically of three lines, (*b*) the lines are of the same length, (c) the length of each of the lines is about two inches, (d) two of the lines are diagonal and one is horizontal, (e) there are three angles, (f) all of the angles are equal, and (g) each of the angles is 60 degrees (it is not necessary for the child to comprehend the numerical equivalent of 60 degrees, only its visual impression). The child who is able to appreciate these relationships and adjust his drawing accordingly will produce the better copy than the child who can guide his hand visually just as well but is unable to organize and conceptualize the task requirements.

In this respect, then, copying activities can be conceived of as involving higher level thought processes than has generally been assumed. Wedell (1973) has also noted that copying tasks can be failed because of other than just visual or visual-motor deficits. His model includes the kinds of organizational planning and decision-making components we have outlined above.

That copying must involve more complex processes than tracing is evident to anyone who has observed children. We also know from our own experiences that it is more difficult to copy figures than it is to trace them. Moreover, Wedell (1964) has found that developmentally the acquisition of tracing skills is much more rapid than copying abilities. Wedell presented children of three age levels (3¾ years, 4½ years, and 5¼ years) with patterns to be traced or copied with pencil and paper or copied with plasticine strips (the latter experimental condition is not particularly relevant to our discussion here). The results are presented in Figure 7.4. As the figure indicates, tracing becomes progressively easier with age in comparison to copying. Between 3¾ years and 4½ years, tracing improves much more dramatically than does copying. These findings are consistent with the notion that copying involves abilities that are less readily influenced by mere practice. If copying involves certain cognitive processes, as we are suggesting here, then it would be expected that improvement would be more gradual.

### The Relation of Visual-Motor Development to Academic Tasks

The child who experiences a visual-motor problem will have difficulty in school. In kindergarten and the primary grades the child is required to engage in numerous activities of a visual-motor nature. Building things with blocks, for example, involves visual-motor coordination. By playing with blocks the child can come to experience more about relationships among objects, their various sizes and shapes. Thus, the child unable to manipulate blocks may be at a disadvantage in being

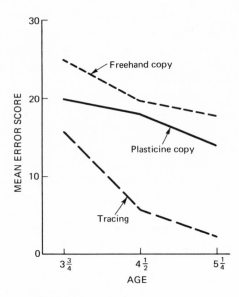

*FIGURE 7.4.*
*Development of children's tracing and*
*pattern copying.*

*Source: K. Wedell, (1965) "Some As-*
*pects of Perceptual-Motor Development in*
*Young Children," in* Learning Problems of
the Cerebral Palsied (*London: Spastics*
*Society). Reprinted by permission.*

able to learn from his environment. The many social relationships that can be engendered while playing with manipulable toys and blocks are also endangered for the child unable to coordinate his eyes and hands.

The role that competitive games and sports play in the social development of children is also important to consider. The child unable to coordinate his eyes and hands in the catching of a ball, for instance, is earmarked for social rejection in our society. Thus, visual-motor incoordination can hinder interpersonal relationships. The child's poor relationship with others and feelings of inadequacy can carry over into the academic situation as well. Feelings of worthlessness can result in poor motivation to do well in school.

Visual-motor deficits can also be a more direct cause of academic problems. Obviously, anything involving the use of pencil and paper will place the visual-motor disabled child at a disadvantage. The frequency with which children must engage in pencil and paper exercises underscores the pedagogical significance of visual-motor disabilities.

The most apparent academic area affected by a visual-motor deficit will be handwriting. Eye-hand coordination is the sine qua non of good handwriting. Figure 7.5 presents examples of the tracing, pattern copying, and handwriting products of two six-year-old children. Although the tracing abilities of the two children are similar, the one child's copying skills are noticeably immature. The fact that the child with poor copying abilities also has poor handwriting is indicative of the relationship between pattern copying and handwriting skills.

In arithmetic computation, too, it has been noted that poor visual-motor coordination can be a detriment to performance (Wedell, 1973). Figure 7.6 presents a hypothetical example of a child's arithmetic work sheet. Would it be any wonder if this child had difficulty adding these numbers?

Poor visual-motor problems can also contribute indirectly to reading and spelling problems. One of the exercises commonly used to help a child learn the proper spelling of words is to have him print them or write them out. If his written production is poor, not only will this exercise be useless but it may actually prove harmful by allowing him to write down letters that only confuse him. Likewise, though there is no research specifically on the subject, it is probable that in the early stages of learning to read—particularly, the identification-of-letters stage—the familiarization with the letters gained from printing them is beneficial for recognizing them visually.

## MOTOR PROBLEMS

Some children exhibit motor difficulties per se, that is, problems of motor coordination that are not due to a disability in combining the visual and motor systems. It is true, however, that there has been little investigation

FIGURE 7.5.
Tracing and handwriting of six-year-old children with poor and good performance on pattern copying.

Source: K. Wedell, "Perceptual-Motor Difficulties," Special Education, 1968, 57, 25–30. Reprinted by permission of the Spastics Society and Association for Special Education.

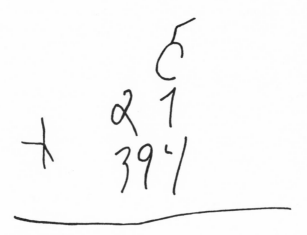

FIGURE 7.6.
Example of a visual-motor disabled child's copying of an
arithmetic problem.

of purely motor problems because on most occasions children engaged
in motor activities are also required to use their visual systems. It is,
therefore, difficult to talk about motor disabilities to the exclusion of the
visual sensory modality.

Most investigators have broken down the motor area into fine motor
and gross motor skills. Fine motor skills refer to movements of the smaller
muscles—tying shoes, handwriting—whereas gross motor activities involve
the larger muscles—throwing a ball, running. Cratty (1973b) suggests,
however, that motor skills can be divided into three groups—those involving (1) large truncal muscles; (2) the intermediate muscles of the limbs;
and (3) the muscles of the hands, fingers, and wrists.

Most attempts to place a movement into a specific category based
on the muscles involved will prove somewhat unsatisfactory. It is more
reasonable to consider activities as having varying degrees of involvement of muscle categories. As Cratty (1973b) states:

> However, once again a close look at muscular activities, including
> sports skills, reveals the difficulty of assigning a single label (fine, inter-
> mediate, gross) to most activities. Balance activities, while usually as-
> signed a place within the "gross" category, actually involve rather finite
> adjustments of the muscle groups surrounding the feet and ankles, as
> well as the larger truncal and leg musculature. . . . Most complex sports
> skills likewise require fine adjustment of the feet and hands, as the
> athlete attempts to run, intercept, and perhaps catch a ball thrown to

him. Similarly, individuals confined to a desk and purportedly engaging in fine motor activity (such as typing or handwriting) frequently complain of backaches and similar discomfort involving the larger truncal muscles. Experimental evidence confirms that a great deal of activity takes place in the larger muscle groups even though an individual is apparently engaging in what most would term fine motor skills. (p. 17)

### The Relation of Motor Development to Academic Tasks

Earlier in this chapter we stated that the child who is experiencing visual-motor problems will quite likely have difficulties in school. In particular, activities requiring the use of pencil and paper will be affected. Likewise, if a fine motor problem prohibits the child from using a pencil, he will encounter numerous failures in school. Fine motor disabilities of the hands, in fact, will lead to many of the same problems indicated for visual-motor disabilities earlier. In addition, self-help skills such as shoe tying, buttoning, and zipping may be affected. Without adequate self-help skills, the child will be susceptible to problems in socialization.

Gross motor difficulties, too, can produce unpleasant socialization experiences for the child. The child who fails in recreational games is a candidate for the possession of feelings of inadequacy. Gross motor disabilities, however, have very little, if any, *direct* influence on academic achievement. Cratty (1973a), for example, supports the position that it is wishful thinking to believe that motor activities in and of themselves will benefit a child in the cognitive sense. He states that only by associating the child's movements with higher level thinking will motor exercises directly benefit intellectual development.

## TACTUAL AND KINESTHETIC PROBLEMS

Closely related to motor problems are tactual and kinesthetic problems. Tactual refers to the sensation of touch and kinesthetic refers to those bodily sensations gained when one moves. For instance, when a person moves his arm in a certain way, he experiences a certain sensation of movement; when he moves his arm in a different manner, he obtains a different sensation.

Kinesthetic and tactual disabilities are apparently not very widespread and therefore there has been relatively little study of them. A. Jean Ayres, however, has written frequently on the subject of tactual and kinesthetic deficiencies. She has referred, for instance, to the rather unusual cases of children who are described as tactually "defensive" (Ayres, 1975). The slightest stimulation of the skin is highly irritating for these children. She also believes that tactile discrimination abilities and kinesthetic abilities are quite often impaired in children who are apraxic, that is, they do not have the ability to perform complex motor acts:

> Of the sensory systems involved in the apraxic child, the discriminative tactile system is the most consistently deficient, but kinesthesis or the perception of joint position and movement is not infrequently poor (Ayres, 1965, 1969, 1971, 1972). Postural responses are usually poorly developed, suggesting involvement of the vestibular and possibly other proprioceptive systems. (Ayres, 1975)

### The  Relation of Tactual and Kinesthetic Development to Academic Achievement

Though the relationship between both tactual and kinesthetic development and higher cognitive thought might not be immediately apparent to most, Ayres does draw the connection: "Sensation from the skin, muscles, joints, gravity and movement receptors of the body have a widespread distribution to academically relevant areas, including the auditory, visual, and motor areas of the cortex" (1975). Ayres thus believes there is a relationship between tactual and kinesthetic development and other areas of development that have a more direct association with academic tasks.

There are at least two areas of academics in which tactual and kinesthetic abilities may play a direct role: writing and spelling. The skill of handwriting undoubtedly is dependent on the child's ability to receive appropriate tactual sensations from the act of holding the pencil. If the child cannot feel the pencil in his hand and the table on which his hand rests, then he will have difficulty in writing with the pencil. Also, kinesthetic sensations accompanying the movement of the hand while writing can be logically associated with handwriting abilities.

Wedell (1973) has also implicated kinesthetic deficits as causal factors with regard to spelling disabilities. He states that one of the ways in which a child "checks" the correctness of his spelling is by the movement sensations that result from the writing of letters. The child unable to recognize the feel of the letters as he forms them may be at a disadvantage with regard to spelling.

### Body Image and Laterality

In the writings of many learning disabilities theorists and practitioners there is thought to be a close relationship between visual-motor,

motor, tactual, and kinesthetic abilities and what have been termed "body image" and laterality. Body image is a rather vaguely defined construct that refers generally to an individual's awareness of his body in terms of the relationship of its parts and the relationship of the body to its spatial environment. The child with an inadequate body image, or body schema, is one who is likely to have difficulty in moving his limbs in an organized way and in judging where his body is in relation to other objects in the environment. Wedell (1973) offers the case of a child who has difficulty in putting on a sweater as an example of a child who might be referred to as having poor body image.

Children with visual-motor disabilities are also frequently described as lacking in laterality—the ability to detect the difference between the left and right side of one's own body. Asked to identify his right hand, for instance, the child with a laterality problem may become disoriented. Kephart (1960), among others, attributed a causal relationship between the ability to differentiate right from left on one's own body and orientation errors of left-right reversal in reading. His training for the child exhibiting reversals in reading thus emphasizes activities constructed for the purpose of teaching the distinction between the body's right and left side. There is no solid research to support Kephart's contention that laterality (left and right on the body) and directionality (left and right on stimuli outside of the body) are causally related.

## STANDARDIZED ASSESSMENT OF VISUAL-MOTOR, MOTOR, TACTUAL, AND KINESTHETIC ABILITIES

### Assessment of Visual-Motor Abilities

There are a number of different instruments and parts of tests designed specifically for the purpose of assessing a child's eye-hand coordination. It is on some of these tests that we will focus our discussion here. The coordination of visual and motor systems in other than the specific integration of eye and hand (e.g., in movement through space) will be covered in the next section on the assessment of motor abilities.

The major distinction that the diagnostician must keep in mind when assessing eye-hand coordination is that a child can perform poorly on a pencil and paper task because he has primarily a visual problem, primarily a visual-motor problem, primarily a motor problem, or some combination of these. Cutler, Cicirelli, and Hirshoren (1973), for example, have investigated the performance of nursery-school children on a test of visual discrimination and one of visual-motor production. Little relationship was found between the two instruments, suggesting that children who might have problems on one might not have problems on the other.

One of the oldest and most established tests of eye-hand functioning is the Bender-Gestalt (Bender, 1938). Originally developed by Lauretta Bender for use with adults, Koppitz (1964) has devised a scoring system applicable to children. The basic format of the test is that the child is shown a group of figures and is asked to copy them. The eight figures are presented in Figure 7.7. The clinician can look at the errors of the child both quantitatively (i.e., number of errors) and qualitatively (i.e.,

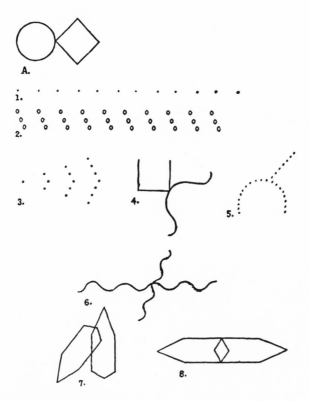

FIGURE 7.7.
Bender-Gestalt test figures.

Source: L. Bender, A Visual-Motor Gestalt Test and Its Clinical Use, *Research Monograph No. 3, p. 4. Copyright 1938, the American Orthopsychiatric Association, Inc. Reproduced by permission.*

kinds of errors). Some of the different types of errors that can be found are: enlargements, compressions, rotations, and distorted angles. While Bender (1970) has praised the Koppitz scoring system, she recommends caution in the use of the Bender-Gestalt with children. She also stresses that when the test is used the examiner should be sure to consider the total functioning of the child.

Several tests on the market are similar in format to the Bender-Gestalt. The Benton Visual Retention Test (Benton, 1963) and the Developmental Test of Visual-Motor Integration (Berry & Buktenica, 1967), for example, are comparable. These instruments are similar in that the child is to draw figures. The Benton differs slightly in that it can be administered by showing and then removing the figures so that the child draws them from memory.

The Eye-Hand Coordination subtest of the Marianne Frostig Developmental Test of Visual Perception is another device frequently used to test eye-hand coordination. On this test, the child is required to draw lines from one point to another on a sheet of paper. The path of the line varies in difficulty from item to item by the number of angles that must be negotiated and the narrowness of the borders within which the line must be drawn.

With regard to the assessment of eye-hand coordination without the use of pencil and paper tasks, the Tower Building subtest of the Stanford-Binet is an example. The young child is required to copy with his own blocks the tower built by the tester. As with all tests, a child may fail this one for a variety of reasons, but failure to build the tower correctly may indicate eye-hand coordination problems.

### Assessment of Motor Abilities

There are fewer well-standardized tests concerned generally with motor development than there are those related to visual-motor development. Instruments used to measure motor abilities actually combine the testing of motor and visual-motor abilities. The Purdue Perceptual-Motor Survey (Roach & Kephart, 1966) is an example. Roach and Kephart have been careful to refer to their instrument as a survey because it does not meet all the criteria necessary to be considered a test. This lack of adequate technical sophistication is indicative of tests in the area of motor development. It is generally recommended that the Purdue Perceptual-Motor Survey be used in the context of a gross screening device.

The Purdue Perceptual-Motor Survey does offer quite a few activities on which to observe the motoric functioning of the child. Tasks are also presented that are primarily visual and visual-motor in nature. The following are the activities of the survey that are concerned principally with motor development (some, of course, also contain visual elements):

1. Walking Board: The child is required to walk forward, backward, and sideways on a balance beam.

2. Jumping: The child is required to hop on both feet, his right foot alone, his left foot alone, and to skip.

3. Identification of Body Parts: The child is asked to touch his shoulders, hips, head, feet, and so forth.

4. Imitation of Movements: The tester makes arm movements while standing in front of the child. The child is then to imitate each of the movements.

5. Obstacle Course: The child must negotiate his body through narrow spaces, that is, over a stick, under a stick, between a wall and a stick.

6. Angels-in-the-Snow: The child, while lying on his back, is required to move his legs and arms into various positions.

### Assessment of Tactual and Kinesthetic Abilities

Few tests assess motor abilities, and fewer still have been devised to test tactual and kinesthetic abilities. Numerous items from visual-motor and motor tests also require the child to use his tactual and kinesthetic senses, but not many attempts have been made to construct specific tests of tactual and kinesthetic abilities. Ayres, however, undoubtedly because of her interest in kinesthetic deficits and tactual problems, such as tactual defensiveness, has included tests dealing with the tactual and kinesthetic senses in her *Southern California Sensory Integration Tests* (Ayres, 1972). At least five tests are designed to measure tactual and kinesthetic abilities: Kinesthesia, Manual Form Perception, Finger Identification, Graphesthesia, Localization of Tactile Stimuli. Here are brief descriptions of these tests:

1. Kinesthesia: With his eyes shielded, the child is required to move his hand to various places on a kinesthesia "chart." For example, the examiner first moves the child's hand and outstretched finger to a certain place on the chart and then guides his hand back to the start. The child is then asked to move his hand back to the place on the chart by himself.

2. Manual Form Perception: Again, the child's eyes are occluded. The examiner places a solid geometric form in one of the child's hands and the child is asked to select from among a number of alternatives the picture of the form identical to the one he is holding.

3. Finger Identification: With his vision occluded, the child is to identify which of his fingers was touched by the tester.

4. Graphesthesia: With eyes shielded, the child sits with his palms down. The examiner "draws" with a pencil eraser a design on the back of one of the child's hands. The child must then reproduce the design.

5. Localization of Tactile Stimuli: The examiner touches the child's visually shielded hand or forearm with a ball-point pen. The child is then required to touch with index finger the place where he was touched.

## EDUCATIONAL PROGRAMS FOR VISUAL-MOTOR, MOTOR, TACTUAL, AND KINESTHETIC DISABILITIES

Many of the programs described in the last chapter on visual-perceptual disabilities are also recommended by their authors for use with children with visual-motor, motor, tactual, and kinesthetic disabilities. Likewise, the reader will note that the programs to be described below also contain many elements developed for the training of visual skills. The educational approaches outlined below, however, are ones whose primary emphases are on motor and visual-motor skills relative to visual skills in isolation. As was noted earlier considerable overlap exists in methods among the programs generally dealing with visual and visual-motor deficits. We have chosen to include a description of a representative sample of these programs. Our treatment is brief, so the reader is encouraged to consult the original sources if he plans to use these programs. The approaches that will be discussed are those of Kephart, Barsch, Cratty, Doman-Delacato, and Fernald.

### Newell Kephart's Approach

As was mentioned earlier, Kephart spent a portion of his professional career in the 1940s in close contact with Heinz Werner and Alfred Strauss at Wayne County Training School in Northville, Michigan. Thus, many of his educational techniques were derived from Werner and Strauss. Until his recent death, Kephart was in charge of the Newell C. Kephart Glen Haven Achievement Center in Fort Collins, Colorado. It is at this center that he put into practice his training activities devised to help perceptually disabled children achieve the perceptual-motor match. His particular approach has been published in the now classic *The Slow Learner in the Classroom* (Kephart, 1960; 2nd. ed., 1971).

Basically, Kephart divided his program into activities involving chalkboard training, sensory-motor training, ocular motor training, and form perception training.

CHALKBOARD TRAINING. Kephart devised a number of elaborate exercises using chalk and chalkboard. He, as well as Getman, noted that a particular advantage of chalkboard over pencil and paper is that spatial directions are more consistent. Up *is* "up" on a chalkboard, whereas up is actually "away from" when a paper is placed on a table before a child. Furthermore, a piece of chalk is easier to hold than a pencil for some children and the movements required are of a grosser nature than those required of pencil and paper.

Different activities for the chalkboard were recommended by Kephart for a variety of purposes: promoting directionality, crossing the midline, orientation, tracing, copying. For inducing directionality the teacher puts dots on the board at random and the child connects one dot to the next one as the teacher puts them on the board. For the child who has problems in crossing the midline, Kephart suggested that at first the child should draw lines to either the right or left of a center line in front of him; gradually, the teacher should require him to draw lines that cross the midline. Numerous other chalkboard activities were described by Kephart for training eye-hand coordination.

SENSORY-MOTOR TRAINING. The activities contained in this portion of Kephart's program were designed to help the child who has difficulty in coordinating movements of his body. The same walking board used to assess children on the Purdue Perceptual-Motor Survey is used here for training posture and balance. The child is asked to walk on the balance beam forward, backward, and sideways. There are a variety of other procedures Kephart recommended for use with the walking board. The balance board, a wooden platform sixteen by sixteen inches, is also used; the child can be asked, for example, to throw and catch a ball while on the balance board platform. Other training exercises include the "angels-in-the snow" routines (also from the Purdue Perceptual-Motor Survey) as well as the trampoline. Activities on the trampoline are meant to promote dynamic balance: "the development of total bodily coordination throughout the gross muscle systems" (Kephart, 1960, p. 224).

OCULAR MOTOR TRAINING. This program was devised for the purpose of helping the child gain control over the movements of his eyes. It includes many activities for the teacher to use in training the child's eye movements. For example, in order to train ocular pursuit one of Kephart's activities is for the teacher to draw a "road" on the board with the flat side of a piece of chalk. The child then takes a toy car and follows the road.

FORM PERCEPTION TRAINING. Training procedures here have been keyed to the developmental level of the child. The exercises include the putting together of puzzles, the construction of designs from match sticks, and putting pegs in a pegboard. For Kephart, because of his belief in the importance of motor activities for visual development, the activities place a heavy emphasis on motoric skills.

### Ray Barsch's Approach

Barsch has articulated a movement approach to education (Barsch, 1976) and advocated what he terms a "Movigenic Curriculum." He has detailed his educational methods in *Achieving Perceptual-Motor Efficiency* (Barsch, 1967). His educational techniques are based upon ten basic constructs:

> (1) the organism is designed for movement (2) the objective of movement is survival (3) movement occurs in an energy surround (4) the mechanism for acquiring information is the percepto-cognitive system (5) the terrain of movement is Space (6) developmental momentum thrusts the learner toward maturity (7) movement occurs in a climate of stress (8) feedback is essential to efficiency (9) development occurs in segments of sequential expansion, and (10) communication of efficiency is derived from the visual spatial phenomenon called language. (p. 329)

There are three basic components of Barsch's Movigenic Curriculum: postural-transport orientations, percepto-cognitive modes, and degrees of freedom. The postural-transport orientations include: muscular strength, dynamic balance, body awareness, spatial awareness, and temporal awareness. The percepto-cognitive modes (perception and cognition are viewed as practically one and the same thing) include the gustatory, olfactory, tactual, kinesthetic, auditory, and visual. What Barsch calls the Degrees of Freedom are bilaterality, rhythm, flexibility, and motor planning. Barsch has included a chapter for each of the above aspects of his program, which contains exercises for use with learning disabled children.

Barsch also sets forth ten guidelines for teachers who use his curriculum:

1. The teacher should be careful to view the child's movement as "efficient-inefficient" rather than as "successful-failing." Efficiency of movement is the goal to be sought.

2. With an increase in efficiency in the child, the teacher should be aware of the complexity of the child's movements. The teacher should evaluate whether the child is achieving more and more complex skills.

3. "Activities must be planned to give the learner ample opportunities to explore his muscular relationships, varying positions of balance, all parts of his body, all positions of space and varying relationships to time" (p. 331).

4. All six of the perceptual modes—gustatory, olfactory, tactual, kinesthetic, auditory, and visual—must be used by the child.

5. "Activities should be provided to deliberately vary the zones of stimulation presenting opportunities in wide assortments of target sources from near, mid, far and remote space" (p. 331).

6. The teacher should provide the child with experiences that necessitate his using a learned task in a variety of ways.

7. The child needs to be encouraged to be the determiner of his own activities. The teacher should give the child a number of activities to choose from and encourage the child's initiative.

8. The teacher must bring about a cognitive ability in the child to plan his own movements.

9. "A spatial orientation can be applied to all types of performance" (p. 332). All academic areas can be considered within a spatial framework.

10. The teacher need not change her own teaching style entirely. The Movigenic Curriculum can be used within the existing framework of the teacher's particular approach.

### Bryant Cratty's Approach

Cratty has written several manuals and books dealing with the training of motor skills. He has devised exercises for the purpose of enhancing motor skills as such (e.g., Cratty, 1967) and also for increasing a child's cognitive abilities (e.g., Cratty, 1973a). With regard to the remediation of motor development, Cratty divides his activities into those for: (a) perceptions of the body and its position in space; (b) balance; (c) locomotion; (d) agility; (e) strength, endurance, and flexibility; (f) catching and throwing balls; (g) manual abilities; and (h) moving and thinking. The specific exercises under each of these headings are very similar to those used for physical education.

To increase a child's cognitive abilities, Cratty maintains that the activity must be associated in some way with the higher thought processes that are to be changed. The activity itself will not increase cognitive capabilities. For example, Cratty (1973a) includes the following game called "Interference":

> **To Enhance:**   Concentration in the presence of distractions, short-term memory, immediate-term memory, ability to mentally rehearse items in a series.
>
> **Participants and Equipment:**   Children ages 5 and older; retarded children ages 8, 9, and older. Variety of playground equipment, ropes, balls, hoops, etc.
>
> **Description:**   Initially a child demonstrates a series of four or five movements, while observers are told that they must remember and later duplicate these movements. Then a second child demonstrates a different series of five movements. Observing children, one by one, are then asked to repeat the first series. Possible interfering effects of second series observed are discussed, with implications for concentration. (p. 35)

### Glen Doman and Carl Delacato's Approach

Doman, a physical therapist, and Delacato, an educational psychologist have posited the most controversial theory and method within the area of learning disabilities and perhaps within the entire field of special education (Delacato, 1959, 1963, 1966). They have founded the Institutes for the Achievement of Human Potential in Philadelphia where they train individuals to carry out their program of "neurological organization."

There are at least three major elements of their approach that have been questioned by numerous authors:

1. The development of the individual, ontogeny, recapitulates the development of the species, phylogeny.
2. The child should be trained to have cerebral dominance, that is, he should be predominantly one-sided with regard to his preferences—right-eyed, right-handed, right-legged.
3. The brain itself is remediated by their procedures.

With respect to the first, Doman and Delacato advocate the once-popular notion that the individual progresses through stages that parallel the evolutionary development of the human species. For example, they presuppose that the child goes through stages equivalent to the fish, amphibian, reptile, and primate before manhood. Their training activities correspond to these levels (e.g., creeping and crawling exercises). Robbins and Glass (1969) present numerous arguments designed to contradict this theory.

Regarding the second element, Doman and Delacato believe strongly in the establishment of a consistent laterality, and they even inhibit some children from using their nonpreferred side in order to bring about laterality. They maintain that this cerebral dominance is necessary in order to learn to read. Robbins and Glass (1969) again question Doman and Delacato's theory regarding the need for a consistent lateral preference.

As to the third, many of the specific activities advocated by Doman and Delacato are the same as those of other perceptual-motor practitioners. The crucial difference in their approach, however, is in their focus on remediation. While individuals such as Barsch, Frostig, Getman, and Kephart have from time to time made enough allusions so that one might infer that they believe their remediation activities influence the activity of the brain, Doman and Delacato make a point of underlining their conviction that their activities remediate the brain. Other perceptual-motor theorists put forth their curriculum within the framework of the behaviors to be improved.

Indicative of the intense feelings that have been aroused concerning the Doman-Delacato treatment method was the unprecedented official statement issued in 1968 by a number of professional organizations regarding the Doman-Delacato procedures. The organizations were: American Academy for Cerebral Palsy, American Academy of Physical Medicine and Rehabilitation, American Congress of Rehabilitation Medicine, Canadian Association for Retarded Children, Canadian Rehabilitation Council for the Disabled, and the National Association for Retarded Children. The statement made by these organizations is a lengthy one, but basically it makes four major points:

1. The promotional methods place parents in an uneasy position if they refuse the treatment.
2. The regimens are so demanding that the parents may neglect other family needs and the child may be inhibited from engaging in normal age-appropriate activities.
3. Their claims of success are exaggerated and undocumented.
4. The theoretical underpinnings of their practices are weak.

### The Efficacy of Perceptual-Motor Training

Considerable controversy has raged over the effectiveness of all the visual perceptual and visual-motor training programs described in this and the last chapter. Not only the Doman-Delacato approach, but perceptual and perceptual-motor training in general has come under attack. Cohen (1969a, 1969b, 1970) in particular has raised adamant questions concerning the value of perceptual training. The debate has reached such intensity that the field of learning disabilities now has two factions: those in favor of perceptual-motor training and those opposed.

Unfortunately, there is really no clear-cut evidence upon which to base judgments in this area. Critics and advocates alike have unwittingly based their arguments on highly questionable research reports. Hallahan and Cruickshank (1973) undertook an extensive review of the literature in order to try to determine the worth of perceptual-motor training. They categorized the studies on the basis of the population studied (e.g., learning disabled, mentally retarded, disadvantaged, and normals) and the program used (e.g., Barsch, Doman-Delacato, Frostig, Getman, Kephart, and a combination of methods).

The results of the review by Hallahan and Cruickshank were both disappointing and startling. Only seven, or 17 percent, of the 42 studies reviewed were free from errors of faulty reporting, unsound methodological procedures, or both. In short, the vast majority were poorly done. With regard to the seven sound studies, there was no consistent trend within this limited sample of reports. Aside from numerous methodological flaws in perceptual-motor training research, there were four main points brought out by the Hallahan and Cruickshank review:

1.  A dilemma exists in this training field with regard to what should be the dependent variable measured. Whether perceptual-motor development should be the target for perceptual-motor training or whether higher cognitive thought—for example, academic achievement—should be the focus of change is a question of considerable importance.

2.  If it is achievement that is to be influenced, then future researchers must take into account the timing of the perceptual-motor treatment and the measure of change. All of the studies assessed achievement immediately after the program ended. It *may* well be, however, that perceptual-motor training brings a child *perceptually* up to a level where he is ready to be taught academics. In other words, a potentially more fruitful research strategy might be to provide perceptual-motor training, then provide academic instruction, then measure academic gains.

3.  The length of the training programs should be of sufficient length and duration to be maximally effective. The mean time of the training programs reviewed was only about 31 hours, a relatively short period of time.

4.  The population studied should be in need of perceptual-motor training. While this point seems hardly worth mentioning, it was almost totally ignored.

With regard to how one should view the efficacy of perceptual-motor training, Hallahan and Cruickshank (1973) concluded:

> Although no persuasive empirical evidence has been brought to the fore in support of perceptual-motor training, neither has there been solid negative evidence. Owing to the lack of satisfactory research studies with proper methodological controls, it is injudicious to decide whole-heartedly that perceptual-motor training deserves or does not deserve approval. The ultimate acceptance or rejection of these theorists and their procedures ought to depend upon systematic, empirical investigations yet to be done.* (p. 216)

Hammill and his colleagues have also questioned the efficacy of perceptual-motor training. They, in fact, have argued that there is no evidence to support the assumption that academic learning is dependent upon underlying psychological processes of any kind (e.g., Hammill & Larsen, 1974).

The burden of proof must ultimately fall on the shoulders of the advocates of perceptual-motor training. Although the history of educational practices is that methods are adopted without first being tested, this attitude must be eliminated. In other words, it should not be left entirely to the critic of a particular method to prove it wrong; proponents of an educational method must demonstrate its efficacy through sound research.

### The VAKT Method

An educational approach that employs the use of the kinesthetic and tactual modalities is the VAKT (visual-auditory-kinesthetic-tactual). Not a method designed to develop kinesthetic and tactual skills, it none-theless uses these two senses in conjunction with visual and auditory perception in order to present the child with a multisensory approach to reading, writing, and spelling. Grace Fernald (1943) is probably the figure most directly associated as an advocate of the VAKT approach, although Gillingham and Stillman (1960) also make use of the kines-thetic and tactual modalities. As Lerner (1971) points out, however, the Gillingham-Stillman method is more of a phonics approach; it places emphasis on learning individual letters and their sounds. Fernald stresses the learning of the whole word.

The steps usually taken in the VAKT approach to teaching reading are:

* D. P. Hallahan & W. M. Cruickshank, *Psychoeducational Foundations of Learning Disabilities* (Englewood Cliffs, N.J.: Prentice-Hall, 1973), p. 216. Reprinted by permission.

1. The child sees the word (visual).
2. The child hears the teacher say the word (auditory).
3. The child himself says the word and thus hears it again (auditory).
4. The child traces the word (either in manuscript or cursive), which has been written for him, and thus feels the movement of his hand and the touch of the letters (kinesthetic and tactual).

There are variations in the above steps, but this is usually the basic sequence of activities. Some variations are to use sandpaper letters to increase the level of tactual stimulation and to repeat some of the above steps—for example, have the child say the word again while tracing. The rationale behind the VAKT method is that by including as many senses as possible the child is being given additional sensory experiences or cues with regard to the word being learned. If the child is weak in any one or two modalities, the others are to help convey the stimulus information.

## APPLIED ANALYSIS
## OF VISUAL-MOTOR, MOTOR, TACTUAL,
## AND KINESTHETIC SKILLS

We have previously commented on the crucial importance for the child's development and academic learning of certain visual-motor, motor, tactual, and kinesthetic skills. Given the importance of these abilities, it is the purpose of applied behavior analysis to investigate how the child's environment can be manipulated in order to insure that he acquires the necessary performances. The applied behavior analysis approach to teaching such skills differs from the others not only in matters of measurement and evaluation but also in not entertaining the assumption that improvement of visual-motor skills in general, or of skills very different from academic tasks, will automatically produce improvement of the performances required for academic achievement. The training of some perceptual skills may ready the child for academic learning, but it will not have a direct benefit on it. It is not assumed, for example, that patterned crawling or practice in walking on a balance beam will affect a child's ability to read or write or count. Rather, the assumption is that one must work directly with those specific skills that are involved in performing academic tasks. If the goal is to teach a child to write, then one must provide instruction in the skills required for forming letters. After specific skills (e.g., writing the letters $a$ to $m$) have been taught, however, one may find that a generalization has been learned (e.g., the child may improve overall in his letter-writing ability and be able to learn new letters more quickly).

Because of its focus on teaching specific skills, applied behavior analysis requires a "task analysis" of the performances to be developed. A task has been analyzed when it has been broken down into prerequisite and component skills to such an extent that the child's errors in performance can be precisely identified and the subskills that he must learn in order to perform adequately are obvious. If a child is not writing legibly, the task of writing may be analyzed into the component skills of:

1. Holding the pencil correctly.
2. Making marks with appropriate pressure on the pencil.
3. Discriminating legibly formed from illegibly formed letters.
4. Forming legible letters when shown a visual model.
5. Properly spacing letters and words.

Each of these five component skills is in itself a task that can be analyzed into component or prerequisite subtasks. Holding the pencil correctly, for example, could be broken down into:

1. Grasping the pencil with the thumb in opposition to the index and middle fingers, the shaft of the pencil forming an angle of approximately 45° with the thumb.
2. Placing the thumb and fingers approximately one inch from the point of the pencil.
3. Curling the fingers naturally toward the palm of the hand.
4. Resting the fourth finger and outside edge of the hand on the paper.

The process of task analysis can be extended indefinitely; it must continue until the teacher or other behavior analyst can identify exactly where the child's performance falters and what must be taught if the child is to reach the instructional objective. Component behaviors, tasks, or skills are an integral part of the terminal performance. Holding the pencil correctly is a component task in the more general task of writing legibly. Prerequisite tasks are not necessarily an integral part of the final performance, but they are necessary antecedents of a component skill. For instance, in learning to put on his shoes a child must learn to match his right shoe with his right foot and his left shoe with his left foot. In obtaining this component skill, one might teach the child first to match cardboard forms of left and right feet to his right and left feet. This matching task with cardboard forms would be prerequisite for learning the final task, but it would not be a component of the final task.

The process of task analysis suggests that one can identify a succession of approximations of the final performance. It also suggests that in order to teach the final performance one could reinforce each successive approximation. This method is precisely what is involved in the process of "shaping" behavior. Behavior shaping, the method of reinforcing successive approximations, is to teaching new behavioral repertoires what stimulus fading is to teaching new discriminations. To use a shaping technique, one must begin with reinforcement of a performance that is already in the individual's repertoire. Then, gradually, the criterion for reinforcement is shifted to closer and closer approximations of the terminal goal. In the case of teaching speech to a nonverbal child, the shaping process may begin with reinforcement of any vocalization. In subsequent teaching sessions, reinforcement may be withheld except for those vocalizations that sound more and more like words. Complex visual-motor skills, such as writing, can be shaped by providing reinforcement first for merely holding the pencil and making lines on the paper and, later, for gradually closer approximations of forming legible letters.

The extent to which tasks must be analyzed and the number of approximations shaped in order to teach a skill will depend on the level of the child's functioning. Tasks must be more finely analyzed and steps in the shaping process must be smaller for younger or more severely handicapped children than for older children and those without handicaps. Like stimulus fading, task analysis and behavior shaping are useful only if they help children to learn at a faster rate. It would be ridiculous to analyze a task and attempt to shape a performance in a child who can in one step master the skill being taught; on the other hand, a task analysis or shaping procedure for a child who is having difficulty in learning is adequate only if the child is performing well on each successive approximation.

In order to reinforce a behavior, one must wait for it to occur; in order to shape a behavior, one must wait specifically for an approximation of the desired performance. That it is possible simply to arrange an environment in which a performance is likely and then wait patiently for approximations that can be reinforced is obvious from the experimental psychology literature. Multitudes of pigeons and rats have been taught, by using behavior shaping, to peck disks or press levers without the experimenter having given them instructions or having shown them how to perform. When a child is being taught a new skill, however, verbal instructions and behavioral examples can in some cases completely eliminate the need for shaping. Explicit instructions alone are sometimes sufficient to induce a desired performance (cf., Berman, 1973; Kauffman, 1975; Lovitt & Smith, 1972). Furthermore, showing children a model or example of how they are to behave can often make it possible for them to acquire instantaneously, through observational learning, a performance that otherwise might take a considerable amount of time to shape (cf., Bandura, 1969; Cullinan, Kauffman, & LeFleur, 1975). Instructions and modeling (behavioral examples or illustrations that are to be imitated) are potentially powerful influences in teaching any skill, but they have been relatively neglected in educational research.

Reinforcement for appropriate performance is a primary factor in teaching, but task analysis, behavior shaping, and modeling are procedures that greatly enhance the value or effectiveness of reinforcement. Task analysis is necessary in order to know precisely what to reinforce. Shaping makes it possible for an individual to acquire gradually and systematically a skill that no amount of reinforcement could induce without successive approximations. Modeling allows the child to acquire immediately an imitative performance that can be reinforced.

Behavior shaping and modeling are particularly germane to the teaching of any skills that require motor or visual-motor acts. However, in the following discussion of applied behavior analysis in specific academic areas, it will be seen that reinforcement, task analysis, shaping, fading, instructions, and modeling can be used effectively in concert.

### Beginning Writing Skills

The work of Staats and his colleagues (Staats, Brewer, & Gross, 1970) has shown that teaching writing skills consists essentially of shaping an imitative motor repertoire. In their work, young culturally deprived children approximately four years old were taught to write the letters of the alphabet. The teacher began by showing the child how to hold a crayon (and, later in the program, a pencil) and trace a line. Next, the child was shown how to trace large letters. After he learned to trace letters, he was taught, through instructions and models, how to copy them, beginning with very large letters that were gradually reduced in size to primary-size type. Appropriate imitations (i.e., tracing or copying the model letters correctly) were reinforced with tokens in much the same manner as responses were reinforced in Staats's reading program described in Chapter 6. The tasks gradually increased in difficulty, and as gradually a greater accuracy of imitation was required in order to obtain reinforcement. As a result of such instruction, the children learned to write the letters of the entire alphabet after several thousand trials. The slow acquisition of a child's writing performance is shown in Figure 7.8 (pp. 144–145). The response numbered 1 was produced when the child was asked to write the letters in his name prior to instruction. The response numbered 2 shows the first trial at tracing the letter *a*. Subsequent trials on copying letter forms show the child's step-by-step acquisition of writing skill. Staats and his associates found that young children learned new letters in fewer trials after they had acquired the ability to copy the first few letters:

> The children were given training in which the stimuli were decreased in size, and they had to imitate longer series of stimulus letters to increasingly stringent standards of exactness. When the child engages in such an extended series of learning trials, his imitational skills become increasingly more precise; that is, his responses come to produce stimuli that match more and more closely the imitational or standard stimulus. It may be added that in this process the child learns not only specific skills, as in imitating the particular letters on which the child is trained. The specific training also yielded general skills in imitation writing. That is, there was an increase in the child's ability to copy a *new* letter when it was first presented. (Staats, et al., 1970, p. 72)

Rayek and Nesselroad (1972) have used even more explicit procedures to teach writing to young handicapped children, and they have obtained good results. Their program includes giving and fading both verbal and visual prompts and reinforcing successive approximations of the terminal goal. Verbal prompts include instructions regarding how to form a letter, and visual prompts include forms to be traced (e.g., lines, which are gradually faded by changing them to dots). The terminal goals include both manuscript and cursive writing. The program combines the use of a number of behavior principles:

> First, writing is taught by shaping procedures. It is the gradual shaping of a motor skill to the point where the response approximates a specific model. Second, letters are made up of stroke elements. A task analysis suggests that the elements requiring the least complex motor responses are the horizontal and vertical lines. Slanted lines and curved lines are more complex. For maximum program efficiency, letters containing common elements are grouped into families and taught together. For instance, all letters using straight lines are taught before letters containing slanted lines. According to the task analysis, letters within a given family are ordered according to their difficulty and assigned in that order. Figure [7.9] shows the stroke elements and the letters and numbers which include them. Third, copying a letter from a visual model precedes writing a letter from dictation. This procedure is used to assure that the child is equipped to make the appropriate strokes prior to writing from dictation. Fourth, writing is functional when it is used in practical ways such as writing one's name, words, or stories. Once these meaningful uses of writing are possible for the child, the social interactions which ensue take over to maintain the behavior. (Rayek & Nesselroad, 1972, pp. 171–172)

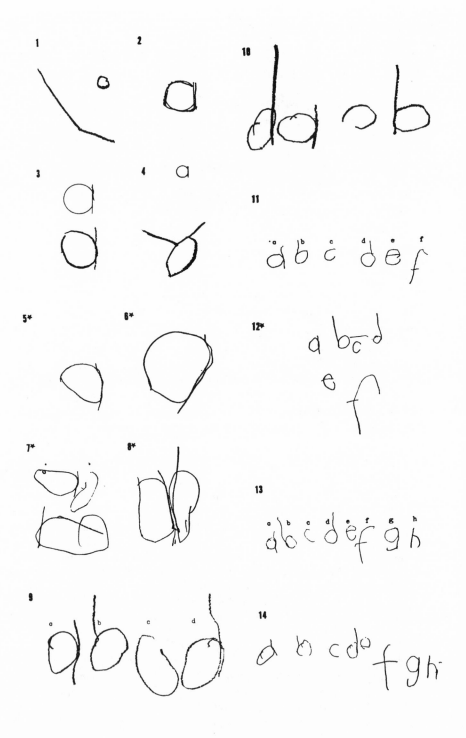

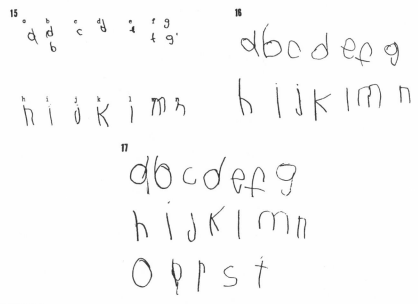

FIGURE 7.8.
Summary of the writing learning of a four-year-old child with an IQ of 89.

Source: A. W. Staats, B. A. Brewer, & M. C. Gross, "Learning and Cognitive Development: Representative Samples, Cumulative-Hierarchical Learning, and Experimental-Longitudinal Methods," Monographs of the Society for Research in Child Development, 1970, Ser. No. 141, Vol. 35, No. 8, p. 69. Reprinted by permission.

In most academic programs manuscript writing (printing) is taught before cursive writing. Lovitt (1973a) and his colleagues, however, have successfully taught cursive writing from the beginning of the school year without taking into consideration what writing instruction the pupils had previously received. Lovitt's research data appear to support Staats's contention that writing learning involves the acquisition of a generalized motor imitation repertoire in which learning to copy specific letters will improve performance on copying other letters.

Procedures for correcting specific writing problems have not been extensively researched. However, reinforcement, explicit instruction, response cost contingencies for errors, and activities such as labeling, tracing, touching, and copying letters have been used to improve handwriting in learning disabled and normal children (Brigham, Finfrock, Breunig, & Bushell, 1972; Fauke, Burnett, Powers, & Sulzer-Azaroff, 1973; Hopkins, Schutte, & Garton, 1971; Lovitt, 1973a).

Lovitt (1973a) has taught typing skills to learning disabled children. Typing does have certain advantages over handwriting, especially

| ELEMENTS | LETTER FAMILIES<br>LETTERS AND NUMBERS |
|---|---|
| $-$  I | i I t T I L H F E I 4 |
| /\ | 7 Z z N V v W w A M<br>Y y X x K k |
| c ɔ O | O o Q C c G D P R B 2<br>3 5 6 8 9 a e d q b p |
| J ſ | J ↓ g f |
| U u | U u |
| n | r n h m |
| S s | S s |

FIGURE 7.9.
*Elements and letter families.*

*Source: E. Rayek & E. Nesselroad. "Application of Behavior Principles to the Teaching of Writing, Spelling, and Composition," in G. Semb (Ed.),* Behavior Analysis and Education—1972 *(Lawrence, Ks.: University of Kansas, Department of Human Development, 1972). Reprinted by permission.*

for individuals who experience difficulty in the visual-motor skills required for writing. Typing is faster (once the basics are learned) and produces a consistent, legible script. Furthermore, typing is an intriguing activity for most children; few will have to be coaxed, prodded, or extrinsically reinforced for learning typing skills.

### Spelling

Spelling is more than a visual-motor task, but visual-motor skills are a prominent part of spelling performance. A common problem in spelling is the reversal of letters, such as *b* for *d*. It appears that such reversals can often be corrected quite easily by the use of explicit instructions and correct models, especially when reinforcement is provided for correct performance (Cooper, 1970). A case in point has been described by Smith and Lovitt (1973). They worked with a ten-year-old boy who often substituted *b* for *d*, usually when *d* was the first letter of the word. Their approach to the problem was simple and direct:

> Every day during [intervention] the experimenter showed Greg the word *dam* written on an index card, and asked him first to read the word, then to name the initial letter of the word. Greg was then instructed to write the word *dam*. The experimenter then showed Greg the word *bam* (written on another index card) and asked him to name the initial letter of that word. Then, pointing to the word *bam*, the experimenter told Greg that he often wrote the word *dam* like this word. Greg was again told to name the first letter of the word *dam*. After he had done so, he was then instructed to write the letter *d*. The experimenter told Greg to be certain to write the word *dam* with a *d* and not with a *b*. (p. 359)

The result of this procedure was that after five days, Greg made no more errors. Also, improvement in other spelling and writing tasks was noted.

As might be expected, spelling accuracy can often be modified by contingencies of reinforcement. Lovitt, Guppy, and Blattner (1969), for example, found that fourth graders' spelling could be improved simply by making free time contingent on accurate performance.

### Reading

Reading ordinarily is considered to be a process of visual discrimination, not a visual-motor skill. However, some reading clinicians, such as Grace Fernald, have thought that reading learning can be enhanced by adding kinesthetic and tactual stimuli to the visual and auditory stimuli. A recent applied behavior analysis project has provided some evidence that tactile stimulation may, in fact, result in faster learning of initial reading discriminations. Massad and Etzel (1972) taught preschool children letter sounds using sandpaper letters and painted (smooth) letters. The children traced both types of letters with their fingers as they called the sounds. It was found that the children learned to discriminate the sandpaper letters in fewer trials and with fewer errors than the painted letters. Apparently, novel or distinctive tactile stimulation associated with visual stimuli can, at least for some children at some stages of learning, be of definite benefit.

### Beginning Arithmetic

The most fundamental arithmetic skill is counting. Staats and his colleagues (Staats, et al., 1970) have shown that learning to count involves learning three distinct performances:

> The child has to learn a sequence of sensorimotor responses that involves attending to the individual objects in the set in order (one at a time, at least at the beginning). He also has to learn a sequence of counting verbal responses. In addition, as a third type of learning, the latter has to be under the control of the former and vice versa. (p. 46)

Specifically, the child must learn (1) the visual-motor skill of touching or moving objects one at a time and in order, (2) the verbal skill of saying the numbers in sequence, and (3) the skill of combining or coordinating the visual-motor and verbal performances. Touching or moving objects in order without the appropriate verbal accompaniment cannot be considered counting. On the other hand, the verbal behavior of saying numbers in order without the corresponding visual-motor performance is (at first) meaningless. In meaningful counting, moving or touching each object is a signal to say the next number, and saying each number is a signal to move or touch the next object. However, it is true that once such a coordinated visual-motor-verbal repertoire is learned, the verbal component alone can be extended meaningfully. For example, after a child has learned to count ten objects, his verbal response alone of counting to twenty may be meaningful.

Staats and his co-workers taught young children to count by systematically developing each of the three skills involved. In the beginning the teacher showed the child a card with pictures of one or two objects on it, and prompted the child to say "One dog," "Two fish," and so forth. When the child could discriminate and label numerosity for one and two objects, a third object was introduced. When "three" was mastered, the pictures were changed to geometric forms. Next, the child was taught to count dots as the teacher uncovered them with her hand. The correct counting performance was modeled by the teacher, and the child was reinforced (with tokens) for imitating. When the child could count four dots, the teacher arranged objects in a row and modeled the behavior of touching and counting them in order. Later, objects were pulled from a row and counted in order. Still later, objects not arranged in order were moved one at a time from a pile and counted. Finally, rote verbal counting was extended through verbal modeling and imitation.

Parsons (1972) and Grimm, Bijou, and Parsons (1973) have used similar procedures in teaching beginning arithmetic skills to handicapped young children. As with beginning writing, these skills were developed by using a number of basic behavior modification techniques in combination: task analysis, reinforcement, shaping, fading, and modeling.

Visual-motor, motor, tactual, and kinesthetic skills appear to be of value in some children's learning of basic computational skills, as well as in counting. Lovitt and his co-workers (Lovitt, 1973a; Smith, Lovitt, & Kidder, 1972) have found that providing objects to manipulate and showing models of problem solutions improved children's computation performance. Finger counting is a part of the arithmetic program described by Parsons (1972).

### Other Motor and
### Visual-Motor Skills

There is ample evidence that a very wide range of motor and visual-motor skills can be changed through the use of reinforcement techniques. Dressing, feeding, climbing, walking, and many other important self-help and play behaviors have been taught or improved by giving positive reinforcement for the desired performance (cf. Dmitriev, 1974; Risley & Baer, 1973). Furthermore, it has been demonstrated that some "creative" behaviors, such as block building (Goetz & Baer, 1973) and easel painting (Goetz & Salmonson, 1972) are modifiable when reinforcement is provided for certain dimensions of performance. The results of the study of block building by Goetz and Baer have already been described (see Figure 5.2). Goetz and Salmonson (1972) found essentially the same relationship between creative easel painting and reinforcement. When the teacher gave positive social reinforcement for specific "creative" forms by describing them explicitly, the children painted more diverse forms than when the teacher made positive comments about the painting in general without calling attention to form diversity—that is, when the teacher specified dimensions of artistic creativity the children were more "creative" painters.

If children have deficits in visual-motor or motor skills, then, their deficits can often be remediated directly and effectively through the use of applied behavior analysis techniques. At this time, the value of perceptual-motor training is not clearly understood. However, careful task analysis and judicious use of modeling, shaping, and reinforcement procedures have shown their worth in many individual cases.

# Distractibility and Hyperactivity

# 8

Children who are identified as learning disabled are frequently described by their teachers and parents as distractible and hyperactive. It is not unusual for the parent to relate numerous incidents from early childhood on which depict a child as an exceedingly rambunctious "pest," always into places where he should not be. This very same child, when confronted with the demands of the school situation, can quickly become a nightmare for even the best of teachers who have not had the background necessary to cope with distractible and hyperactive children. It only takes one of these children in a classroom to create chaos.

As is the case with so many of the handicaps included within the realm of learning disabilities, distractibility and hyperactivity were first noted and studied by Werner and Strauss (Chapter 1). In fact, these particular behaviors are so much identified with the efforts of these scientists that a child who exhibits them is frequently identified as manifesting the Strauss Syndrome. The term "Strauss Syndrome" has been used rather loosely. Ingredients of the syndrome usually include one or more of the following (depending upon who is using the term):

1. Distractibility
2. Hyperactivity
3. Perceptual-motor problems
4. Brain damage

The most frequent usage of the term, however, usually limits the characteristics to hyperactivity and distractibility. No definitive research data on this subject exist, but teacher reports and clinical observations usually place the two behaviors together. It does, of course, make sense that a child who wanders aimlessly and speedily about his environment would also have a short attention span.

## DISTRACTIBILITY

Interest in the psychological variable of attention has had a rather unusual history. With the rise of the behavioristic school of thought during the first half of this century, the construct of attention was not pursued. The behaviorists' concern for only those behaviors that are observable and measurable led them to scorn such a vague notion as attention. Since the 1950s, and especially the 1960s, however, attention has become an extremely popular variable for study. To a large extent, the objections raised by the behaviorists regarding observability and measurability have been met.

### The Importance of Attention for Psychological Theories and Academic Achievement

So popular has attention become that all but a very few modern theories of perceptual, cognitive, and social development rely heavily upon it. To list but five.

1. Wohlwill's (1970) conceptualization of cognitive development makes attention the sine qua non of conceptual functioning.
2. Gibson's (1969) theory of perceptual development is constructed to a great extent upon attentional mechanisms; the child, for example, must attend to distinctive features.
3. Fantz (1966), along with others who study infants, has assigned attention a crucial role in perceptual development in infancy.
4. Zeaman and House (1963), whose work we will describe later, view mental retardation itself as synonomous with poor attention skills.
5. Bandura's (1969) theory of the development of imitation (a most central construct for Bandura) is largely dependent upon the development of attention.

In the classroom situation, it is logical that attending skills are necessary for the child to achieve. The child who cannot attend for more than a few seconds or even minutes will find classroom learning difficult. Empirical support for the relationship between attention and academic achievement comes from a study by Lahaderne (1968) who observed the attending behaviors of children in four sixth-grade classrooms. Lahaderne also assessed attitudes toward school as well as intelligence and academic achievement. His results indicate that attention was related to achievement and that this relationship was largely independent of IQ and attitudes toward school.

The work of Staats (Staats, 1968a, b; Staats, Brewer, & Gross, 1970), some aspects of which we have discussed in previous chapters, also promotes the importance of attention in early reading acquisition. As Hallahan and Cruickshank (1973) point out in their discussion of studies made by Staats and his associates:

> One of their experiments is particularly relevant to this point. Within a behavior modification framework, preschool children were taught by reinforcement to learn to read the letters of the alphabet, starting with the letter A and proceeding to Z.
> Plotting the learning curves of the children, Staats et al. found that, for those children who successfully completed the alphabet, the first letters required a greater number of learning trials than did the latter ones. Too, there was a gradual decrease in the number of learning trials needed for acquisition of a letter as the children progressed from A to Z. The crucial finding was that the difference in the learning rate of those children who learned to read and those who did not occurred primarily at the beginning letters, the latter children requiring many more learning trials for the initial letters. Staats, in a previous investigation . . . , had found that the attainment of an alphabet-reading repertoire in children is characterized by a learning-how-to-learn process. Referring to this finding and the above-mentioned difference between the fast and slow learners, Staats et al. concluded that attention is important in the early stages of alphabet learning. In other words, attention appeared to be an important factor accounting for the difference between those children who learned the alphabet and those who did not. The slow learners did not learn to direct their attention to the task at hand.* (p. 236)

### Distractibility As an "Overriding Disability"

The obvious importance of attending skills to so many facets of learning makes it imperative that the teacher consider the child's attentional abilities when devising an educational program for him. Many apparent disabilities may actually be the result of an attentional deficit.

---

* D P. Hallahan & W. M. Cruickshank, *Psychoeducational Foundations of Learning Disabilities* (Englewood Cliffs, N.J.: Prentice-Hall, 1973), p. 236. Reprinted by permission.

This is why we refer to the potential of distractibility to be an "overriding disability." Because of its central role in so much of psychological and educational functioning, it may itself be the cause of any number of disabilities. The child exhibiting difficulties on tasks involving eye-hand coordination, for example, *may* have more of an attentional problem, which causes him to do poorly, than a perceptual-motor deficit.

### Assessment of Attention

In previous chapters pertaining to various learning disabilities an extensive section was presented on standardized instruments for the assessment of the disability in question. In this chapter the section on instruments will be brief: there are no commonly used, standardized tests for attention. Several experimental measures, some of which we will discuss later, do exist, but none has been constructed for diagnostic purposes. Much research has been conducted, however, using the Wechsler Intelligence Scale for Children (WISC) that indicates certain subtests can be used to assess the attentional abilities of children. Huelsman (1970) undertook an extensive review of studies comparing the WISC scores of achievers and underachievers. He found that the low achievers consistently scored poorly in arithmetic, coding, and digit span—three subtests that have been frequently reported as being dependent on attending abilities.

### The Normal Development of Attention

VISUAL ATTENTION.  The study of visual attention has experienced a period of rapid growth since the mid-1960s. The reason for this expansion is due, as noted above, to an increase in interest in attention as a factor in learning and to an increase in sophistication regarding the measurement of attention. Particularly with regard to the developmental period of infancy, technological advances have been made that make attention more amenable to objective measurement. Besides the use of cameras, which can record the eye movements of infants, investigators have used a more precise measure of attention: heart rate. While it is informative to know where the infant gazes, the study of eye movements in connection with attention in infancy suffers because it is difficult to tell whether the infant is actually "attending" to where his eyes are gazing. It has been found, however, that one can gauge the infant's attention fairly accurately by monitoring his heart rate. When an infant attends to an object in his environment, his heart rate decelerates rapidly. Numerous investigators have just begun to explore attentional development in infancy; we will refer later to this work as it relates specifically to learning disabled children.

John Hagen and his colleagues, among others, have conducted a number of studies of the development of attentional abilities in younger and older children (Druker & Hagen, 1969; Hagen, 1967; Hagen & Frisch, 1968; Hagen & Sabo, 1967; Maccoby & Hagen, 1965). Other investigators, using the same task in different experimental paradigms and with some different populations, have essentially replicated their results with regard to normal children (Hallahan, Kauffman, & Ball, 1973; Hallahan, Kauffman, & Ball, 1974b; Hallahan, Stainback, Ball, & Kauffman, 1973). Children develop visual selective attention skills rather gradually until about the age of twelve to thirteen, when there is a dramatic increase in selective attention ability.

The experimental task used by Hagen consists of cards, each containing the picture of an animal and a familiar household object. The child is presented with a series of these cards, each one being shown to him for two seconds and then turned facedown in a row in front of him. The child is told to pay attention to where in the series the animals are. After a series of from about three to six cards, the child is shown a cue card and asked to point to where in the facedown array that particular animal is. The child is given twelve of these series and the proportion he correctly remembers (i.e., the proportion of the times he can remember the position of the facedown card matching the cue card) is termed his *central recall* score. After the twelve series, the child is asked to remember the correct pairings of the animals and the objects (each animal was always paired with the same object), even though he had been instructed to pay attention only to the animals. The proportion correct on this task is his *incidental recall* score. When performances on the two tasks are compared, a developmental increase in selective attention (better recall on the central relative to the incidental) is demonstrated, especially at about twelve to thirteen years of age when incidental recall has been found in some studies to decline. Figure 8.1 is an example of the developmental findings for normal children.

AUDITORY ATTENTION. An auditory analogue of the above visual task has been developed and administered to children of various age levels (Hallahan, Kauffman, & Ball, 1974a). The findings were generally the same as in the visual domain except that the increase in auditory selective attention was more gradual and did not show the pronounced increase at the older ages. Maccoby (1967), using a dichotic listening task, has also found a gradual rise in auditory selective attention. The dichotic listening task presents a taped message in a man's voice to one ear and a message in a woman's voice in the other ear. The child is required to pay attention to the one and ignore the other.

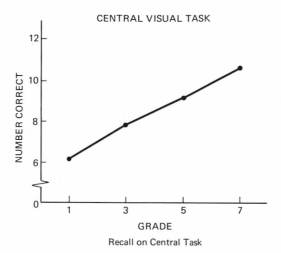

Recall on Central Task

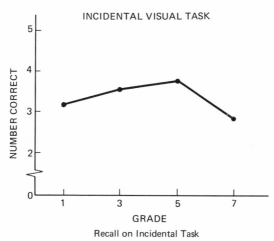

Recall on Incidental Task

*FIGURE 8.1.*
*Recall on central and incidental visual tasks as a function of age.*

Source: E. E. Maccoby & J. W. Hagen, "Effects of
Distraction upon Central versus Incidental Recall:
Developmental Trends," Journal of Experimental
Child Psychology, 1965, 2, 280–289. Reprinted by
permission.

## Attention in the Disabled

THE RETARDED.   As we discussed in the first chapter, the research
of Werner and Strauss was crucial to the development of the field of
learning disabilities. The particular aspect of their work with which we

are concerned here is their investigation of figure-background discrimination in the retarded. The two child psychologists looked at figure-background ability in a number of modalities, but their most intensive investigations were in the visual realm. They presented slides of familiar objects embedded in a background to their subjects at very fast exposure times (see Figure 8.2 for examples of the figure-background slides). Slides were presented to each child and on the basis of the answer to the question, "What did you see?" they found two different kinds of retardates. One group of children tended to report the correct figure; the other group tended to refer to the background only.* The latter group, it was concluded from this experimental and other clinical evidence, was highly distractible and needed a different educational program (we will discuss this program later).

Another team of researchers has obtained evidence which they believe indicates that retardates, in general, suffer from an attentional deficit. Zeaman and House (1963) have conducted investigations of the discrimination learning of retarded children. Their evidence suggests that once the retarded child learns to attend to the relevant dimension (e.g., color, size, form) that discriminates two objects, he learns just as rapidly as his normal peers of the same mental age.

Because the subjects in the studies conducted by Werner and Strauss and by Zeaman and House all resided in institutions, it is dangerous to generalize about all retardates. This caution is particularly valid in light of Zigler's (Balla, Butterfield, & Zigler, 1974; Zigler, 1969) strong case for the deleterious effects of institutionalization. Hagen and Huntsman (1971), using the central-incidental task described earlier, have found an attention deficit in institutionalized, but not community-residing, retardates. To complicate matters further, however, Hagen, Hallahan, and Kauffman (1974) have found some tentative evidence to suggest that the social class of the retardate before he enters the institution *may* be more important than the institutionalization per se.

Even though the subtle nuances of attentional problems in the retarded must await further research, it is safe to say that the evidence now available points to the conclusion that there are at least some retardates who are inattentive. Distractibility appears to be a significant problem for some retarded children.

THE LEARNING DISABLED. Although teacher and clinical reports have pointed to the distractibility of the learning disabled, it has not been until recently that empirical evidence has begun to accrue which indi-

---

* As we noted in the first chapter, Werner and Strauss believed a basic etiological difference between the two was that the latter were brain damaged. This is now considered questionable because of the inadequate criteria they used for diagnosis.

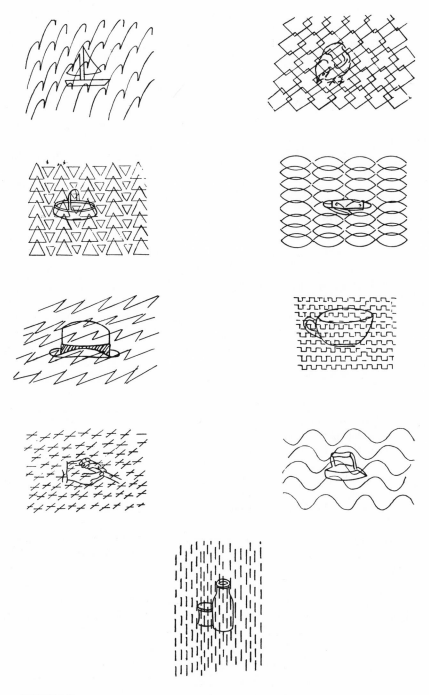

FIGURE 8.2.
Werner-Strauss figure-background slides to test pure visual perception.

Source: A. A. Strauss & L. E. Lehtinen, Psychopathology and Education of the Brain-Injured Child, Vol. 1 (New York: Grune & Stratton, 1947). Reprinted by permission.

cates that many learning disabled children are highly distractible. Halla-han, Kauffman, and Ball (1973) compared sixth grade over- and under-achievers using the central-incidental tasks and found the latter to be deficient in selective attention. In other data collected on learning disabled children using the central-incidental tasks, Hallahan (1975) found further evidence of a selective attention deficit in learning disabled children.

Tarver and Hallahan (1974) have reviewed a number of studies that have experimentally placed learning disabled children in situations where there are potential distractors (Alwitt, 1966; Browning, 1967a; Douglas, 1972; Elkind, Larson, & Van Doorninck, 1965; Hallahan, Kauffman, & Ball, 1973; Keogh & Donlon, 1972; Mondani & Tutko, 1969; Sabatino & Ysseldyke, 1972; Silverman, Davids, & Andrews, 1963). The tentative conclusions reached were:

> Children with learning disabilities were consistently found to be highly distractible when measures of distractibility were congruent with Cruick-shank's definition of distractibility—inability to filter out extraneous stimuli and focus selectively on the task. . . . On the other hand, they were consistently found to be no more highly distracted than normal controls by lights, noises, etc. . . . Browning's (1967b) post hoc hyporesponsiveness hypothesis offers one explanation for these seemingly inconsistent findings. . . . Browning (1967b) suggests that the stimulus intensity of the flashing lights, etc., is sufficient to alert the children with learning disabilities, resulting in increased responsiveness (i.e., more responses) and improved performance.
>
> Another post hoc interpretation can be suggested. The evidence indicates that learning disabled children have difficulty in distinguishing between which aspects of a stimulus situation are relevant and which are irrelevant. When relevant and irrelevant stimuli are easily distinguishable (i.e., when the irrelevant stimuli consist of qualities of high intensity and the relevant do not or vice versa) then the learning disabled children would be predicted to perform better than when the relevant and irrelevant stimuli are of relatively equal intensity. (Tarver & Hallahan, 1974, p. 567)

Earlier we mentioned that the technique of measuring the amount of heart rate deceleration is a method that is being used more and more in the measurement of attention, particularly in infants. Sroufe, Sonies, West, and Wright (1973) used heart rate deceleration to measure attentional responses in learning disabled and normal children aged seven to ten years. They found significantly less heart rate deceleration, that is, less attention, in learning disabled children compared with normal children. Lewis (1975) has reviewed the research and presented data on infants with various kinds of disabilities and has concluded that measures such as heart rate deceleration taken in infancy hold much promise in terms of early prediction of later learning problems.

Yet another experimental measure has been used to find learning disabled children deficient in an ability closely related to attention. Using the Matching Familiar Figures (MFF) test developed by Kagan (1966), Keogh and Donlon (1972) and Hallahan, Kauffman, and Ball (1973) found learning disabled children to be more impulsive and less reflective than normals. The MFF requires the child to match a standard figure with one exactly like it from among many alternatives. Impulsives respond quickly and make many errors; reflectives respond slowly, evaluating the alternatives, and make few errors. The finding that learning disabled children are more likely to be impulsive is consistent with the other studies indicating their distractibility.

## EDUCATION OF
## THE DISTRACTIBLE CHILD

As mentioned in the first chapter, Werner and Strauss, and later Cruickshank, made educational recommendations for the distractible and hyperactive child. Specifically, three major programming considerations were outlined by Cruickshank in his Montgomery County Project:

1. A structured program.
2. Reduced environmental stimulation.
3. Enhancement of the stimulus value of the teaching materials.

### A Structured Program

Because the distractible child is so much at the mercy of his impulses, the recommended program for him is one involving a heavy emphasis on structure. Unable to provide his own structure, the distractible child can become quite disoriented in a classroom environment which promotes the idea of having the child make a number of decisions for himself. Many kinds of classrooms that may be completely appropriate for the average child—an open, nondirective classroom for example—may be most harmful for the impulse-ridden, distractible child. Cruickshank provides an example of what is involved in a structured program:

> Specifically, what is meant by a structured program? For example, upon coming into the classroom the child will hang his hat and coat on a given hook—not on any hook of his choice, but on the same hook every

day. He will place his lunch box, if he brings one, on a specific shelf each day. He will then . . . follow the teacher's instructions concerning learning tasks, use of toilet, luncheon activities, and all other experiences until the close of the school day. The day's program will be so completely simplified and so devoid of choice (or conflict) situations that the possibility of failure experience will be almost completely minimized. The learning tasks will be within the learning capacity and within the limits of frustration and attention span of the child. This will mean that a careful study of the child's attention span will have to be made. If it is determined that he has an attention span of four minutes, then all teaching tasks should be restricted to four minutes.* (Cruickshank, Bentzen, Ratzeburg, & Tannhauser, 1961, p. 18)

### Reduced Environmental Stimulation and Enhancement of Teaching Materials

Cruickshank also recommends that the distractible child be placed in a classroom that is as devoid as possible of extraneous environmental stimuli. Cruickshank implemented many of the suggestions of Werner and Strauss as well as adding some innovations of his own into the classroom. Some of the major modifications recommended for the classroom were:

1. The walls and ceiling should be sound-treated.
2. The floor should be carpeted.
3. The windows should be opaque so that they will admit light but the child cannot see objects on the outside.
4. Book shelves and cupboards should have doors so that objects on them can be covered.
5. Bulletin boards should be covered or not decorated except for specific, brief periods of the day.
6. Cubicles, three-sided work areas, should be used for the most distractible children when involved in tasks requiring concentration.

Not all of the classroom, however, was designed to be bland. To contrast with the blandness of those aspects of the environment not involved in the teaching activity itself, the material directly necessary for instruction was made to draw the child's attention to it. The use of vivid colors to highlight the instructional materials was thus suggested. The distractible child in learning to read, for example, would be presented with a few words, or maybe only one word, per page and these words

* W. M. Cruickshank, F. A. Bentzen, F. H. Ratzeburg, & M. T. Tannhauser, *A Teaching Method for Brain-Injured and Hyperactive Children* (Syracuse: Syracuse University Press, 1961), p. 18. Reprinted by permission.

would be in bold colors. This modification of the reading task was introduced purposely to contrast with the usual reading text wherein a page of print might contain many words plus miscellaneous pictures.

### The Efficacy of the Reduced
### Environmental Stimuli Program

Cruickshank undertook a demonstration-pilot study of the above-outlined procedures (Cruickshank, Bentzen, Ratzeburg, & Tannhauser, 1961). A comparison was made of children in the modified classrooms and those in nonmodified classrooms. The results after one year of the program were not overwhelmingly positive. The experimental group made gains in perceptual-motor abilities, as assessed by the Bender-Gestalt, and on the degree of distractibility, as measured by the figure-background test used by Werner and Strauss. But no gains were made in intelligence or academic achievement. After one year, the children left the experimental program and the gains were erased. This regression is not unusual with regard to this kind of research; it has also been found in other settings. For example, children in compensatory preschool programs, which induce gains, lose their advantage once the program ends and they enter the traditionally run classrooms. The results of the project after one year were disappointing, but the pilot nature of the program should be kept in mind. Cruickshank (1975) has described the logistical and administrative problems faced by his research team. Unfortunately, the difficulties he encountered are far from rare in the area of field-based research.

Other researchers have also attempted to evaluate the efficacy of aspects of the Cruickshank program. Hallahan and Kauffman (1975b) have reviewed these efforts (Gorton, 1972; Jenkins, Gorrafa, & Griffiths, 1972; Rost & Charles, 1967; Shores & Haubrich, 1969; Slater, 1968; Sommervill, Warnberg, & Bost, 1973). As was the case with the perceptual-motor efficacy studies, there were numerous methodological problems:

1.  None of the purported efficacy studies was an exact replication of the *total* program devised by Cruickshank. The major component that the researchers concentrated on was stimulus reduction.

2.  The stimulus reduction employed varied widely in kind and probably in quantity and quality. The specific methods used ranged from total seclusion of individual children to attempts to seclude an entire classroom.

3.  There are serious questions with respect to how distractible the children studied really were.

4.  The duration of the studies was usually short.

Because of the above limitations, the following two conclusions from the review of these studies of reduced environmental stimuli *must be treated as tentative*:

1. They generally supported the notion that attending skills were increased.
2. In terms of academic achievement and other higher level measures, no advantage was found.

### The Efficacy of Stimulus-Enriched Teaching Materials

No investigations have been made of Cruickshank's recommendation of the specific use of teaching materials that are highly stimulating. Nonetheless, there is a great deal of related research to substantiate the use of such material. There is a body of literature to show that children at a very early age demonstrate marked preferences for attending to different aspects of stimuli (Pick & Pick, 1970). Some children, for example, are more attracted by the size dimension of objects or figures whereas others direct their attention more toward the color dimension. (Developmental studies have found that on the average, children attend more to color at early ages and then shift at about six years of age to prefer the dimension of form.) That a child required to use materials that "play to his strength" should do better is only logical. Empirical research also has demonstrated that children exposed to tasks involving the stimulus dimension of their choice are more apt to perform better than when they use nonpreferred dimensions (Odom & Corbin, 1973).

The task of learning to read involves form discrimination. As we have just pointed out, however, some children—the majority at about six years of age—are more apt to attend to colors. The teacher, it would seem, would be using the psychological characteristics of his children to his advantage if he were to present color-dominant children with letters differing in color as well as form. Particularly, those letters that are more difficult to discriminate could be presented in different colors. Stevenson (1972) has reviewed the literature on the use of color cues in discrimination and has arrived at the same conclusion. A recommendation he makes is that letters such as *b* and *d* should be presented in different colors. Based on research, this recommendation is appropriate for the average child and would be exceedingly apt for a distractible child, especially if he has a preference for the color dimension. As Hallahan and Kauffman (1975b) have noted, the use of color cues might be of most benefit if applied to those features of the letter that distinguish it from other letters with which it is likely to be confused:

In the example of "b" and "d" the particular side of the "o" on which the "l" falls is the distinctive feature with regard to the particular name of the letter. Since attention to such distinctive features is so important to learning, it can be suggested that rather than printing the whole letter in color the teacher might highlight the "l" of "b" and "d" by presenting it in a bright color. The hypothesized result would be that such a technique would draw the child's attention to the crucial portion of the two letters which differentiate them. (p. 231)

### Using Language to Increase a Child's Attention

There is a wealth of data that suggests that a viable teaching technique for the inattentive child is for the teacher to encourage him to use language in order to help him direct his attention. Studies using experimental tasks demonstrate the value of language cues (e.g., Balling & Myers, 1971; Furth & Milgram, 1973; Hagen, Hargrave, & Ross, 1973; Hagen & Kingsley, 1968; Hagen, Meacham, & Mesibov, 1970; Kingsley & Hagen, 1969; Yussen, 1972). Instructing the child to rehearse verbally those aspects of academic tasks to which he should attend would appear to be a wise teaching strategy.

If, for example, the child is having difficulty attending to his math problems, the teacher might have him verbally rehearse out loud, or to himself, the numbers of the problems. Arithmetic problems of the story-problem variety are especially dependent upon skills of concentration for solution. The child must maintain his attention to a number of details before he arrrives at his final answer. The teacher might ask the distractible child who has verbal facility to verbalize his process of solution in order to help him concentrate on the relevant details of the problem. Such a technique also allows the teacher to pinpoint the particular stage of the problem that the child fails rather than just knowing that he has produced a final answer that is wrong.

The distractible child who has difficulty in handwriting because he cannot maintain his attention on the task may also profit from using language. By saying aloud or to himself the letters as he forms them, he may be better able to concentrate on his writing activities. Spelling, also, is an activity that can be aided by having the child verbally rehearse the letters in the word to be spelled. It has also been reported by teachers that the age-old procedure of having a child read aloud is especially beneficial for the distractible child.

Not only the child's use of language, but also the teacher's use of language can be an effective method of inducing the child to be attentive. Simple as it may seem, it is surprising how often teachers fail to take advantage of verbally telling the child what to do. The use of clear-cut, concise instructions can help the teacher to direct the child's information-seeking behavior. For the disoriented, distractible child, concrete instructions may be all the more helpful. With regard to the impulsivity-reflectivity dimension, reflective behavior is induced best by instructing the child in the appropriate strategy of attending to the various alternatives before responding. It is, however, not enough to tell him to slow down before responding; to do so may result in his being slower, but he is still likely to make just as many errors. Suggestions directed to the child on how he should attend while slowing down have proven effective (see Epstein, Hallahan, & Kauffman, 1975, for a review of this literature).

### Applied Behavior Analysis
### of Attention and Distractibility

As we discussed in Chapter 1, the highly structured approach of Cruickshank, Haring, Whelan, and others set the stage for the application of behavior modification with hyperactive and distractible children. It is, perhaps, in the sphere of the child's attention to academic tasks that the link between the structured approach and behavior modification is clearest. In the structured approach the teacher's *differential attention* to "on task" behavior is used as a key instrument in teaching children attention and study skills. That is, when the child is given a task to do, the teacher attends differentially to the child, depending on the child's behavior. When the child works appropriately on the task, the teacher attends to (praises, touches, looks at) him; when he engages in other than work behaviors, the teacher ignores him completely.

This simple contingent relationship between the child's behavior and the teacher's attention is exemplified in an early report by Zimmerman and Zimmerman (1962). The subjects of their study were two institutionalized emotionally disturbed boys about eleven years old. In the first boy, the problem was that when asked to spell a word he had previously studied, "he would pause for several seconds, screw up his face, and mutter letters unrelated to the word" (p. 59). At first, the teacher would try to help the child by asking him to sound out the word or by giving him other clues or encouragement. However, this teacher "help" did not improve the child's behavior. The teacher then began to withhold all attention until the child, complying with her instruction to write a word, wrote the word correctly; she would then respond immediately with smiles and praise. The child's bizarre inattention ceased within a month. In the case of the second boy, the problem consisted of temper tantrums, irrelevant verbalizations, and baby talk. As with the first child, the teacher began to attend to him only when his behavior was appropriate and to ignore all undesirable responses. The result was the same as in the first case—the child learned to behave appropriately.

The behavior principles that account for the success of such early efforts to modify behavior are clear. Positive reinforcers in the form of teacher attention were provided for desirable behaviors and withheld following unwanted responses—positive reinforcement strengthened appropriate behavior while undesirable responses were placed on extinction. The same behavior principles undergird numerous more recent studies in which the attending behaviors of children have been improved. The major differences between the earlier structured approach and the more recent applied behavior analysis techniques are to be found in the more explicit reinforcement contingencies and more precise measurement techniques of applied behavior analysis.

As we have commented elsewhere:

> The behavior modification approach to problems of attention assumes that attending is comprised, at least in part, of behaviors that can be measured directly. Behaviors such as looking at the teacher, following directions, engaging in a single activity, writing answers, or in some other manner giving correct responses or exhibiting task-oriented activity have been recorded as measures of attention in the classroom. A behavior modification analysis of attention implies that such attending responses are a function of specific consequences which can be varied systematically to increase or decrease attending behavior (Martin & Powers, 1967). A number of studies have shown that task attention, study behavior, or orientation to teacher can be increased by reinforcing those behaviors with teacher attention or other social or material consequences. These studies have demonstrated the effectiveness of a variety of reinforcement procedures in different settings and with children varying in age, behavioral description, and diagnostic label (Hallahan & Kauffman, 1975b, p. 239)

Among the many studies of reinforcement of task attention or study behavior is a now classic report by Hall, Lund, and Jackson (1968). One of the six subjects of their study was Levi, a first grader selected because he was often disruptive. Each day during the experiment, an observer recorded Levi's attention to the teacher and his academic tasks. Every ten seconds, the observer recorded whether or not Levi was attending, and the percent of study behavior (i.e., percent of ten-second intervals Levi was studying) was plotted for each day. Figure 8.3 shows the results of differential teacher attention for study and nonstudy behavior. During baseline sessions, the teacher gave Levi almost no attention when he was studying but frequently attended to him when he was disruptive (i.e., not studying, making noise, or disturbing others). When the teacher ignored Levi's disruptive and inattentive actions and attended to him frequently while he was engaged in study behaviors, his study behavior increased dramatically (as shown in Reinforcement$_1$). A reversal of the

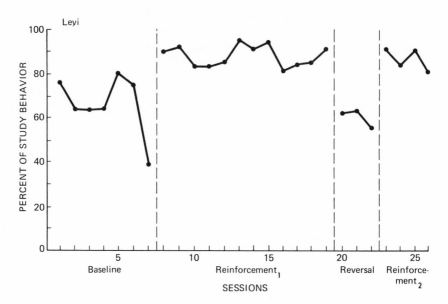

FIGURE 8.3.
*Record of study behavior for Levi, an often disruptive first grader.*

*Source: R. V. Hall, D. Lund, & D. Jackson, "Effects of Teacher Attention on Study Behavior," Journal of Applied Behavior Analysis, 1968, 1, p. 9. Reprinted by permission.*

relationship between teacher attention and study behavior (i.e., providing teacher attention for nonstudy behavior and ignoring studying) produced a reversal in Levi's percent of study behavior—it dropped from about 90 percent to about 60 percent. Reinstatement of teacher attention for study behavior (Reinforcement$_2$) resulted in Levi's once more becoming studious. Hall and his co-workers obtained essentially the same results with the other five children included in their report.

A number of researchers and special educators have shown that extrinsic reinforcers, such as food, money, and tokens which can be used to purchase privileges or prizes, can be used to increase the attentiveness of distractible children (see Hallahan & Kauffman, 1975, for a review of these studies). Hewett's Santa Monica Project is particularly noteworthy as a special education program in which the effects of token reinforcement for attention were examined. Hewett devised an "engineered classroom" which included a highly differentiated physical environment, academic program, and structure which could be tailored to the needs of children functioning at widely differing developmental levels. A central theme in the engineered classroom was a developmental sequence of educational goals, beginning with the most basic goals of getting the child to pay attention, respond to tasks, and follow directions and ending with the goal of the child's becoming a self-motivated learner for the sake of achievement alone. For each level in his sequence of goals Hewett specified the problem presented by the child, the educational task that must be taught, the type of reward that children functioning at that level would likely respond to, and the amount of structure or type of demands the teacher would need to use in order to accomplish the goal. Although Hewett's developmental sequence has undergone several revisions (cf. Hewett, 1974), Table 8.1 summarizes major aspects of the hierarchy of goals as it has been most widely published.

The physical environment of the engineered classroom was carefully planned to facilitate children's learning at each level and their progression through the levels of the developmental sequence of goals. As may be seen in Figure 8.4, the classroom was arranged into three major centers, each of which was designed with certain goals and tasks in mind. The "order center," consisting simply of tables, chairs, and a storage cabinet, was the area in which attention, response, and order levels were emphasized. Here was the focus of activity for children who exhibited problems of distractibility and hyperactivity. Attention, response, and order activities emphasized listening to and looking at the teacher or tasks, making or attempting to make correct responses, following instructions, and completing tasks. Although relatively little structure (i.e., relatively few demands) was imposed at the initial level of attention, the teacher's demands on the child were gradually and systematically increased so that "what" and "how" the child was expected to do as well as "when" and "where" he was to respond were explicitly stated at the order level.

A token reinforcement system played a very prominent part in the daily schedule of activities in Hewett's program.

> The engineered classroom day revolves around the child's receiving check marks for various accomplishments. Each morning as he enters the door the child picks up a Work Record card from the Work Record holder nearby. . . . As the child goes through the day he is given check marks reflecting his accomplishments and classroom functioning. Cards filled with check marks can later be exchanged for tangible rewards such as candy and trinkets. . . . Usually, a possible ten check marks are given by either the teacher or aide following each 15-minute work period in the classroom. During the time devoted to giving check marks (usually five minutes) all work done within the preceding work period is corrected and the new assignment for the next 15 minutes is given. This allows three 15-minute work periods and three five-minute check-mark-giving periods during each class hour.

TABLE 8.1    Summary of the Developmental Sequence of Educational Goals

| Level | Attention | Response | Order | Exploratory | Social | Mastery | Achievement |
|---|---|---|---|---|---|---|---|
| Child's problem | Inattention due to withdrawal or resistance | Lack of involvement and unwillingness to respond in learning | Inability to follow directions | Incomplete or inaccurate knowledge of environment | Failure to value social approval or disapproval | Deficits in basic adaptive and school skills not in keeping with IQ | Lack of self motivation for learning |
| Educational task | Get child to pay attention to teacher and task | Get child to respond to tasks he likes and which offer promise of success | Get child to complete tasks with specific starting points and steps leading to a conclusion | Increase child's efficiency as an explorer and get him involved in multisensory exploration of his environment | Get child to work for teacher and peer group approval and to avoid their disapproval | Remediation of basic skill deficiencies | Development of interest in acquiring knowledge |
| Learner reward | Provided by tangible rewards (e.g., food, money, tokens) | Provided by gaining social attention | Provided through task completion | Provided by sensory stimulation | Provided by social approval | Provided through task accuracy | Provided through intellectual task success |
| Teacher structure | Minimal | Still limited | Emphasized | Emphasized | Based on standards of social appropriateness | Based on curriculum assignments | Minimal |

Source: Reprinted from F. M. Hewett, "Educational Engineering with Emotionally Disturbed Children," Exceptional Children, 1967, 33, p. 461 by permission of The Council for Exceptional Children.

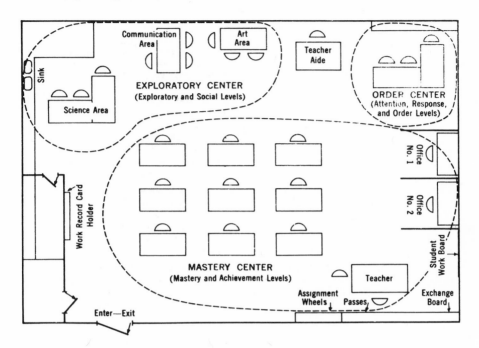

*FIGURE 8.4.*
*Floor plan of Hewett's engineered classroom.*

*Source: Reprinted from F. M. Hewett, "Educational Engineering with Emotionally Disturbed Children," Exceptional Children, 1967, 33, p. 463 by permission of The Council for Exceptional Children.*

Two check marks are given if the child started his work, three if he "followed through" on an assignment, and a possible five bonus check marks are administered for "being a student." In the engineered classroom "being a student" refers . . . to how well the child respected limits of time, space, and activity and the working rights of others. . . . For some extremely inattentive children, the bonus check marks may be given "Because you put your name on the paper and paid attention to your work," even though no actual work was accomplished. For those children with response problems, the five check marks may be given "Because you tried to do the assignment," regardless of the number of problems correct.* (Hewett, 1968, pp. 247–249)

An outline of the Hewett schedule of activities is presented in Table 8.2.

One of the variables included in the evaluation of Hewett's Santa Monica Project was task attention, defined as eye, head, and body orien-

* From Frank M. Hewett, *The Emotionally Disturbed Child in the Classroom,* pp. 247–249. Copyright © 1968 by Allyn and Bacon, Inc. Reprinted by permission.

TABLE 8.2      Hewett Classroom Schedule and Provision for Check Marks

| Time | Activity | Possible Check Marks and Criteria |
|------|----------|-----------------------------------|
| 8:30 A.M | Coming in room, taking seat, and flag salute | *5 for being ready to work*<br>3: Coming on time<br>2: Picking up card and going to seat |
| 8:35 A.M | Order | *10 for doing order worksheet*<br>2: Starting<br>3: Following through<br>5: Bonus for "being a student" |
| 8:40 A.M. | Reading (skill reading, individual reading, work study, or story writing) | *10 check marks following each of three 15-minute work periods (same criteria as above)* |
| 9:40 A.M. | Recess (outside room) | *10 check marks for recess behavior*<br>2: Leaving the room<br>5: Behavior during recess<br>3: Returning and being ready to work |
| 9:50 A.M. | Arithmetic (skill arithmetic and individual arithmetic) | *10 check marks each 15 minutes (same criteria as for reading)* |
| 10:50 A.M | Recess (nutrition— inside room) | *10 check marks for recess behavior*<br>5: Behavior during recess<br>5: Being ready to return to work |
| 11:00 A.M. | Physical Education (outside room) | *10 check marks for behavior during period*<br>2: Leaving the room<br>5: Behavior during the period<br>3: Returning and being ready to work |
| 11:20 A.M. | Group listening to teacher read story or record | *10 check marks for behavior during period* |
| 11:30 A.M. | Exploratory (science, art, and communication) | *10 check marks each 15 minutes (same criteria as reading and arithmetic)* |
| 12:20 P.M. | Check out | Total number of check marks received for the day are graphed on the child's Work Report on his desk |

*Source: Frank M. Hewett,* The Emotionally Disturbed Child in the Classroom, *table X1.1, 274. Copyright © 1968 by Allyn and Bacon, Inc. Reprinted by permission.*

tation to the teacher or task. The level of attending behavior, so defined, was found to be significantly higher in experimental (engineered) classrooms than in control classrooms in which check marks were not given.

Attending behavior defined as visual orientation toward the teacher or task materials does not, of course, imply *meaningful* attention to the task. Children can be looking at the teacher or their books while thinking about something else. Correct performance of a task would seem to necessitate meaningful attention, but this is not necessarily so. Recent work by Sidman and Willson-Morris (1974) has indicated that it is sometimes possible to respond correctly while attending to unknown or irrelevant aspects of the task (e.g., it may be possible to answer comprehension questions correctly without having read the material from which the questions were drawn). Thus, it is clear that neither reinforcing attending behaviors nor reinforcing correct performance is always sufficient to improve a child's attending skills. Nevertheless, it is clear that one can make the following statements in the light of research: (a) reinforcement of attending behaviors may be helpful for the child who spends a great proportion of his time in off-task activities because it brings him into closer contact with the task and makes meaningful attention possible; (b) reinforcement of correct academic responses may increase the attending behaviors of children if they have the necessary attentional strategies to complete the task correctly; (c) children may need to be taught specific attentional strategies in order to learn attention to meaningful stimuli or stimulus dimensions; and (d) tasks must be so analyzed as to eliminate the possibility that the child can perform correctly without attending to the relevant stimuli.

One strategy to increase attention which we mentioned earlier in this chapter involves verbalization. Two applied behavior analysis studies have shed additional light on the facilitative effect of verbalization on children's performance in arithmetic. Lovitt and Curtiss (1968) worked with an eleven-year-old boy whose accuracy in arithmetic computation was erratic. They first obtained baseline data from his performance on problems of the type $\square - 2 = 6$. After establishing his correct and error rates, as shown in Figure 8.5, they required the child to verbalize each problem (e.g., "Some number minus two equals six.") before writing his answer. As the graph reveals, this verbalization procedure increased the child's correct rate and decreased his error rate. Furthermore, when he was no longer required to verbalize each problem before writing the answer, his performance continued to improve. Lovitt and Curtiss found essentially the same effect in two other experiments with the same child involving problems of the type $\square - 20 = 40$ and $4 - 3 = 9 - \square$

Parsons (1972) compared a child's performance in arithmetic using two different instructional programs: In Program A the child was required to circle the operation sign ($+$ or $-$) before completing the problem; in Program B the child was required both to circle the operation sign and to name it ("plus" or "minus"). Figure 8.6 shows that Program B, in which verbalization of the sign was required, produced much better performance. As Parsons summarized:

> These results suggest that for attending to be optimal, the child must make more than an overt response; he must respond differentially to the materials. Reinforcing correct solutions was not enough to increase attending once it deteriorated (Program A—terminal problems). However, reinforcing correct solutions did maintain efficient attending once

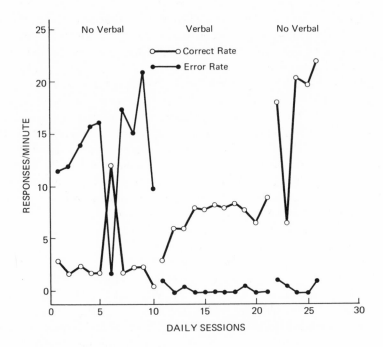

FIGURE 8.5.
Correct answer and error rates for the subject during the three phases of a nonverbal experiment in which the mathematics problems were of the class [    ] —2=6.

Source: T. C. Lovitt & K. Curtiss, "Effects of Manipulating an Antecedent Event on Mathematics Response Rate," Journal of Applied Behavior Analysis, 1968, 1, p. 331. Reprinted by permission.

the child had responded differently to the two operation signs (Program B). (p. 194)

## HYPERACTIVITY

Even though hyperactivity is mentioned at least as frequently as distractibility as a behavioral problem and both distractibility and hyperactivity are frequently associated, there have been less systematic research and fewer educational recommendations made for hyperactivity as compared with distractibility. With regard to the educational aspects, this statement has to be modified somewhat because many of the educational strategies devised to reduce distractibility are also purported to decrease

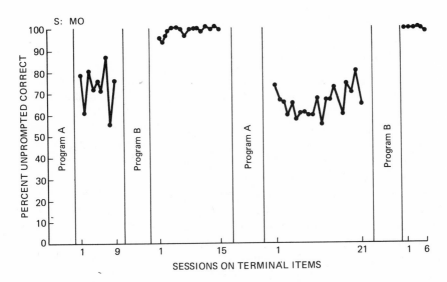

FIGURE 8.6.
One child's accuracy performance following nonverbalized activity (Program A) and verbalized activity (Program B).

Source: J. A. Parsons, "The Reciprocal Modification of Arithmetic Behavior and Program Development," in G. Semb (Ed.), Behavior Analysis and Education—1972 (Lawrence, Ks.: University of Kansas, Department of Human Development, 1972), p. 195. Reprinted by permission.

hyperactivity. The educational approach of Cruickshank, for example, is geared for both distractibility and hyperactivity. The amount of motor activity during specific educational treatment has not been looked at very often.

Perhaps the major reason why hyperactivity has not been examined more than it has is because a variety of measurement problems are associated with motor activity. There are basically two means of measuring motoric activity: (a) human observation of the child (or children) in question and (b) mechanical recording devices. Both techniques are fraught with pitfalls. Observational methods require numerous man-hours and involve critical questions of reliability that need to be addressed. Mechanical devices are expensive, are susceptible to failure, and may result in the child acting differently. One device, for instance, requires the child to wear an experimental wristwatch on his arm or leg—or both. It has not been infrequently reported that some children take a great deal of pleasure in shaking their arms in order to see the watch hand move around (and thus record excessive movement).

### The Use of Language
### to Control Hyperactivity

Besides the "reduced environmental stimuli" approach to reducing hyperactivity, verbal control can be an effective control over motor activity. A Soviet investigator, A. R. Luria (1961), has conducted some classic studies investigating the role of the child's own language in regulating his motor performance. Luria's theory posits that it is not until the child has a well-developed usage of language that he can become proficient at controlling his motor behavior.

Other studies indicate that young children can be trained to use their own language as a controller of their motor performance (Bem, 1967; Birch, 1966; Lovaas, 1964). Hyperactive children have also successfully been taught to use this technique (Meichenbaum & Goodman, 1969; Palkes, Stewart, & Freedman, 1971; Palkes, Stewart, & Kahana, 1968). The educational implication of these studies is that

> training hyperactive children to verbalize may be one method of reducing inappropriate motoric behavior. In the early stages, it may be necessary to require the severely hyperactive child to verbalize each of the steps in a sequence of behaviors before attempting each step. It may be that only after much training in this overt verbalization can he gradually come to use these language cues covertly. (Hallahan & Kauffman, 1975b, p. 245)

### Medication

It is becoming a common practice for children who are exceedingly hyperactive and distractible to be put under medication in order to help them concentrate and decrease their hyperactivity. Paradoxically, it is usually the stimulant drugs—for example, Ritalin and amphetamines—that are used for the purpose of calming hyperactive children. Just why stimulants usually have the reverse effect on children that they do on adults is still unknown, though many speculative, neurological explanations do exist.

The use of drugs with children has not gone without criticism. Once the practice of prescribing them for hyperactive children became a fairly common practice—some estimate that as many as 200,000 children are being treated with drugs (Sroufe, 1975)—a heated controversy arose regarding a wide variety of aspects surrounding their use. Questions of possible drug abuse, harmful side effects, advertising practices, and so forth, have been brought up. The debate reached such proportions that a panel of experts from numerous disciplines convened in January, 1971 at a meeting sponsored by the Office of Child Development and the Office of the Assistant Secretary for Health and Scientific Affairs, Department of Health, Education, and Welfare. The panel—composed of Daniel X. Freedman (Chairman), T. Berry Brazelton, James Comer, William Cruickshank, E. Perry Crump, Barbara Fish, George H. Garrison, Frank Hewett, Leo E. Hollister, Conan Kornetsky, Edward T. Ladd, Robert J. Levine, Patricia Morisey, Irving Schulman, and Martin H. Smith — submitted a *Report of the Conference on the Use of Stimulant Drugs in the Treatment of Behaviorally Disturbed Young School Children*. Some of the major conclusions reached were:

1.  The physician should monitor closely the dosage in order to control side effects.

2.  Clinical and research experience do not lend credence to the notion that there is any association between prescribed drug use for young children and later drug abuse.

3.  To be on the safe side, some precautions with regard to abuse need to be pointed out. The child should not be given sole responsibility for administering his own medication. The drug itself does not usually need to be brought to school. Common sense considerations regarding drugs in the medicine cabinet should be followed.

4.  The medication does not handicap the child emotionally.

5.  Parents should not be coerced into using drugs for the children by school personnel.

6.  Pharmaceutical companies should not engage in unethical promotion tactics and should advertise only through medical channels.

7.  More research is needed.

8.  "In summary, there is a place for stimulant medications in the treatment of the hyperkinetic behavioral disturbance, but these medications are not the only form of effective treatment."

Although the panel of experts who prepared the above statements have collectively acquired a number of years of experience related to drug treatment, the issue of drug use is still not at rest. The controversy continues and is likely to continue until more research is conducted. Sroufe (1975), for example, has taken a serious look at the research into drug treatment and has, in general, postulated that all of the evidence is not yet in. Well-controlled, systematic studies are lacking. The key points Sroufe makes are:

1.  While short-term drug effects have been studied, there is a paucity of long-term studies (only one study was found by Sroufe in which the drug period lasted longer than eight weeks).

2. There is a paucity of adequate research on short-term physical side effects and none on long-term physical side effects (e.g., loss of appetite and insomnia).

3. The drug efficacy studies conducted thus far have relied heavily upon looking at children's performance on repetitive, low-level tasks. Little is known about the effects of drugs on higher conceptual thought.

4. Placebo effects (positive effects that sometimes occur even though the "medication" given to the patient is not what he thinks it is; in some research studies a "placebo control group" is used to insure that the effects of the drug, if they occur, are not the result of the patient "feeling" he should do better because he is under medication) are still unresolved in terms of stimulant drug studies.

5. There is little solid research to indicate that drugs are more or less effective than behavior modification.

6. There needs to be well-controlled investigation of the relationship between the early use of prescribed medication and the potential for later drug abuse.

7. It may be that drugs are too effective in the sense that they appear to offer an apparently quick and easy solution to a problem that needs to be approached on a variety of fronts. In other words, it might be that drugs afford an easy excuse for educational professionals to shirk their duties.

Sroufe's position is notably more pessimistic than that of the panel of experts even though the panel is also cautious with regard to its statements on drug use. It may be that a partial reason for the discrepancy is that Sroufe's analysis is focused more on the experimental adequacy of the drug studies whereas the report of the conference appears to be more influenced by years of clinical experience.

The volatile nature of the debate over the use of drugs makes it imperative that knowledgeable teachers be aware of the issues. At this point, there is no single piece of advice on this matter that will give them a clear-cut idea of where to stand on the issue. It *is* important that teachers be aware of the *potential* power and danger of drugs and that they leave final decisions on these matters to qualified physicians.

### Applied Behavior Analysis of Hyperactivity

Disruptive or inappropriate classroom behaviors, such as out-of-seat behavior, unnecessary movement, noise-making, talking out, throwing tantrums, fighting, and so on are often associated with hyperactivity, and measurement of these behaviors is frequently a part of the behavior modification approach to the hyperactive child. Many of the same techniques that are effective in the treatment of inattention and distractibility are, as we have previously stated, also effective in reducing the problem of hyperactivity. The case of Levi in the study by Hall, and his colleagues (1968) is a case in point. When Levi's teacher shifted her attention from inattentive, disruptive behaviors to attentive, study behaviors, not only did Levi's study behavior improve (as shown in Figure 8.3) but his disruptive behavior declined, as can be seen in Figure 8.7.

Time after time it has been shown that differential social attention from the teacher, parent, or other person caring for the child has had a salutary effect on disruptive or disturbing behavior (cf., Becker, 1971; Krumboltz & Krumboltz, 1972). The essential elements of good classroom control appear to be: (a) making clear rules regarding behavior, (b) giving frequent praise to the children who follow the rules, (c) ignoring disruptive or inappropriate behavior unless it is dangerous or intolerable, and (d) when misbehavior cannot be allowed to continue, giving soft, private reprimands to the rule-violator (Madsen, Becker, & Thomas, 1968; Madsen, Madsen, Saudargas, Hammond, Smith, & Edgar, 1970).

Although the aforementioned elements of classroom control may be used to improve the behavior of most children, they are clearly insuffi-

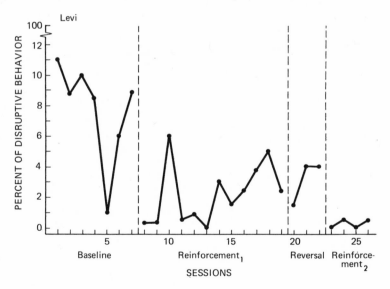

FIGURE 8.7.
Record of disruptive behavior for Levi, a first grader.

Source: R. V. Hall, D. Lund, & D. Jackson, "Effects of Teacher Attention on Study Behavior," Journal of Applied Behavior Analysis, 1968, 1, p. 10. Reprinted by permission.

cient tools for controlling the behavior of some hyperactive youngsters. More incisive methods of behavior modification are often successful with such children. These methods may involve using stronger reinforcers than social attention. Token reinforcers, games, and other material rewards or activities, given contingent on appropriate or nonhyperactive behavior, are often sufficient to change behavior in a desirable direction. The control of persistently occurring behaviors that are inimical to classroom order and learning sometimes requires punishment, either in the form of response cost or application of punishing stimuli. In some cases, it has been found that enlisting the child's parents or peers as agents of reinforcement is of value. Finally, because children learn a great deal by observing and imitating others, peers and adults have effectively served as exemplars for hyperactive children. (We have previously reviewed the applied behavior analysis research related to these methods [Hallahan & Kauffman, 1975b]. We shall return to a discussion of behavior problems related to hyperactivity and behavior modification procedures for dealing with them in Chapter 10).

In short, hyperactive behavior is susceptible to direct measurement and influence through environmental manipulation. Although factors other than reinforcement may contribute to its etiology and amelioration or cure, it is clear that reinforcement techniques available to teachers and parents are effective antidotes for hyperactivity.

# Language
# Disabilities

# 9

It has been pointed out in previous chapters, that the child with a visual, motor, or visual-motor handicap has captured most of the attention of those in the field of learning disabilities; the child with a language disability has been relatively neglected. In an analysis of the learning disabilities literature from 1966 to 1970, Hallahan and Cruickshank (1973) found that there were more than three times as many journal articles dealing with perceptual-motor behavior as there were with language. The literature on brain-damaged, mentally retarded children also reflected a minimal interest in language disabilities—no doubt because the historical origins of the field of learning disabilities are in the field of mental retardation. This neglect of language considerations has been unfortunate when one realizes the basic importance of language in everyday functioning. Language is one of the primary behaviors that separates humans from the lower animals. Language is an ability of great significance in the child's chances for success in school. Language is a great facilitator in terms of the acquisition of new knowledge. Language is *the* major component of the vast majority of intelligence tests. There are a myriad of reasons why language disabilities should be taken seriously by professionals within learning disabilities. It is not because a low proportion of learning disabled children have language problems that there is so little interest. Teachers frequently indicate that their learning disabled youngsters have language problems, and one estimate has stated that 50 percent of learning disabled children have language disabilities (Marge, 1972).

We are talking here about *relative* emphases. There have, of course, been some theoretical and practical efforts undertaken on behalf of children with language disabilities. Within the past few years especially an awareness has grown of the need to consider language problems. One of the reasons for this upsurge in interest has probably been the expanding body of knowledge within the field of psycholinguistics. Since the early 1960s many advances have been made concerning normal language development. Until recently, very little was known about language development, particularly language acquisition.


## NORMAL LANGUAGE DEVELOPMENT

Numerous investigators have now charted the major milestones in the development of language in children (see Eisenson, 1972; Lenneberg, 1967; and Menyuk, 1972 for a thorough discussion of these stages.). At birth, the infant engages in crying. Starting with the birth cry, believed to be a reflex response to the pain of breathing on his own, the infant for several weeks engages in crying as a response to discomfort. Eisenson (1972) has termed this "undifferentiated" crying in that the infant's cries are indistinguishable on the basis of the various states of discomfort.

At about two months of age, two responses begin to occur in the infant. Cooing sounds emerge and the infant's crying begins to be differentiated. A qualitative difference becomes apparent among the different situations that evoke crying.

From about three to six months of age the infant engages in babbling. Eisenson believes this to be a crucial stage in terms of later language development in that the child's babbling comes under the control of reinforcement. Eisenson cites Lewis's (1959) observations that while innate factors set the stage for the infant's babbling it can be increased or decreased by reinforcement. This line of reasoning, of course, leads to a consideration of this stage as a *possible* source of language disabilities.

The child enters a stage of echolalia, according to Eisenson, at about eight to nine months. At this point, the infant engages in imitating speech sounds. If an adult says something, the child will at times attempt to say the same thing.

At about one year of age the child utters his first words. Primitive sentences are formed at about eighteen months. From this point on, language acquisition occurs exceedingly rapidly in terms of the complexities of the language that are to be mastered. By three or four years, the child is able to use most of the basic syntactical structures of the language. Marge (1972) states that the child at about three years can use all of the basic syntax required to produce simple sentences up to a length of ten to eleven words. By four to five years, practically all of the syntactical complexities have been mastered.

## Competence Versus Performance
## and Comprehension Versus Production

The above general sequence refers primarily to the child's ability to speak the language. Language theorists have pointed out that one should draw a distinction both between comprehension and production and competency and performance. With regard to the competency and performance distinction, what the psycholinguists are usually interested in is the child's competency with regard to such variables as syntax. Unfortunately, competency is an elusive construct (i.e., difficult to measure), and one usually has to rely upon *measurement* of a child's performance in order to *infer* his competency based upon that performance. Chomsky (1965) and McNeill (1970) have discussed thoroughly the distinction between competence and performance. McNeill, for example, states:

> A sharp distinction between competence and performance has been traditional in linguistics since Saussure's *Cours de linguistique générale* (1916) and was first drawn at least as early as the eighteenth century (Chomsky, 1966). One can think about language in either of two ways. There are, first of all, actual acts of speaking and learning, taking place in time, subject to various distractions, limited by memory and by the general weakness of the human flesh. . . . Performance is linguistic behavior, either encoding or decoding speech. . . . At the present time there are no theories of linguistic performance. (p. 1139)

This distinction between competence and performance (which can be receptive or productive) should alert the teacher to recognize that poor language performance may be indicative of other than inadequate language competence. In other words, just because a child has poor language (receptive-productive) skills one cannot assume that the child is deficient in language competence, that is, that the child cannot understand and use the language appropriately under optimum conditions.

Often confused with this competence-performance issue is the dichotomy of comprehension versus production. Comprehension refers to the child's ability to understand what is spoken to him whereas production refers to the child's language utterances. The competency-performance issue is the more general of the two in that it applies to both comprehension and production. The comprehension-production distinction is concerned with the more concrete differentiation between the child's listening (comprehension) and speaking (production).

The practical importance of the comprehension-production differentiation is that comprehension develops prior to production. Eisenson (1972) provides an example of this:

Almost all children can detect fine shades of differences before they can themselves produce them. A child may persist in his "kicky" for *kitty*, but reject this pronunciation from an adult; he may still produce "wawi-pop" at age five but resent such an offering from an older person. What the child is demonstrating by this apparently inconsistent language behavior is that at age four or five he has better phonemic discrimination, and so better expectations in regard to listening, than he has motor control over his own productions. (p. 17)

Fraser, Bellugi, and Brown (1963) experimentally demonstrated the order of development of comprehension and production. They required children to pick pictures that went with a particular sentence (comprehension) or to make up sentences describing the pictures. Their results confirmed what experience with young children predicts—comprehension precedes production.

The significance of the order of development of comprehension and production is that it is logical to assume that production depends to some extent upon comprehension. In other words, for the child to speak well he must first have good comprehension. The speech of deaf children, of course, bears out this premise. In addition, the fact that the rank order of the proficiency of both perception and production of the features of language (e.g., nasality, voicing, continuancy, place) have been found to be virtually the same (Menyuk, 1972) points to the conclusion that speaking skills are dependent upon listening abilities.

The above discussion underscores the significance of auditory abilities for the development of language. If a child has an auditory perceptual problem, it is logical to assume that he might also have poor productive as well as receptive language abilities.

### Phonemic Development

Phonemic development refers to "the emergence of the sound units of a language" (McNeill, 1970, p. 1130). As noted above, some of the first sounds produced by the infant are crying, cooing, and babbling. How the child arrives at understanding and producing the sounds used in language is the study of phonemic development. In terms of the perception of sounds, Menyuk (1972) notes that shortly after birth the infant is capable of discriminating between sounds on the bases of frequency, intensity, and duration. She also cites the study of Lewis (1936) who found that at about two to six months of age the infant can discriminate different patterns of intonation and stress and can discriminate between speech and nonspeech sounds and friendly and unfriendly voices. Menyuk also states that the very young infant attends more to those sounds within the frequency range of speech and thus may be preprogrammed for learning speech sounds.

Perhaps the most important theorist and researcher in the field of phonemic development is Jakobson (1941, 1968) who has put forward a theory of distinctive features of sounds. As discussed in the chapter on visual disabilities, this concept of distinctive features has also been used by Eleanor Gibson in the realm of visual development. Jakobson's position is that the child learns the different speech sounds on the basis of attributes that distinguish the various sounds. Some of the features learned are consonantal, nasal, strident, and voiced.

As with the distinctive features in visual perception, the distinctive features of speech can be used to predict which sounds will be more difficult to discriminate. In terms of production, research indicates that the first sounds the child utters are those that are highly discriminable on the basis of distinctive features. That the infant's first words are often "mama" and "papa" is predicted by Jakobson's analysis because, as Menyuk points out, the features

> are composed of repetitions of the maximally contrasting segments C, V (or + consonantal/ − vocalic, − consonantal/ + vocalic), and the labial (lip) sounds (p, m). These sounds represent the greatest degree of closure of the vocal tract for speech whereas the vowel /a/ represents the greatest degree of opening. (1972, p. 23)

The child who has not captured the ability to produce phonemes appropriately is commonly referred to as a child with articulation problems. It is important to distinguish here between comprehension and production problems. Even though a child can auditorially discriminate sounds, he may, because of motor problems, be unable to produce them. Another child, however, may misarticulate because of an inability to comprehend speech sounds in his environment. This latter difficulty is probably the more serious of the two because poor auditory discrimination skills could handicap the child from learning other aspects of language such as syntax and semantics.

### Syntactical Development

Syntax refers to the way in which speakers go about putting words and phrases together to produce sentences. Before the age of three or four, when he has mastered most of the basic grammatical structures, the child passes through at least two major stages in syntax development. Additional research will undoubtedly discover more fine-grained stages, but the principal milestones most language authorities refer to are holophrastic speech and telegraphic speech.

A growing body of data suggests that some of the first one-word utterances spoken by the young child are more than mere labeling responses. McNeill (1970) believes that the child's one-word productions are holophrastic predicates—they stand for sentences. These utterances are, according to de Laguna (1927) and McNeill (1970), "comments made by the child on the situation in which he finds himself. The holophrastic word is the comment; together with the extralinguistic context, the topic of the comment, it forms a rudimentary kind of proposition, and thus amounts to a full sentence conceptually" (McNeill, p. 1076).

When the child first begins to string words together he enters a stage commonly referred to as "telegraphic" speech. He tends to leave out certain words and word endings. However, the utterances are remarkably understandable because he tends for the most part to omit the nonessential aspects of the construction. At about eighteen months of age a rudimentary form of syntax is evident in the child's first two-word utterances. Braine (1963) has charted this development and refers to the construction of "pivot" and "open" classes of words. The young child has one class of words—the pivot class—in which a small number of words are used frequently. The open class contains many more words than the pivot.

Pivot class words never appear alone but are always produced in combination with open class words, which however, sometimes do appear alone or together with other open class words. While the position of the pivot class may be either before or after an open class word, any one individual word in a pivot or open class always appears in the same position. Certain words are more likely to be either a pivot or open class word, (e.g., nouns are frequently open class words and articles are frequently pivot class words) but there is some variation among children. The important thing to remember, however, is that each child forms his two-word utterances within the framework of a certain set of rules. That this is more than mere imitation of adult productions is suggested by the fact that some children have been found to speak in a word order different from adults. Based upon the sentence, "The shoe is all gone," the child is likely to say, for example, "Allgone shoe" instead of "Shoe allgone" (McNeill, 1970). The available evidence indicates, then, that at as young an age as eighteen months the normal child has an established grammatical repertoire.

### Morphological Development

The child also develops rules of inflection at a very early age. By four to five years of age the normal child has acquired most of the proper word inflections. Berko (1958), in a classic study, showed children pictures of "nonsense" objects with instructions like "Here is a wug. Here are two others, there are two _____." The appropriate answer is the /z/

("zzz") sound added to wug (i.e., wugs). This study demonstrated that young children acquire the basic morphological rules at an early age.

## DEVIANT LANGUAGE DEVELOPMENT
## IN LEARNING DISABILITIES

Unfortunately, there is a dearth of empirical information on the language disabilities of children who have been identified as learning disabled. The problem is truly one of lack of interest in investigating these disabilities, because experience in classrooms for the learning disabled readily reveals a multitude of comprehension and production difficulties.

The few studies that have been conducted verify the observation that as a group learning disabled children have more language problems than normal children. Denner (1970), for instance, administered a test of syntactic comprehension to normal children and to children identified as "problem readers." The experimenter showed a series of logograph cards to each child and the child was to perform the act (e.g., "Walk around the teacher") which the logograph-sentence indicated. Although Denner does not report the IQ scores of the normal and problem readers, making it impossible to know if the two groups were equated, the results are suggestive of a syntactic comprehension deficiency in poor readers. Guthrie (1973), on the other hand, found that disabled readers performed similarly to normals in syntactic processing during silent reading. Also, Bartel, Grill, and Bartel (1973) demonstrated that, as a group, learning disabled children are deficient in language performance, but not competency. Oakan, Wiener, and Croner (1971) studied the phonemic aspects of reading and concluded that the reading disabled child may be unable to use the intonational patterns of pitch, stress, and pauses to organize the input of words he reads.

The above studies, so few in number and somewhat contradictory in conclusions, point to a need for further research in this area. Studies looking at the early development of syntax and morphology are needed. It would be of interest, for example, to know if the stage of holophrastic speech is evident in the young learning disabled child or to know if he differs in any way in his formation (or nonformation) of pivot and open class words. Berko's test of morphological endings would also be an appropriate device to administer. Lovell and Bradbury (1967), for instance, have used Berko's test to find a group of educable mentally retarded children deficient in morphological development. It would also be of interest to know if language disabled children generate the same grammatical sentences as those of normal children. Menyuk (1972) has cited some suggestive evidence that the child with phonemic problems and the child with syntactic problems also speak according to a set of rules. In other words, the child with language disabilities may have his own grammatical rules (the wrong ones) that govern how he talks.

### Work on Aphasia

Though the field of learning disabilities suffers from a lack of basic and applied research into language disabilities, the field of speech pathology has generated considerably more work on speech and language problems. At one time a careful distinction was made between problems that a *speech* clinician should handle and those that he should not. Problems of motor production, such as articulation, were the chief domain of the speech clinician. Over the past few years, however, the role of the speech therapist has expanded to include children with a wide variety of language disabilities—phonemic, syntactical, prosodic, and morphological problems. While certainly not steeped in definitive knowledge regarding language problems, this new breed of "speech and language pathologist" frequently has the background training to deal with the language problems of learning disabled children. A certain amount of professional jealousy has been evident between speech therapists and learning disabilities teachers, but there is no doubt that they are both frequently dealing with the same kinds of language characteristics in children.

Some of the work most applicable to the language disabilities of learning disabled children has been carried out in the field of childhood aphasia. One of the leading authorities in this field, Jon Eisenson, views the developmentally aphasic child as very similar to the child with learning disabilities. He uses the term developmental aphasia interchangeably with the terms congenital aphasia and dyslogia and defines it as referring

> to the impairment for a child to acquire symbols for a language system. The impairment must be of sufficient degree to interfere with the child's ability to communicate. The use of the term developmental aphasia, or one of its synonyms, implies that the child's perceptual abilities for auditory (speech) events underlies his impairment for the acquisition of auditory symbols. His expressive disturbances are a manifestation of his intake or decoding impairment. A child cannot produce language if he cannot decode the speech to which he is exposed, or if the speech remains for him sounds without sense. An aphasic child may, in addition, have dysarthria and dyspraxia, impairments in the ability to control his articulatory mechanism. . . . These productive impairments are not, per se, aphasic but are motor difficulties. (Eisenson, 1972, pp. 68–69)

Other behavioral characteristics which Eisenson ascribes to children with developmental aphasia are similar to those attributed to children with learning disabilities. Some of the characteristics listed by Eisenson are:

1. Perceptual disabilities in one or more, but not all, sensory modalities.
2. Auditory disabilities, especially in phonemic discrimination and sequencing.
3. Sequencing problems.
4. "Intellectual inefficiency" in relation to intellectual potential.

This fourth characteristic is analogous to the characteristic of underachievement so integral to the definition of learning disabilities. With regard to neurological findings, too, the developmentally aphasic child exhibits characteristics indicative of those children labeled minimally brain injured.

The key point Eisenson makes with regard to developmental aphasia is that there are very few children with expressive problems who do not also possess comprehension difficulties. Eisenson sees auditory perceptual disabilities as the prime causal factor in most language problems. The following statement by Eisenson underscores the emphasis he places on auditory abilities:

> In order for a child to acquire (learn and produce) an oral language code, he must have the following capacities.
>
> 1. He must be able to receive stimuli that occur in a sequence or order.
>
> 2. He must be able to hold the sequence in mind, to hold the sequential impression, so that its components may be integrated in some pattern. This may be achieved either by memory or by the application of a rule plus memory.
>
> 3. He must be able to scan the pattern from within so that it may be compared with other stored patterns or other remembered impressions.
>
> 4. He must be able to respond differentially, to assign meaning on some level, to the identified pattern or impression.
>
> 5. In order to speak he must have an oral-articulatory system, or an equivalent manual system if he is deaf, to provide a flow or sequence of movements that constitute an utterance, audible and/or visible. (Eisenson, 1972, p. 28)

## INTERACTION OF LANGUAGE DISABILITIES WITH OTHER AREAS OF DEVELOPMENT

### Language and Cognition

A considerable amount of discussion has taken place in the psycholinguistic literature regarding the interaction of language and thought. Whether one causes or influences the other or whether there is an interaction between the two has been the topic of some controversy. The Soviet psychologist Vygotsky (1962) believes, for example, that speech becomes interiorized as inner speech, which is the equivalent of cognition. McNeill (1970) argues that the acquisition of language is a cognitive act in itself and, therefore, that cognition influences language. No matter which particular position is adopted, it is apparent that some interaction exists between language and thought. In terms of language disabilities, the more it can be assumed that language influences thought the more it can be assumed that the child with language disabilities will also be likely to suffer cognitively.

A well-formulated position suggesting that both language and cognition exert influence on one another is that of Jerome Bruner's (Bruner, Olver, & Greenfield, 1966). Bruner asserts that the child has to reach a certain level of cognitive development before language is possible. Once language begins to be acquired, the child can then use it to achieve higher levels of conceptual thought.

Two of the primary psychological activities that Bruner believes language makes possible are analysis and synthesis. This occurs because language is discrete rather than continuous:

> *Discreteness* in language refers to the fact that at the sound level, as at the level of meaning, the material of human language is discontinuous: there is no intermediate step between *bin* and *pin* that produces a word: /b/ and /p/ are discontinuous phonemes, and, should one voice a word that was a sound midway between, the hearer will interpret it as one phoneme or the other. So too with words or morphemes. . . . What this imposes on the speaker of human language is the requirement that he analyze the domain of sound and of sense into discontinuous components that can then be constituted into a message. . . . Analysis and synthesis are literally *forced* on anyone who would speak human language. Language, then, breaks up the natural unity of the perceptual world—or at least imposes another structure on it. (Bruner, Olver, & Greenfield, 1966, pp. 40–41)

Using Bruner's conceptualization of the role of language, it would, thus, be predicted that the child with language disabilities would also have perceptual and conceptual problems.

An interesting and provocative model of language acquisition that takes into account an interaction between cognition and language has been presented by Nelson (1973). The components of this interaction system are shown in Figure 9.1. The model depicts an interaction between the cognitive structure the child brings to the language learning situation and parental strategies in teaching language. The result of this interaction is the child's own strategy for learning language.

There are three major components of the interaction process: (1) language function, (2) cognitive-linguistic match, and (3) control and

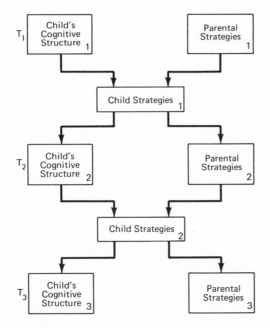

FIGURE 9.1.

*Schematic model of the interactive language-learning process. The model proceeds sequentially with the child's strategies for learning language at time 2 ($T_2$) being formed by the interaction between the child's cognitive structure and parental strategies at time 1 ($T_1$).*

Source: K. Nelson, "Structure and Strategy in Learning to Talk," Monographs of the Society for Research in Child Development, 1973, 38, Ser. No. 149, p. 96. Reprinted by permission.

feedback. With regard to language function, Nelson states that the child believes that language can serve primarily one of two types of function: expressive and referential. In the expressive, the child uses language primarily as a means of social interaction; in the referential, language is used to talk about objects. The cognitive-linguistic match refers to the match between the child's functional use of language and that of the adults closest to him. For example, if he uses language primarily as an expressive means and his mother uses it referentially, there would be a mismatch. Control and feedback describe the extent to which the adult accepts (through different kinds of positive reinforcement) or rejects the child's utterances.

Nelson has collected data from children and their mothers and has presented some case studies that are suggestive of what are the most and least beneficial interaction patterns. She found, for instance, that children who use language referentially are the large vocabulary builders. She also found mismatched uses between parent and child and rejection of the child's use of language to be correlated with poor language development. With regard to specific interaction patterns, what Nelson calls the "Match-Referential-Acceptance" pattern was found to be most beneficial and the "Mismatch-Expressive-Rejection" pattern the least beneficial. The other interaction patterns resulted in language acquisition somewhere between these two patterns.

Besides providing a framework for consideration of how language is acquired, Nelson's model has implications for the relationship between cognition and language:

> First, the basic prerequisite of language learning is conceptualization (a point emphasized by Lenneberg [1967]). Thus, those children who are more advanced in this process will be more advanced in language. Children who are intellectually deficient will be slow in all phases of learning to talk. Moreover, the present model shows why some children who are not inherently slow learners or poor conceptualizers may be slow in learning the language because of deviant conceptual systems [e.g., Mismatch-Referential-Acceptance and Mismatch-Expressive-Acceptance]. (Nelson, 1973, p. 117)

Another aspect of Nelson's model, which will be discussed later but should be pointed out here, is that it assumes children's language learning is highly child-directed. The adult can be a facilitator or inhibitor of the child's language development, but the model does not allow much room for the adult, under relatively normal circumstances, to make any drastic changes in the child's approach. In other words, Nelson assumes that the adult can have very little success in imposing his functional view of language on the child.

## Language and Other Aspects of Psychological Development

Besides the broad topic of cognitive development, there are a number of other areas of development with which language is intimately linked. The ability to use language appears to be a powerful tool that can help the child in a variety of interactions with his environment. Above we mentioned that the acquisition of language makes it possible for the child to analyze and synthesize perceptual events. Stevenson

(1972) has reviewed a number of studies that indicate verbal labeling of stimuli can significantly affect the perceptual processes involved in visual discrimination. If children are given labels that are quite different for different figures, then these figures are more easily discriminated. The evidence above suggests that the language disabled child could be a prime candidate for perceptual problems.

In Chapter 8 we cited Luria's work on the verbal control of motor behavior, suggesting that language deficiencies could result in an inability to control motoric responses, which in turn results in hyperactivity. Luria's work indicates that for the child who is just acquiring language the verbal stimulus acts more as an exciter or initiator of action. In other words, when commanded to stop doing something, most one-year-old children not only will continue but will have a tendency to emit the response even more. Luria theorizes that with age the child interiorizes language and becomes capable of controlling his own actions through language. This position, of course, suggests that some hyperactive children's problems may be due to a language breakdown.

There is also substantial evidence to indicate that language can be influential in aiding a child in his memory abilities. This field of study has come to be known as "verbal mediation." John Hagen, among others, has investigated the development of verbal mediation in children (Hagen & Kingsley, 1968; Hagen, Meacham, & Mesibov, 1970; Kingsley & Hagen, 1969), and he has concluded that a child's memory for visual material can be increased by inducing him to label the stimuli. This increase in performance, however, is evident for normal children of ages six, seven, and eight; the remembering abilities of older children and adults were decreased by induced labeling. Hagen theorizes that children over eight have their own spontaneous, covert rehearsal strategies and overt labeling interferes with these processes. Hagen's research suggests that language abilities can influence memory abilities. In terms of teaching, however, the teacher should use induced labeling as an instructional strategy for those children who are in need of it. Children with inefficient or nonexistent verbal rehearsal strategies would be expected to benefit from instructions in the use of verbal labels.

### Language and Academic Performance

The academic skill most directly related to language ability is that of reading. Eleanor Gibson, even though her major field of study is that of visual perception, recognizes the importance of language abilities in her theory of reading. Her conceptualization of the acquisition of reading places language at the beginning and end of the stages required for reading. As the developmental psychologists Pick and Pick (1970) describe her work:

> Eleanor Gibson has conducted extensive theoretical and experimental analyses of the stages of reading and learning to read (Gibson, 1965; Gibson, 1969). In her view, the first phase of learning to read is acquiring the spoken language. Learning to read then involves learning to decode the written language to speech. This mastery of the written language proceeds through three generally sequential stages. The first is learning to discriminate among the written elements—the letters of the alphabet. Second, the child must learn to decode the letters to the sounds of speech. Finally, as he becomes a skilled reader he learns to use all the "rules" in the language such as spelling structure and grammatical structure. In short, he learns to process larger and more complicated units of the written language. (p. 814)

Pick and Pick have reviewed several studies which support the notion that a child's understanding of grammatical structure is an aid in the act of reading. Better readers, for example, are more aware of their own reading errors when these errors are grammatically inappropriate with regard to the text (Weber, 1967). Pick and Pick hypothesize that syntactical structure is influential in the formation of perceptual units by the reader. The skilled reader does not focus on every single letter, but processes larger perceptual chunks. These chunks are dependent upon grammatical rules.

Pick and Pick also indicate that studies of eye-voice span in reading indicate that a child's understanding of grammatical rules helps his reading. Eye-voice span refers to the fact that when reading the individual's eye generally gets ahead of his voice when he reads aloud. Pick and Pick cite studies (Levin & Turner, 1966; Levin & Kaplan, 1966) demonstrating that the eye-voice span is influenced by the grammatical structure of the sentence being read. The eye tends to "span" ahead to the end of phrases. The child with poor syntactical knowledge might, thus, be at a disadvantage in this eye-voice span process.

### Auditory Abilities and Academic Performance

Because language comprehension precedes language production and because language comprehension is to some extent dependent upon auditory abilities, it is logical that auditory disabilities would also result in academic problems, particularly reading. Most theories of learning to read emphasize the importance of auditory skills. Gibson, for example, stresses the importance in early reading acquisition of decoding the letters of the alphabet with regard to the sounds of speech. If one's speech pro-

duction or comprehension is inadequate, it would obviously make it difficult to arrive at grapheme-phoneme (what is written-what is spoken or
heard) correspondence.

Gibson, Osser, and Pick (1963) performed an experiment demonstrating that the "pronouncability" of words influences how accurately
they are read. Children presented with nonsense words that were pronouncable—for example "raf"—and unpronouncable—"rfa"— were able to
perceive the pronouncable stimuli more accurately. It therefore appears
that a child's ability to take advantage of grapheme-phoneme correspondence will influence his reading ability.

Hammill and Larsen (1974) have, in an extensive review of cor-
relational studies between various auditory perceptual abilities and reading achievement, attacked the position that auditory disabilities result
in reading disabilities. They note that very few of the studies demonstrate
a high correlation between the two. What should be kept in mind, however, is that reading problems can stem from a wide variety of disabilities
—language, visual, memory, attentional. The multi-causal nature of reading disabilities could result in a low correlation between any one psychological variable—say, auditory perception—and reading. Another way of
stating this point is that some of the poor readers in the studies reviewed
by Hammill and Larsen could have had good auditory perception but
also have had other psychological characteristics that cause poor reading.
The children with poor auditory perceptual abilities could still, in general,
have had poor reading abilities. What are needed are studies of good
versus poor auditory-ability subjects. While Hammill and Larsen's review should caution one against believing auditory abilities to be the
only factor involved in reading disabilities, it does not discount the possibility that auditory perception influences reading ability.

## STANDARDIZED ASSESSMENT
## OF LANGUAGE DISABILITIES

Traditionally, a child's language ability was assumed to be best assessed
by observing his IQ score. Because intelligence tests rely heavily upon
language abilities, the IQ score was presumably a good indication of
verbal ability. With the recognition by those in the field of learning disabilities of specific kinds of abilities, coupled with the consideration of
such variables as syntactical development within psycholinguistics, there
has begun to develop a number of language tests that purport to measure
specific aspects of language abilities.

With regard to the receptive aspect of language, tests of auditory
discrimination have been devised. Two such tests are the *Auditory Discrimination Test* (Wepman, 1958) and the *Goldman-Fristoe-Woodcock*

*Test of Auditory Discrimination* (Goldman, Fristoe, & Woodcock, 1970). Wepman's Auditory Discrimination Test is one of the most frequently used to determine auditory perceptual ability. It consists of presenting a child from five to eight years of age with three- to five-letter word pairs and asking him whether the two words are alike or different. The words are either the same or different with regard to the beginning or ending consonants or the vowel (e.g., "mop-pop," "rap-rat," "bed-bad").

The Goldman-Fristoe-Woodcock Test is designed for the purpose of assessing the auditory discrimination ability of individuals four years old and older. The test is administered via a tape recorder in order to control for the effects of the examiner's voice. The stimuli used are words. Presented with a word, the subject is required to select one picture (from among four) which corresponds with the word. The pictures depict words in which all the initial or final consonants differ. In an attempt to simulate real-life conditions, a subtest is included which is administered with background noise. The test items are categorized on the basis of distinctive features so that it is possible to assess which distinctive features are the ones an individual child might miss.

Though the above tests examine auditory discrimination, the *Peabody Picture Vocabulary Test* (Dunn, 1959) and the *Durrell Listening-Reading Series* (Durrell, Hayes, & Brassard, 1969) are tests of more general receptive skills. For a quick assessment of a child's listening vocabulary, the Peabody Picture Vocabulary Test is often used. It is for use with children from two and one-half to 18 years of age. On each item, the child is shown four pictures and given the name of an object or concept. He is to choose the picture that goes best with the word given by the examiner. Frequently used to provide a quick indication of a child's IQ, it can also indicate, along with other tests, the child's level of vocabulary comprehension.

The Durrell Listening-Reading Series was constructed in order to compare a child's listening and reading skills. The authors maintain that a child's potential level of reading can be estimated by how he does on the listening portion. In addition to this purpose, which in itself may be questionable (Bormuth, 1972), the listening portion can be used alone to assess a child's language comprehension skills. At the primary level the child must decide whether a word or sentence read to him belongs to one of three specified categories. At the intermediate level the child matches a word with one of four categories. Further, the child is read a story and then asked a number of questions about it. At the advanced level, the child is given listening tasks that require even greater concentration.

Within the realm of speech tests a measure of articulation is the *Goldman-Fristoe Test of Articulation* (Goldman & Fristoe, 1969). This test for individuals two years and older requires the examinee to produce twenty-three phonemes and twelve blends in response to a series of pictures. The child is also told two stories, each of which has pictures that go along with the story. The child is then asked to recount the story and the examiner looks for the child's production of specific phonemes. As two reviewers (Byrne, 1972; Sherman, 1970) have noted, this part of the test is extremely difficult to score. The last part of the test requires the examinee to imitate those phonemes he missed on the first two sections.

Few tests are designed to measure a child's syntactical ability. Besides the experimental, nonstandardized test of Berko (discussed above) and the Grammatic Closure subtest of the Illinois Test of Psycholinguistic Abilities (ITPA; discussed below), Irwin, Moore, and Rampp (1972) also cite the *Northwestern Syntax Screening Test* (Lee, 1970).

The language test that has received the most mention and discussion within the field of learning disabilities is the ITPA (Kirk, McCarthy, & Kirk, 1961; rev. ed., 1968). The development of the ITPA has, as was pointed out in Chapter 1, done much to further the development of the field of learning disabilities (see also Kirk, 1976). It has, in particular, stressed the notion of intra-individual assessment and testing for educational purposes. Because of its integral association with the field of learning disabilities, we will discuss the ITPA in some detail.

The ITPA is composed of twelve subtests for use with children from two to ten years of age. The subtests were devised to fit Osgood's (1957a, 1957b) communications model, which is composed of (*a*) channels of communication, (*b*) psycholinguistic processes, and (*c*) levels of organization. Channels refer to the various sensory modalities through which information can pass (e.g., visual or auditory). The processes are receptive (input of information), expressive (output of information), and organizing (internal manipulation of concepts and linguistic skills). The organizational levels are the representational and the automatic. The representational deals with symbolic behavior; the automatic is concerned with chains of habit.

Six subtests can be given at the representational level. Two are in the receptive domain: "Visual Reception" and "Auditory Reception." "Visual Association" and "Auditory Association" are in the organizing process, and "Verbal Expression" and "Motor Expression" are within the expressive processes. Six abilities are purportedly assessed at the automatic level, where purely receptive and expressive abilities have not been included: "Visual Sequential Memory," "Auditory Sequential Memory," "Visual Closure," "Auditory Closure," "Grammatic Closure," and "Sound Blending." Here is a rundown on these twelve subtests.

Visual Reception is a subtest in which the examiner presents the child with a picture of an object and then shows him pictures of a number of objects from which the child must choose one like the stimulus object. The items gradually become more difficult. At first the child must find another example of the stimulus object; later, he must choose on the basis of functional similarity.

Auditory Reception items are composed of questions such as "Do airplanes fly?" "Do cars talk?" The simple yes or no required keeps the expressive process to a minimum.

On the easier items of Visual Association, the child is presented with the picture of an object and four alternatives. He is asked to choose the one that "goes with" the stimulus object. Later, he is shown two objects that go together and is requested to pick from alternatives an object that goes with a stimulus object in the same way the first two stimuli go together.

Auditory Association requires the child to complete verbal analogies. The ability assessed is on the surface similar to the *Miller Analogies Test,* a test frequently used to establish admissions criteria for entrance into university graduate programs.

For Verbal Expression the examiner presents the child with concrete objects one at a time and then asks the child questions to get him to tell about each one. An elaborate scoring system assesses the quality of the child's responses.

On the Motor Expression subtest the child is shown pictures of objects one at a time. He is then required to show what one does with each of them. The ability assessed is that of expressing motorically what each of the objects is used for.

Visual Sequential Memory requires the child to reproduce from memory a sequence of geometric shapes. The examiner shows a picture of a series of these shapes, and then the child is to reconstruct them with chips that have the geometric shapes on them.

Auditory Sequential Memory is similar to the Digit Span subtests from the WISC and Stanford-Binet. A series of numbers is read to the child and he is to repeat them in order. The numbers are presented at a rate of two per second, differing from the WISC and Binet in which the examiner presents the digits at a rate of one per second.

On Visual Closure, the child is shown figures such as dogs and is then asked within 30 seconds to find as many of them as possible from among a morass of objects. The dogs are partially hidden, and so the child must be able to "close" on them visually to do well.

On Auditory Closure, words are said by the examiner with some of the sounds missing. The child is asked what the words are.

Grammatic Closure is constructed for the determination of the child's ability to use morphological rules. He is shown pictures that require him to use different parts of speech. While being shown a picture of two beds, for example, he must complete the sentence, "Here are two _____."

The Sound Blending subtest has items in which the examiner says the separate sounds of a word and the child must blend them together in order to recognize and say the word. Because of the difficulty involved in learning how to administer this subtest, a phonograph record is provided with a model for practice.

Hallahan and Cruickshank (1973) have reviewed the research literature on the ITPA, and their conclusions can be summarized by the following two points:

1. The subtests are not completely independent. Especially at the younger age levels, the separate subtests do not appear to be assessing distinct areas of ability.
2. Some of the abilities assessed may not correspond with the subtest names. For example, on the Visual Closure subtest, a child might also do poorly because of a distractibility problem.

## TRAINING CHILDREN WITH LANGUAGE DISABILITIES

### Behavioristic versus Nativistic Theories

To a great extent, how the teacher views the process of language acquisition will influence how he goes about teaching language to the child. In other words, his conceptualization of normal language development will color his approach toward attempting to increase a child's language skills. While there is an increasing number of theoretical explanations on how language is acquired, most positions fall within two major camps.

Many theorists believe that learning principles can be used to explain language acquisition. Skinner (1957), in his now classic *Verbal Behavior*, was the first to popularize the notion that operant conditioning is the primary means of learning language. Since then, others have expanded upon his ideas (e.g., Jenkins & Palermo, 1964; Staats, 1968a). These theories can all be subsumed under the broad umbrella term "behavioristic" theories.

For a few years the behavioristic account of language went relatively uncontested. Vocal critics within the expanding field of psycholinguistics then came to the fore. Many of them have relied upon the revolutionary ideas of Noam Chomsky (1957, 1965). Chomsky, in fact, was one of the first to attack the behavioristic position in his review of Skinner's book (Chomsky, 1959). One of the leading advocates of this nonbehavioristic position is David McNeill (1966, 1970). Though the behaviorists stress the importance of the environment, McNeill and others emphasize the role of innate abilities which the child brings to the language learning situations. To the nonbehaviorists, in other words, many aspects of language learning are innately "wired in." McNeill and other psycholinguists believe that because the child generates novel sentences never heard before, his action represents a strong case against the behavioristic explanation.

The "nativistic" position holds that there are two basic structures in language—"deep" and "surface." As Palermo (1970) describes them:

> Many linguists have argued for some time that one must postulate an underlying abstract structure for language which is different from the actual manifestations of language in the speech of those who use the language. The postulation of an underlying abstract system . . . is required by paraphrase and ambiguity. Since all speakers of English know that the sentence "John ran the race" means the same thing as "The race was run by John," there must be some underlying abstract relation between the two sentences. Similarly, "Elmer selected a tie" is a paraphrase of "Elmer picked out a tie." In the first case, the underlying abstract relations involve syntax; in the second case, . . . semantics. In both cases, linguists have made some progress in demonstrating that there are abstract structures underlying such sentences and that there are rules that can be applied to show the relation between the two structures.
>
> The rules are general, in the sense that they apply to an infinite number of sentences. . . . The abstract underlying structures are referred to as *deep structures*, the manifestations are referred to as *surface structures*, and the rules relating the two kinds of structures are called *transformational* rules.* (pp. 473–474)

The child, the nativists hold, possesses an innate ability with regard to deep structure. The fact that the child constructs his own grammar in the space of only a couple of years or so is used as evidence for the notion that the child brings his own innate capacities to the situation.

With regard to how one views the manner in which a child's language abilities can be augmented, the behavioristic and nativistic camps again differ. The behaviorists advocate a much more directive teaching approach. They assume that the adult or teacher can make a crucial

---

* D. S. Palermo, Language acquisition, in H. W. Reese & L. P. Lipsitt, (Eds.), *Experimental Child Psychology* (New York: Academic Press, 1970). p. 474. Reprinted by permission.

difference in increasing the child's acquisition of language. The nativists believe environment is important, but their approach is much more child-centered. The adult, for the most part, must wait for the child to respond before he attempts to teach him. For example, McNeill (1970) states:

> A language is thus acquired through [the child's] discovering the relations that exist between the surface structure of its sentences and the universal aspects of the deep structure, the latter being a manifestation of children's own capacities. The interaction between children's innate capacities and their linguistic experience occurs at this point, in the acquisition of transformations—and it is here that parental speech must make its contribution. (p. 1088).

One of the primary means nativists use to encourage the child's language acquisition is "expansion." Expansion is child-centered. The process of expansion refers to the adult's responding in an interpretative way to the child's utterances. The adult expands upon the limited grammatical statement of the child. For example, if the child says "Doggie gone," the adult might say "Yes, the doggie is gone." Studies of the effectiveness of expansions (Cazden, 1965), however, have not given clear-cut support to the notion that they are helpful. One explanation forwarded has been that there is considerable room for error in expanding on a child's speech. In the above example, for instance, the child might really have meant "The doggie is *not* gone." The adult's response would thus be confusing.

The purported mechanism of expansion and the model of Nelson (1973) mentioned earlier are examples of the nativists' child-centered approaches to language acquisition. The behaviorists have devised approaches that are more adult-directed (we will discuss these in a later section of this chapter). The approaches we will take up next have not been aligned exclusively with either the behaviorist or the nativist position. To a great extent they are atheoretical in that they are built primarily upon clinical and classroom experience.

### Remedial Approaches and Programs

Earlier in the chapter, we discussed Eisenson's theoretical formulations regarding what he terms developmental aphasia. Ingram and Eisenson have also developed a number of training activities for aphasic children (Ingram & Eisenson, 1972). They believe that one must look for certain signs of justification before using direct intervention for aphasia. One such sign would be the child's failure to experience the rapid growth in vocabulary that usually occurs between two and three years of age. A child should also combine two and three word utterances once he has a vocabulary of fifty words or more. The child should at least be able to discriminate speech-sound sequences of three phonemes. Lastly, before implementing a training program for aphasia, it should be determined that the child's problem is not primarily one of apraxia (problem in moving motor muscles involved in speech).

Ingram and Eisenson have designed training activities that in a very general way are based upon the developmental level of the child. For example, they have divided their training suggestions on the basis of the child's average words per utterance. Different activities, in other words, are recommended for children at different stages of development, and the level is usually assessed by measuring the length of the child's sentences. While the specific activities may vary depending upon the child's age, the overall approach remains the same. It is the prime objective of their program to have the child produce utterances that are a step above what he can already do. Ingram and Eisenson state that situations should be created in which the child will use language, though they are not overly specific about how one goes about creating them.

Helmer Myklebust has also written extensively about remediation of language disabilities (Johnson & Myklebust, 1967). Myklebust arrived at his interest in language-impaired, learning disabled children through his early work with the deaf. He found children in his clinic who were able to hear but were still poor in "auditory language" (receptive language or comprehension).

One of the main theoretical constructs proposed by Myklebust is that of semi-autonomous systems. There are, he believes, neurological systems that can function either independently or in consort. Independent functioning is referred to as intraneurosensory learning, while combined functioning is termed interneurosensory learning. According to Myklebust, the latter—for example, a combination of the visual and auditory modalities—is very difficult for some learning disabled children. A multi-sensory approach—Fernald's VAKT for instance—would therefore be difficult for these children.

In general, Johnson and Myklebust consider remedial techniques for two kinds of language problems: receptive and expressive. They have devised a number of training activities for both. With regard to working with receptive language problems, some of the major guidelines they have outlined are:

1.  Training should begin early; a "wait and see" approach should be avoided.
2.  Training in comprehension skills should come before training in expressive skills.

3. The material worked with should be meaningful. Drill on nonsense words or separate sounds should be avoided. Whole words and sentences are what should be used.

4. The introduction of new vocabulary and concepts should be gradual and explicit.

5. The use of language and the experience it relates to should be close in time.

6. Repetition of the training activities is necessary.

7. Words sounding different should be taught first, whereas the more difficult task of discriminating similar sounds should be left until later.

With regard to expressive problems, Johnson and Myklebust have concentrated their efforts on three major types:

(1) The first group has a deficit primarily in *reauditorization* and word selection. These children understand and recognize words but they cannot remember (or retrieve) them for spontaneous usage.

(2) The second group has difficulty learning to say words; they comprehend and reauditorize but cannot execute the motor patterns necessary for speaking. There is no paralysis but they cannot voluntarily initiate the movements of the tongue and lips because of an *apraxia.*

(3) The third group has *defective syntax.* They are able to use single words and short phrases but are unable to plan and organize words for the expression of ideas in complete sentences. They omit or distort the order of words, use incorrect verb tenses, and make other grammatical, syntactical errors long after such skills have been acquired by normal children. (Johnson & Myklebust, 1967, p. 114)

Because the first and third kinds are the most relevant for learning disabled children, we will describe Johnson and Myklebust's approach toward them. Some of the general educational procedures they recommend for the child with reauditorization problems are:

1. Meaningful and not nonsense words should be used.

2. Words should be used in context, and visual cues should be used to help the child remember words.

3. Rapid naming drills are sometimes useful.

4. The child should be taught self-monitoring skills.

5. The child should be encouraged to use new words frequently.

The educational recommendations of Johnson and Myklebust for the child with syntax problems are for the purpose of developing *"a correct, natural, spontaneous flow of language"* (p. 136). Johnson and

Myklebust state that their approach is similar to audio-lingual methods used in teaching foreign languages. They do not advocate teaching specific grammatical rules to the child but believe that there should be a structured procedure for enabling the child to learn.

> The teacher should *provide a series of sentences auditorially, sufficiently structured with experience so the child will retain and internalize various sentence plans.* It might appear that these principles are similar to those for language learning in any child. While it is true that in general the goals are the same, the experiences and the sentences must be much more closely planned and coordinated. Simultaneity, auditory stimulation, structure, and repetition are critical. The normal child abstracts grammatical principles by making spontaneous associations, but those with learning disabilities must have many more concrete presentations. (Johnson & Myklebust, 1967, p. 137)

Mildred McGinnis, also originally working with the deaf, has formulated a program for children with receptive and expressive aphasia (McGinnis, 1963). She devised what has been referred to as the "Association Method." Myers and Hammill (1969) state that it is called the Association Method because its goal is to have the child associate each of the skills necessary for receptive and expressive language. As they have also stated, the method is based upon the following five principles:

1. Words are taught by a phonetic or elemental approach.

2. Each sound is learned through emphasis on precise articulation production.

3. The correct articulation of each sound is associated with its corresponding letter-symbol written in cursive script.

4. Expression is used as the foundation or starting point in building language.

5. Systematic sensorimotor association is utilized. (Myers & Hammill, 1969, p. 191)

In contrast with Myklebust's approach McGinnis's is oriented toward having the child learn to produce single sounds. These sounds, however, are then put together by the child to form words.

Many training activities have been designed for use in conjunction with the ITPA. Based upon the profile of a child, the teacher is given a number of remedial exercises. Kirk and Kirk (1971) have written a book containing specific activities for the different deficit areas assessed by the ITPA. Karnes (1968) too has a book of exercises. Also, Minskoff, Wiseman, and Minskoff (1974) have published an educational package based on the ITPA.

## APPLIED ANALYSIS
## OF LANGUAGE BEHAVIOR

Previously in this chapter we referred to behavioristic theories of language acquisition. From a behavioral perspective language learning involves the acquisition of verbal behavior through reinforcement processes. Both receptive language (i.e., decoding or understanding) and expressive language (i.e., encoding or expression) require the learning of a great number of verbal discriminations. These discriminations can be taught by arranging appropriate prompts and reinforcing consequences. In other words, according to the theoretical position of Skinner (1957), Staats (1968a), and other behaviorists, there is no essential difference between the learning processes underlying verbal behavior and those underlying nonlanguage behavior. Though the details of behavioristic theories of language are beyond the scope of this volume, practical applications of behavior principles to children's language learning are not. We will discuss applied behavior analysis of language under the following topics: following instructions, reading comprehension, written composition, and expressive oral language.

### Following Instructions

Nothing so terrifies the beginning teacher as a situation in which the children in his charge refuse to follow instructions. If his directions to stop a misbehavior or to work on an academic task are ignored or followed by open defiance, such as guffaws, insults, or taunts, the end of classroom control and academic learning is sure to follow. Teachers of ED, LD, and EMR children, perhaps to a greater extent than teachers of ordinary pupils, are haunted by the nightmare of an out-of-control classroom in which their instructions are of no avail. Not infrequently, special education teachers have quit the profession in despair or been forced out of the schools because their verbal commands and requests have seemingly fallen on deaf ears.

If teaching and learning are to occur, then, there must be at least a modicum of compliance with the teacher's instructions. This assumption is challenged by some critics of behavior modification and even by some critics of traditional education, who charge that schools are repressive institutions that are turning children into mindless automatons. While the majority of teachers would not, in our opinion, view children's compliance with reasonable instructions as inherently evil, neither have most teachers been particularly skillful in getting their pupils to obey:

"Those teachers who value instructional control nevertheless do not usually apply systematic reinforcing consequences for such compliance, often resorting instead to reasoning, nagging, and threats contingent on noncompliance" (Baer, Rowbury, & Baer, 1973, p. 289).

When children do not follow instructions, their lack of compliance may indicate that they do not understand the language of the teacher. Those who have worked with ED, LD, and EMR children (e.g., Cruickshank, et al., 1961; Johnson & Myklebust, 1967; Haring & Phillips, 1962) have noted that instructions must be kept particularly brief, simple, and direct if they are to be effective. The tendency of many teachers to drown their directions in a sea of verbiage must be kept in check. Part of the structured approach to teaching is excising irrelevant or distracting verbalization from the child's environment. In addition to simplifying instructions, other behavioral strategies can be employed in teaching receptive language (including how to follow directions). Lovaas (1966, 1969), for example, has detailed the way in which reinforcement, shaping, and fading can be used in training psychotic children to follow instructions. However, little of the applied behavior analysis literature has dealt with the problem of developing instructional control in those children who behave normally in most respects but do not comprehend clear instructions— probably because such children are a rarity.

It is, to be sure, possible that a child can understand the meaning of the teacher's instructions but be unable to perform the desired response. It may seem inane to call attention to the fact that it is of no use to tell a child to do something he cannot. But consider that in a class of twenty or more children, instructions to perform a given task may be appropriate for many or most of them while at the same time be calling on some children to perform what for them is an impossible feat. It is a reality that in today's educational system many teachers are frustrated by children who do not follow instructions simply because they cannot. Identifying precisely what the child can and cannot do and tailoring instructions to the individual's capabilities are necessary steps in establishing instructional control.

The most significant factor in teaching children to follow directions may be reinforcement. When reinforcement is provided for compliance and withheld for noncompliance, children tend to follow instructions to a much greater extent than when compliance is not reinforced. This procedure has been shown to be true in experimental studies with kindergarten children (Schutte & Hopkins, 1970), behaviorally deviant preschoolers (Baer, Rowbury, & Baer, 1973), and eight- to fifteen-year-old retarded children (Zimmerman, Zimmerman, & Russell, 1969). The reinforcers may be differential teacher attention, special activities, or tokens. What is important is that the child receive reinforcement for compliance and none for noncompliance. With some extremely oppositional children it may be necessary to use time-out for noncompliance (cf. Baer, et al., 1973).

In summary, it is apparent that if one wishes to better the chances that children will follow instructions, one should take care to use language the child can understand, to make sure that the child can perform as directed, and to provide reinforcement for compliance. Assuming that the child can and will follow instructions, questions remain regarding how best to instruct and the effects of instructions on desirable performances. Few investigations of how best to instruct have been conducted, but two recent studies have provided interesting data regarding the effects of instructions.

In Chapter 5 we mentioned a study by Lovitt and Smith (1972) in which the effects of instructions on a learning disabled child's verbal behavior were noted. By merely telling the child how to respond, Lovitt and Smith dramatically changed his verbal descriptions of pictures. In one condition of their experiment the child was told:

> "Most of your sentences have started with 'this is.' 'This is' is a way to start a sentence; however, there are many different ways to start sentences. Today, let's try to start our sentences in many different ways." (p. 688)

In another of the experimental conditions the child was told:

> "You are making sentences. You have learned to start your sentences in many different ways. However, many of your sentences are very short. For example, look at this [picture] card. . . . I could say: 'This is a woodpecker.' That is a sentence, but it only has four words and doesn't tell me very much. I could say: 'This is a red-headed woodpecker looking for bugs to eat.' Now, we have an 11 word sentence that tells me more. Let's see if you can start your sentences in many different ways *and* make your sentences longer so they tell me more." (p. 688)

With only these instructions and no reinforcement of any kind the child changed his expressive oral language responses as directed. Furthermore, generalization of improvement was noted—the child used more words to describe pictures when instructions were no longer used.

Working with two special-class EMR junior high-school students, Knapczyk and Livingston (1974) noted the effects of prompting question-asking (i.e., instructing the pupils to ask questions) on reading comprehension and on on-task behavior as well as on question-asking during reading instruction. Throughout baseline sessions, no prompts (directions) were given, but the frequency of question-asking, percent of time on task, and accuracy of reading comprehension were recorded. During training sessions, prompts similar to the following were used: "Today, I would like you to ask a question if there is a word you don't know or direction you don't understand" (Knapczyk & Livingston, 1974, p. 117). For one of the two students a return to baseline conditions was carried out, and subsequently the training condition was reinstituted. Thus, as may be observed from Figures 9.2, 9.3, and 9.4, the authors employed a combination withdrawal and multiple baseline (multiple subject) design. The effects of these simple instructions (and, of course, promptly answering questions asked by the pupils) on all three measures were strong and salutary. As shown in Figure 9.2, both students asked more questions when instructed to do so. Both students also attended

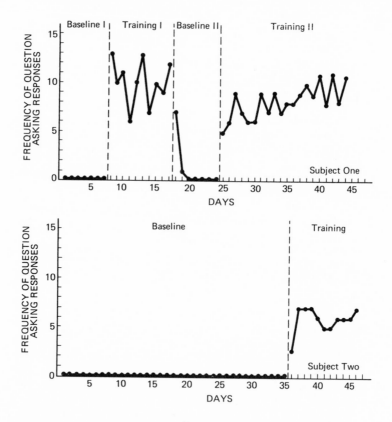

FIGURE 9.2.

Frequency of question-asking responses during baseline and training sessions in reading for two EMR students.

Source: D. R. Knapczyk & G. Livingston, "The Effects of Prompting Question-Asking upon On-Task Behavior and Reading Comprehension," Journal of Applied Behavior Analysis, 1974, 7, p. 118. Copyright 1974 by the Society for the Experimental Analysis of Behavior, Inc. Reprinted by permission.

more to the academic task, as shown in Figure 9.3. Finally, as illustrated in Figure 9.4, accuracy on reading comprehension tasks was improved for both pupils.

The results obtained by Knapczyk and Livingston are particularly germane to this chapter. Not only did the authors demonstrate the usefulness of a simple teaching procedure with EMR children, but they also observed effects on important language variables—question-asking and reading comprehension. Furthermore, the particular instructions chosen appeared to set in motion a sequence of teacher-pupil interactions that facilitated language usage.

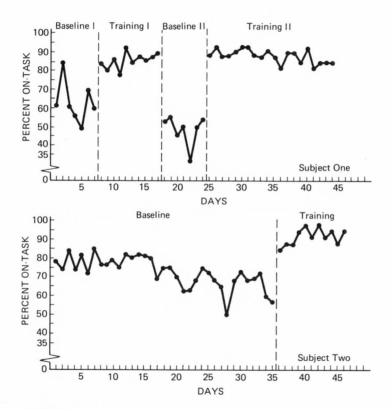

FIGURE 9.3.

Percent of on-task behavior observed during the 50-minute reading period for two EMR students.

Source: D. R. Knapczyk & G. Livingston, "The Effects of Prompting Question-Asking upon On-Task Behavior and Reading Comprehension," Journal of Applied Behavior Analysis, 1974, 7, p. 119. Copyright 1974 by the Society for the Experimental Analysis of Behavior, Inc. Reprinted by permission.

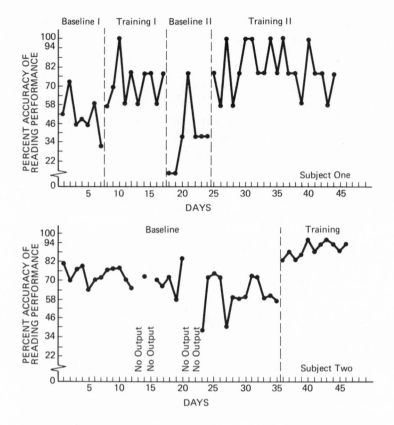

**FIGURE 9.4.**

*Percent of performance on assigned reading comprehension tasks during training sessions for two EMR students.*

*Source: D. R. Knapczyk & G. Livingston, "The Effects of Prompting Question-Asking upon On-Task Behavior and Reading Comprehension," Journal of Applied Behavior Analysis, 1974, 7, p. 120. Copyright 1974 by the Society for the Experimental Analysis of Behavior, Inc. Reprinted by permission.*

A response chain between the teacher and subjects was structured by this procedure: student raises his hand, teacher acknowledges, student asks a question, and teacher provides information. This chain provides the subjects with a clear mode of both securing information about the work assigned and obtaining teacher acknowledgment of the work performed. Both of these factors may have served to maintain question-asking and to reinforce on-task behavior and appropriate reading skills.

Similarly, the information obtained by the subjects from this feedback procedure may have affected performance, since verification of appropriate responses was immediate. Remedial information concerning the task was provided by the teacher as difficulties were observed. Also, feedback to the teacher from questions asked could facilitate more effective instructional procedures for these subjects than was provided during baseline. (Knapczyk & Livingston, 1974, pp. 119–120)

## Reading Comprehension

Crucial components of reading include visual discrimination and the learning of grapheme-phoneme correspondences, as we discussed in Chapter 6. Yet reading involves much more than merely saying sounds or words. Reading also requires a conceptual understanding of what is read. As we have seen in the work of Knapczyk and Livingston (1974), applied behavior analysis may reveal factors that enhance or improve reading comprehension.

Not surprisingly, it has been found by a number of educators that the accuracy with which children answer comprehension questions about what they have read can be improved by providing reinforcement for correct answers. In Chapter 5 we briefly described a study conducted by Lahey, McNees, and Brown (1973) in which pennies and praise were provided as reinforcers contingent on correct answers to comprehension questions. Other investigations (e.g., Knapczyk & Livingston, 1973; Lovitt, 1973a) have also demonstrated that comprehension performance can be improved by reinforcement. Also, it should be remembered that the highly successful reading technique devised by Staats (exemplified by Ryback & Staats, 1970) employed token reinforcement for correct answers to comprehension questions.

It must be recognized, though, that reinforcement for correct answers can only provide *motivation* for comprehension. Motivation is extremely important, and, judging from the success of reinforcement in improving correctness in the studies mentioned here, may be lower than desirable in many classroom situations. Motivation alone, however, is inadequate as a basis for teaching reading comprehension skills. Even the motivated child may fail to acquire the cognitive skills necessary for reading comprehension unless a careful instructional program is provided. Much of the work in this field has involved programmed instruction, in which specific comprehension skills are taught step-by-step (e.g., Bijou, Birnbrauer, Kidder, & Tague, 1966). Recently, Strang (1972a, b) and Wolf (Strang & Wolf, 1971) have used an automated device (i.e., teaching machine) to teach a variety of reading skills to reading-deficient elementary pupils from poverty backgrounds. Using relatively inexpensive components (e.g., slide projector, tape recorder, and electrical circuitry that is readily available), Strang has developed what amounts to an automated tutoring system that can be arranged to perform precisely and reliably many of the teaching functions usually performed by human teachers. His reading program has included a motivational component—

that is, extrinsic back-up reinforcers such as money for correct responses. Reading rate, comprehension, and practical reading skills (e.g., reading want ads, extracting facts from an encyclopedia, using a card catalog) have been improved using this system. In the area of reading comprehension, Strang has taught three specific skills: reproducing facts from a reading passage (reproductive comprehension); remembering a sequence of events (successive or sequence comprehension); and extracting the main idea or interpreting a passage (interpretive comprehension).

### Written Composition

Experienced teachers from the elementary-school level to colleges and universities know how difficult it is to teach the skills of written composition. Students too, at every level, have felt the sting of criticism of their efforts to express themselves in writing. It is not uncommon to hear the opinion that facility with written language is a "gift"—it cannot be learned, and a lack of ability to write lucidly is a woe that one must patiently endure. An applied behavior analysis perspective on the problem, however, leads to a more optimistic view. If one accepts the proposition that language is learned rather than innate, then it follows that the individual's environment can be so arranged to insure the acquisition of language skills, including skills in written expression.

Several applied behavior analysts have shown that aspects of written expression, composition, or "creative" writing can be influenced significantly by certain teaching and motivation techniques. In a nonremedial six-week summer school session for children in grades four through six, Maloney and Hopkins (1973) were able to alter the sentence structure children used in written stories. Each day a different noun was written on the chalkboard and the pupils were given forty minutes to compose a ten-sentence story, using the noun as the story topic. During the baseline phase no special instructions were given, but certain aspects of composition were scored for each child (e.g., the number of different adjectives or action verbs used in the story).

After five days the class (fourteen pupils) was divided into two "teams" and a "good writing game" was played each day. Points were awarded for specific aspects of composition, and the team accumulating a specified number of points earned five minutes extra recess and a small candy treat (both teams could "win" if the necessary points were earned). Before each writing task the teacher wrote examples of the desired behavior on the board after students verbalized them. On days six through nine, points were given for every different adjective used in a story; on days ten through thirteen, for each different action word used; and on days fourteen through seventeen, for different adjectives, action verbs, and sentence beginnings. Figure 9.5 describes the results averaged for the fourteen children (most of the children's performances were typified by the means for the group). When the use of different adjectives was prompted and reinforced, the children used more adjectives that were different; when the use of different action verbs was called for and rewarded, the children increased their use of different action verbs. Finally, it may be seen from Figure 9.5 that children responded by varying

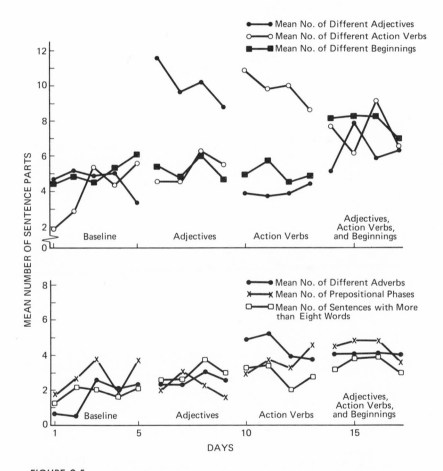

FIGURE 9.5.

(Above): mean number of different adjectives, different action verbs, and different beginnings for 14 ten-sentence stories during a 17-day period; (below): mean number of different adverbs, prepositional phrases, and sentences with more than eight words for 14 ten-sentence stories during a 17-day period.

Source: K. B. Maloney & B. L. Hopkins, "The Modification of Sentence Structure and its Relationship to Subjective Judgments of Creativity in Writing," Journal of Applied Behavior Analysis, 1973, 6, p. 429. Copyright 1973 by the Society for the Experimental Analysis of Behavior, Inc. Reprinted by permission.

TABLE 9.1     Representative stories—neither the best nor the worst—by fifth-grade,
"adjustment" class boys under a token reinforcement program.

---

**Student A Group A**

*Baseline Story:* I like to play football, Sometimes I like to play baseball, Some-times I go to the boys Club. I like boy Club. because we can play pool, hockey, basketball, swimming Gym.

*Story from New Words Condition:* "My Classroom" In my class we have Arts and Craft. We make molds, beans, flowers, houses out of sticks, pictures, Art, paint-ing. We move the board. We have locks on our door and cabinet. We have lots and lots. of things. We go on trips. We went to the Planetarium, and the Museum of Natural History and the Bronx Zoo. We are the only class that have Arts and Craft, and three other classes. We have multiplication, Divide, Adding. We have Morning Block. We play a game that nobody ever played before. It's bonus and jackpot prizes. We earn points by doing our work. And we play a lot of games on Wednesdays we go out side to play games. We Read Reader Digest And Science Readers I did not do my morning Assignment because my Mother came in to talk to Mr. Kramer. Just now Principal walked in. He is seeing how we work. He likes the class. The End

**Student B Group B**

*Baseline Story:* I like to play football with my friend I like to go swiming in the boys school

*Story from New Words Condition:* If I were President the U.S.A. there wouldn't be no Black Panthers and there wouldn't be no President in the city. And there would be no war. And policement wouldn't use clubs without trouble. And there wouldn't be more school in new united states. There wouldn't be no junkies in the United States of America.

**Student C Group C**

*Baseline Story:* I like to go swimming. I like to rid Bikes. I like to run all day. I like to Play games. Jailbrabk pull off. round-up tag. freexze tag Pull of is My Favorite games.

*Story from Number of Words Condition: The Spring Thing:* Me and my mother is going to the Spring Festival. My Mother is bringing a Cake to the Festival. We are going to sell horse and we sell dogs and we seld fishes and we sell clowns. We have fun makeing molds and we have fun makeing wheelbarrels. I painted brick for the Festival. It is nice to make nice things. We made sticks and we made churches. Tim is bringing cookies and a cake. Terrence is bring a cake also. Eddie is bring a cake and some cookies for the Festival. We is selling necklaces braclert and rings. It is going to be a beautiful show at the Festival. We are selling Our thing to put basket-ball hoops and baseball fields. We is going to eat food at the Festival. I am going to sell my Clown at the Festival. Eddie made a robot for the Festival. We made different kinds of things, I have made plenty things for the Class Room. I would like to sell My Clown for a one $1.00 piece.

---

*Source: T. A. Brigham, P. S. Graubard, & A. Stans, "Analysis of the Effects of Se-quential Reinforcement Contingencies on Aspects of Composition," Journal of Applied Behavior Analysis, 1972, 5, p. 428. Copyright 1972 by the Society for the Experi-mental Analysis of Behavior, Inc. Reprinted by permission.*

adjectives, action verbs, and sentence beginnings in the final condition, and that other aspects of sentence structure and composition (i.e., ad-verbs, prepositional phrases, and sentence length) improved concur-rently. Clearly, these children changed their written compositions to conform to environmental manipulations. Left unclear, however, is whether these changes were produced by instructions, examples, reinforcement, or some combination of these factors.

Brigham, Graubard, and Stans (1972) modified certain aspects of the written compositions of thirteen fifth-grade boys in an "adjustment" class. The pupils had been placed in the class for academic and behavior problems, and as a group they were more than two years behind academically. A token reinforcement program was an integral part of classroom routine. Under baseline conditions, students were given writing assignments and received token reinforcers for "good work" (i.e., sitting down, paying attention, staying in seat, completing the assignment, etc.). During the successive three phases of the study, the boys were given points contingent on specific composition variables: in the first phase, a point for each word written; in the next phase, an additional two points for each different word; and in the final phase, three more points for each new (i.e., never previously used by the child in any composition) word used. In general, it was found that the reinforcement contingencies influenced the children's written productions. Samples of the students' work are presented in Table 9.1.

It appears that many teachers harbor misconceptions about creative writing and its relationship to reinforcement. As Brigham and his associates (1972) put it: "Many teachers in [free schools and British Infant Schools] fervently believe that there is a reservoir of 'creativity' within children—that if only teachers would leave children alone, original and scintillating stories would soon appear" (p. 429). The evidence to date suggests that in contrast with leaving children alone, the teacher can encourage "creative" composition by providing directive guidance and reinforcement. Furthermore, the common assumption that attention to the mechanics of composition (punctuation, capitalization, etc.) will inhibit creativity is refuted by the finding of Lovitt and his colleagues (Lovitt, 1973a), namely, that feedback on mechanics had a positive effect on mechanics *and* content.

### Expressive Oral Language

Ordinarily, children who have *severe* deficits in oral language are diagnosed as severely mentally retarded, brain-damaged, severely emotionally disturbed, severely hearing impaired, or some combination of these. They are seldom considered to be EMR, LD, or only mildly or moderately ED. Those children with mild or moderate oral language or speech deficits may be diagnosed as ED, LD, or EMR, but their difficulties in oral communication are usually thought to be the proper concern of the speech pathologist as well as of special education teachers.

For severe language problems, behavioral methods for teaching specific language skills to autistic and severely retarded children have been developed (see Baer & Guess, 1971; Bricker & Bricker, 1975; Garcia, Guess, & Byrnes, 1973; Gray, 1970; Guess, 1969; Guess & Baer, 1973; Hartung, 1970; Lovaas, 1966, 1969; Risley & Wolf, 1967; Sailor, Guess, & Baer, 1973; Wheeler & Sulzer, 1970). Aside from the operant conditioning research and teaching methods used by speech pathologists and clinicians, most of the behavior analysis techniques applied to mild or moderate oral language deficits have involved culturally disadvantaged preschool children. (We have previously discussed a noteworthy exception, the study of Lovitt and Smith in which instructions were used to change a child's expressive oral language.)

Risley and his co-workers have, since 1968, conducted a series of investigations into how the language of disadvantaged children can be modified in a preschool program. In the first of these, Hart and Risley (1968) studied methods for teaching children to use adjective-noun combinations in their spontaneous speech (e.g., "I want the red trike" rather than a request that did not name both the object and its color). They found that providing children with social and intellectual stimulation (e.g., teaching children the color names of objects during group instruction) and praising them for their use of adjectives were insufficient to increase the use of adjectives or adjective-noun combinations in their spontaneous speech. The children could be taught the desired language responses in the group-teaching situation, but their use of the language patterns did not generalize to free-play activities. They therefore initiated a procedure in which the children could use certain materials and equipment only after they had asked for the object by name and described its color.

> Outdoor items such as trikes, wagons, balls, and shovels were not placed outside the storage shed as usual; rather, a child wanting to use them had to ask a teacher for them and employ an appropriate color-noun combination. A child desiring a snack from the basket held by the teacher had to ask, not for a snack or a cookie, but for a "brown" cookie (if the cookies were of that color), or a "yellow" banana. Indoors, items such as dress-up clothes in the doll house, pegboard materials, parquetry blocks, toy animals, and cars, *etc.*, all had to be named by a color-noun combination before a child was allowed to use them. These materials were not removed from the children's reach; rather, when a child approached one of these materials, a teacher put her hand on the material the child was reaching for. (Hart & Risley, 1968, p. 113)

This teaching technique, in which the use of materials was made contingent on color-noun naming, was very successful in inducing children to use color-noun combinations in their everyday language. Hart and Risley suggested two implications of their results for preschool teachers. First, it appears that language responses like those taught in their study may be learned most efficiently in a "natural" or functional environment in which the contingencies applied to pre-academic behaviors approximate those that operate outside the preschool. Second, preschool materials may be reinforcers for many young children, and for some they may be even more powerful reinforcers than social rewards or food. Thus, teachers should look for ways in which to use natural reinforcers, such as contingent access to materials or activities, to facilitate the acquisition of functional language responses, such as description of objects in the environment.

Reynolds and Risley (1968) worked with a four-year-old girl who very seldom talked. In order to increase her talking, they made the teacher's attention, in the form of praising, giving equipment, assisting, and so forth, contingent on the child's verbalization. In addition, whenever the verbalization consisted of a request for materials, the teacher would provide the materials only after the child had answered one or more questions (e.g., "What are you going to paint?" or "What else do you need besides the paint brush?"). This procedure produced a dramatic increase in the child's verbalizations. Her talking decreased to near zero when the teacher's attention was made contingent on nonverbalization and increased dramatically again when the teacher's attention was once more made contingent on talking. Further analyses showed that the material reinforcers (i.e., access to materials and equipment) were critical in establishing and maintaining the child's verbal behavior.

In a subsequent project, Risley and Hart (1968) explored ways in which to make children's nonverbal behavior (using a preschool material) correspond to their verbal behavior (reporting on their use of the material). Not surprisingly, it was found that when children were reinforced (with a snack) for reporting their use of a material regardless of whether or not they had actually used the material, the correspondence between their verbal and nonverbal behavior was low. On the other hand, when the children received reinforcement only if their reports of using materials matched their actual use of them, there was close correspondence between their use of materials and their verbal statements about their behavior. Once correspondence between verbal and nonverbal behavior had been established, reinforcement of "saying" was sufficient to change "doing"—that is, children's nonverbal behavior could be modified indirectly by changing what they said. It is obviously of social importance to be able to depend upon correspondence between the verbal and nonverbal behavior of individuals and to be able to change a person's nonverbal behavior by altering what he says. Risley and Hart have provided some direction for teachers who wish to teach children to make saying correspond with doing.

Modeling and imitation are used in almost all language training programs: the teacher presents a language model that the child is to imitate. Risley and Reynolds (1970) investigated the use of emphasis (i.e., stressing particular syllables, words, or phrases) as a method of determining which parts of a verbal presentation disadvantaged pre-schoolers would imitate. The teacher read sentences composed of short phrases (e.g., "Children can swim in the summer," or "I talked to my brother") and asked the children to repeat each sentence. No differential reinforcement for accurate imitation was given, but the teacher stressed (i.e., emphasized) certain words as she read each sentence. The pro-portion of words stressed in each sentence was systematically varied, and the effects on imitation were measured. Stress was effective in determin-ing *which* parts of a sentence would be imitated, but this was true only when relatively few words were stressed. In other words, if too many words in a sentence were stressed, the emphasis was of no value in increasing imitation. The fewer the number of words stressed in a sen-tence, the greater the probability that the child would imitate them. Furthermore, if only one word in a phrase was stressed, the child was more likely to imitate not only that word but the entire phrase. Thus, it was shown that emphasis can be useful in increasing imitation, so long as it is not overdone.

In a more recent study, Hart and Risley (1974) again used pre-school materials to modify the language of twelve disadvantaged preschoolers. Three experimental conditions were in effect in succession: (1) a material was made available only after the child had named it; (2) a material was made available only after the child had used an adjective-noun combination in describing it; and (3) a material was made available only after the child had used a compound sentence in request-ing it (e.g., "I want a ball so I can bounce it"). For each experimental condition the teacher provided prompts as necessary. As shown in Table 9.2, there were four levels of teacher behavior. If the child did not ask for a material with the appropriate language within 30 seconds, a prompt was given, the nature of the prompt depending on the child's verbali-zation. For example, under the adjective-noun condition, Level 3, if the child said "I want a car" the teacher would respond "I have red cars and blue cars," and so on, and wait for the child to say, "I want a red (or blue) car." The effects of these procedures are shown in Figure 9.6. The graph shows that the contingencies had a pronounced effect on the chil-dren's language. As Hart and Risley (1974) summarized,

This study replicates and extends the Hart and Risley (1968) study in demonstrating that the free-play periods of preschoolers can be used

TABLE 9.2      Levels of Teacher Behavior During Experimental Conditions

| | *Materials Contingent On* | | |
| | Nouns | *Adjective-Noun Combinations* | *Compound Sentences* |
|---|---|---|---|
| Level 1 | Waiting for 30 seconds | Waiting for 30 seconds | Waiting for 30 seconds |
| Level 2 | "What do you want?" "What do you need?" | "What kind?" | "Why?" "What for?" |
| Level 3 | "What is that called?" | Offering alternatives: "I have red cars and blue cars," *etc.* | "Say the whole thing." |
| Level 4 | Imitation by child of teacher verbalization: "This is a car. Say 'car.' " | Imitation by child of teacher verbalization: "Say the whole thing, 'a red car.' " | Imitation by child of teacher verbalization: "You need to say, 'I want a car so I can play with it.' " |

*Source: B. Hart & T. R. Risley, "Using Preschool Materials to Modify the Language of Disadvantaged Children," Journal of Applied Behavior Analysis, 1974, 7, 246. Copyright 1974 by the Society for the Experimental Analysis of Behavior, Inc. Reprinted by permission.*

as powerful incidental teaching periods by capitalizing upon moments when children request new play materials to teach them systematically more elaborate language. It also demonstrates that, in accordance with the findings of previous research (Allen *et al.*, 1967; Buell *et al.*, 1968; Reynolds and Risley, 1968), the experimental manipulations in the present study had no apparent adverse effects on related behaviors. The proportion or type of teacher-child interaction was not measurably affected by the experimental manipulations. Nor did the requirements for obtaining play materials result in the children's preferring to play with a set of materials that continued to be free of such requirements. (p. 255)

### Contributions of Bereiter, Engelmann, and Becker

In the mid 1960s, a small group of individuals at the University of Illinois began formulating an approach to language training that was to have a profound influence on education for culturally disadvantaged children and on the development of a behavioral model for teaching all basic academic skills. Carl Bereiter and Siegfried Engelmann began with the assumption that culturally deprived children are, essentially, language deprived children:

The language deficiencies of disadvantaged children [are] seen to consist not of deficiencies in vocabulary and grammar as such but of failure to master certain uses of language. Language for the disadvantaged child seems to be an aspect of social behavior which is not of vital importance. The disadvantaged child masters a language that is adequate for main-

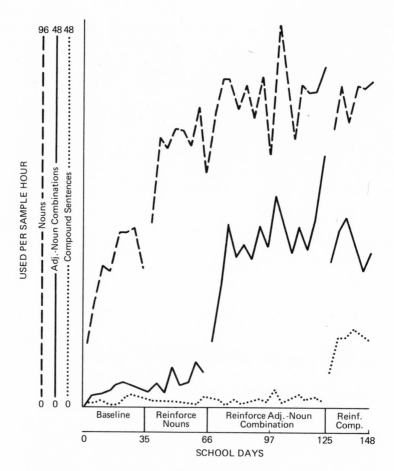

FIGURE 9.6.

Average use of nouns (broken line), adjective-noun combinations (solid
line), and compound sentences (dotted line) per 15-minute sample by 12
children across experimental conditions. The experimental conditions were:
baseline (days 1 to 34); access to preschool materials contingent on use of
a noun (days 35 to 65); access to preschool materials contingent on use
of an adjective-noun combination (days 66 to 124); and access to
preschool materials contingent on use of a compound sentence (days 125
to 148). Note the different scale for nouns versus adjective-noun
combinations and compound sentences.

Source: B. Hart & T. R. Risley, "Using Preschool Materials to Modify
the Language of Disadvantaged Children," Journal of Applied Behavior
Analysis, 1974, 7, p. 249. Copyright 1974 by the Society for the Experimental Analysis of Behavior, Inc. Reprinted by permission.

taining social relationships and for meeting his social and material needs,
but he does not learn how to use language for obtaining and transmitting

information, for monitoring his own behavior, and for carrying on verbal reasoning. In short, he fails to master the cognitive uses of language, which are the uses that are of primary importance in school. (Bereiter & Engelmann, 1966, p. 42)

In order to teach the specific language (i.e., cognitive) skills that are required for success in school, Bereiter and Engelmann (1966, undated) developed a highly directive teaching strategy and many learning activities. Their program included activities in reading, arithmetic, and music as well as in receptive and expressive oral language. Engelmann (1969) has further articulated procedures for teaching reading and arithmetic in the primary grades.

The work of Bereiter and Engelmann was extended by the collaboration of Wesley C. Becker, Engelmann, and others in developing the DISTAR* programs. In DISTAR, teaching is highly structured and sequential. The children are taught in small groups of four to six pupils, and each pupil is expected to respond to instruction according to rules established and modeled by the teacher. Appropriate behavior and correct responses are reinforced with praise or food (e.g., raisins or juice), or both. Children who misbehave are ignored or prompted unobtrusively while those who are well behaved are reinforced, thus providing both a model for the miscreant and vicarious reinforcement for good behavior. Such an instructional system not only produces significant academic gains in most children but also discourages unruly behavior (e.g., Kauffman & Hallahan, 1973).

The teacher using the Bereiter-Engelmann or DISTAR methods must have a well-developed repertoire of specific teaching skills to be successful. Osborn (1968) has summarized the skills needed for small-group teaching techniques. The teacher must be able to:

a) Diagnose and evaluate what the child knows that is relevant to what she is going to teach;

b) Decide on the learning tasks of a period and teach them, not letting the children distract her with chance remarks from the intended program;

c) Speak quickly and distinctly, changing tasks frequently;

d) Restructure and reorganize presentation when children are not learning;

e) Present learning tasks in the most simple and logical way possible, adding only one new concept at a time;

* Direct Instructional System for Teaching Arithmetic and Reading (DISTAR) is published by Science Research Associates. The DISTAR programs are available for several levels of arithmetic, reading, and language.

f) Give instant feedback to children, correct wrong responses, praise correct responses;

g) Intercept wrong responses, when possible, before or while they are being made;

h) Give the answer to a child who seems about to make a mistake or who is silent;

i) Get the attention of misbehaving or distracted children by touching them on the shoulder or knees instead of interrupting the lesson with verbal admonishments;

j) Move on to new tasks when children have mastered a task and do not spend time drilling on material the children already know. (p. 45)

Becker, Engelmann, and Thomas (1971) have outlined in some detail the general teaching model on which the work of Bereiter, Engelmann, and Becker is based. The model makes explicit use of antecedent stimuli (i.e., directions, cues, prompts), behavioral goals, and consequences (i.e., corrections, reinforcement). In short, it consists of the systematic application of operant learning principles to teaching the basic academic skills. Consequently, their teaching model and instructional systems have particular applicability to the education of those children who have difficulty learning, regardless of whether they are labeled culturally disadvantaged, ED, LD, or EMR for administrative purposes.

# Social-Emotional Disabilities

# 10

The child's social development encompasses all of the topics we have discussed in preceding chapters. Perceptual, language, cognitive, and motor skills are inextricably intertwined with the development of social skills. Social growth demands that the child learn interpersonal skills involving his family, peers, and the society of which he is a part, that he learn ethical and moral values, adopt behavior consistent with his sex role, develop self-control, and so on. How quickly or adequately he learns such social responses will depend in part on his perceptual, conceptual, language, and motor development, for these skills are mediators of many social interactions. The child learns many social skills and values through language interactions with his parents, and indeed many of his social interactions *are* language interactions. Motor skills are required for social play, and the child deficient in motor skills is a likely candidate for social isolation or ostracism. Perceptual or cognitive deficits, which prevent the child from achieving academically, may also have a highly deleterious effect on his social adaptation to school. Because nearly every aspect of a child's development occurs in a social context or is of concern because of social standards or values, a theory of social development is, in a very real sense, a theory of child development. Nevertheless, it is possible to focus attention on those behaviors that constitute interpersonal interactions. In this chapter we will concern ourselves primarily with behaviors that are peculiar to the interaction of two or more people and that are of concern because of social standards or expectations.

Normal social behavior is defined by social and cultural standards. These standards vary among cultures and social groups and change with such factors as time, socio-economic conditions, and political realities. One cannot, therefore, arbitrarily classify a given social behavior as desirable or undesirable but must take into account the context in which the behavior occurs.

> In our country, attitudes toward the behavior of children in school have changed dramatically over the last century. Gnagey (1969) reports that S. L. Pressey found a list of misbehaviors and recommended punishments published in North Carolina in 1848. Among them were:
>
>> Playing cards at school (10 lashes)
>> Swearing at school (8 lashes)
>> Drinking liquor at school (8 lashes)
>> Telling lies (7 lashes)
>> Boys and girls playing together (4 lashes)
>> Quarreling (4 lashes)
>> Wearing long fingernails (2 lashes)
>> Blotting one's copybook (2 lashes)
>> Neglecting to bow when going home (2 lashes)
>
> Today, many Americans would be more likely to recommend lashes for wearing long hair or for a student's *insistence* on bowing when going home. (Payne, Kauffman, Brown, & DeMott, 1974, p. 12)

Furthermore, the behavior of delivering lashes to schoolchildren would now be seen as inappropriate by most Americans. The point to be made is that when and where a behavior occurs will influence how it is evaluated. Normality of social behavior, then, must be defined with specific situational variables in mind. In this chapter we will not attempt to trace the course of normal social development, given the prevailing standards and values of a social or cultural group. We will, however, examine the development of certain undesirable social behaviors that, if chronic or exhibited to a marked degree, are typically a cause for concern among parents, peers, school personnel, and other socialization agents. Such social behaviors are frequently referred to as "psychopathological," inferring that they reflect mental ill health or morbid cognitive processes. We will not focus our discussion on the types of psychopathological disorders often associated with *severe* emotional disturbance (e.g., psychopathy, sociopathy, schizophrenia, autism, etc.) or *severe* mental retardation. Rather, our discussion will be concerned primarily with the milder deviations in social development frequently associated with the learning disabled, educable mentally retarded, or mildly to moderately emotionally disturbed child.

Since the beginning of the twentieth century, interest in children's behavior disorders has grown, and for the past twenty years a significant part of the research in child development has pertained to childhood psychopathology. A number of theories of psychopathology have been formulated in attempts to explain the origins of problem behavior. These theories range from Freudian psychoanalytic theory, which is based almost solely on the conjectural analysis of case studies (cf. Bettelheim, 1955, 1970), to Skinnerian behavioral theory, which is based on a rather tenuous extrapolation from data obtained in the laboratory or during the course of treatment of behavior problems (cf. Bijou & Baer, 1961; Ferster, 1961). Not one of these theories has led to the empirical verification of the *etiology* of behavior disorders, although the behavioral approach to *intervention* has been demonstrated empirically to be highly effective (Becker, 1971; Thoresen, 1973). Our view is that it is most fruitful at this time to attend carefully to those data obtained through empirical research and to set aside most speculation or theorizing about causes until a firmer foundation of empirical data is laid.

## DIMENSIONS OF DISORDERED SOCIAL BEHAVIOR

Systems of classification in psychiatry and psychopathology have never been satisfactory. No system exists in which an individual can be *reliably* assigned to a category of disorder, much less to a category that accurately depicts his behavior, reveals the etiology, implies a specific treatment, and provides a prognosis (Katz, Cole, & Barton, 1965; Menninger, 1963; Ullmann & Krasner, 1969). This situation applies to children as well as adults. Indeed, the problem of classification of childhood behavior disorders is exacerbated by the short history of child psychology and psychiatry, by the normal transience of symptomatology during the developmental period, and by the tendency of many child psychologists to be "developmentally optimistic" regarding the behavior problems of children —that is to adopt the attitude, "Don't worry, he'll grow out of it."

Demographic studies of normal children's behavior problems have indicated that normal children are far from problem-free. The California Growth Study (MacFarlane, Allen, & Honzik, 1954) and research by Lapouse and Monk (1958), for example, have shown that it is common for children to exhibit behaviors that their parents consider to be undesirable—temper tantrums, overactivity, food finickiness, specific fears, excessive shyness or withdrawal, lying—at some time during their development. Moreover, normal children themselves are aware that their behavior is now and then a problem (Griffiths, 1952). Obviously, then, the presence at some point in the child's life of undesirable behavior, such as excessive timidity, overaggressiveness, tantrums, thumb-sucking, and so on, cannot in itself be a criterion for the presence of psychopathology. It is only when children exhibit such problems to a marked degree and over a relatively long period of time that their behavior can be considered indicative of "emotional disturbance" or disorder (Bower, 1969). Furthermore, children are almost always judged to be in need of psychotherapy or other intervention on the basis of a cluster or multiplicity of behavior difficulties rather than on the basis of a single problem behavior.

The behavioral characteristics of schoolchildren whose social development may warrant special attention have been summarized by Bower (1969):

1. *An inability to learn which cannot be explained by intellectual, sensory, or health factors.* An inability to learn is perhaps the single most significant characteristic of emotionally handicapped children in school. Such nonlearning may be manifested as an inability to profit from experience as well as inability to master skill subjects. The non-learner seldom escapes recognition. Achievement tests often confirm what the teacher has long suspected. If all other major causative factors have been ruled out, emotional conflicts or resistances can be ruled in.

2. *An inability to build or maintain satisfactory interpersonal relationships with peers and teachers.* It isn't getting along with others that is significant here. Satisfactory interpersonal relations refers to the ability to demonstrate sympathy and warmth toward others, the ability to stand alone when necessary, the ability to have close friends, the ability to be aggressively constructive, and the ability to enjoy working and playing with others as well as enjoying working and playing by oneself. In most instances, children who are unable to build or maintain satisfactory interpersonal relationships are most visible to their peers. Teachers are also able to identify many such children after a period of observation.

3. *Inappropriate types of behavior or feelings under normal conditions.* Inappropriateness of behavior or feelings can often be sensed by the teacher and peer groups. "He acts funny," another child may say. The teacher may find some children reacting disproportionately to a simple command such as "Please take your seat." What is appropriate or inappropriate is best judged by the teacher using her professional training, her daily and long-term observation of the child, and her experience working and interacting with the appropriate behavior of large numbers of normal children.

4. *A general, pervasive mood of unhappiness or depression.* Children who are unhappy most of the time may demonstrate such feelings in expressive play, art work, written composition, or in discussion periods. They seldom smile and usually lack a *joie de vivre* in their schoolwork or social relationships. In the middle or upper grades a self-inventory is usually helpful in confirming suspicions about such feelings.

5. *A tendency to develop physical symptoms, pains, or fears associated*

*with personal or school problems.* This tendency is often noted by the school nurse and parent. Illness may be continually associated with school pressures or develop when a child's confidence in himself is under stress. In some cases, such illnesses or fears may not be apparent to the teacher; peers, however, are often aware of children who are sick before or after tests or have headaches before recitations. Speech difficulties which may be the symptoms of emotional distress are usually most visible to the teacher and parent.

The significant characteristics of children indicating a need for closer scrutiny by a teacher are inability to learn, unsatisfactory interpersonal relationships, inappropriate behavior, unhappiness, and repetitive illness.\* (pp. 22–23)

From Bower's research on early identification of emotionally disturbed children, one may expect approximately 10 percent of the children in an average classroom to demonstrate significant problems in one or more of these areas. Among problem students, boys typically outnumber girls by a ratio of four or five to one. As we shall point out in the discussion that follows, many of the behavior problems that characterize emotionally handicapped youngsters are also characteristic, though possibly to a lesser degree, in children who are considered learning disabled or mentally retarded.

### Multivariate Statistical Analysis

In an attempt to identify types or clusters of deviant behaviors on an empirical basis, researchers have turned to quantitative methods of determining interrelationships among behavior problems. These methods are "multivariate" in that a large number of variables are intercorrelated using complex statistical procedures such as factor analysis. The results of these statistical procedures reveal which behavior problems tend to cluster or occur together, that is, to form a syndrome. In early studies (e.g., Ackerson, 1942; Hewitt & Jenkins, 1946), behavior traits obtained from children's case histories were listed and then "clustered" by visual inspection of the data. Since Peterson's (1961) initial factor analytic study, however, researchers have relied upon statistical techniques to reveal the interrelationships among problem behaviors.

Peterson began by examining the referral problems listed in more than 400 case folders obtained from a child guidance clinic. On the basis of the frequency with which these problems occurred, he selected fifty-

\* E. M. Bower, *Early Identification of Emotionally Handicapped Children in School,* 2d ed. (Springfield, Ill.: Charles C. Thomas, 1969), pp. 22–23. Reprinted by permission.

eight items describing behavioral difficulties and compiled them in a check-list. The format of the checklist required ratings of 0 (no problem), 1 (mild problem), or 2 (severe problem) for each of the fifty-eight items. The checklist was completed by twenty-eight teachers of more than 800 children in kindergarten through sixth grade, and the scores were then factor analyzed. Peterson's interpretation of the factor analysis suggested the existence of two major factors: a "conduct problem," which implied a tendency to express impulses against society, and a "personality problem" or neuroticism, which constituted a variety of elements suggesting low self-esteem, social withdrawal, and dysphoria. Boys showed more conduct problems than girls at all grade levels. However, it was found that al-though boys exhibited more personality problems in the lower grades, girls showed more personality problems than boys after third grade.

A number of studies following the pattern set by Peterson have yielded essentially the same results. Using the Behavior Problem Check-list developed by Quay and Peterson (1967), these studies have estab-lished the existence of two pervasive and prominent patterns of deviant behavior (those labeled by Peterson as "conduct problem" and "person-ality problem") plus a third and usually less prominent dimension that may be labeled "inadequacy" or "immaturity." Quay (1972) has summar-ized the results of these studies. Tables 10.1, 10.2, and 10.3 provide a synopsis of the behavior traits, life history characteristics, and question-naire responses identified in representative studies in which the Peterson and Quay checklist analysis technique was employed and in which the three dimensions of deviant behavior—conduct disorder, personality dis-order, and inadequacy-immaturity—were found.

Investigations into the types of problem behavior exhibited by spe-cial education students have shown that the same three dimensions apply. Quay, Morse, and Cutler (1966) found that in classes for the emotionally disturbed, conduct problems and inadequacy-immaturity were the pre-dominant types of behavioral difficulties with the dimension of personal-ity problem accounting for a smaller portion of the children's troubles. In a study of youngsters with special learning disabilities, Paraskevo-poulos and McCarthy (1969) found that teachers and mothers of the children identified behavior problems that fell into the same clusters and patterns.

In Chapter 3, we suggested that emotionally disturbed and learning disabled children as groups could be placed along a continuum of mal-adaptive behavior (see Figure 3.4). We also suggested that ED children could reasonably be assumed to fall on the continuum more toward the maladaptive side of the scale than LD children. Research by McCarthy and Paraskevopoulos (1969) supports our suggestion. They compared the behavior ratings of learning disabled, emotionally disturbed, and average

TABLE 10.1     Selected Behavior Traits, Life History Characteristics, and Questionnaire Responses Associated with Conduct Disorder

| Behavior Traits | Representative Studies[a] | | | | | | | |
|---|---|---|---|---|---|---|---|---|
| Disobedience | 1, | 4, | 6, | 8, | 9, | 15 | | |
| Disruptiveness | 1, | 4, | 6, | 8, | 9, | 15 | | |
| Fighting | 1, | 4, | 6, | 8, | 9, | 2, | 5, | 15 |
| Destructiveness | 1, | 4, | 6, | 8, | 9, | 7 | | |
| Temper Tantrums | 1, | 4, | 6, | 8, | 9, | 15 | | |
| Irresponsibility | 1, | 4, | 6, | 8, | 9 | | | |
| Impertinent | 1, | 4, | 6, | 8, | 9, | 3, | 7 | |
| Jealous | 1, | 3, | 4, | 9 | | | | |
| Shows signs of anger | 3, | 5 | | | | | | |
| Acts bossy | 5, | 7 | | | | | | |
| Profanity | 1, | 8, | 3, | 9 | | | | |
| Attention seeking | 1, | 3, | 4, | 6, | 7, | 8, | 9 | |
| Boisterous | 1, | 4, | 6, | 7, | 8, | 9 | | |

| Life History Characteristics | Representative Studies[a] | | | |
|---|---|---|---|---|
| Assaultive | 8, | 10, | 11, | 12 |
| Defies authority | 8, | 10, | 11, | 12 |
| Inadequate guilt feelings | 10, | 12 | | |
| Irritable | 11, | 12 | | |
| Quarrelsome | 8, | 11 | | |

| Questionnaire Responses | Representative Studies[a] |
|---|---|
| I do what I want to whether anybody likes it or not | 13,   14 |
| It's dumb to trust other people | 13,   14 |
| The only way to settle anything is to lick the guy | 13,   14 |
| I'm too tough a guy to get along with most kids | 13,   14 |
| If you don't have enough to live on, it's okay to steal | 13,   14 |
| I go out of my way to meet trouble rather than try to escape it | 13,   14 |

[a] Representative studies are as follows: 1. Peterson et al. (1961), 2. Patterson (1964), 3. Dreger et al. (1964), 4. Quay (1964a), 5. Spivack & Spotts (1965), 6. Quay & Quay, (1965), 7. Ross, Lacey, & Parton (1965), 8. Quay (1966), 9. Lessing & Zagorin (1971), 10. Hewitt & Jenkins (1946), 11. Quay (1964b), 12. Achenbach (1966), 13. Peterson, Quay, & Cameron (1959), 14. Peterson, Quay, & Tiffany (1961), and 15. Brady (1970).

Source: H. C. Quay, "Patterns of Aggression, Withdrawal and Immaturity," in H. C. Quay & J. S. Werry (Eds.), Psychopathological Disorders of Childhood (New York: Wiley, 1972). Reprinted by permission.

children and found that, in fact, the distribution of scores over the three factors was strikingly similar for ED and LD children. It is not surprising, given this similarity in *types* of behavior exhibited, that ED and LD children have been rather difficult to differentiate for purposes of placement and education. However, McCarthy and Paraskevopoulos did find that ED children exhibited all types of deviant behavior at a higher *level* than LD children, suggesting that ED and LD youngsters differ in the

TABLE 10.2    Selected Behavior Traits, Life History Characteristics, and Questionnaire
Responses Associated with Personality Disorder

| Behavior Traits | Representative Studies[a] | | | | | | | | | |
|---|---|---|---|---|---|---|---|---|---|---|
| Feelings of inferiority | 1, | | | 4, | 6, | 7, | | 9 | | |
| Self-consciousness | 1, | | | 4, | 6, | 7, | 8, | 9, | 15 | |
| Social withdrawal | 1, | 2, | 3, | 4, | 6, | 7, | 8, | | 15 | |
| Shyness | 1, | | 3, | 4, | 6, | | 8, | 9, | 15 | |
| Anxiety | 1, | 2, | | 4, | | | 8, | | 15 | |
| Crying | 1, | | | | | | 8, | 9 | | |
| Shyness (sic) | 1, | 2, | | 4, | 6, | | | | 15 | |
| Hypersensitive | 1, | | | 4, | | 7, | 8, | 9, | 15 | |
| Seldom smiles | | 2 | | | | | | | | |
| Chews fingernails | | 2 | | | | | | | | |
| Depression, chronic sadness | 1, | | | 4, | | | 8, | | 15 | |

| Life History Characteristics | Representative Studies[a] | | |
|---|---|---|---|
| Seclusive | 8 | 10 | 11 |
| Shy | 8 | 10 | 11 |
| Sensitive | | 10 | 11 |
| Worries | | 10 | 11 |
| Timid | | | 11 |
| Has anxiety over own behavior | | | 11 |

| Questionnaire Responses | Representative Studies[a] |
|---|---|
| I don't think I'm quite as happy as others seems to be | 13, 14 |
| I often feel as though I have done something wrong or wicked | 13, 14 |
| I seem to do things I regret more often than most people do | 13, 14 |
| I just don't seem to get the breaks other people do | 13, 14 |
| People often talk about me behind my back | 13, 14 |
| I have more than my share of things to worry about | 13 |

[a] Representative studies are as follows: 1. Peterson et al. (1961), 2. Patterson
(1964), 3. Dreger et al. (1964), 4. Quay (1964a), 5. Spivack & Spotts (1965), 6. Quay
& Quay (1965), 7. Ross, Lacey, & Parton (1965), 8. Quay (1966), 9. Lessing &
Zagorin (1971), 10. Hewitt & Jenkins (1947), 11. Quay (1964b), 12. Achenbach
(1966), 13. Peterson, Quay, & Cameron (1959), 14. Peterson, Quay, & Tiffany (1961),
and 15. Brady (1970).

Source: H. C. Quay, "Patterns of Aggression, Withdrawal and Immaturity," in H. C.
Quay & J. S. Werry (Eds.), Psychopathological Disorders of Childhood (New York:
Wiley, 1972). Reprinted by permission.

severity or number of problems, as shown in Figure 10.1. These findings
were summarized by McCarthy and Paraskevopoulos (1969) as follows:

> In addition to differences in *levels* of behavior, important differences
> in *profiles* were found. Analyses of intragroup differences on the three
> factors suggested that (a) the emotionally disturbed children as a group
> exhibit more conduct problem behavior than either immature or person-

TABLE 10.3    Selected Behavior Traits and Life History Characteristics Associated with Immaturity

| Behavior Traits | | | | | | | | | | |
|---|---|---|---|---|---|---|---|---|---|---|
| | 1 | 2 | 3 | 4 | 5 | 6 | 7 | 8 | 9 | 12 | 13 |
| Preoccupation | 1 | | | | 5 | 6 | | | 9 | 12 | |
| Short attention span | 1 | | 3 | | 5 | 6 | | | 9 | | 13 |
| Clumsiness | 1 | | 3 | | | | | 8 | 9 | | 13 |
| Passivity | 1 | 2 | 3 | | 5 | 6 | | | | | 13 |
| Daydreaming | 1 | | | | 5 | 6 | | | 9 | 12 | 13 |
| Sluggish | 1 | | | | | 6 | | | 9 | 12 | |
| Drowsiness | 1 | | | | | 6 | | | | 12 | |
| Prefers younger playmates | 1 | | 3 | 4 | | | | 8 | | | |
| Masturbation | | 2 | 3 | | | | | | | | |
| Giggles | | 2 | | | | | | | | | |
| Easily flustered | | | 3 | | | | | | | | |
| Chews objects | | 2 | | | | | 7 | | | | |
| Picked on by others | | | | 4 | | | 7 | | | | |
| Plays with toys in class | | | | | | | 7 | | | | |

| Life History Characteristics | Representative Studies [a] | |
|---|---|---|
| Habitually truant from home | 10 | |
| Unable to cope with a complex world | 10 | |
| Incompetent, immature | 10 | |
| Not accepted by delinquent subgroup | 10 | |
| Engages in furtive stealing | | 11 |

[a] Representative studies are as follows: 1. Peterson et al. (1961). 2. Patterson (1964), 3. Quay (1964a), 4. Dreger et al. (1964), 5. Quay & Quay (1965). 6. Quay, Morse, & Cutler (1966), 7. Pimm, Quay, & Werry (1969), 8. Miller (1967), 9. Lessing & Zagorin (1971), 10. Quay (1964b), 11. Quay (1966), 12. Brady (1970), 13. Conners (1969).

*Source: H. C. Quay, "Patterns of Aggression, Withdrawal and Immaturity," in H. C. Quay & J. S. Werry (Eds.), Psychopathological Disorders of Childhood (New York: Wiley, 1972). Reprinted by permission.*

ality problem behavior, and they are more immature than neurotic; (b) the learning disabled children as a group also manifest more conduct problem behaviors than immature or neurotic behaviors, with both of the latter dimensions being perceived as present to the same degree; and (c) teachers of regular classes perceive either fewer problems and/or problems of less severity than do teachers of the other two groups, with these problem behaviors distributed relatively evenly over the three factors. Conduct problem behavior characterized by restlessness, disruptiveness, attention seeking, fighting, irresponsibility, tension, hyperactivity, distractibility, jealousy, etc., appears to be the main characteristic of both emotionally disturbed and learning disabled children. (p. 73)

Although we cannot offer research data in support of our contention that educable mentally retarded children fall along the same continuum

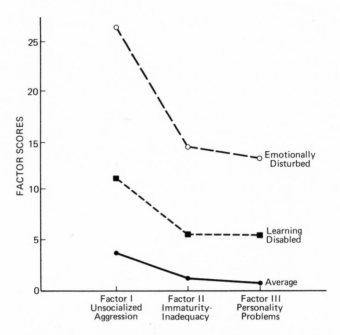

*FIGURE 10.1.*

*Mean factor scores for emotionally disturbed, learning disabled, and average children on the Behavior Problem Checklist.*

Source: *Reprinted from J. McCarthy & J. Paraskevopoulos, "Behavior Pattern of Learning Disabled, Emotionally Disturbed, and Average Children,"* Exceptional Children, *1969, 36, p. 71 by permission of The Council for Exceptional Children.*

of disordered behavior as ED and LD children (see Chapter 3), it is our considered judgment that this similarity in social behavior is a reasonable assertion. We base the assertion on three observations: (1) the generality and stability of the behavioral dimensions identified in ED, LD, delinquent, and normal populations, (2) the difficulty in differentially diagnosing a child as ED, LD, or EMR, and (3) our own informal observations of EMR children's behavior.

In summary, although it is not now possible to classify children meaningfully as falling into diagnostic categories of psychopathology, it is possible to identify the types of behavior children exhibit. It appears that among children who exhibit behavior problems, three basic patterns are predominant: aggression (i.e., conduct problems), withdrawal (i.e., personality problems or neuroticism), and immaturity. Research indicates that conduct problems are most salient in ED and LD populations and that the ED children differ from LD children primarily in the degree or number of problems exhibited.

## DEVELOPMENT AND CONTROL
## OF AGGRESSION

Although the research of Quay, Peterson, and others makes clear that a significant number of ED and LD children are perceived by their teachers as immature or withdrawn, their research also makes obvious the fact that the teacher of ED or LD children must be prepared for much behavior of the hyperaggressive, acting-out type. Overly aggressive behavior in children is of concern not only because of its pernicious influence in the classroom, but also because it is a poor augury for their emotional status as adults (as we shall see in our discussion of longitudinal studies of behavior disorders). And there exists in America today a growing anxiety over the level of violence in our society. Aggression, as we shall use the term here, refers to behavior that elicits escape, avoidance, or counteraggressive responses from another person. A "victim" and a "victimizer," then, are always involved in behavior that is aggressive.

The origin of aggressive behavior has not been irrefutably established. Several empirically researchable theories of aggression have been advanced, however. The frustration-aggression hypothesis, first articulated by Dollard, Doob, Miller, Mowrer, and Sears (1939), proposes that frustration (i.e., thwarting or blocking the attainment of a goal) inevitably leads to aggression. It suggests also that underlying all aggression is some prior frustration. Recent research has indicated rather clearly that the relationship between frustration and aggression is not so simple. Most frustrations appear to be aversive in nature, and such unpleasant stimuli generally provide the occasion for aggression. Nevertheless, there is ample evidence that aggression is not an inevitable consequence of being thwarted (cf. Berkowitz, 1973). Children can be taught to react in nonaggressive ways to frustration or to inhibit aggression. Furthermore, if the child's perceptions of frustration are altered, aggression may not follow frustration. For example, children may be reinforced for constructive or cooperative behavior under frustrating circumstances or they may be told the reason for a frustrating event's occurrence, thereby decreasing the likelihood of an aggressive response.

Another theory is that aggression is learned by observing aggressive acts. A rather large body of research is available to suggest that children do exhibit higher levels of aggressive behavior after having viewed others performing acts of aggression, regardless of whether the aggressive models were observed live or on film or whether the filmed models were humans or cartoon characters (Bandura, 1969; Feshbach, 1970). When the model has been rewarded for his aggression or received no consequences, children have tended to perform more imitative aggressive acts than when the model has received punishment. A recent study by Friedrich and Stein (1973) has added to the evidence that watching televised violence heightens aggression in preschool children. In their study preschoolers watched aggressive cartoons ("Batman" and "Superman"), prosocial shows ("Mister Rogers' Neighborhood") or neutral films during a summer nursery-school program. The effects of watching these programs were measured during free play in the nursery school. It was found that the aggressive programs produced a sharp decline in tolerance of delay and frustration and increased interpersonal aggression in those children who were already above average in aggression. The prosocial programs, on the other hand, increased positive interpersonal behaviors, but only for children from lower socio-economic levels. The effects on children of viewing televised violence is a topic to which we will return later.

Perhaps the most rigorous studies of children's aggression have been conducted by Gerald Patterson and his associates, Bricker, Cobb, and Littman. Patterson, Littman, and Bricker (1967) measured the aggressive behaviors shown by children in two nursery-school classes and examined the antecedent events and consequences surrounding aggressive acts. They found that when aggressive behaviors were followed by positive reinforcement from the peer group, aggressive behavior increased. When aggression was followed by a negative reinforcer, however, (e.g., teacher intervention or the victim's counterattack), the next act of aggression was likely to be a different type of response or to be directed toward a different victim.

> The data also showed that children who initially displayed low rates of aggressive behaviors were conditioned by the peer group to show dramatic acceleration in the frequency of initiation of these behaviors. The acceleration in these behaviors was a function of the frequency with which a child was victimized by the aggressive behaviors of other children and the frequency with which the victim successfully counterattacked. (Patterson, Littman, & Bricker, 1967, p. 39)

The work of Patterson and his colleagues suggested a theory of aggression in which reinforcement plays the predominant role. A subsequent naturalistic study of twenty-four families by Patterson and Cobb (1971) pointed to the role of *negative reinforcement* (i.e., contingent removal or termination of an aversive stimulus) in producing aggression. Briefly, Patterson and Cobb's hypothesis, which is based on a large amount of empirical data, is that aggressive children train their parents and peers to react to them with counteraggression. In effect, the aggressive child becomes embroiled in coercive interactions with others, and the result is an escalation of violence.

In the coercion process, behavior is controlled by the presentation and withdrawal of aversive stimuli. The process begins when one member presents what another member *perceives* as an aversive stimulus. His reaction in turn, is to present an aversive response to the other person. The interchange continues until one member withdraws his aversive stimulus, at which point the other reciprocates and withdraws his. Thus, there are *two* identical sets of escape processes, one for each member of the dyad; each member provides aversive stimuli for the other. By the same token, each is reinforced by the withdrawal of the aversive stimulus presented by the other. If either member does not terminate, then the interaction is likely to continue with a steady escalation of the intensity of the pain being delivered. (p. 83)

When a child is attacked by a peer, he may quickly learn that a counterattack will terminate his tormentor's aggression. After several successful and rewarding counterattacks, he may begin launching attacks of his own. Eventually, his victim's reactions may come to serve as positive reinforcers for his attacks, and the very presence of the victim may then provide the occasion for aggression. Thus, the aggressor is trained and trains others in coercive techniques. Tedeschi, Smith, and Brown (1974) also have suggested that coercive power is the essential element in aggressive interactions.

Parents may, according to Patterson and Cobb, be shaped to initiate physical assaults on their children by the children themselves. The mother or father may learn that aversive child behavior (e.g., crying, whining, arguing, messing about) can be quickly terminated by hitting. If the child begins to stop his aversive actions only after suffering hits of increasing force, the vicious cycle of coercion may begin.

Patterson and his fellow researchers do not pretend to have shown conclusively that their theory of coercion or training in aggression by negative reinforcement is correct. The theory represents speculation based on a large amount of data. These data do show convincingly, however, that in family interactions aggressive behaviors such as hitting are increased in probability when they are followed by aversive events—aggression almost invariably increases aggression.

### Control of Aggression

Most of our discussion of the control of aggression will be found in the concluding section of this chapter, "Applied Analysis of Social Behavior." We will summarize here, however, the findings regarding several important issues.

Theories of aggressive behavior that include concepts of "drive" or "instinct" or some other *something* that accumulates within the organism lead to the assumption that aggression can be reduced by draining off this store. The term most often applied to the draining off or purging of the aggression "reservoir" is *catharsis*. It is suggested that catharsis can be achieved through *sublimation* (e.g., engaging in contact sports where aggression serves some socially sanctioned or constructive purpose), *displacement* (e.g., aggressing against a substitute and socially acceptable target, such as a punching bag or doll), or *fantasy* (e.g., watching movies in which aggression is portrayed or imagining aggressive acts). Yet as Berkowitz (1973) has noted, "The catharsis idea has become practically a cultural truism, but unfortunately has been validated more by social consensus than by careful empirical research and penetrating analysis" (p. 103). The vast bulk of the evidence weighs against the catharsis hypothesis. In fact, Berkowitz (1973) has expressed the belief, based on his reviews (cf. also Berkowitz, 1962), that attempts to use catharsis as a means of reducing aggression would only lead to *increased* aggression. Berkowitz's belief seems clearly to be supported by the research of Patterson (Patterson & Cobb, 1971; Patterson, et al., 1967) and Friedrich and Stein (1973).

Several nonpunative methods of reducing aggression have been suggested. Berkowitz (1973) has raised the question of *stimulus satiation* —if children are repeatedly exposed to aggressive stimuli, will these stimuli eventually lessen in their ability to induce aggression? The research of Friedrich and Stein is relevant here. They found that children of higher socio-economic status who watched less violent television at home tended to be more aggressive after watching televised aggression. Their data did not strongly support the idea that children become sated on violence, however. "Even those groups with extensive histories of viewing violence showed some behavioral changes in response to such programs in the nursery school" (Friedrich & Stein, 1973, p. 59).

Quick and temporary removal from an aggression-evoking situation can be an effective means of reducing aggressive behavior (as we will discuss in more detail in our comments regarding "time-out" in the last section of this chapter). If the child can be made cognitively aware of the harmful consequences of aggressive behavior, that aggression is "bad" or "immoral," that the potential victim has desirable qualities, or that he shares common goals or emotions with the victim, he may be less likely to aggress. It is of utmost importance *not* to provide reinforcement for aggressive acts, but adults who are unresponsive or extremely permissive regarding aggression run the serious risk that their nonresponsiveness will be interpreted by the child as tacit approval (Berkowitz, 1973).

Punishment of aggression is fraught with difficulties, too. The punishing agent provides an aggressive model that the child may imitate, particularly in his interactions with weaker or lower social status children.

Furthermore, punishment involves events that are aversive (i.e., the presentation of negative reinforcers or withdrawal of positive reinforcers) and, as we have already discussed, aversive events breed coercion. Nevertheless, punishment should not be completely ruled out as a control technique. If the punishment is consistent, not excessively intense, delivered by a person who is usually warm and loving, and if reinforcement is available for alternative nonaggressive responses, punishment may be a useful control technique that does not produce undue adverse side effects (see Baer, 1971; Becker, 1964; Berkowitz, 1973).

## MORAL DEVELOPMENT

Since the mid-1950s there has been an upsurge of research into the development of conscience and moral values. The Watergate affair and its aftermath have undoubtedly kindled a new spark of interest in the topic of how people acquire and maintain standards of moral character and moral ideology. The topic is of particular interest to those who deal with children whose social behavior is chronically a source of consternation or a cause for rebuke. Moral behavior and moral training are of concern not only to parents, but also to educators; and they are of concern not only in our society which is dominated by democratic institutions and ideals, but also in the Soviet Union where the classroom is designed explicitly to produce good socialist citizens (cf. Bronfenbrenner, 1962; Iakobson, 1968; Smirnov, 1964). The topic of moral development is an extremely broad and complex one, encompassing behavioral, emotional, and judgmental aspects of a wide range of conduct, including aggression, cheating, altruism, and so on. Consequently, we will confine ourselves here to a brief sketch of some theoretical issues and summaries. In the next two sections of this chapter we will address the topics of family and school influences on social development, including aspects of moral behavior.

### Development of Moral Judgment

Moral judgment refers not to moral knowledge (i.e., awareness of social rules or expectations) but to the child's interpretation and use of rules in conflict situations and the reasons he gives for moral actions. Much of the theoretical basis for the current perspective on the development of moral judgment was provided by Piaget (1932, 1948). In brief, Piaget's contention—based partly on his questioning of Swiss children about their beliefs regarding the rules of the game of marbles—is that children three to eight years of age tend to hold that moral rules are fixed and eternal. They have this opinion because their cognitive limitations prevent them from distinguishing clearly between their own experience and that of others and between objective and subjective reality. Furthermore, the young child sees his parents as the perfect and sacred source of moral authority. At about the age of eight or ten, Piaget says, children naturally develop a belief in "autonomous" justice morality which represents a logical form of concern for reciprocity and equality among individuals. This higher level of moral judgment is derived from the interaction of the child with his peers.

The view of Piaget and his followers regarding age changes in several aspects of moral judgment have been summarized by Kohlberg (1964) as follows:

1. *Intentionality in judgment.* Young children tend to judge an act as bad mainly in terms of its actual physical consequences, whereas older children judge an act as bad in terms of the intent to do harm. As an example, children were asked who was worse—a child who broke five cups while helping his mother set the table or a boy who broke one cup while stealing some jam. Almost all four-year-olds say the child who committed the larger accidental damage was worse (as do about 60 per cent of six-year-olds); whereas the majority of nine-year-olds say the "thief" was worse (Boehm and Nass, 1962; Caruso, 1943; Janis, 1961; Lerner, 1937a; MacRae, 1954; Piaget, 1932).

2. *Relativism in judgment.* The young child views an act as either totally right or totally wrong, and thinks everyone views it in the same way. If the young child does recognize a conflict in views, he believes the adult's view is always the right one. In contrast, the older child is aware of possible diversity in views of right and wrong. As an example, children were told a story in which a lazy pupil is forbidden by his teacher to receive any help in his homework. A friendly classmate does help the pupil. The children were then asked whether the friendly classmate thinks he is right or wrong for helping, whether the lazy pupil would think he was right or wrong, what the teacher would think, and so on. The majority of six-year-olds expected only one judgment on which everyone would agree; for example, they would say that the helping classmate would think he was wrong to help. By age nine, a majority of children recognized that there would be more than one perspective on moral value in the situation (Lerner, 1937b; MacRae, 1954).

3. *Independence of sanctions.* The young child says an act is bad because it will elicit punishment; the older child says an act is bad because it violates a rule, does harm to others, and so forth (Kohlberg, 1963). For example, young children were asked to judge a help-

ful, obedient act (attentively watching a baby brother while the mother is away) followed by punishment (the mother returns and spanks the baby-sitting child). Many four-year-olds simply say the obedient boy was bad because he got punished, ignoring his act. More mature four to five-year-olds say the boy was bad because he must have done something bad to get punished; that is, they invent a misdeed to account for the punishment. By age seven, a majority say the boy was good, not bad, even though he was punished (Kohlberg, 1963).

4. *Use of reciprocity.* Four-year-old children do not use reciprocity as a reason for consideration of others, whereas children of seven and older frequently do. Even seven-year-olds show mainly selfish and concrete reciprocity concerns, including anticipation of retaliation and anticipation of return of favors. Most ten-year-olds who were asked "What would the Golden Rule say to do if a boy came up and hit you?" interpreted the Golden Rule in terms of concrete reciprocity and said, "Hit him back. Do unto others as they do unto you." By age eleven to thirteen most children can clearly judge in terms of ideal reciprocity, in terms of putting oneself in the place of someone in a different position, and in terms of sentiments of gratitude for past affection and favors (Kohlberg, 1958; Durkin, 1959).

5. *Use of punishment as restitution and reform.* Young children advocate severe painful punishment after stories of misdeeds; older children increasingly favor milder punishments leading to restitution to the victim and to the reform of the culprit (Harrower, 1934; Piaget, 1932; Johnson, 1962).

6. *Naturalistic views of misfortune.* Six to seven-year-old children have some tendency to view physical accidents and misfortunes occurring after misdeeds as punishments willed by God or by natural objects ("immanent justice"). Older children do not confuse natural misfortunes with punishment (Caruso, 1943; Lerner, 1937a; MacRae, 1954; Medinnus, 1959).[*] (pp. 396–398)

Kohlberg (1964, 1969) and Turiel (1973, 1974) have outlined stages of moral development based on Piaget's observations. Six stages have been briefly defined by Turiel (1974):

Stage 1:   Obedience and punishment orientation. Egocentric deference to superior power or prestige, or a trouble-avoiding set. Objective responsibility.

Stage 2:   Naively egoistic orientation. Right action is that instrumentally satisfying the self's needs and occasionally those of others.

[*] L. Kohlberg, "Development of Moral Character and Moral Ideology," in M. L. Hoffman and L. W. Hoffman (Eds.), *Review of Child Development Research*, Volume I, prepared under the auspices of the Society for Research in Child Development, © 1964 by Russell Sage Foundation and reprinted by permission.

Awareness of relativism of value to each actor's needs and perspective. Naive egalitarianism and orientation to exchange and reciprocity.

*Stage 3:* Good-boy orientation. Orientation to approval and to pleasing and helping others. Conformity to stereotypical images of majority or natural role behavior, and judgment by intentions.

*Stage 4:* Authority and social-order maintaining orientation. Orientation toward authority, fixed rules, and the maintenance of the social order. Right behavior consists of doing one's duty, showing respect for authority, and maintaining the given social order for its own sake. Morality is not based on individual or personal values and judgments.

*Stage 5:* Contractual legalistic orientation. Right action is defined in terms of individual rights and of standards which have been initially examined and agreed upon by the whole society. Emphasis is upon procedural rules for reaching consensus and ensuring general welfare. Concern with establishing and maintaining individual rights, equality, and liberty. Distinctions are made between values having universal, prescriptive applicability and values specific to a given society.

*Stage 6:* The universal-ethical-principle orientation. Right is defined by the decision of conscience in accord with self-chosen ethical principles appealing to logical comprehensiveness, universality, and consistency. These principles are abstract; they are not concrete moral rules. These are universal principles of justice, of the reciprocity and equality of human rights, and of respect for the dignity of human beings and individual persons.* (pp. 14–15)

## Development of Moral Attitudes and Emotions

The development of moral judgment is related to but not synonomous with the development of conscience, character, superego, or feelings of guilt, anxiety, or remorse following transgression. It has been found that young children typically fantasize that punishment will follow transgression. As children grow older, fantasies of confession, guilt, or self-criticism increase (cf. Kohlberg, 1964). Apparently, as children mature and experience punishment and blame associated with transgression they come to internalize the standards of external authority. Parents, peers, and other socialization agents undoubtedly induce moral attitudes or sensitize the child to moral precepts through punishment,

* E. Turiel, "Conflict and Transition in Adolescent Moral Development," *Child Development*, 1974, 45, 14–15. Reprinted by permission.

love, withdrawal, reasoning, modeling, and encouraging the child to "take the role of the other" in situations of moral conflict. But the exact relationship between moral attitudes and such induction and sensitization processes is not known. As we shall see later in this chapter, however, there is some evidence that induction (i.e., reasoning, love-oriented techniques) is superior to sensitization (i.e., punishing, power-assertive techniques) in developing desirable attitudes toward transgression.

### Development of Moral Behavior

A child's moral judgment and attitude may not, of course, match his moral conduct. Children frequently express "good" moral judgment and sentiment, but commit moral transgressions when faced with a conflict situation (e.g., a situation in which they can be either honest or cheat and "get away with it"). The exact relationship between cognitive development and the development of moral judgment and moral conduct is not fully understood (cf. Stephens, McLaughlin, Hunt, Mahoney, Kohlberg, Moore, & Aronfreed, 1974). Even so, it is generally believed that children of higher intelligence, social class, and peer group status tend to be more advanced in both moral judgment and moral conduct, though judgment and conduct appear to respond differentially to situational factors.

> The picture of moral development emerging from the moral judgment findings contrasts in several ways with the picture derived from the findings on moral conduct. Judgment does not appear to become "moral" until early adolescence, while "morality" of conduct appears to develop early. Individual differences in level of moral judgment are quite general and stable; morality of conduct is more specific to the situation and more unstable over time. Moral judgment appears to develop in the same direction regardless of social groups; moral conduct appears to develop in line with specific social class and peer-group norms.* (Kohlberg, 1964, p. 408)

The impact of moral education or "character education" by parents, schools, and churches on children's moral conduct appears to be very weak. Future research, however, may conceivably establish long-range effects that have not appeared in evaluations of immediate conformity to moral codes (Kohlberg, 1964). It does seem obvious that the family and the school are the source of much moralizing, and that parents and

---

* L. Kohlberg, "Development of Moral Character and Moral Ideology," in M. L. Hoffman and L. W. Hoffman (Eds.), *Review of Child Development Research*, Volume I, prepared under the auspices of the Society for Research in Child Development, © 1964 by Russell Sage Foundation and reprinted by permission.

teachers as socialization agents are likely to be profoundly influential in establishing moral conduct, although the effects of explicit moral instruction sessions seem to be rather frail or distant.

*How,* not whether, parents and teachers will influence moral conduct is the question at hand. At present it appears that much of the child's moral training involves punishment, threat of punishment, or rebuke. This approach to moral training seems to produce inferior results compared with an approach that induces moral conduct through reasoning and explanation (cf. Hoffman, 1970; Leizer & Rogers, 1974). Goldiamond (1968) has advanced the notion that moral education could be made effective by using positive reinforcement for desirable moral choices rather than punishment or threat, the effects of which are often destructive:

> Laboratory research in behavior analysis suggests that we might turn our attention to the possibility of establishing moral and other discriminations without extinction and aversive control, but using errorless procedures that provide continual reinforcement. It may thereby be possible to program behavioral relations with the environment which are dictated by conscience, which are moral, and which are altruistic, but at the same time are spontaneous, existential and free, since they have been programmed without fear or threat. (p. 70)

The behavioral analysis of moral conduct and the application of that analysis to moral training are still only suggestive. More positive and effectual methods of moral education are needed. The behavioral approach offers a ray of hope.

## FAMILY INFLUENCES ON SOCIALIZATION

It is well known that "in all societies, the nuclear family is the initial matrix within which personality is rooted and nourished" (Clausen, 1966, p. 1). Frequent topics for investigation have included models of parent and child behavior (Schaefer, 1971), parent-child similarity and imitation (Hetherington, 1967), family structure and its effects on personality development (Clausen, 1966), the relationship of interactions in families to child psychopathology (Hetherington & Martin, 1972; Mishler & Waxler, 1968), the application of social learning principles to family life (Patterson, 1971), and parental discipline (Becker, 1964). We shall focus our attention here on parental discipline and its effects on children's aggression and moral development.

Becker (1964) has drawn a model of parental behavior in which various types of parents can be located according to their discipline techniques. His three-dimensional model (Figure 10.2) includes the continua of warmth versus hostility, restrictiveness versus permissiveness, and calm detachment versus anxious emotional involvement.

The warmth versus hostility dimension is defined at the warm end by variables of the following sort: accepting, affectionate, approving, understanding, child-centered, frequent use of explanations, positive response to dependency behavior, high use of reasons in discipline, high use of praise in discipline, low use of physical punishment, and (for mothers) low criticism of husband. The hostility end of the dimension would be defined by the opposite characteristics. The restrictiveness versus permissiveness dimension is defined at the restrictive end by: many restrictions and strict enforcement of demands in the areas of sex play, modesty

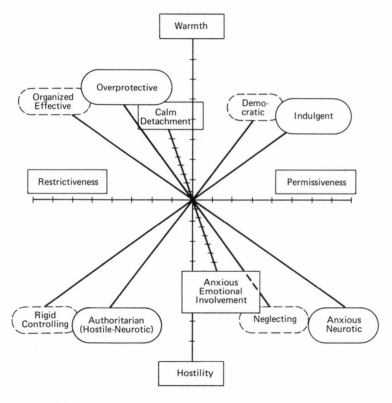

FIGURE 10.2.
Becker's hypothetical model for parental behavior.

Source: W. C. Becker, "Consequences of Different Kinds of Parental Discipline," in M. L. Hoffman and L. W. Hoffman, Review of Child Development Research, Volume I, p. 175, prepared under the auspices of the Society for Research in Child Development, © 1964 by Russell Sage Foundation. Reprinted by permission.

behavior, table manners, toilet training, neatness, orderliness, care of household furniture, noise, obedience, aggression to sibs, aggression to peers, and aggression to parents. Anxious emotional involvement versus calm-detachment is defined at the anxious end by: high emotionality in relation to child, babying, ˙protectiveness, and solicitousness for the child's welfare. . . . For example, both the democratic parent and the indulgent parent (by definition) are high on the dimensions of warmth and permissiveness, but the indulgent parent is high on emotional involvement while the democratic parent tends to be low on this dimension (calm-detached). Both the organized-effective ˎparent and the overprotective parent are high on warmth and restrictiveness, but the overprotective parent again shows more emotional involvement than the organized-effective parent. The argument can be thus carried around the model, showing how the typical concepts for types of parents can be thought of as being defined by various combinations of three dimensions of parent behavior.* (Becker, 1964, pp. 174–175)

The calm detachment-emotional involvement dimension has not been adequately researched, but supporting evidence is available regarding statements of the consequences of restrictive versus permissive and warm versus hostile discipline. It is not surprising, in view of our previous discussion in this chapter, that parents who use hostile, power-assertive techniques of discipline tend to produce aggression and resistance to authority in their children, whereas parents who employ warm, love-oriented techniques tend to encourage a higher level of prosocial behavior and self-responsibility. Too, as might have been expected, power-assertive techniques tend to sensitize children to the fear of punishment and expectation of the hostility of external authority, whereas love-oriented techniques tend to induce feelings of guilt and internalized reactions to transgression. Restrictive discipline techniques generally foster inhibited behavior, whereas permissive discipline usually produces uninhibited behavior in children (Becker, 1964).

The interactive effects of warm versus hostile and restrictive versus permissive discipline may be more important than their simple effects. Table 10.4 is a summary (after Becker, 1964, p. 198) of findings related to these interactive effects.

Another factor affecting child behavior is consistency in parental discipline. It seems quite clear that inconsistent discipline has a deleterious effect, producing increased levels of aggression, conflict, and delinquency and less than optimal moral development. Yet, as Becker (1964) has pointed out, inconsistency can take many forms and little is

---

* W. C. Becker, "Consequences of Different Kinds of Parental Discipline," in M. L. Hoffman & L. W. Hoffman (Eds.), *Review of Child Development Research*, Volume 1, pp. 174–175, © 1964 by Russell Sage Foundation and reprinted with permission.

TABLE 10.4    Interactions in the Consequences of Warmth vs. Hostility and
Restrictiveness vs. Permissiveness in Parental Discipline

|  | *Restrictiveness* | *Permissiveness* |
|---|---|---|
| Warmth | Submissiveness<br>Dependence<br>Politeness<br>Neatness<br>Obedience<br>Minimum aggression<br>Maximum rule enforcement<br>   for boys<br>Dependence<br>Unfriendliness<br>Lack of creativity<br>Maximal compliance | Activeness<br>Social outgoingness and friendliness<br>Creativity<br>Successful aggression<br>Minimal rule enforcement for boys<br>Facilitation of adult role-taking<br>Minimal self-aggression for boys<br>Independence<br>Low projective hostility |
| Hostility | Neuroticism<br>Quarreling and shyness with<br>   peers<br>Social withdrawal<br>Inhibition of adult role-taking<br>Maximal self-aggression for boys | Delinquency<br>Noncompliance<br>Maximal aggression |

Source: W. C. Becker, "Consequences of Different Kinds of Parental Discipline," in
M. L. Hoffman and L. W. Hoffman, Review of Child Development Research, Volume I, p. 198, prepared under the auspices of the Society for Research in Child
Development, © 1964 by Russell Sage Foundation. Reprinted by permission.

known regarding the differential effects of specific types of inconsistent
discipline. Parental discipline can be inconsistent in that one parent is
restrictive and the other permissive or one hostile and the other warm
and loving. Inconsistency may also take the form of capriciousness, the
parent at one time permitting or rewarding a behavior and at another
time rebuking or severely punishing it. Or inconsistency could arise in
the discrepancy between what a parent says (e.g., threatening punishment) and what he does (e.g., not following through on the threat). In
any event, there is little reason to doubt the harmful effect of any type of
inconsistency in discipline. While rigidity is not an appropriate goal and
perfect consistency is an unattainable goal, parents and teachers would
be well advised to examine carefully the consistency with which they
apply expectations and consequences for their children's behavior.

## THE SCHOOL AS
## A SOCIALIZATION AGENT

It is not an unheard opinion that the family has such a pervasive
influence on children's behavior that the school is essentially a powerless
instrument for change. This opinion is based on an underestimation of

the centrality of school in the life of the child after the age of five or six. Failure at school is tantamount to failure at life for most children, whereas school success enhances the child's self-realization. Hewett (1968) has expressed confidence in the value of school even for seriously emotionally disturbed children:

> Despite the 19 or 20 hours emotionally disturbed children must spend outside the school each day, often in deplorable surroundings and malignant family relationships, the author is convinced four to six positive hours in the classroom can make a significant difference in their lives* (p. 40).

Similar confidence in the ability of school to be a significant force for desirable behavior change has been expressed by others who have been involved in the education of disturbed children (cf. Kauffman & Lewis, 1974).

The social structure of the classroom and the sociopsychological relationships that develop among the teacher and pupils are complex phenomena that have been under study for at least thirty years. It is possible now to make some generalizations regarding certain facets of the socialization process in the classroom with a relatively high degree of confidence. One of these generalizations is related to our previous discussion of aggression: A teacher's use of punishment and negative reinforcement as primary control techniques will produce the same effects as the use of these techniques by parents, namely counteraggression and coercion. Alternatively, if positive reinforcement of appropriate behavior is stressed, it is likely that aggressive and disruptive behavior will subside (Becker, 1971; O'Leary & O'Leary, 1972; Worell & Nelson, 1974). The teacher who wishes to be a good influence on the child's social development, therefore, should be extremely cautious in the use of punishment and unflagging in the use of positive reinforcement for appropriate behavior.

Another generalization that seems clearly to be supported by research involves the circular, self-perpetuating nature of social adjustment in the classroom. A child who enters the classroom with upper-middle class status, good health, high intelligence, and well-developed social skills is likely to have high self-esteem and to perceive others and their reactions to him accurately. His perceptions of social situations and interactions are likely to serve him well. If he behaves in a way that induces a positive response from the environment he tends to repeat that

---

* From Frank M. Hewett, *The Emotionally Disturbed Child in the Classroom*, p. 40. Copyright © 1968 by Allyn and Bacon, Inc. Reprinted by permission.

approach, and if his behavior receives a negative evaluation he will be perceptive and confident enough to try a new approach. His intelligence, sensitivity, and adaptability make him a positive social stimulus to others; they reciprocally strengthen the very behaviors that increase his social status and personal satisfactions by their responses to him. On the other hand, children who enter the classroom with sociopsychological deficiences—for example, children who might be considered ED, LD, or EMR—immediately risk being pulled into a spiral of increasing maladjustment (see Long, 1974). As one group of child psychologists has put it:

> Consider the child who enters the classroom with less vigorous health, with limited intellect, inadequate interpersonal skills, from the lower classes. He is likely to have a low level of self-esteem and relatively high anxiety. The data indicate that he is likely to initiate interaction with his peers and the teacher with awkwardness, and that he is likely to induce responses which are, at best, a restrained embarrassment, or at worst, hostile ridicule. He is likely to feel humiliated to some degree, and is likely to respond with some degree of either aggression or withdrawal, or both in alternation. If he responds with aggression, he is likely to promote counteraggression. If he responds with withdrawal, he is likely to promote some form of passive rejection or counterwithdrawal. It has even been noted (Lippitt and Gold, 1959) that the low-status boys—often aggressive and troublesome—evoke more criticism from the teacher than do their high-status classmates; while the low-status girls— often overdependent and passive—receive more support from the teacher. Although the teacher's reaction is understandable, it increases hostility and dependency, respectively. The response of the others—peers or teacher—to this child's interaction attempts are not likely to increase his self-esteem or his interpersonal skills. He is likely to distort his perception of the responses by denial or projection in order to protect whatever limited self-esteem he can marshall in the face of his rejection by others. His utilization of his intelligence is likely to be reduced. Again, a self-sustaining circular process is established. Rejection breeds defensiveness, perceptual distortions, further aggression or withdrawal, and reduction in self-esteem. Further aggression or withdrawal and further counteraggression or passive rejection complete the circle, and symptoms of emotional conflict and disturbance appear.* (Glidewell, Kantor, Smith, & Stringer, 1966, p. 248)

The structured approach of Haring and Phillips (1962) to educating children with social behavior deficits was designed specifically

---

* J. C. Glidewell, M. B. Kantor, L. M. Smith, & L. A. Stringer, "Socialization and Social Structure in the Classroom," in L. W. Hoffman & M. L. Hoffman (Eds.), *Review of Child Development Research*, Volume 2, p. 248, © 1966 by Russell Sage Foundation and reprinted by permission.

to interfere in such a maladaptive cycle of behavior. Their assumption was that children live by their assertions about how events occur. Emotionally disturbed children, they hypothesized, became entrapped in a vicious cycle of making assertions that are inappropriate (and, therefore, usually disconfirmed), experiencing the anxiety and distortion of social perception that results from disconfirmation, and making more mistakes based on these unreliable perceptions. Haring and Phillips interfered in this maladaptive cycle by "structuring" the classroom environment, that is, by making the expectations for the child and the consequences for his behavior very clear and consistent or predictable. In this kind of environment the child could gradually learn the consequences of his actions and bring his perceptions into line with reality. Eventually, it was hoped, he would learn the skills of self-management and the interpersonal skills that would allow him to enter the self-enhancing cycle of behavior-environment interactions—those that seem so natural to the child with good social adjustment.

As we mentioned in Chapter 1, Haring and Phillips, Cruickshank, Whelan, and others provided a foundation of classroom management procedures that may be seen as a simple form of current applied behavior analysis. The structured approach and, as we shall see later in this chapter, applied behavior analysis are powerful methods for remediating children's social excesses and deficits and for helping them to enter what Baer and Wolf (1970) have described as a "natural community of reinforcement."

## LONGITUDINAL STUDIES
## OF BEHAVIOR DISORDERS

Robins (1972) has noted that longitudinal or follow-up studies can be conducted to answer a variety of research questions: Who in a certain population will develop psychopathology? What hereditary factors, social settings, early behavior, or child-rearing practices predispose individuals to psychopathological disorders? How long do behavior disorders persist? How effective is a given treatment? What behavior in children predicts adult adjustment? It is our purpose here to suggest answers to only two questions: (1) What early behaviors of the child predict the gloomiest picture of his later adjustment? and (2) What child-rearing practices bode ill for children who are difficult to manage?

For many years it was a popular belief that the aggressive or conduct-disordered child, although an immediate source of pain to others, was not so seriously maladjusted as the shy, withdrawn child. There was suspicion that the quietness and seclusiveness of the personality-problem

or neurotic child were precursors of schizophrenia or other serious psychiatric disorders in adulthood. It now appears that exactly the reverse
is true. Childhood "neuroticism" does not seem to predict adult maladjustment, but conduct problems—hostility, aggression, destructiveness,
antisocial behavior—and school failure seem to foretell grave difficulties
later in life, especially for boys (Robins, 1966, 1972; Watt, Stolorow,
Lubensky, & McClelland, 1970; White & Charry, 1966). Hyperactivity
and learning problems in the early school years, characteristics frequently
associated with the diagnosis of learning disability, do not lead to an
optimistic prediction for children's later school adjustment (Minde,
Lewin, Weiss, Lavigueur, Douglas, & Sykes, 1971; Rubin & Balow, 1971).
This is not surprising in view of the fact that "the ability of the child
to learn . . . school tasks no doubt constitutes a major criterion for adjustment, since for the child there is basically one set of outside norms
(the school) and one essential job (academic success)" (Glavin, 1972,
p. 375).

The most serious difficulties of children in relation to their later
social adjustment are conduct disorders and school failure: The evidence
for this assertion is convincing. Given that the most prevalent type of
behavior in classes for ED, LD, and (we suspect) EMR children is conduct disorder and academic incompetence, the heavy responsibility of
the teacher is obvious.

In a longitudinal study in which the course of development of 136
children was followed from early infancy, Thomas, Chess, and Birch
(1968) examined the interactive effects of temperament and environmental influences on behavior. They were particularly interested in temperament because of their belief that environmental influences alone are
insufficient to explain the range and variability in individual children's
behavior.

> Temperament is the *behavioral style* of the individual child—the *how*
> rather than the *what* (abilities and content) or *why* (motivations) of be-
> havior. Temperament is a phenomenologic term used to describe the
> characteristic tempo, rhythmicity, adaptability, energy expenditure,
> mood, and focus of attention of a child independently of the content of
> any specific behavior.* (p. 4)

Careful analysis of clinical data obtained over a period of more than
a decade led Thomas and his co-workers to identify two basic patterns of
temperament: "easy children" and "difficult children." Most of the easy

* Reprinted by permission of New York University Press from *Temperament
and Behavior Disorders in Children* by Alexander Thomas et al., © 1968 by New
York University.

children did not develop behavior problems. They were easy to care for; predominantly positive in mood; very regular, low, or mild in their reactions; quickly adaptable; and unusually positive in approaching new situations. Experienced mothers recognized their good fortune in having an "easy" baby, and these children often contributed to their mothers' convictions that they were good, effective, or skillful parents. In contrast, the difficult children were characterized by irregularity in biological functions; predominantly negative (i.e., withdrawn) in their responses to new stimuli; slow to adapt to changes of environment, frequently expressed a negative mood; and intense in their reactions. The characteristics of difficult children were observed by their mothers and the researchers before the children were two years of age, and it was many of these youngsters who later developed behavior disorders. The development of behavior disorders in difficult children was not inevitable, however. Behavioral dysfunction was seen to be the result of interaction between the temperamental characteristics of the child and his environment, particularly the reactions of his parents. Furthermore, this interaction implied a *reciprocal* influence in which the child's temperament was modified by parental behavior and vice versa.

> The differences in the developmental courses of difficult children which result from differences in parent-child interactions are illustrated by the contrasting behavioral courses of two of the study children. Both youngsters, one a girl and the other a boy, showed similar characteristics of behavioral functioning in the early years of life, with irregular sleep patterns, constipation and painful evacuations at times, slow acceptance of new foods, prolonged adjustment periods to new routines, and frequent and loud periods of crying. Adaptation to nursery school in the fourth year was also a problem for both children. Parental attitudes and practices, however, differed greatly. The girl's father was usually angry with her. In speaking of her, he gave the impression of disliking the youngster and was punitive and spent little or no recreational time with her. The mother was more concerned for the child, more understanding, and more permissive, but quite inconsistent. There was only one area in which there was firm but quiet parental consistency, namely, with regard to safety rules. The boy's parents, on the other hand, were unusually tolerant and consistent. The child's lengthy adjustment periods were accepted calmly; his strident altercations with his younger siblings were dealt with good-humoredly. The parents waited out his negative moods without getting angry. They tended to be very permissive, but set safety limits and consistently pointed out the needs and rights of his peers at play.
> By the age of five and a half years, these two children, whose initial characteristics had been so similar, showed marked differences in behavior. The boy's initial difficulties in nursery school had disappeared,

he was a constructive member of his class, had a group of friends with whom he exchanged visits, and functioned smoothly in most areas of daily living. The girl, on the other hand, had developed a number of symptoms of increasing severity. These included explosive anger, negativism, fear of the dark, encopresis, thumb-sucking, insatiable demands for toys and sweets, poor peer relationships, and protective lying. It is of interest that there was no symptomatology of negativism in the one area where parental practice had been firmly consistent, i.e., safety rules.

The boy, though his early handling had been difficult for his parents, was never considered by them to have a behavioral disturbance. They understood that the youngster's troublesome behavior was the expression of his own characteristics. With this constructive parental approach, these troublesome items of behavior did not become transformed into symptoms of a behavior disorder. The girl, in contrast, suffered the consequences of parental functioning which was excessively stressful for a child with her temperamental attributes and developed a neurotic behavior disorder.* (Thomas, et al., 1968, pp. 82–83)

Interaction of temperament and environment, rather than physiological status or environmental demand alone, was apparently the most viable explanation for behavioral development even in the children with brain damage (Thomas, et al., 1968). Thus, one cannot in all cases set an arbitrary standard for parenting behavior that is "good" or "bad" aside from the extant behavioral patterns of the child. Nevertheless, the cases described by Thomas, Chess, and Birch do clearly illustrate the devastating effects of two parenting variables—inconsistency and a hostile, punitive approach to discipline—on the child's development. The observations of these researchers are entirely consistent with the findings regarding inconsistency, punishment, and aggression that we discussed earlier.

## ASSESSMENT OF SOCIAL BEHAVIOR

Traditionally, the child's social behavior has been assessed by means of psychological testing and clinical observation or interviews. The validity and reliability of these methods, and consequently their usefulness in designing psychoeducational interventions, are limited (cf. Levine, 1966; O'Leary, 1972). Three types of assessment that have shown greater promise or actual value in education are "screening," "behavior rating," and "target assessment." Screening has as its objective the early identifi-

---

* Reprinted by permission of New York University Press from *Temperament and Behavior Disorders in Children* by Alexander Thomas et al., © 1968 by New York University.

cation of children's social problems or the early detecting of those children who are likely to develop significant problems. In screening, the person using the assessment device is cast in the role Bower (1969) describes as a "suspectition." Behavior rating scales rely on the somewhat subjective evaluation of a child's behavior by a parent, teacher, other adult, or peer. Descriptors are provided, and the rater must decide whether or not or to what degree the child's behavior fits the description. Some screening techniques rely heavily upon rating scales or consist entirely of them, but not all behavior rating scales were designed as screening instruments. Target assessment refers to the precise definition and continuous recording of specific behaviors in order to assess their quantitative level and any changes which may occur. This is the method of assessment associated with applied behavior analysis.

### Screening

A number of screening tests designed to select children with potential academic learning problems are designed to assess the child's social status or skills as well (e.g., *A Psychoeducational Inventory of Basic Learning Abilities*, Valett, 1968; *First Grade Screening Test*, Pate & Webb, 1969). Long, Fagen, and Stevens (1971) have devised a screening instrument to identify resourceful (normal), marginal (weak in some areas, but can make a successful adjustment with proper handling in the regular classroom), and vulnerable (failure seems inevitable without special education) pupils. The screening instrument is comprised of several different elements involving ratings by the pupil himself, the teacher, and the school nurse or someone else who can identify significant events in the child's life history. However, the best-known instrument designed explicitly for screening children for potential social learning problems is Bower and Lambert's (1962) *A Process for In-School Screening of Children with Emotional Handicaps.* The process includes a behavior rating of pupils by the teacher for children in kindergarten through grade twelve. For each of eight descriptive statements (e.g., "This pupil gets into fights or quarrels with other pupils more often than others") the teacher must decide which pupils best fit and which least fit the description. Also included in the process is a peer rating and a self-rating system formulated with the age of the children in mind. For kindergarten through third grade the peer rating is called "Class Pictures" and requires that each child in the class identify the classmate he thinks would act like a specified child in a series of pictures depicting adaptive and maladaptive behavior. The self-rating for kindergarten through grade three, "Picture Game," requires each child to sort a group of pictures into "sad" and "happy" piles. For grades four through seven, the peer rating consists of having each child in the class choose the classmate he thinks would be best cast in a specified role (e.g., "A mean, cruel boss") or choose the role he thinks others would choose for him in "A Class Play." Children in grades four through seven complete the self-rating ("Self-Test") part of the process by rating descriptors (e.g., "This boy daydreams a lot") in terms of whether he would like very much to be or would very much not want to be like the boy (or girl) described. For older children, grades seven through twelve, the "Self-Test" is essentially the same. The peer rating for older children is a "Student Survey" in which each pupil names another he believes is best described by a statement (e.g., "A student who is good in school work"). If the child is rated in negative terms by his peers, himself, and his teacher, it is quite likely that his behavior should be evaluated further; one would be justified in *suspecting,* but not concluding, that he has a social-emotional disability. Teacher ratings alone, however, have been shown to be quite effective in identifying troubled children, especially those with conduct disorders (Bower, 1969; Nelson, 1971).

Early identification has been viewed by many as an important aspect of helping children with learning or behavior disorders. It has also been considered the most significant factor in primary prevention. Keogh and Becker (1973) have pointed out that early detection carries with it some dangers as well as benefits, however. If the child is identified early as a member of a highly stigmatized group or if he is identified but appropriate remedial services are not available for him, then the psychological damage to him and his family may be greater than the benefits. As Wallace and Kauffman (1973) have also noted:

> Until very recently . . . few schools have attempted to use any systematic procedures to identify incipient problems because special services have been available only for those children with the most obvious and disturbing learning deficits (Morse, Cutler, & Fink, 1964). There is little point in identifying problems for which no services are available. Identification under such circumstances highlights the inadequacy of the schools and tends to create pressure for inappropriate solutions. (pp. 82–83)

## Rating Scales

Several behavior rating scales have been developed for the purpose of evaluating children's current behavioral status and their response to treatment programs (Haring & Phillips, 1962; Hewett, 1968; Quay & Peterson, 1967; Spivack & Spotts, 1966; Walker, 1969). Most of these scales consist of a series of statements (e.g., "This student showed concern with progress in arithmetic." "Expresses fears that are unreasonable") or traits (e.g., "Child's ability and willingness to help others") on which the teacher, parent, or other adult must rate the child according to a numerical value (e.g., 1: never, 2: rarely, 3: sometimes, 4: often, 5: always). The numerical score of the child or the average score for a group is then used as a quantitative description of behavior. Although such rating scales obviously are limited by the rater's subjectivity in assigning a quantitative value to a rather vague or global characteristic, they have been useful to some extent in the evaluation of educational programs (e.g., Haring & Phillips, 1962; Hewett, 1968). The checklist developed by Quay and Peterson (1967), which defines behaviors relatively objectively and requires quantitative judgment over a rather restricted range, obviously has been of value in identifying dimensions of disordered behavior.

### Target Assessment

The assessment technique that is of greatest utility, at least from the educator's viewpoint, is target assessment. This is the technique also that demands the greatest amount of individualization, for it entails describing and recording that specific behavior of the individual child which is constituting a problem. The problem must be defined as an observable event that can be measured reliably in terms of its frequency, rate (i.e., frequency per unit time), or percentage. If such data are obtained and plotted over a succession of days, one obtains a useful assessment of the level of the problem behavior and can estimate also any changes resulting from an intervention program. The value of this type of assessment should be obvious in our discussion of applied behavior analysis in this and other chapters.

## PROGRAMS TO
## DEVELOP SOCIAL SKILLS

The usual school curriculum, especially reading and social studies, provides opportunities for discussion of social behavior, feelings, motivations, and so on. Furthermore, classroom incidents, such as teasing, bullying, sharing, cooperating, provide the perceptive and competent teacher with frequent opportunities to discuss social learning or teach social skills. The usual curriculum and classroom incidents, however, relegate social learning to the realm of the adventitious or incidental. Clearly, it would be desirable, at least for those children with social learning deficits, to have a planned program for teaching specific social skills.

In the early 1960s, Ojemann (Hawkins & Ojemann, 1960; Kremenak & Ojemann, 1965; Ojemann, 1961) developed a human behavior curriculum in conjunction with the Preventive Psychiatry Research Program at the University of Iowa. His program was designed to replace children's "nonthinking" (surface) analysis of social problems with a "thinking" (causal) one. Stories, incidents, cartoons, problems, and activities provided the beginning point for a discussion that sought to bring out the dynamic reasons for behavior. "Learning what emotions people have is not sufficient. The many different ways in which emotional behavior may develop, the variety of alternative ways of meeting emotional problems, and the probable effects of the various alternative ways need emphasis" (Ojemann, 1961, p. 386). Ojemann's approach was basically one of looking for psychiatric-dynamic "causal" factors, such as feelings of inferiority and rejection, in children's behavior. The assumption underlying this approach is that through gaining *insight* into the dynamics of behavior the child will learn how to behave more adaptively. This assumption has not received convincing support from research data (see Becker, 1971; Hobbs, 1974; Worell & Nelson, 1974).

More recently, Long and his colleagues (Fagen, Long, & Stevens, 1975; Long, 1974) have developed a curriculum for teaching self-control skills. The capacity for self-control is seen as a composite of eight different skill areas that can be taught in units, as shown in Table 10.5. For each curriculum unit specific activities are provided. Many of these activities are games or tasks than can easily be integrated into the regular academic curriculum. A number of the activities are similar or identical to those suggested by others for the remediation of perceptual, perceptual-motor, or academic difficulties (e.g., identifying foreground objects and hidden-figure tasks for mastering figure-ground discrimination, which is Unit 2 in the Selection area of the curriculum in Table 10.5). The purposes of teaching these skills are primarily related to the control of disruptive classroom behavior and to adequate school performance:

1. To reduce disruptiveness, improve school adjustment, and prevent behavior and learning disorders.

2. To strengthen the emotional and cognitive capacities which children need in order to cope with school requirements.

3. To build control skills which allow for an effective and socially acceptable choice of action.

4. To enhance value for the teacher-learner and educational process.

5. To promote a more desirable educational balance between cognitive and affective development than that which currently exists. (Fagen, Long, & Stevens, 1975, pp. 7–8)

TABLE 10.5    Self-Control Curriculum: Overview of Curriculum Areas and Units

| Curriculum Area | Curriculum Unit |
| --- | --- |
| Selection | 1. Focusing and concentration<br>2. Mastering figure-ground discrimination<br>3. Mastering distractions and interference<br>4. Processing complex patterns |
| Storage | 1. Developing visual memory<br>2. Developing auditory memory |
| Sequencing and ordering | 1. Developing time orientation<br>2. Developing auditory-visual sequencing<br>3. Developing sequential planning |
| Anticipating consequences | 1. Developing alternatives<br>2. Evaluating consequences |
| Appreciating feelings | 1. Identifying feelings<br>2. Developing positive feelings<br>3. Managing feelings<br>4. Reinterpreting feeling events |
| Managing frustration | 1. Accepting feelings of frustration<br>2. Building coping resources<br>3. Tolerating frustration |
| Inhibition and delay | 1. Controlling action<br>2. Developing part-goals |
| Relaxation | 1. Developing body relaxation<br>2. Developing thought relaxation<br>3. Developing movement relaxation |

Source: S. A. Fagen, N. J. Long, & D. J. Stevens, Teaching Children Self-Control: Preventing Emotional and Learning Problems in the Elementary School (Columbus, Ohio: Charles E. Merrill, 1975), p. 77. Reprinted by permission.

The rationale for the self-control curriculum was derived from the "psychoeducational" approach to behavior management which emphasizes the roles of feelings, self-understanding, introspection, and insight. However, the curriculum designers did integrate the affective domain with the cognitive and combine specific socio-emotional activities with more traditional academic tasks.

Taken together, the eight skills represent an integration of cognitive and affective factors which mediate possibilities for regulating action. The presence of these skills enables a learner to make personally and socially acceptable choices regarding task requirements—choices which preclude the feelings of inadequacy which so often accompany task performance or nonperformance. Through mastery of these self-control skills, the learner incorporates the necessary self-pride and respect for open-minded reflection on available alternatives.

The self-control curriculum focuses on the internal or mediating processes for skill achievement. Thus, tasks are predominantly process-oriented, with few activities requiring correct answers or narrow outputs.

We affirm that inner experiences (affects or thoughts) can be treated operationally so that significant improvement can occur in process skills which mediate response outcomes. (Fagen, Long, & Stevens, 1975, p. 44)

A social learning curriculum has been prepared by Goldstein (1974). Although the curriculum was developed primarily out of Goldstein's concern for the social learning deficits of the educable mentally retarded children be taught (see Goldstein, 1975), it is designed with all special students in mind, LD and ED as well as EMR. The goal of the social learning curriculum is to teach children to think critically and act independently to such an extent that they can become socially and occupationally competent. This means that children must be taught behaviors that range from managing their own personal affairs (e.g., finances, leisure time, communication, travel, health) to maintaining themselves independently. The curriculum is organized into ten phases, each containing fifteen to twenty lessons. These phases are: perceiving individuality, recognizing the environment, recognizing interdependence, recognizing the body, recognizing and reacting to emotions, recognizing what the senses do, communicating with others, getting along with others, identifying helpers, and maintaining body functions. Behavioral objectives are stated for each phase and each lesson. For example, the overall objective for Phase 5, Recognizing and Reacting to Emotions, is stated: "The student should be able to identify specific emotions; causes of and changes in emotions; consequences of emotional reactions; degrees of emotions; and moods created by emotions." For Phase 2, Recognizing the Environment, Lesson 8 is entitled Borrowing and Taking and has this objective: "The student should be able to explain the difference between borrowing and taking." The entire curriculum is in the form of a kit, complete with detailed lesson plans, stimulus pictures to provoke discussion, duplicating masters and overhead projection transparencies, and supplementary books for integrating the lessons with other curriculum areas.

## APPLIED ANALYSIS
## OF SOCIAL BEHAVIOR

Most of the responses that have been altered through the use of behavior modification techniques can be classified under the broad rubric of "social behavior." Consequently, the literature on the modification of behaviors that are social in nature is voluminous (cf. Bandura, 1969). It is only very recently that applied behavior analysts have begun to devote a significant proportion of their efforts to the assay of academic learning.

(See Kauffman, 1975, for a review of applied analysis of academic behavior.) Even in special education the majority of the behavior modification studies have been either of behaviors that are socially desirable or of behaviors that are troublesome primarily because of social expectations (cf. Kazdin & Craighead, 1973). We cannot, therefore, discuss here all of the topics or issues relevant to the applied analysis of social behavior. We will present selected studies on several topics that are pertinent to our previous discussion of social development.

### Control of Aggressive, Hyperactive, and Disruptive Behavior

Aggressiveness, hyperactivity, and disruptiveness are behavioral characteristics often seen in the same child. Behavior management techniques that are successful in reducing one of these types of behavior are likely to be effective with the others. Behavior analysts have devised several methods for dealing with such problems. These methods are not mutually exclusive, but rather are often used in combination, especially in cases where behavior problems are severe.

REINFORCEMENT OF INCOMPATIBLE BEHAVIORS. The essence of this method is *differential* attention or reinforcement. Undesirable behavior is ignored (i.e., placed on an *extinction* schedule) while at the same time desirable behavior is attended to or reinforced. Thus the undesirable behavior is weakened in two ways: it is not reinforced, and other desirable behaviors incompatible with it are strengthened.

In Chapter 8 we discussed the case of Levi (Hall, et al., 1968) as an illustration of the effects of differential teacher attention on disruptive behavior (see Figure 8.7). Another well-known project in which differential teacher attention was used to lessen problem behavior is a study of the control of aggression in a nursery school class (Brown & Elliott, 1965). Certain acts of physical aggression (e.g., pushes, hits) and verbal aggression (e.g., threats) were counted by observers. When the teachers ignored these aggressive acts and attended (i.e., looked, touched, and talked) to children when they were engaged in behaviors incompatible with aggression, such as cooperative play, aggression was dramatically reduced.

Differential reinforcement of behaviors incompatible with aggression, hyperactivity, and disruption may involve reinforcers other than teacher attention. Patterson and his colleagues (Patterson, 1965; Patterson, Cobb, & Ray, 1972; Patterson, Jones, Whittier, & Wright, 1965; Patterson, Shaw, & Ebner, 1969; Ray, Shaw, & Cobb, 1970) have used a "work box" to provide powerful rewards for the desirable behavior of typically aggressive and hyperactive children. The work box consists of a small box placed on a child's desk. It contains a counter and a light or buzzer that can be activated by remote control. (In the case reported by Patterson, et al., 1965, only a buzzer was used.) It is explained to the child and his classmates that whenever he has been working (i.e., sitting still and attending) for a few minutes the counter will turn and the light will flash or the buzzer will sound. The "points" earned on the counter can be exchanged for extra recess time, candy, trinkets, or pennies which the entire class will share. Then, contingent on the child's exhibiting desirable behavior for a short time, the counter is advanced. Gradually, the period of appropriate behavior required for advancement of the counter is lengthened. Eventually, the work box is faded out and teacher-dispensed points take its place. It appears that part of the reason for success of this procedure involves a change in the child's social status among his peers. Aggressive, hyperactive children seldom are popular among their classmates. However, when such a child becomes the source of rewards for his classmates, the behavior that earns the rewards (e.g., quiet study behavior) is likely to be reinforced by other children.

Patterson's work box represents a somewhat novel way of rewarding behavior incompatible with aggression and disruption. Other techniques that incorporate novel contingencies or "good behavior games" (e.g., Barrish, Saunders, & Wolf, 1969; Kauffman & Hallahan, 1973) also have been successful in the control of "acting-out" behavior. The essential feature of all these techniques is the explicit and effective reinforcement of behavior that precludes the child's engaging in aggression, disruption, or other undesirable acts. A corollary feature is the nonreinforcement of undesirable behavior.

TIME-OUT.   Although reinforcement for appropriate behavior will resolve many behavior problems, it is clearly insufficient in some cases. Some situations require direct suppression of the maladaptive behavior by some type of punishment.

Punishment can take several forms (e.g., presentation of aversive stimuli or response cost), but we will discuss only time-out, that is, punishment involving contingent removal of the child from the situation or removal of the opportunity to obtain reinforcers (see Chapter 5). In its usual application time-out involves removing the child from the situation in which he exhibited inappropriate behavior and placing him in relative isolation for a brief time. This procedure is mildly aversive for most children and has been quite successful in reducing the occurrence of dangerous or intolerable behavior in most cases (Leitenberg, 1965). The isolation area may be a small, bare, lighted room or booth or a screened-off area of the classroom. The period of time the child is kept in the time-out area has ranged from one to thirty minutes. It has been found that for many children very short time-outs are as effective as longer ones (White, Nielson, & Johnson, 1972), and that after a time-out has followed misbehavior for several days, it need not be applied to every instance of the inappropriate conduct in order to be effective (Clark, Rowbury, Baer, & Baer, 1973).

In the context of our previous discussion in this chapter regarding aggression, time-out would seem to be a particularly useful and productive way of dealing with severe conduct problems—it plays down the use of aversive stimuli which seem to elicit counteraggression and coercion. Furthermore, it has been used very successfully with a wide variety of specific behaviors and age levels and in a wide variety of settings, including the regular classroom, the home, and institutions (see Patterson, et al., 1972; Clark, et al., 1973).

Two points regarding time-out must be kept in mind: First, time-out for inappropriate behavior is of no value without reinforcement for good behavior; and second, time-out need not involve removing or isolating the child. An example of how reinforcement and a time-out contingency that did not require isolating the child were combined has been provided by Kubany, Weiss, and Sloggett (1971). They were faced with the problem behavior of Henry, a bright (I.Q. 120) six-year-old whom they described as hyperactive, loud, demanding, oppositional, and disruptive. He would not sit at his desk, which he separated from the other children and piled with debris. Ordinarily, he refused any school work, except reading aloud to the class. Much of his time was spent drawing pictures of sea life on the chalkboard and narrating stories about them. Then too,

> Henry's incessant talking and loud outbursts made it almost impossible for the teacher to carry out her routine. His misbehavior was all the more salient as the class was in general well behaved. Some of Henry's deviant behaviors were smearing and spraying paint on desks and floors, unraveling rolls of tape, destroying a pegboard with a hammer, chipping away at the sidewalk outside the classroom with a screwdriver and hammer, throwing temper tantrums during which he turned over desks and chairs, not returning to the classroom after recess, sometimes from morning recess not until lunch-time. This caused considerable consternation among school personnel since they are responsible for students' well-being throughout the school day. When asked what Henry liked to do, the teacher included "swearing" and "tipping over his chair." When we came upon the scene, Henry's mother was about to take him to a child psychiatrist, and school administrators were considering a plan to place him on a half-day schedule or possibly even to remove him from the public school and place him in a special class for emotionally handicapped children. (p. 174)

Henry's teacher had tried scolding and reprimanding him, only to find that his behavior became even worse. During the time that baseline data were recorded, she usually ignored his misbehavior, but Henry received much attention from his peers. Kubany and his associates designed an intervention procedure with several considerations in mind: the necessity for a time-out contingency for Henry's misbehavior, the peer attention he was receiving for misbehavior, and the impossibility of isolating Henry during time-out because of the nature of the school setting. They obtained a large (nine inch by nine inch) fifteen-minute electric timer and fitted it with a false face with numbers one through six at two-minute intervals and a red star at the end of the series. "Henry's Clock" was printed across the center of the timer. On the first day of the intervention procedure the teacher explained the contingencies to the entire class. The procedure was in effect only from the end of the afternoon recess until the end of the school day, the most troublesome time. As long as Henry was in his seat and quiet the clock was running and a treat (variety of trinkets and candies) was dropped in a "Sharing Jar" for each two minutes of running time (a treat was given for each fifteen minutes of running time after the first day). Henry was allowed to distribute the treats to the rest of the class at the end of the day. Each time the clock reached the end of a cycle Henry also earned a red star, which was placed on a "Good Behavior Chart" posted at the front of the room. The earned treats and stars constituted reinforcement for behavior incompatible with disruption. Time-out was provided for disruptive behavior by the teacher's turning off the clock until Henry had behaved appropriately for fifteen seconds—that is, as long as Henry was misbehaving the clock was off, time did not accumulate, and treats and stars were not earned and thus he was "in time-out." The rather dramatic effects of this intervention are shown in Figure 10.3. A "reversal" (i.e., return to baseline conditions) and reinstatement of the reinforcement-time-out contingency demonstrated the causal relationship between the intervention procedure and behavioral improvement. Henry's overall behavior improved so markedly that the Kubany team judged special class placement to be obviated.

TOKEN REINFORCEMENT.    The work of Patterson and his co-workers and Kubany and his involved allowing children to earn one commodity (points or time) that could be exchanged for another (trinkets, candy, recess). In essence, this constituted "token" reinforcement in which earned reinforcers were exchanged for other "back-up" reinforcers. Token reinforcement can become a "token economy" in which the medium of exchange becomes a veritable monetary system with many of the complexities that that implies. The medium of exchange in token economies has varied widely and has included check marks, plastic chips, foreign coins, holes punched in cards, and other materials. Backup reinforcers have

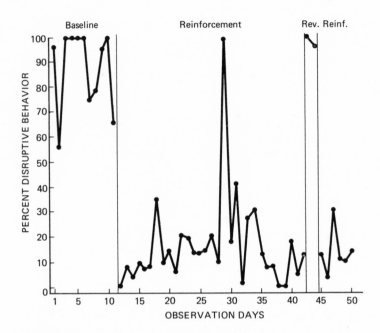

*FIGURE 10.3.*
*Henry's disruptive behavior during baseline, reinforcement, reversal, and reinforcement phases*

Source: E. S. Kubany, L. E. Weiss, & B. B. Sloggett, "The Good Behavior Clock: A Reinforcement/Time-Out Procedure for Reducing Disruptive Classroom Behavior," Journal of Behavior Therapy and Experimental Psychiatry, 1971, 2, p. 175. Reprinted by permission.

included activities intrinsic to the classroom (e.g., recess, play materials, curriculum materials, certain privileges) and miscellaneous tangible items, including food, toys, and clothing. A broad range of behaviors, including aggressive and disruptive behaviors, in a broad range of settings, including regular and special classrooms, have been modified using token reinforcement. There is no doubt that token reinforcement is a powerful tool for changing social behavior, but it is also very clear that a token system is a complex instrument that can easily go awry without careful planning and management (cf. Kazdin & Bootzin, 1972; O'Leary & Drabman, 1971; Stainback, Payne, Stainback, & Payne, 1973).

CONTINGENCY CONTRACTING. A contingency contract spells out in detail the arrangement between a child's behavior and its consequences. When contingency contracts are drawn systematically, there is value in the explication of consequences for behavior (Cantrell, Cantrell, Huddleston,

& Woolridge, 1969; Homme, 1969; Patterson, et al., 1972; Tharp & Wetzel, 1969). Of course, the contract must call for a reasonable standard of conduct and offer a fair reward from both the child's and the adult's viewpoints. In some cases there may be a need for negotiation of the terms of the contract. Naturally, the terms must be adhered to if the agreement is to be effective. Contingency contracts have been most widely used with older children who have fairly sophisticated verbal and reasoning skills. Contracts can vary greatly in complexity, however, and very simple terms can be stated for younger children. Patterson, Cobb, and Ray (1972) have provided an example of a contract (Figure 10.4) designed for a ten-year-old boy who had physically attacked other children (causing them to need medical care), stolen bicycles, and destroyed school property. Note that the contract involves the child's parents as well as school personnel and that token reinforcers (specifically, a response cost contingency involving points that can "buy" time to watch television) and time-out are included in the arrangement.

CONTINGENCIES MANAGED BY PARENTS. Experience has shown that many parents can be effective in administering reinforcement and time-out contingencies arranged by school or clinic personnel and, with proper instruction and advice, devise useful contingencies of their own (Csapo, 1973; Hawkins, Peterson, Schweid, & Bijou, 1966; Kauffman & Scranton, 1974; Kroth, Whelan, & Stables, 1970; O'Leary, O'Leary, & Becker, 1967; Patterson, 1973; Sluyter & Hawkins, 1972; Straughan, 1964; Zeilberger, Sampen, & Sloane, 1968). In fact, quite a few excellent manuals for use in parent education are now available (e.g., Madsen & Madsen, 1972; Patterson, 1971; Patterson & Gullion, 1968). The teacher who does not attempt to enlist the aid of a child's parents in managing problem conduct risks foregoing a useful partnership.

PEER INFLUENCE. As a child matures he gives up many attachments to his parents and increasingly comes under the control of his peers. In some of the studies presented in this chapter peer reaction was seen to be a significant factor in control of the problem behavior. It is obvious that in nearly every case of disordered behavior the responses of the child's peers will be of some influence. In some instances the peer group is all important and little can be done to improve the situation unless the child's peers are involved in an intervention technique. Worell and Nelson (1974) have suggested that "peer power is effected by means of three major channels: (1) modeling, or observing and imitating one another; (2) reinforcement through verbal and nonverbal approval or disapproval of one another's behavior; and (3) direct instruction and transmission of peer culture, mores, and regulations" (p. 230). Several

The following is a contract between Sam and his teacher, his principal, and his counselor, in order for Sam to learn ways to behave during school. Sam will earn points during the school hours so that he can do some of the things he enjoys at home. The total number of points which can be earned each day is 50. The behaviors are the following:

Talking in a normal tone of voice, e.g., not yelling.

Cooperating with his teacher, e.g., not arguing and doing what is asked on the playground and in the halls.

Minding other teachers.

Remaining in chair unless school work requires moving in the classroom, e.g., not roaming around the room.

Talking to other children at proper times, e.g., not disturbing other children when they work.

Following his teacher's directions for work, e.g., doing the work assigned.

Sam will start with a total of 50 points each day and will lose a point for each time he does not follow the above rules. Each time he loses a point, he is to be placed in Time Out for five minutes. At the end of each school day his teacher will call his mother to give her a total of points earned for that day. Sam will be allowed five minutes of TV for each point.

For the following behaviors Sam is to be sent home from school for the day:

1. Destroying property.
2. Fighting with other children to the point of hurting them.
3. Taking property belonging to someone else.
4. Swearing.
5. Refusing to go into Time Out.

When Sam is sent home his principal will call his father to tell him what Sam has done. His principal will then call his mother so she will know that Sam is being set home. When Sam arrives home, he is to do some task around the house or yard until school is out, at which time he can follow the normal routine of the household except watching TV that night.

When Sam does not follow the rules of the lunchroom he is to be sent from the lunchroom to the principal's office without finishing his meal.

His mother will keep the number of points earned each day in order to assess Sam's progress. His mother will also continue to teach Sam reading skills until such time as he is able to handle reading material in the classroom. The therapist will continue to supervise Sam's mother until the reading program is completed. (To be signed by all parties.)

Date _Feb. 3, 1971_

Sam _Sam_
Mother _Mom_
Father _Dad_
Teacher _Mrs. Hansen_
Principal _Mr. Dean_

FIGURE 10.4.

Sam's contract.

Source: G. R. Patterson, J. A. Cobb, & R. S. Ray, "Direct Intervention in the Classroom: A Set of Procedures for the Aggressive Child," in F. W. Clark, D. R. Evans, & L. A. Hamerlynck (Eds.), Implementing Behavioral Programs for Schools and Clinics (Champaign, Ill.: Research Press, 1972), pp. 166–167. Reprinted by permission.

studies have shown that peers, even at the elementary-school level, can function effectively as reinforcement agents and contribute to the reduction of inappropriate behavior (e.g., Csapo, 1972; Nelson, Worell, & Polsgrove, 1973; Packard, 1970; Surratt, Ulrich, & Hawkins, 1969).

### Facilitation of
### Desirable Social Behavior

Amid concern for reducing behavior problems it is easy to lose sight of the fact that applied behavior analysis can be attuned as easily to the teaching of desirable social behaviors as to the elimination of maladaptive responses. While it is true that procedures designed to teach adaptive behavior are often employed because a maladaptive response or behavior deficit has come to the teacher's attention, it is also true that in some cases the *focus* is on the adaptive behavior acquired and its importance in the child's further development.

Hall and Broden (1967), for example, deliberately developed the social play of a nine-year-old brain-injured boy. True, this child did exhibit marked perceptual problems, impaired gross and fine motor coordination, impulsivity, perseveration, tantrums, and expressive language difficulties. Too, he had a history of premature birth and depressed functioning in the neonatal period and had been diagnosed as having probable central nervous system dysfunction. Nevertheless, it was thought that properly arranged contingencies of reinforcement would result in his learning to play more of the time with other children and facilitate his further social development. Baseline observation showed that the child spent an average of only about 17 percent of his play time in social (i.e., parallel or cooperative) play; he was, for practical purposes, a social isolate (see Figure 10.5). It was noted also that he received considerable teacher attention during "isolate" play, often in the form of invitations or encouragement to join other children in their play activities. Under the assumption that the teachers' attention was a reinforcer for this child (and, ironically, the very reinforcer sustaining his social isolation), it was decided that when he was engaged in isolate play he would be ignored, but that his social play would be attended to by the teachers. The result of making teacher attention contingent on social play can be seen in Section B of Figure 10.5. It should be noted that social play did not increase during the first three days of the first reinforcement phase. This seemed to be due to the fact that the child seldom played with his peers and, therefore, had few opportunities to be reinforced. After session eleven (point *a* in the figure), the teachers used a shaping procedure in which they reinforced successive approximations of social play—looking at, approaching, and playing with his classmates. This shaping pro-

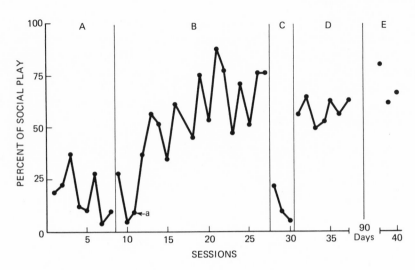

FIGURE 10.5.

*Record of a brain-injured, nine-year-old's rates of social play: A: Baseline period—prior to experimental procedures; B: Reinforcement period—social reinforcement of social play by boy's teachers; C: Reversal period—reinforcement of nonsocial play; D: Return to reinforcement period—reinforcement of social play; E: Post-experiment period—three months after termination of the experiment.*

Source: R. V. Hall & M. Broden, "Behavior Changes in Brain-Injured Children through Social Reinforcement," Journal of Experimental Child Psychology, 1967, 5, p. 474. Reprinted by permission.

cedure seemed to be an effective "primer" for social play. Predictably, when the contingencies of reinforcement were reversed, and the child received teacher attention only for isolate play, social play dropped drastically (Section C). Reinstatement of the teacher attention contingency for social play confirmed the functional relationship between teacher attention and the child's social behavior. Hall and Broden obtained post-experimental data that indicated the social gains of the child were not lost (Section E). At the end of the experiment the teachers noted that the child laughed more, that he was more cooperative in other activities, that his peers seemed to enjoy him more, and that he engaged in more physical contact with his classmates.

Hart, Reynolds, Baer, Brawley, and Harris (1968) also found that contingent teacher attention, in the form of supplying equipment or materials, smiling at, laughing or conversing with, or admiring the child, was effective in increasing social play. Noncontingent social attention from the teacher (i.e., attention given randomly throughout the day regardless of the child's behavior), on the other hand, did not improve the child's behavior.

Factors other than contingent teacher attention for desirable behavior have been shown in behavior analyses to contribute to children's social development. Buell, Stoddard, Harris, and Baer (1968) found, for example, that by socially reinforcing a preschool girl for using outdoor play equipment teachers contributed not only to her motor development but also to her social contacts and interactions with other children. More recently, Quilitch and Risley (1973) have shown that the types of toys or play materials provided for children also influence social interaction, that is, certain toys are "social toys" and others are "isolate toys." Wahler (1967) demonstrated that even at the preschool level a child's peers control powerful social reinforcers and that children can be induced to facilitate their classmates' adaptive social behavior by providing contingent attention.

### Ethical and Moral Aspects
### of Applied Behavior Analysis

Behavior modification technology is still in its infancy, but already there is concern about the dangers inherent in its application (Bandura, 1969; Kauffman, 1973; Risley & Baer, 1973; Roos, 1974). This concern is understandable and desirable. The technology is very powerful and, if misused, could conceivably result in disastrous consequences. For example, coercion, loss of personal freedom, learning of undesirable behaviors, long-term decrements in reinforcer effectiveness could occur. The problems faced here, however, are no different from the problems presented by any other technology. Any technology may carry with it both immediate benefits and immediate or long-range potential dangers (Kauffman, 1973).

As Risley and Baer (1973) have pointed out, the decision to modify behavior is inescapable. Behavior principles operate regardless of whether one chooses to let them operate randomly or to control them systematically. Principles or laws of behavior are not "good" or "bad" in themselves; only the decisions made by people to control or not to control them can be judged as moral or immoral. The responsibility for moral judgment and moral behavior, then, is cast squarely on the shoulders of those who use behavior modification technology. Roos (1974) has commented:

> As increasing control is gained over our destiny, behavioral scientists are being confronted with ethical and moral issues which have taunted man since the beginning of history. All ethical and moral responsibilities for the effects of our technology could be avoided by rationalizing that scientists are only tools of society—technicians charged with implementing

cultural decisions. Though probably attractive to many, this would be a naive and irresponsible refuge from reality. (p. 6)

For teachers, who each day must decide which behaviors of the children in their charge should be facilitated and which should be inhibited, the moral question is pervasive. "It may be that the essential moral problem facing application of behavior modification is deciding which behaviors we shall now modify, and in what direction" (Risley & Baer, 1973, p. 324). We believe that teachers of children with learning disabilities have a special obligation to consider carefully their decisions regarding what and how children should be taught.

# References

ACHENBACH, T. M. The classification of children's psychiatric symptoms: A factor analytic study. *Psychological Monographs*, 1966, *80*, 6.

ACKERSON, L. *Children's behavior problems*. Chicago: University of Chicago Press, 1942.

AHRENS, R. Beitrage zur entwicklung des physiognomie—und mimikerkennes. *Zertschrift f. Exp. w. angew. Psychol.*, 1954, *2*, 412–454, 599–633.

ALLEN, K. E., Henke, L. B., Harris, F. R., Baer, D. M., & Reynolds, N. J. Control of hyperactivity by social reinforcement of attending behavior. *Journal of Educational Psychology*, 1967, *58*, 231–237.

ALWITT, L. F. Attention on a visual task among non-readers and readers. *Perceptual and Motor Skills*, 1966, *23*, 361–362.

AYRES, A. J. Patterns of perceptual-motor dysfunction in children: A factor analytic study. *Perceptual and Motor Skills*, 1965, *20*, 335–368.

AYRES, A. J. Deficits in sensory integration in educationally handicapped children. *Journal of Learning Disabilities*, 1969, *2*, 160–168.

AYRES, A. J. Characteristics of types of sensory integrative dysfunction. *American Journal of Occupational Therapy*, 1971, *25*, 329–334.

AYRES, A. J. *Southern California Sensory Integration Tests*. Los Angeles: Western Psychological Services, 1972.

AYRES, A. J. Sensorimotor foundations of academic ability. In W. M. Cruickshank & D. P. Hallahan (Eds.), *Perceptual and learning disabilities in children*. Vol. 2: *Research and Theory*. Syracuse, N. Y.: Syracuse University Press, 1975.

BAER, A. M., ROWBURY, T., & BAER, D. M. The development of instructional control over classroom activities of deviant preschool children. *Journal of Applied Behavior Analysis*, 1973, *6*, 289–298.

BAER, D. M. Let's take another look at punishment. *Psychology Today*, 1971, 5 (5), 32–37, 111.

BAER, D. M., & Guess, D. Receptive training of adjectival inflections in mental retardates. *Journal of Applied Behavior Analysis*, 1971, 4, 129–139.

BAER, D. M., & WOLF, M. M. The entry into natural communities of reinforcement. In R. Ulrich, T. Stachnik, & J. Mabry (Eds.), *Control of human behavior* (Vol. 2). Glenview, Ill.: Scott, Foresman, 1970.

BAER, D. M., WOLF, M. M., & RISLEY, T. R. Some current dimensions of applied behavior analysis. *Journal of Applied Behavior Analysis*, 1968, 1, 91–97.

BAKWIN, H., & BAKWIN, R. M. *Behavior disorders in children* (4th ed.). Philadelphia: Saunders, 1972.

BALLA, D. A., BUTTERFIELD, E. C., & ZIGLER, E. Effects of institutionalization on retarded children: A longitudinal cross-institutional investigation. *American Journal of Mental Deficiency*, 1974, 78, 530–549.

BALLING, J. D., & MYERS, N. A. Memory and attention in children's double-alternation learning. *Journal of Experimental Child Psychology*, 1971, 11, 448–460.

BANDURA, A. *Principles of behavior modification*. New York: Holt, Rinehart, & Winston, 1969.

BARRISH, H. H., SAUNDERS, M., & WOLF, M. M. Good behavior game: Effects of individual contingencies for group consequences on disruptive behavior in the classroom. *Journal of Applied Behavior Analysis*, 1969, 2, 119–124.

BARSCH, R. H. Achieving perceptual-motor efficiency. Seattle: Special Child Publications, 1967.

BARSCH, R. H. Ray H. Barsch. In J. M. Kauffman & D. P. Hallahan (Eds.), *Teaching children with learning disabilities: Personal perspectives*. Columbus, Ohio: Charles E. Merrill, 1976.

BARTEL, N. R., GRILL, J. J., & BARTEL, H. W. The syntactic-paradigmatic shift in learning disabled and normal children. *Journal of Learning Disabilities*, 1973, 6, 518–523.

BECKER, W. C. Consequences of different kinds of parental discipline. In M. L. Hoffman & L. W. Hoffman (Eds.), *Review of child development research* (Vol. 1). New York: Russell Sage Foundation, 1964.

BECKER, W. C. (Ed.). *An empirical basis for change in education: Selections on behavioral psychology for teachers*. Chicago: Science Research Associates, 1971.

BECKER, W. C. Applications of behavior principles in typical classrooms. In C. Thoresen (Ed.), *Behavior modification in education*. Seventy-second yearbook of the National Society for the Study of Education, Part I. Chicago: University of Chicago Press, 1973.

BECKER, W. C., Engelmann, S., & Thomas, D. R. *Teaching: A course in applied psychology*. Chicago: Science Research Associates, 1971.

BEERY, K. E., & BUKTENICA, N. *Developmental Test of Visual-Motor Integration*. Chicago: Follett Publishers, 1967.

BEM, S. L. Verbal self-control: The establishment of effective self-instruction. *Journal of Experimental Psychology*, 1967, *74*, 485–491.

BENDER, L. *A Visual-Motor Gestalt Test and its clinical uses*. Research Monograph No. 3. New York: American Orthopsychiatric Association, 1938.

BENDER, L. Use of the Visual Motor Gestalt Test in the diagnosis of learning disabilities. *Journal of Special Education*, 1970, *4*, 29–39.

BENTON, A. L. *The Revised Benton Visual Retention Test*. New York: Psychological Corp., 1963.

BEREITER, C., & ENGELMANN, S. *Teaching disadvantaged children in the preschool*. Englewood Cliffs, N.J.: Prentice-Hall, 1966.

BEREITER, C., & ENGELMANN, S. *Language learning activities for the disadvantaged child*. New York: Anti-Defamation League of B'nai B'rith (undated).

BERKO, J. The child's learning of English morphology. *Word*, 1958, *14*, 150–177.

BERKOWITZ, L. *Aggression: A social psychological analysis*. New York: McGraw-Hill, 1962.

BERKOWITZ, L. Control of aggression. In B. M. Caldwell & H. N. Ricciuti (Eds.), *Review of child development research* (Vol. 3). Chicago: University of Chicago Press, 1973.

BERMAN, M. L. Instructions and behavior change: A taxonomy. *Exceptional Children*, 1973, *39*, 644–650.

BETTELHEIM, B. *Truants from life*. New York: Free Press, 1955.

BETTELHEIM, B. Listening to children. In P. A. Gallagher & L. L. Edwards (Eds.), *Educating the emotionally disturbed: Theory to practice*. Lawrence, Kans.: University of Kansas, 1970.

BIJOU, S. W. Studies in the experimental development of left-right concepts in retarded children using fading techniques. In N. R. Ellis (Ed.), *International review of research in mental retardation* (Vol. 3). New York: Academic Press, 1968.

BIJOU, S. W. Environment and intelligence: A behavioral analysis. In R. Cancro (Ed.), *Intelligence: Genetic and environmental influences*. New York: Grune & Stratton, 1971.

BIJOU, S. W., & BAER, D. M. *Child development: A systematic and empirical theory*. Englewood Cliffs, N.J.: Prentice-Hall, 1961.

BIJOU, S. W., & BAER, D. M. Operant methods in child behavior and development. In W. K. Honig (Ed.), *Operant behavior: Areas of research and application*. New York: Appleton-Century-Crofts, 1966.

BIJOU, S. W., & BAER, D. M. (Eds.). *Child development: Readings in experimental analysis*. Englewood Cliffs, N.J.: Prentice-Hall, 1967.

BIJOU, S. W., BIRNBRAUER, J. S., KIDDER, J. D., & TAGUE, C. Programmed instruction as an approach to teaching of reading, writing, and arithmetic to retarded children. *Psychological Record*, 1966, *16*, 505–522.

BIJOU, S. W., PETERSON, R. F., HARRIS, F. R., ALLEN, K. E., & JOHNSTON, M. S. Methodology for experimental studies of young children in natural settings. *Psychological Record*, 1969, *19*, 177–210.

BIRCH, D. Verbal control of nonverbal behavior. *Journal of Experimental Child Psychology*, 1966, *4*, 266–275.

BIRCH, H. G. *Brain damage in children: The biological and social aspects.* Baltimore: Williams and Wilkins, 1964.

BLAKE, K. A., AARON, I. E., & WESTBROOK, H. R. Learning of basal reading skills by mentally handicapped and non-mentally handicapped children. *Journal of Research and Development in Education*, 1969, *2*, 3–120.

BOEHM, L., & NASS, M. L. Social class differences in conscience development. *Child Development*, 1962, *33*, 565–575.

BORMUTH, J. R. Review of "Durrell Listening-Reading Series." In O. K. Buros (Ed.), *The seventh mental measurement yearbook.* Highland Park, N.J.: Gryphon Press, 1972.

BORTNER, M., & BIRCH, H. G. Perceptual and perceptual-motor dissociation in cerebral palsied children. *Journal of Nervous and Mental Diseases*, 1962, *134*, 103–108.

BOWER, E. M. *Early identification of emotionally handicapped children in school* (2nd ed.). Springfield, Ill.: Charles C. Thomas, 1969.

BOWER, E. M., & LAMBERT, N. M. *A Process for In-School Screening of Children with Emotional Handicaps.* Princeton, N.J.: Educational Testing Service, 1962.

BRADY, R. C. *Effects of success and failure on impulsivity and distractibility of three types of educationally handicapped children.* Unpublished doctoral dissertation, University of Southern California, 1970.

BRAINE, M. D. S. The ontogeny of English phrase structure. The first phase. *Language*, 1963, *39*, 1–13.

BRICKER, W. A., & BRICKER, D. D. A program of language training for the severely language handicapped child. *Exceptional Children*, 1970, *37*, 101–111.

BRICKER, W. A., & BRICKER, D. D. William A. Bricker and Diane D. Bricker: Mental retardation and complex human behavior. In J. M. Kauffman & J. S. Payne (Eds.), *Mental retardation: Introduction and personal perspectives.* Columbus, Ohio: Charles E. Merrill, 1975.

BRIGHAM, T. A., FINFROCK, S. R., BREUNIG, M. K., & BUSHELL, D. The use of programmed materials in the analysis of academic contingencies. *Journal of Applied Behavior Analysis*, 1972, *5*, 177–182.

BRIGHAM, T. A., GRAUBARD, P. S., & STANS, A. Analysis of the effects of sequential reinforcement contingencies on aspects of composition. *Journal of Applied Behavior Analysis*, 1972, *5*, 421–429.

BROCA, P. Remarques sur le siège de la faculté du langage articulé suivé d'une observation d'aphemie. *Bulletin Societé Anatomique de Paris,* 1861, *36,* 331.

BRONFENBRENNER, U. Soviet methods of character education: Some implications for research. *American Psychologist,* 1962, *17,* 550–565.

BROWN, P., & ELLIOTT, R. Control of aggression in a nursery school class. *Journal of Experimental Child Psychology,* 1965, *2,* 103–107.

BROWNING, R. M. Effect of irrelevant peripheral visual stimuli on discrimination learning in minimally brain-damaged children. *Journal of Consulting Psychology,* 1967, *31,* 371–376. (a)

BROWNING, R. M. Hypo-responsiveness as a behavioral correlate of brain damage in children. *Psychological Reports,* 1967, *20,* 251–259. (b)

BRUININCKS, R. H., & WEATHERMAN, R. F. *Handicapped children and special education program needs in northeast Minnesota.* Minneapolis: Department of Special Education, University of Minnesota, 1970.

BRUNER, J. S., OLVER, R. R., & GREENFIELD, P. M. *Studies in cognitive growth.* New York: Wiley, 1966.

BUELL, J., STODDARD, P., HARRIS, F. R., & BAER, D. M. Collateral social development accompanying reinforcement of outdoor play in a preschool child. *Journal of Applied Behavior Analysis,* 1968, *1,* 167–173.

BURKS, H. H. *The Burks Behavior Rating Scale.* El Monte, Calif.: Arden Press, 1969.

BUSH, W. J., & GILES, M. T. *Aids to psycholinguistic teaching.* Columbus, Ohio: Charles E. Merrill, 1969.

BYRNE, M. C. Review of "Goldman-Fristoe Test of Articulation" In O. K. Buros (Ed.), *The seventh mental measurements yearbook.* Highland Park, N.J.: Gryphon Press, 1972.

CANTRELL, R. P., CANTRELL, M. L., HUDDLESTON, C., & WOOLRIDGE, R. Contingency contracting with school problems. *Journal of Applied Behavior Analysis,* 1969, *2,* 215–220.

CARUSO, I. H. La notion de la responsabilité et de la justice immanente chez l'enfant. *Archives de Psychologie,* 1943, *29,* entire No. 114.

CAZDEN, C. *Environmental assistance to the child's acquisition of grammar.* Unpublished doctoral dissertation, Harvard University, 1965.

*Central processing dysfunctions in children: A review of research.* Phase 3 of a three-phase project. National Institute of Neurological Diseases and Stroke, Monograph No. 9, 1969.

CHALL, J. *Learning to read.* New York: McGraw-Hill, 1967.

CHOMSKY, N. A. Review of *Verbal behavior* by B. F. Skinner, *Language,* 1959, *35,* 26–58.

CHOMSKY, N. A. *Syntactic Structures.* The Hague: Monton, 1957.

CHOMSKY, N. A. *Aspects of the theory of syntax.* Cambridge: MIT Press, 1965.

CHOMSKY, N. A. *Cartesian linguistics.* New York: Harper & Row, 1966.

CLARK, H. B., ROWBURY, T., BAER, A. M., & BAER, D. M. Timeout as a punishing stimulus in continuous and intermittent schedules. *Journal of Applied Behavior Analysis*, 1973, *6*, 443–455.

CLAUSEN, J. A. Family structure, socialization and personality. In M. L. Hoffman & L. W. Hoffman (Eds.), *Review of child development research* (Vol. 2). New York: Russell Sage Foundation, 1966.

COHEN, S. A. Comments from Dr. Cohen. *Journal of Learning Disabilities*, 1969, *2*, 661. (a).

COHEN, S. A. Studies in visual perception and reading in disadvantaged children. *Journal of Learning Disabilities*, 1969, *2*, 498–507. (b)

COHEN, S. A. Cause versus treatment in reading achievement. *Journal of Learning Disabilities*, 1970, *3*, 163–166.

CONNERS, C. K. A teacher rating scale for use in drug studies with children. *American Journal of Psychiatry*, 1969, *126*, 152–156.

COOPER, J. O. Eliminating letter and number reversal errors with modeling and reinforcement procedures. (Doctoral dissertation, University of Kansas, 1970; Ann Arbor, Mich.: University Microfilms No. 71–13, 390.

COOPER, J. O. *Measurement and analysis of behavioral techniques.* Columbus, Ohio: Charles E. Merrill, 1975.

COREY, J. R., & SHAMOW, J. The effects of fading on the acquisition and retention of oral reading. *Journal of Applied Behavior Analysis*, 1972, *5*, 311–315.

CRATTY, B. J. *Developmental sequences of perceptual-motor tasks.* Freeport, Long Island, New York: Educational Activities, 1967.

CRATTY, B. J. *Intelligence in action.* Englewood Cliffs, N.J.: Prentice-Hall, 1973. (a)

CRATTY, B. J. *Teaching motor skills.* Englewood Cliffs, N.J.: Prentice-Hall, 1973. (b)

CRUICKSHANK, W. M. (Ed.), *The teacher of brain-injured children: A discussion of the bases for competency.* Syracuse: Syracuse University Press, 1966.

CRUICKSHANK, W. M. The development of education for exceptional children. In W. M. Cruickshank & G. O. Johnson (Eds.), *Education of exceptional children and youth* (2nd ed.). Englewood Cliffs, N.J.: Prentice-Hall, 1967.

CRUICKSHANK, W. M. The learning environment. In W. M. Cruickshank & D. P. Hallahan (Eds.), *Perceptual and learning disabilities in children*, (Vol. 1), *Psychoeducational practices.* Syracuse: Syracuse University Press, 1975.

CRUICKSHANK, W. M. William M. Cruickshank. In J. M. Kauffman & D. P. Hallahan (Eds.), *Teaching children with learning disabilities: Personal perspectives.* Columbus, Ohio: Charles E. Merrill, 1976.

CRUICKSHANK, W. M., BENTZEN, F. A., RATZEBURG, F. H., & TANNHAUSER, M. T. *A teaching method for brain-injured and hyperactive children.* Syracuse: Syracuse University Press, 1961.

CRUICKSHANK, W. M., BICE, H. V., & WALLEN, N. E. *Perception and cerebral palsy.* Syracuse: Syracuse University Press, 1957.

CRUICKSHANK, W. M., & HALLAHAN, D. P. Alfred A. Strauss: Pioneer in learning disabilities. *Exceptional Children*, 1973, *39*, 321–327.

CSAPO, M. Peer models reverse the "one bad apple spoils the barrel" theory. *Teaching Exceptional Children*, 1972, *5*(1), 20–24.

CSAPO, M. Parent-teacher intervention with inappropriate behavior. *Elementary School Guidance and Counseling*, 1973, *7*, 198–203.

CULLINAN, D., KAUFFMAN, J. M., & LaFLEUR, N. K. Modeling: Research with implications for special education. *Journal of Special Education*, 1975, *9*, 209–221.

CUTLER, C. M., CICIRELLI, V. G., & HIRSHOREN, A. Comparison of discrimination and reproduction tests of children's perception. *Perceptual and Motor Skills*, 1973, *37*, 163–166.

DEITZ, S. M., & REPP, A. C. Decreasing classroom misbehavior through the use of DRL schedules of reinforcement. *Journal of Applied Behavior Analysis*, 1973, *6*, 457–463.

DELACATO, C. H. *The treatment and prevention of reading problems: The neurological approach.* Springfield, Ill.: Charles C. Thomas, 1959.

DELACATO, C. H. *The diagnosis and treatment of speech and reading problems.* Springfield, Ill.: Charles C. Thomas, 1963.

DELACATO, C. H. *Neurological organization and reading.* Springfield, Ill.: Charles C. Thomas, 1966.

DeMOTT, R. Visually impaired. In N. G. Haring (Ed.) *Behavior of exceptional children.* Columbus, Ohio: Charles E. Merrill, 1974.

DENNER, B. Representational and syntactic competence of problem readers. *Child Development*, 1970, *41*, 881–887.

DMITRIEV, V. Motor and cognitive development in early education. In N. G. Haring (Ed.), *Behavior of exceptional children: An introduction to special education.* Columbus, Ohio: Charles E. Merrill, 1974.

DOLLARD, J., DOOB, L., MILLER, N., MOWRER, O., & SEARS, R. *Frustration and aggression.* New Haven: Yale University Press, 1939.

DOUGLAS, V. S. Stop, look, and listen: The problem of sustained attention and impulse control in hyperactive and normal children. *Canadian Journal of Behavioral Science*, 1972, *4*, 259–282.

DREGER, R. M., LEWIS, P. M., RICH, T. A., MILLER, K. S., REID, M. P., OVERDALE, D. C., TAFFEL, C., & FLEMMING, E. L. Behavioral classification project. *Journal of Consulting Psychology*, 1964, *28*, 1–13.

DREW, C. J., FRESTON, C. W., & LOGAN, D. R. Criteria and reference in evaluation. *Focus on Exceptional Children*, 1972, *4*, 1–10.

DRUKER, J. F., & HAGEN, J. W. Developmental trends in the processing of task-relevant and task-irrelevant information. *Child Development*, 1969, *40*, 371–382.

DUNN, L. M. *Peabody Picture Vocabulary Test*, Circle Pines, Minn.: American Guidance Service, 1959.

DUNN, L. M. Children with moderate and severe general learning disabilities.

In L. M. Dunn (Ed.), *Exceptional children in the schools* (2nd. ed.). New York: Holt, Rinehart, & Winston, 1973.

DURKIN, D. Children's concepts of justice: A comparison with Piaget data. *Child Development,* 1959, *30,* 59–67.

DURRELL, D. D., HAYES, M. T., & BRASSARD, M. B. *Durrell Listening-Reading Series,* New York: Harcourt Brace Jovanovich, 1970.

EISENSON, J. *Aphasia in children.* New York: Harper & Row, 1972.

ELKIND, D., LARSON, M., & VAN DOORNINCK, W. Perceptual decentration learning and performance in slow and average readers. *Journal of Educational Psychology,* 1965, *56,* 50–56.

ENGELMANN, S. *Preventing failure in the primary grades.* Chicago: Science Research Associates, 1969.

EPSTEIN, M. H., HALLAHAN, D. P., & KAUFFMAN, J. M. Implications of the reflectivity-impulsivity dimension for special education. *Journal of Special Education,* 1975, *9,* 11–25.

ESTES, W. K. *Learning theory and mental development.* New York: Academic Press, 1970.

FAGEN, S. A., LONG, N. J., & STEVENS, D. J. *Teaching children self-control: Preventing emotional and learning problems in the elementary school.* Columbus, Ohio: Charles E. Merrill, 1975.

FANTZ, R. L. Pattern vision in young infants. *Psychological Record,* 1958, *8,* 43–47.

FANTZ, R. L. The origin of form perception. *Scientific American,* 1961, *204,* 66–72.

FANTZ, R. L. Pattern vision in newborn infants. *Science,* 1963, *140,* 296–297.

FANTZ, R. L. Pattern discrimination and selective attention as determinants of perceptual development in children. In A. H. Kidd & J. R. Riviore (Eds.), *Perceptual development in children.* New York: International Universities Press, 1966.

FANTZ, R. L., ORDY, J. M., & UDELF, M. S. Maturation of pattern vision in infants during the first six months. *Journal of Comparative and Physiological Psychology,* 1962, *55,* 907–917.

FAUKE, J., BURNETT, J., POWERS, M. A., & SULZER-AZAROFF, B. Improvement of handwriting and letter recognition skills: A behavior modification procedure. *Journal of Learning Disabilities,* 1973, *6,* 25–29.

FERNALD, G. *Remedial techniques in basic school subjects.* New York: McGraw-Hill, 1943.

FERSTER, C. B. Positive reinforcement and behavioral deficits of autistic children. *Child Development,* 1961, *32,* 437–456.

FESHBACH, S. Aggression. In P. H. Mussen (Ed.), *Carmichael's manual of child psychology* (3rd ed.; Vol. 2). New York: Wiley, 1970.

FRASER, C., BELLUGI, V., & BROWN, R. Control of grammar in imitation, comprehension and production. *Journal of Verbal Learning and Verbal Behavior,* 1963, *2,* 121–135.

FRIEDRICH, L. K., & STEIN, A. H. Aggressive and prosocial television programs and the natural behavior of preschool children. *Monographs of the Society for Research in Child Development,* 1973, 38 (4, 1–63, Serial No. 151).

FROSTIG, M. Marianne Frostig. In J. M. Kauffman & D. P. Hallahan (Eds.), *Teaching children with learning disabilities: Personal perspectives.* Columbus, Ohio: Charles E. Merrill, 1976.

FROSTIG, M., & HORNE, D. *The Frostig program for the development of visual perception: Teacher's guide.* Chicago: Follett, 1964.

FROSTIG, M., LEFEVER, D. W., & WHITTLESEY, J. R. B. *The Marianne Frostig developmental test of visual perception.* Palo Alto: Consulting Psychology Press, 1964.

FURTH, H. G., & MILGRAM, N. A. Labeling and grouping effects in the recall of pictures by children. *Child Development,* 1973, 44, 511–518.

GAGNE, R., & GIBSON, J. J. Research on the recognition of aircraft. In J. J. Gibson (Ed.), *Motion picture training and research.* Report No. 7, Army Air Force Aviation Psychology, Program, Research Reports. Washington, D.C.: U.S. Government Printing Office, 1947.

GALLAGHER, J. J. Children with developmental imbalances: A psychoeducational definition. In W. M. Cruickshank (Ed.), *The teacher of brain-injured children: A discussion of the bases for competency,* Syracuse: Syracuse University Press, 1966.

GALLAGHER, J. J. James J. Gallagher. In J. M. Kauffman & D. P. Hallahan (Eds.), *Teaching children with learning disabilities: Personal perspectives.* Columbus, Ohio: Charles E. Merrill, 1976.

GARCIA, E., GUESS, D., & BYRNES, J. Development of syntax in a retarded girl using procedures of imitation, reinforcement, and modelling. *Journal of Applied Behavior Analysis,* 1973, 6, 299–310.

GETMAN, G. N. The visuomotor complex in the acquisition of learning skills. In J. Hellmuth (Ed.), *Learning disorders* (Vol. 1). Seattle: Special Child Publications, 1965.

GETMAN, G. N. Gerald N. Getman, In J. M. Kauffman & D. P. Hallahan (Eds.), *Teaching children with learning disabilities: Personal perspectives.* Columbus, Ohio: Charles E. Merrill, 1976.

GETMAN, G. N., KANE, E. R., HALGREN, M. R., & McKEE, G. W. *The physiology of readiness: An action program for the development of perception in children.* Minneapolis: Publications to Accelerate School Success, Inc., 1964.

GIBSON, E. J. Development of perception: Discrimination of depth compared with discrimination of graphic symbols. In J. C. Wright and J. Kagan (Eds.), *Basic cognitive processes in children. Monographs of the Society for Research in Child Development,* 1963, 28, (2, Serial No. 86).

GIBSON, E. J. Learning to read. *Science,* 1965, 148, 1066–1072.

GIBSON, E. J. *Principles of perceptual learning and development.* Englewood Cliffs, N.J.: Prentice-Hall, 1969.

GIBSON, E. J., GIBSON, J. J., PICK, A. D., & OSSER, H. A. developmental study of the discrimination of letter-like forms. *Journal of Comparative and Physiological Psychology,* 1962, 55, 897–906.

GIBSON, E. J., OSSER, H., & PICK, A. D. A study in the development of grapheme-phoneme correspondence. *Journal of Verbal Learning and Verbal Behavior,* 1963, 2, 142–146.

GILLINGHAM, A., & STILLMAN, B. *Remedial training for children with specific disability in reading, spelling, penmanship.* Cambridge, Mass.: Educators Publishing Service, 1960.

GINSBERG, B. E., & LAUGHLIN, W. S. Race and intelligence, what do we really know? In R. Cancro (Ed.), *Intelligence: Genetic and environmental influences.* New York: Grune & Stratton, 1971.

GLAVIN, J. P. Persistence of behavior disorders in children. *Exceptional Children,* 1972, 38, 367–376.

GLIDEWELL, J. C., KANTOR, M. B., SMITH, L. M., & STRINGER, L. A. Socialization and social structure in the classroom. In L. W. Hoffman & M. L. Hoffman (Eds.), *Review of child development research* (Vol. 2). New York: Russell Sage Foundation, 1966.

GNAGEY, W. J. *The psychology of discipline in the classroom.* New York: Macmillan, 1969.

GOETZ, E. M., & BAER, D. M. Social control of form diversity and the emergence of new forms in children's blockbuilding. *Journal of Applied Behavior Analysis,* 1973, 6, 209–217.

GOETZ, E. M., & SALMONSON, M. M. The effect of general and descriptive reinforcement on "creativity" in easel painting. In G. Semb (Ed.), *Behavior analysis and education—1972.* Lawrence, Kans.: Kansas University Department of Human Development, 1972.

GOLDIAMOND, I. Moral behavior: A functional analysis. *Psychology Today,* 1968, 2(4), 31–34, 70.

GOLDMAN, R., & FRISTOE, M. *Goldman – Fristoe Test of Articulation.* Circle Pines, Minn.: American Guidance Service, 1969.

GOLDMAN, R., FRISTOE, M., & WOODCOCK, R. W. *Goldman-Fristoe-Woodcock Test of Auditory Discrimination.* Circle Pines, Minn.: American Guidance Service, 1970.

GOLDSTEIN, H. *The social learning curriculum.* Columbus, Ohio: Charles E. Merrill, 1974.

GOLDSTEIN, H. Herbert Goldstein: Social learning of the mentally retarded. In J. M. Kauffman & J. S. Payne (Eds.), *Mental retardation: Introduction and personal perspectives.* Columbus, Ohio: Charles E. Merrill, 1975.

GOLDSTEIN, K. *The organism.* New York: American Book, 1939.

GOLLIN, E. S. Some research problems for developmental psychology. *Child Development,* 1956, 27, 223–235.

GOLLIN, E. S. Developmental studies of visual recognition of incomplete objects. *Perceptual and Motor Skills,* 1960, 11, 289–298.

GOODALL, K. Shapers at work. *Psychology Today,* 1972, *6* (6), 53–63, 132–138.

GORDON, E. W. Methodological problems and pseudoissues in the nature-nurture controversy. In R. Cancro (Ed.), *Intelligence: Genetic and Environmental influences.* New York: Grune & Stratton, 1971.

GORTON, C. E. The effects of various classroom environments on performance of a mental task by mentally retarded and normal children. *Education and Training of the Mentally Retarded,* 1972, *7,* 32–38.

GRAY, B. B. Language acquisition through programmed conditioning. In R. H. Bradfield (Ed.), *Behavior modification: The human endeavor.* San Rafael, Calif.: Dimensions, 1970.

GRIFFITHS, W. *Behavior difficulties of children as perceived and judged by parents, teachers, and children themselves.* Minneapolis: University of Minnesota, 1952.

GRIMM, J. A., BIJOU, S. W., & PARSONS, J. A. A problem-solving model for teaching remedial arithmetic to handicapped young children. *Journal of Abnormal Child Psychology,* 1973, *1,* 26–39.

GUESS, D. A functional analysis of receptive language and productive speech: Acquisition of the plural morpheme. *Journal of Applied Behavior Analysis,* 1969, *2,* 55–64.

GUESS, D., & BAER, D. M. An analysis of individual differences in generalization between receptive and productive language in retarded children. *Journal of Applied Behavior Analysis,* 1973, *5,* 311–329.

GUILFORD, J. P. The structure of intellect. *Psychological Bulletin,* 1956, *52,* 267–293.

GUTHRIE, J. T. Reading comprehension and syntactic responses in good and poor readers. *Journal of Educational Psychology,* 1973, *65,* 294–299.

HAGEN, J. W. The effect of distraction on selective attention. *Child Development,* 1967, *38,* 685–694.

HAGEN, J. W., & FRISCH, S. R. The effect of incidental cues on selective attention. Report No. 57, USPHS Grant HDO 1368. Ann Arbor: Center for Human Growth and Development, University of Michigan, 1968.

HAGEN, J. W., HALLAHAN, D. P., & KAUFFMAN, J. M. *Selective attention performance of institutionalized, retarded children and normals equated on mental and chronological age.* Unpublished manuscript, 1974.

HAGEN, J. W., HARGRAVE, S., & ROSS, W. Prompting and rehearsal on short-term memory. *Child Development,* 1973, *44,* 201–204.

HAGEN, J. W., & HUNTSMAN, N. J. Selective attention in mental retardates. *Developmental Psychology,* 1971, *5,* 151–160.

HAGEN, J. W., & KINGSLEY, P. R. Labeling effects on short-term memory. *Child Development,* 1968, *39,* 113–121.

HAGEN, J. W., MEACHAM, J. A., & MESIBOV, G. Verbal labeling, rehearsal, and short-term memory. *Cognitive Psychology,* 1970, *1,* 47–58.

HAGEN, J. W., & SABO, R. A. A developmental study of selective attention. *Merrill-Palmer Quarterly,* 1967, *13,* 159–172.

HALL, R. V. *Managing behavior*. Lawrence, Kans.: H & H Enterprises, 1971.

HALL, R. V., AXELROD, S., FOUNDOPULOS, M., SHELLMAN, J., CAMPBELL, R. A., & CRANSTON, S. S. The effective use of punishment in the classroom. *Educational Technology*, 1971, *11*(4), 24–26.

HALL, R. V., & BRODEN, M. Behavior changes in brain-injured children through social reinforcement. *Journal of Experimental Child Psychology*, 1967, *5*, 463–479.

HALL, R. V., CRISTLER, C., CRANSTON, S. S., & TUCKER, B. Teachers and parents as researchers using multiple baseline designs. *Journal of Applied Behavior Analysis*, 1970, *3*, 247–255.

HALL, R. V., LUND, D., & JACKSON, D. Effects of teacher attention on study behavior. *Journal of Applied Behavior Analysis*, 1968, *1*, 1–12.

HALLAHAN, D. P. Cognitive styles: Pre-school implications for the disadvantaged. *Journal of Learning Disabilities*, 1970, *3*, 4–9.

HALLAHAN, D. P. Distractibility in the learning disabled child. In W. M. Cruickshank & D. P. Hallahan (Eds.), *Perceptual and learning disabilities in children*, (Vol. 2), *Research and theory*. Syracuse: Syracuse University Press, 1975.

HALLAHAN, D. P., & CRUICKSHANK, W. M. *Psychoeducational foundations of learning disabilities*. Englewood Cliffs, N.J.: Prentice-Hall, 1973.

HALLAHAN, D. P., & KAUFFMAN, J. M. *Learning disabilities: A behavioral definition*. Paper presented at Second International Scientific Conference on Learning Disabilities, Brussels, Jan. 3–7, 1975. (a)

HALLAHAN, D. P., & KAUFFMAN, J. M. Research on the education of distractible and hyperactive children. In W. M. Cruickshank & D. P. Hallahan (Eds.), *Perceptual and learning disabilities in children*. (Vol. 2), *Research and theory*. Syracuse: Syracuse University Press, 1975. (b)

HALLAHAN, D. P., KAUFFMAN, J. M., & BALL, D. W. Selective attention and cognitive tempo of low achieving and high achieving sixth grade males. *Perceptual and Motor Skills*, 1973, *36*, 579–583.

HALLAHAN, D. P., KAUFFMAN, J. M., & BALL, D. W. Developmental trends in recall of central and incidental auditory material. *Journal of Experimental Child Psychology*, 1974, *17*, 409–421. (a)

HALLAHAN, D. P., KAUFFMAN, J. M., & BALL, D. W. Effects of stimulus attenuation on selective attention performance of children. *Journal of Genetic Psychology*, 1974, *125*, 71–77. (b)

HALLAHAN, D. P., STAINBACK, S. B., BALL, D. W., & KAUFFMAN, J. M. Selective attention in cerebral palsied and normal children. *Journal of Abnormal Child Psychology*, 1973, *1*, 280–291.

HALLGREN, B. Specific dyslexia (congenital word blindness: A clinical and genetic study). *Acta Psychiatrica et Neurologica*, 1950, Suppl. 65.

HAMMILL, D., & LARSEN, S. The relationship of selected auditory perceptual skills and reading ability. *Journal of Learning Disabilities*, 1974, *7*, 429–436.

HARING, N. G. (Ed.) *Behavior of exceptional children: An introduction to special education.* Columbus, Ohio: Charles E. Merrill, 1974. (a)

HARING, N. G. Norris G. Haring. In J. M. Kauffman & C. D. Lewis (Eds.), *Teaching children with behavior disorders: Personal perspectives.* Columbus, Ohio: Charles E. Merrill, 1974. (b)

HARING, N. G., & HAYDEN, A. H. (Eds.) *The improvement of instruction.* Seattle: Special Child, 1972.

HARING, N. G., & LOVITT, T. C. Operant methodology and educational technology in special education. In N. G. Haring & R. L. Schiefelbusch (Eds.), *Methods in special education.* New York: McGraw-Hill, 1967.

HARING, N. G., & PHILLIPS, E. L. *Educating emotionally disturbed children.* New York: McGraw-Hill, 1962.

HARING, N. G., & PHILLIPS, E. L. *Analysis and modification of classroom behavior.* Englewood Cliffs, N.J.: Prentice-Hall, 1972.

HARING, N. G., & WHELAN, R. J. Experimental methods in education and management. In N. J. Long, W. C. Morse, & R. G. Newman (Eds.), *Conflict in the classroom.* Belmont, Calif.: Wadsworth, 1965.

HARRIS, F. R., WOLF, M. N., & BAER, D. M. Effects of adult social reinforcement on child behavior. In S. W. Bijou & D. M. Baer (Eds.), *Child development: Readings in experimental analysis.* Englewood Cliffs, N.J.: Prentice-Hall, 1967.

HARROWER, M. E. Social status and moral development. *British Journal of Educational Psychology,* 1934, *4,* 75–95.

HART, B. M., REYNOLDS, N. J., BAER, D. M., BRAWLEY, E. R., & HARRIS, F. R. Effect of contingent and non-contingent social reinforcement on the cooperative play of a preschool child. *Journal of Applied Behavior Analysis,* 1968, *1,* 73–76.

HART, B. M. & RISLEY, T. R. Establishing use of descriptive adjectives in the spontaneous speech of disadvantaged preschool children. *Journal of Applied Behavior Analysis,* 1968, *1,* 109–120.

HART, B. M., & RISLEY, T. R. Using preschool materials to modify the language of disadvantaged children. *Journal of Applied Behavior Analysis,* 1974, *7,* 243–256.

HARTUNG, J. R. A review of procedures to increase verbal imitation skills and functional speech in autistic children. *Journal of Speech and Hearing Disorders,* 1970, *5,* 203–217.

HASAZI, J. E., & HASAZI, S. E. Effects of teacher attention on digit-reversal behavior in an elementary school child. *Journal of Applied Behavior Analysis,* 1972, *5,* 157–162.

HAWKINS, A. S., & OJEMANN, R. H. *A teaching program in human behavior and mental health,* (Book 5), *Handbook for fifth grade teachers.* Iowa City: State University of Iowa, 1960.

HAWKINS, R. P., PETERSON, R. F., SCHWEID, E., & BIJOU, S. W. Behavior therapy in the home: Amelioration of problem parent-child relations with the parent in a therapeutic role. *Journal of Experimental Child Psychology*, 1966, *4*, 99–107.

HEAD, H. *Aphasia and kindred disorders of speech* (Vols. 1 and 2). London: Cambridge University Press, 1926.

HELD, K., & HEIN, A. Movement produced stimulation in the development of visually guided behavior. *Journal of Comparative and Physiological Psychology*, 1963, *56*, 872–876.

HENDRICKSON, L. N., & MUEHL, S. The effect of attention and motor response pretraining on learning to discriminate b and d in kindergarten children. *Journal of Educational Psychology*, 1962, *53*, 236–241.

HESS, R. D., & SHIPMAN, V. C. Maternal influences upon early learning: The cognitive environments of urban preschool children. In R. D. Hess & R. M. Bear (Eds.), *Early education*. Chicago: Aldine, 1968.

HETHERINGTON, E. M. The effects of familial variables on sex typing, on parent-child similarity, and on imitation in children. In J. P. Hill (Ed.), *Minnesota symposia on child psychology* (Vol. 1). Minneapolis: University of Minnesota Press, 1967.

HETHERINGTON, E. M., & MARTIN, B. Family interaction and psychopathology in children. In H. C. Quay & J. S. Werry (Eds.), *Psychopathological disorders of childhood*. New York: Wiley, 1972.

HEWETT, F. M. Educational engineering with emotionally disturbed children. *Exceptional Children*, 1967, *33*, 459–467.

HEWETT, F. M. *The emotionally disturbed child in the classroom*. Boston: Allyn & Bacon, 1968.

HEWETT, F. M. Frank M. Hewett. In J. M. Kauffman & C. D. Lewis (Eds.), *Teaching children with behavior disorders: Personal perspectives*. Columbus, Ohio: Charles E. Merrill, 1974.

HEWETT, F. M., TAYLOR, F., & ARTUSO, A. The Madison Plan really swings. *Today's Education*, 1970, *59*, 15–17.

HEWITT, L. E., & JENKINS, R. L. *Fundamental patterns of maladjustment: The dynamics of their origin*. Springfield: State of Illinois, 1946.

HINSHELWOOD, J. *Congenital word blindness*. London: Lewis, 1917.

HOBBS, N. J. Nicholas J. Hobbs. In J. M. Kauffman & C. D. Lewis (Eds.), *Teaching children with behavior disorders: Personal perspectives*. Columbus, Ohio: Charles E. Merrill, 1974.

HOFFMAN, M. L. Moral development. In P. H. Mussen (Ed.), *Carmichael's manual of child psychology* (3rd ed.; Vol. 2). New York: Wiley, 1970.

HOMME, L. *How to use contingency contracting in the classroom*. Champaign, Ill.: Research Press, 1969.

HOPKINS, B. L., SCHUTTE, R. C., & GARTON, K. L. The effects of access to a playroom on the rate and quality of printing and writing of first and second grade students. *Journal of Applied Behavior Analysis*, 1971, *4*, 77–87.

HUELSMAN, C. B. The WISC subtest syndrome for disabled readers. *Perceptual and Motor Skills*, 1970, *30*, 535–550.

HUNT, J., McV. *Intelligence and experience*. New York: Ronald Press, 1961.

HUTTENLOCHER, J. Discrimination of figure orientation: Effects of relative position. *Journal of Comparative and Physiological Psychology*, 1967, *63*, 359–361.

IAKOBSON, P. N. Social psychology and problems of character education. *Soviet Education*, 1968, *10*(6), 19–27.

INGRAM, D., & EISENSON, J. Therapeutic approaches III: Establishing and developing language in congenitally aphasic children. In J. Eisenson (Ed.), *Aphasia in children*. New York: Harper & Row, 1972.

IRWIN, J. V., MOORE, J. M., & RAMPP, D. L. Nonmedical diagnosis and evaluation. In J. V. Irwin & M. Marge (Eds.), *Principles of childhood language disabilities*. Englewood Cliffs, N.J.: Prentice-Hall, 1972.

JACKSON, J. H. On the physiology of language. *Brain*, 1915, *38*, 59–64.

JAKOBSON, R. *Kindersprache, aphasie, und allgemeine lantgesetze*. Uppsala: Almgrist and Weksell, 1941.

JAKOBSON, R. Child language, aphasia, and general sound laws. (A. Keiler, trans.). The Hague: Monton, 1968.

JANIS, M. The development of moral judgment in preschool children. New Haven: Yale University Child Study Center, 1961 (dittoed).

JENKINS, J. J., & PALERMO, D. S. Mediation processes and the acquisition of linguistic structure. In U. Bellugi & R. Brown (Eds.), The acquisition of language. *Monographs of the Society for Research in Child Development*, 1964, *29*, (1, Whole No. 92).

JENKINS, J. R., GORRAFA, Q., & GRIFFITHS, S. Another look at isolation effects. *American Journal of Mental Deficiency*, 1972, *76*, 591–593.

JENSEN, A. How much can we boost IQ and scholastic achievement? *Harvard Educational Review*, 1969, *39*, 1–123.

JOHNSON, D. J., & MYKLEBUST, H. R. *Learning disabilities: Educational principles and practices*. New York: Grune & Stratton, 1967.

JOHNSON, R. A. A study of children's moral judgments. *Child Development*, 1962, *33*, 327–354.

KAGAN, J. Developmental studies in reflection and analysis. In A. Kidd & J. Riviore (Eds.), *Perceptual development in children*. New York: International Universities Press, 1966.

KAGAN, J., & Lewis, M. Studies of attention in the human infant. *Merrill-Palmer Quarterly of Behavior and Development*, 1965, *11*, 95–127.

KALLMANN, F. J. The genetics of human behavior. *American Journal of Psychiatry*, 1956, *113*, 496–501.

KARNES, M. B. *Helping young children develop language skills*. Washington, D.C.: Council for Exceptional Children, 1968.

KATZ, M. M., Cole, J. O., & BARTON, W. E. (Eds.), *The role and methodology of classification in psychiatry and psychopathology*. Washington, D.C.: U.S. Department of Health, Education, and Welfare, 1965.

KAUFFMAN, J. M. Psychoeducational technology: Criteria for assessment and control in special education. *Focus on Exceptional Children*, 1973, 5(3), 1–5.

KAUFFMAN, J. M. Behavior modification. In W. M. Cruickshank & D. P. Hallahan (Eds.), *Perceptual and learning disabilities in children*, (Vol. 2), *Research and theory*. Syracuse: Syracuse University Press, 1975.

KAUFFMAN, J. M., & HALLAHAN, D. P. Control of rough physical behavior using novel contingencies and directive teaching. *Perceptual and Motor Skills*, 1973, *36*, 1225–1226.

KAUFFMAN, J. M., & HALLAHAN, D. P. The medical model and the science of special education. *Exceptional Children*, 1974, *41*, 97–102.

KAUFFMAN, J. M., KNEEDLER, R. D., GAMACHE, R., & HALLAHAN, D. P. Effects of imitation on children's subsequent imitative behavior. Unpublished manuscript. University of Virginia, 1975.

KAUFFMAN, J. M., LaFLEUR, N. K., HALLAHAN, D. P., & CHANES, C. M. Imitation as a consequence for children's behavior: Two experimental case studies. *Behavior Therapy*, 1975, *6*, 535–542.

KAUFFMAN, J. M., & LEWIS, C. D. (Eds.) *Teaching children with behavior disorders: Personal perspectives*. Columbus, Ohio: Charles E. Merrill, 1974.

KAUFFMAN, J. M., & Scranton, T. R. Parent control of thumb-sucking in the home. *Child Study Journal*, 1974, *4*, 1–10.

KAZDIN, A. E. Methodological and assessment considerations in evaluating reinforcement programs in applied settings. *Journal of Applied Behavior Analysis*, 1973, *6*, 517–531.

KAZDIN, A. E., & BOOTZIN, R. R. The token economy: An evaluative review. *Journal of Applied Behavior Analysis*, 1972, *5*, 343–372.

KAZDIN, A. E., & CRAIGHEAD, W. E. Behavior modification in special education. In L. Mann & D. A. Sabatino (Eds.), *The first review of special education* (Vol. 2). Philadelphia: Journal of Special Education Press, 1973.

KEOGH, B. K., & BECKER, L. D. Early detection of learning problems: Questions, cautions, and guidelines. *Exceptional Children*, 1973, *40*, 5–11.

KEOGH, B. K., & DONLON, G. M. Field independence, impulsivity, and learning disabilities. *Journal of Learning Disabilities*, 1972, *5*, 331–336.

KEPHART, N. C. *The slow learner in the classroom*. Columbus, Ohio: Charles E. Merrill, 1960.

KEPHART, N. C. *The slow learner in the classroom* (2nd ed.). Columbus, Ohio: Charles E. Merrill, 1971.

KEPHART, N. C. The perceptual-motor match. In W. M. Cruickshank & D. P. Hallahan (Eds.), *Perceptual and learning disabilities in children*. Vol. I: *Psychoeducational practices*. Syracuse, N.Y.: Syracuse University Press, 1975.

KEPHART, N. C., & STRAUSS, A. A. A clinical factor influencing variations in IQ. *American Journal of Orthopsychiatry*, 1940, *10*, 345–350.

KINGSLEY, P. R., & HAGEN, J. W. Induced versus spontaneous rehearsal in short-term memory in nursery school children. *Developmental Psychology,* 1969, *1,* 40–46.

KIRK, S. A. Research in education. In H. A. Stevens & R. Heber (Eds.), *Mental retardation.* Chicago: University of Chicago Press, 1964.

KIRK, S. A. Samuel A. Kirk. In J. M. Kauffman & D. P. Hallahan (Eds.), *Teaching children with learning disabilities: Personal perspectives.* Columbus, Ohio: Charles E. Merrill, 1976.

KIRK, S. A., & KIRK, W. *Psycholinguistic learning disabilities: Diagnosis and remediation.* Urbana: University of Illinois Press, 1971.

KIRK, S. A., McCARTHY, J. J., & KIRK, W. D. *Illinois test of psychcolinguistic abilities* (Experimental ed.). Urbana: University of Illinois Press, 1961.

KIRK, S. A., McCARTHY, J. J., & KIRK, W. D. *Illinois test of psycholinguistic abilities* (Rev. ed.). Urbana: University of Illinois Press, 1968.

KLAUS, R., & GRAY, S. The early training project for disadvantaged children: A report after five years. *Monographs of the Society for Research in Child Development,* 1968, *33* (4, Serial No. 120).

KNAPCZYK, D. R., & LIVINGSTON, G. Self-recording and student teacher supervision: Variables within a token economy structure. *Journal of Applied Behavior Analysis,* 1973, *6,* 481–486.

KNAPCZYK, D. R., & LIVINGSTON, G. The effects of prompting question-asking upon on-task behavior and reading comprehension. *Journal of Applied Behavior Analysis,* 1974, *7,* 115–121.

KOHLBERG, L. *The development of modes of moral thinking and choice in the years ten to sixteen.* Unpublished doctoral dissertation, University of Chicago, 1958.

KOHLBERG, L. The development of children's orientations toward a moral order: I. Sequence in the development of moral thought. *Vita Humana,* 1963, *6,* 11–33.

KOHLBERG, L. Development of moral character and moral ideology. In M. L. Hoffman & L. W. Hoffman (Eds.), *Review of child development research* (Vol. 1). New York: Russell Sage Foundation, 1964.

KOHLBERG, L. Montessori with the culturally disadvantaged: A cognitive-developmental interpretation and some research findings. In R. D. Hess & R. M. Bear (Eds.), *Early Education.* Chicago: Aldine, 1968.

KOHLBERG, L. *Stage and sequence: The developmental approach to morality.* New York: Holt, Rinehart, & Winston, 1969.

KOPPITZ, E. M. *The Bender Gestalt test for young children.* New York: Grune & Stratton, 1964.

KREMENAK, S., & OJEMANN, R. H. *Learning: The on-your-own series. Programs A, B, & C.* Iowa City: University of Iowa, 1965.

KROTH, R., WHELAN, R. J., & STABLES, J. M. Teacher application of behavior principles in home and classroom environments. *Focus on Exceptional Children,* 1970, *1,* 1–10.

KRUMBOLTZ, J. D., & KRUMBOLTZ, H. B. *Changing children's behavior.* Englewood Cliffs, N.J.: Prentice-Hall, 1972.

KUBANY, E. S., WEISS, L. E., & SLOGGETT, B. B. The good behavior clock: A reinforcement/time out procedure for reducing disruptive classroom behavior. *Journal of Behavior Therapy and Experimental Psychiatry,* 1971, *2,* 173–179.

DE LAGUNA, G. A. *Speech: Its function and development.* Bloomington: Indiana University Press, 1927.

LAHADERNE, H. M. Attitudinal and intellectual correlates of attention: A study of four sixth-grade classrooms. *Journal of Educational Psychology,* 1968, *59,* 320–324.

LAHEY,B. B., MCNEES, M. P. & BROWN, C. C. Modification of deficits in reading for comprehension. *Journal of Applied Behavior Analysis,* 1973, *6,* 475–480.

LAPOUSE, R., & MONK, M. An epidemiologic study of behavior characteristics in children. *American Journal of Public Health,* 1958, *48,* 1134–1144.

LAVRENT'EVA, T. V., & RUZSKAYA, A. G. Comparative analysis of touch and vision: Communication v. simultaneous intersensory comparison of form at a preschool age. *Dokl. Akad. Pedagog.* NAUK RSFSR, 1960, *44,* 73–76.

LEE, L. *Northwestern Syntax Screening Test.* Evanston, Ill.: Northwestern University Press, 1970.

LEITENBERG, H. Is time out from positive reinforcement an aversive event? *Psychological Bulletin,* 1965, *64,* 428–441.

LEITENBERG, H. The use of single-case methodology in psychotherapy research. *Journal of Abnormal Psychology,* 1973, *82,* 87–101.

LEIZER, J. I., & ROGERS, R. W. Effects of method of discipline, timing of punishment, and timing of test on resistance to temptation. *Child Development,* 1974, *45,* 790–793.

LENNEBERG, E. H. *Biological foundations of language.* New York: Wiley, 1967.

LENT, J. R. James R. Lent: Teaching daily living skills. In J. M. Kauffman & J. S. Payne (Eds.), *Mental retardation: Introduction and personal perspectives.* Columbus, Ohio: Charles E. Merrill, 1975.

LERNER, E. *Constraint areas and the moral judgment of children.* Menasha, Wis.: George Banta, 1937. (a)

LERNER, E. Perspectives in moral reasoning. *American Journal of Sociology,* 1937, *43,* 249–269. (b)

LERNER, J. W. *Children with learning disabilities: Theories, diagnosis, and teaching strategy.* Boston: Houghton Mifflin, 1971.

LESSING, E., & ZAGORIN, S. Dimensions of psychopathology in middle childhood as evaluated by three symptom checklists. *Educational and Psychological Measurement,* 1971, *31,* 175–198.

LEVIN, H., & KAPLAN, E. *Studies of oral reading, X: The eye-voice span for active and passive sentences.* Unpublished manuscript, Cornell University, 1967.

LEVIN, H., & TURNER, E. Sentence structure and the eye-voice span. *Project Literacy Reports* (Cornell University), 1966, No. 7, 79–87.

LEVINE, M. Psychological testing of children. In L. W. Hoffman & M. L. Hoffman (Eds.), *Review of child development research* (Vol. 2). New York: Russell Sage Foundation, 1966.

LEWIS, M. *Infant speech.* London: Kegan Paul, Trench, Truber, & Co., 1936.

LEWIS, M. *How children learn to speak.* New York: Basic Books, 1959.

LEWIS, M. *Exploratory studies in the development of a face schema.* Paper presented at the American Psychological Association, Chicago, September, 1965.

LEWIS, M. Development of attention and perception in the infant and young child. In W. M. Cruickshank & D. P. Hallahan (Eds.), *Perceptual and learning problems in children,* (Vol. 2), *Research and theory.* Syracuse: Syracuse University Press, 1975.

LINDSLEY, O. R. Direct measurement and prosthesis of retarded behavior. *Journal of Education,* 1964, *147,* 62–81.

LIPPITT, R., & GOLD, M. Classroom social structure as a mental health problem. *Journal of Social Issues,* 1959, *15,* 40–58.

LONG, N. J. Nicholas J. Long. In J. M. Kauffman & C. D. Lewis (Eds.), *Teaching children with behavior disorders: Personal perspectives.* Columbus, Ohio: Charles E. Merrill, 1974.

LONG, N. J., FAGEN, S., & STEVENS, D. *Psychoeducational Screening System for Identifying Resourceful, Marginal, and Vulnerable Pupils in the Primary Grades.* Washington, D.C.: Psychoeducational Resources, 1971.

LOVAAS, O. I. Cue properties of words: The control of operant responding by rate and content of verbal operants. *Child Development,* 1964, *35,* 245–256.

LOVAAS, O. I. A program for the establishment of speech in psychotic children. In J. K. Wing (Ed.), *Early childhood autism: Clinical, educational, and social aspects.* New York: Pergamon, 1966.

LOVAAS, O. I. *Behavior modification: Teaching language to psychotic children.* Instructional film, 45 min., 16 mm—sound, color. Englewood Cliffs, N.J.: Prentice-Hall, 1969.

LOVELL, K., & BRADBURY, B. The learning of English morphology in educationally subnormal special school children. *American Journal of Mental Deficiency,* 1967, *71,* 609–615.

LOVITT, T. C. Assessment of children with learning disabilities. *Exceptional Children,* 1967, *34,* 233–239.

LOVITT, T. C. Operant conditioning techniques for children with learning disabilities. *Journal of Special Education,* 1968, *2,* 283–289.

LOVITT, T. C. Behavior modification: The current scene. *Exceptional Children,* 1970, *37,* 85–91.

Lovitt, T. C. *Applied behavior analysis techniques and curriculum research.* Report submitted to the National Institute of Education, 1973. (a)

Lovitt, T. C. Self-management projects with children with behavioral disabilities. *Journal of Learning Disabilities,* 1973, *6,* 138–150. (b)

Lovitt, T. C. Thomas C. Lovitt. In J. M. Kauffman & D. P. Hallahan (Eds.), *Teaching children with learning disabilities: Personal perspectives.* Columbus, Ohio: Charles E. Merrill, 1976.

Lovitt, T. C., & Curtiss, K. Effects of manipulating an antecedent event on mathematics response rate. *Journal of Applied Behavior Analysis,* 1968, *1,* 329–333.

Lovitt, T. C., Guppy, T. E., & Blattner, J. E. The use of a free-time contingency with fourth graders to increase spelling accuracy. *Behaviour Research and Therapy,* 1969, *7,* 151–156.

Lovitt, T. C., & Smith, J. O. Effects of instructions on an individual's verbal behavior. *Exceptional Children,* 1972, *38,* 685–693.

Luria, A. R. *The role of speech in the regulation of normal and abnormal behavior.* New York: Liverwright, 1961.

McCarthy, J., & Paraskevopoulos, J. Behavior patterns of learning disabled, emotionally disturbed, and average children. *Exceptional Children,* 1969, *36,* 69–74.

Maccoby, E. E. Selective auditory attention in children. In L. P. Lipsitt & C. C. Spiker (Eds.), *Recent advances in child development and behavior* (Vol. 3). New York: Academic Press, 1967.

Maccoby, E. E., & Hagen, J. W. Effects of distraction upon central versus incidental recall: Developmental trends. *Journal of Experimental Child Psychology,* 1965, *2,* 280–289.

MacFarlane, J., Allen, L., & Honzik, M. *A developmental study of the behavior problems of normal children between twenty-one months and fourteen years.* Berkeley and Los Angeles: University of California Press, 1954.

McGinnis, M. A. *Aphasic children.* Washington, D.C.: Volta Bureau, 1963.

McIntosh, D. K., & Dunn, L. M. Children with major specific learning disabilities. In L. M. Dunn (Ed.), *Exceptional children in the schools* (2nd ed.). New York: Holt, Rinehart, & Winston, 1973.

MacMillan, D. L., Forness, S. R., & Trumbull, B. M. The role of punishment in the classroom. *Exceptional Children,* 1973, *40,* 85–96.

McNeill, D. Developmental psycholinguistics. In F. Smith & G. A. Miller (Eds.), *The genesis of language: A psycholinguistic approach.* Cambridge: MIT Press, 1966.

McNeill, D. The development of language. In P. H. Mussen (Ed.), *Carmichael's manual of child psychology* (3rd ed.). New York: Wiley, 1970.

MacRae, R. A test of Piaget's theories of moral development. *Journal of Abnormal and Social Psychology,* 1954, *49,* 14–18.

Madsen, C. H., Becker, W. C., & Thomas, D. R. Rules, praise, and ignoring:

Elements of elementary classroom control. *Journal of Applied Behavior Analysis*, 1968, *1*, 139–150.

MADSEN, C. H., MADSEN, C. K., SAUDARGAS, R. A., HAMMOND, W. R., SMITH, J. B., & EDGAR, D. E. Classroom RAID (Rules, Approval, Ignore, Disapproval): A cooperative approach for professionals and volunteers. *Journal of School Psychology*, 1970, *8*, 180–185.

MADSEN, C. K., & MADSEN, C. H. *Parents/children/discipline*. Boston: Allyn & Bacon, 1972.

MALONEY, K. B., & HOPKINS, B. L. The modification of sentence structure and its relationship to subjective judgments of creativity in writing. *Journal of Applied Behavior Analysis*, 1973, *6*, 425–433.

MARGE, M. The general problem of language disabilities in children. In J. V. Irwin & M. Marge (Eds.), *Principles of childhood language disabilities*. Englewood Cliffs, N.J.: Prentice-Hall, 1972.

MARTIN, G. L., & POWERS, R. B. Attention span: an operant conditioning analysis. *Exceptional Children*, 1967, *33*, 565–570.

MASSAD, V. I., & ETZEL, B. C. Acquisition of phonetic sounds by preschool children. In G. Semb (Ed.), *Behavior analysis and education—1972*. Lawrence, Kans.: Kansas University Department of Human Development, 1972.

MEDINNUS, G. R. Immanent justice in children: A review of the literature and additional data. *Journal of Genetic Psychology*, 1959, *90*, 253–262.

MEEHL, P. E. Schizotaxia, schizotypy, schizophrenia. *American Psychologist*, 1962, *17*, 827–838.

MEICHENBAUM, D., & GOODMAN, J. Reflection-impulsivity and verbal control of motor behavior. *Child Development*, 1969, *40*, 785–797.

MEIER, J. H. Prevalence and characteristics of learning disabilities found in second grade children. *Journal of Learning Disabilities*, 1971, *4*, 1–16.

MENNINGER, K. *The vital balance*. New York: Viking, 1963.

MENYUK, P. *The development of speech*. New York: Bobbs-Merrill, Co., 1972.

MEYEN, E. L., & HIERONYMOUS, A. N. The age placement of academic skills in curriculum for EMR. *Exceptional Children*, 1970, *36*, 333–339.

MILLER, L. C. Dimensions of psychopathology in middle childhood. *Psychological Reports*, 1967, *21*, 897–903.

MINDE, K., LEWIN, D., WEISS, G., LAVIGUEUR, H., DOUGLAS, V., & SYKES, E. The hyperactive child in elementary school: A 5 year controlled followup. *Exceptional Children*, 1971, *38*, 215–221.

*Minimal brain dysfunction in children: Terminology and identification*. Phase 1 of a three-phase project. Washington, D.C.: U.S. Dept. of HEW, 1966. (NINDB Monog. No. 3).

*Minimal brain dysfunction national project on learning disabilities in children*. Task Force II. U.S. Public Health Service Publication, No. 2015, 1969.

MINSKOFF, E. H., WISEMAN, D. E., & MINSKOFF, J. G. *The MWM Program for*

*Developing Language Abilities*. Ridgefield, N.J.: Educational Performance Associates, 1974.

MISHLER, E. G., & WAXLER, N. E. *Interaction in families: An experimental study of family processes in schizophrenia*. New York: Wiley, 1968.

MONDANI, M. S., & TUTKO, T. A. Relationship of academic underachievement to incidental learning. *Journal of Consulting and Clinical Psychology*, 1969, *33*, 558–560.

MOONEY, C. H. Recognition of novel visual configurations with and without eye movements. *Journal of Experimental Psychology*, 1958, *56*, 133–138.

MORSE, W. C., CUTLER, R. L., & FINK, A. H. *Public school classes for the emotionally handicapped: A research analysis*. Washington, D.C.: Council for Exceptional Children, 1964.

MYERS, P. S., & HAMMILL, D. D. *Methods for learning disorders*. New York: Wiley, 1969.

MYKLEBUST, H. R. Learning disabilities: Definition and overview. In H. R. Myklebust (Ed.), *Progress in learning disabilities*. New York: Grune & Stratton, 1968.

MYKLEBUST, H. R., & BOSHES, B. *Minimal brain damage in children*. Final Report, Contract 108-65-142, Neurological and Sensory Disease Control Program. Washington, D.C.: Department of Health, Education, and Welfare, 1969.

National Advisory Committee on Handicapped Children, Conference sponsored by Bureau of Education for the Handicapped, U.S. Office of Education, Washington, D.C.; Sept. 28, 1967.

National Advisory Committee on Handicapped Children. *Special education for handicapped children: First annual report*, Washington, D.C.: U.S. Department of Health, Education, and Welfare, 1968.

NELSON, C. M. Techniques for screening conduct disturbed children. *Exceptional Children*, 1971, *37*, 501–507.

NELSON, C. M., WORELL, J., & POLSGROVE, L. Behaviorally disordered peers as contingency managers. *Behavior Therapy*, 1973, *4*, 270–276.

NELSON, K. Structure and strategy in learning to talk. *Monographs of the Society for Research in Child Development*, 1973, *38* (1 and 2 Serial No. 149).

NEWBROUGH, J. R., & KELLY, J. A. A study of reading achievement in a population of school children. In J. Money (Ed.), *Reading disability, progress and research needs in dyslexia*. Baltimore: Johns Hopkins Press, 1962.

NORRIE, E. Ordblindhedens. In S. J. Thompson, *Reading disability*. Springfield, Ill.: Charles C. Thomas, 1959.

OAKAN, R., WIENER, M., & CROMER, W. Identification, organization and reading comprehension for good and poor readers. *Journal of Educational Psychology*, 1971, *62*, 71–78.

ODOM, R. D., & CORBIN, D. W. Perceptual salience and children's multidimensional problem solving. *Child Development*, 1973, *44*, 425–432.

O'GRADY, D. J. Psycholinguistic abilities in learning disabled, emotionally disturbed, and normal children. *Journal of Special Education,* 1974, *8,* 157–165.

OJEMANN, R. H. Investiagtions on the effects of teaching an understanding and appreciation of behavior dynamics. In G. Caplan (Ed.), *Prevention of mental disorders in children.* New York: Basic Books, 1961.

O'LEARY, K. D. The assessment of psychopathology in children. In H. C. Quay & J. S. Werry (Eds.), *Psychopatholigical disorders of childhood.* New York: Wiley, 1972.

O'LEARY, K. D., & DRABMAN, R. Token reinforcement programs in the classroom: A review. *Psychological Bulletin,* 1971, *75,* 379–398.

O'LEARY, K. D., & O'LEARY, S. G. (Eds.). *Classroom management: The successful use of behavior modification.* New York: Pergamon, 1972.

O'LEARY, K. D., O'LEARY, S. G., & BECKER, W. C. Modification of a deviant sibling interaction pattern in the home. *Behaviour Research and Therapy,* 1967, *5,* 113–120.

ORTON, S. *Reading, writing, and speech problems in children.* New York: Norton, 1937.

OSBORN, J. Teaching a teaching language to disadvantaged children. In M. A. Brottman (Ed.), Language remediation for the disadvantaged preschool child. *Monographs of the Society for Research in Child Development,* 1968, *33*(8, 36–48, Serial No. 124).

OSGOOD, C. E. A behavioristic analysis of perception and language as cognitive phenomena. In J. S. Bruner (Ed.), *Contemporary approaches to cognition.* Cambridge: Harvard University Press, 1957.

OWEN, F. W., ADAMS, P. A., FORREST, T., STOLZ, L. M., & FISHER, S. Learning disorders in children: Sibling studies. *Monographs of the Society for Research in Child Development,* 1971, *36*(4, Serial No. 144).

PACKARD, R. G. The control of "classroom attention": A group contingency for complex behavior. *Journal of Applied Behavior Analysis,* 1970, *3,* 13–28.

PALKES, H., STEWART, M., & FREEDMAN, J. Improvement in maze performance of hyperactive boys as a function of verbal-training procedures. *The Journal of Special Education,* 1971, *5,* 337–342.

PALKES, H., STEWART, M., & KAHANA, B. Porteus maze performance of hyperactive boys after training in self-directed verbal commands. *Child Development,* 1968, *39,* 817–826.

PARASKEVOPOULOS, J., & McCARTHY, J. Behavior patterns of children with special learning disabilities. *Psychology in the Schools,* 1969, 7, 42–46.

PARSONS, J. A. The reciprocal modification of arithmetic behavior and program development. In G. Semb (Ed.), *Behavior analysis and education—1972.* Lawrence, Kans.: Kansas University Department of Human Development, 1972.

PATE, J. E., & WEBB, W. W. *First Grade Screening Test. Circle Pines,* Minn.: American Guidance Service, 1969.

PATTERSON, G. R. An empirical approach to the classification of disturbed children. *Journal of Clinical Psychology*, 1964, *20*, 326–337.

PATTERSON, G. R. An application of conditioning techniques to the control of a hyperactive child. In L. Krasner & L. Ullmann (Eds.), *Case studies in behavior modification*. New York: Holt, Rinehart, & Winston, 1965.

PATTERSON, G. R. *Families: Applications of social learning to family life*. Champaign, Ill.: Research Press, 1971.

PATTERSON, G. R. Reprogramming the families of aggressive boys. In C. Thoresen (Ed.), *Behavior modification in education*. Seventy-second yearbook of the National Society for the Study of Education, Part 1. Chicago: University of Chicago Press, 1973.

PATTERSON, G. R., & COBB, J. A. A dyadic analysis of "aggressive" behaviors. In J. P. Hill (Ed.), *Minnesota symposia on child psychology* (Vol. 5). Minneapolis: University of Minnesota Press, 1971.

PATTERSON, G. R., COBB, J. A., & RAY, R. S. Direct intervention in the classroom: A set of procedures for the aggressive child. In F. W. Clark, D. R. Evans, L. A. Hamerlynck (Eds.), *Implementing behavioral programs for schools and clinics*. Champaign, Ill.: Research Press, 1972.

PATTERSON, G. R., & GULLION, M. E. *Living with children: New methods for parents and teachers*. Champaign, Ill.: Research Press, 1968.

PATTERSON, G. R., JONES, R., WHITTIER, J., & WRIGHT, M. A. A behavior modification technique for the hyperactive child. *Behaviour Research and Therapy*, 1965, *2*, 217–226.

PATTERSON, G. R., LITTMAN, R. A., & BRICKER, W. A. Assertive behavior in children: A step toward a theory of aggression. *Monographs of the Society for Research in Child Development*, 1967, *32* (5, 1–43, Serial No. 113).

PATTERSON, G. R., SHAW, D. A., & EBNER, M. J. Teachers, peers, and parents as agents of change in the classroom. In F. A. M. Benson (Ed.), *Modifying deviant social behaviors in various classroom settings*. Eugene: University of Oregon Department of Special Education, 1969.

PAYNE, J. S., KAUFFMAN, J. M., BROWN, G. B., & DeMOTT, R. M. *Exceptional children in focus*. Columbus, Ohio: Charles E. Merrill, 1974.

PETER, L. J. *Prescriptive teaching*. New York: McGraw-Hill, 1965.

PETERSON, D. R. Behavior problems of middle childhood. *Journal of Consulting Psychology*, 1961, *25*, 205–209.

PETERSON, D. R., BECKER, W. C., SHOEMAKER, D. J., LURIA, Z., & HELLMER, L. A. Child behavior problems and parental attitudes. *Child Development*, 1961, *32*, 151–162.

PETERSON, D. R., QUAY, H. C., & CAMERON, G. R. Personality and background factors in juvenile delinquency as inferred from questionnaire responses. *Journal of Consulting Psychology*, 1959, *23*, 392–399.

PETERSON, D. R., QUAY, H. C., & TIFFANY, T. C. Personality factors related to juvenile delinquency. *Child Development*, 1961, *32*, 355–372.

PIAGET, J. *The moral judgment of the child.* Glencoe, Ill.: Free Press, 1948. (Originally published 1932.)

PIAGET, J., & VINH-BANG. Comparisons des mouvements oculaires et des centrations du regard chez l'enfant et chez l'adulte. *Archives de Psychologie,* 1961, *38,* 167–200.

PICK, H. L., & PICK, A. D. Sensory and perceptual development. In P. H. Mussen (Ed.), *Carmichael's manual of child psychology* (3rd ed.). New York: Wiley, 1970.

PIMM, J. B., QUAY, H. C., & WERRY, J. S. Dimensions of problem behavior in first grade children. *Psychology in the Schools,* 1967, *4,* 155–157.

QUAY, H. C. Personality dimensions in delinquent males as inferred from the factor analysis of behavior ratings. *Journal of Research in Crime and Delinquency,* 1964, *1,* 33–37. (a)

QUAY, H. C. Dimensions of personality in delinquent boys as inferred from the factor analysis of case history data. *Child Development,* 1964, *35,* 479–484. (b)

QUAY, H. C. Personality patterns in preadolescent delinquent boys. *Educational and Psychological Measurement,* 1966, *26,* 99–110.

QUAY, H. C. Patterns of aggression, withdrawal, and immaturity. In H. C. Quay & J. S. Werry (Eds.), *Psychopathological disorders of childhood.* New York: Wiley, 1972.

QUAY, H. C., MORSE, W. C., & CUTLER, R. L. Personality patterns of pupils in special classes for the emotionally disturbed. *Exceptional Children,* 1966, *32,* 297–301.

QUAY, H. C., & PETERSON, D. R. *Behavior problem checklist.* Champaign, Ill.: Children's Research Center, University of Illinois, 1967.

QUAY, H. C., & QUAY, L. C. Behavior problems in early adolescence. *Child Development,* 1965, *36,* 215–220.

QUILITCH, H. R., & RISLEY, T. R. The effects of play materials on social play. *Journal of Applied Behavior Analysis,* 1973, *6,* 573–578.

RAPAPORT, D., GILL, M. M., & SCHAFER, R. *Diagnostic psychological testing* (Rev. ed. by R. R. Holt; 2nd ed.). New York: International Universities Press, 1968.

RAY, R. S., SHAW, D. A., & COBB, J. A. The work box: An innovation in teaching attentional behavior. *The School Counselor,* 1970, *18,* 15–35.

RAYEK, E., & NESSELROAD, E. Application of behavior principles to the teaching of writing, spelling, and composition. In G. Semb (Ed.), *Behavior analysis and education—1972.* Lawrence, Kans.: Kansas University Department of Human Development, 1972.

REESE, H. W., & LIPSITT, L. P. (Eds.) *Experimental child psychology.* New York: Academic Press, 1970.

*Report of the Conference on the Use of Stimulant Drugs in the Treatment of Behaviorally Disturbed Young School Children.* Sponsored by the Office of Child Development and the Office of the Assistant Secretary for Health and Scientific Affairs, HEW, Washington, D.C., Jan. 11–12, 1971.

REYNOLDS, N. J., & RISLEY, T. R. The role of social and material reinforcers in increasing talking of a disadvantaged preschool child. *Journal of Applied Behavior Analysis,* 1968, *1,* 253–262.

RISLEY, T. R., & BAER, D. M. Operant behavior modification: The deliberate development of behavior. In B. M. Caldwell & H. N. Ricciuti (Eds.), *Review of child development research* (Vol. 3). Chicago: University of Chicago Press, 1973.

RISLEY, T. R., & HART, B. Developing correspondence between the non-verbal and verbal behavior of preschool children. *Journal of Applied Behavior Analysis,* 1968, *1,* 267–281.

RISLEY, T. R., & REYNOLDS, N. J. Emphasis as a prompt for verbal imitation. *Journal of Applied Behavior Analysis,* 1970, *3,* 185–190.

RISLEY, T. R., & WOLF, M. M. Establishing functional speech in echolalic children. *Behaviour Research and Therapy,* 1967, *5,* 73–88.

ROACH, E., & KEPHART, N. *The Purdue-Perceptual-Motor Survey.* Columbus, Ohio: Charles E. Merrill, 1966.

ROBINS, L. N. *Deviant children grown up.* Baltimore: Williams & Wilkins, 1966.

ROBINS, L. N. Follow-up studies of behavior disorders in children. In H. C. Quay & J. S. Werry (Eds.), *Psychopathological disorders of childhood.* New York: Wiley, 1972.

ROBBINS, M., & GLASS, G. V. The Doman-Delacato rationale: A critical analysis. In J. Hellmuth (Ed.), *Educational Therapy* (Vol. 2). Seattle: Special Child Publications, 1969.

ROOS, P. Human rights and behavior modification. *Mental Retardation,* 1974, *12,* 3–6.

ROSENZWEIG, M. R. Environmental complexity, cerebral change, and behavior. *American Psychologist,* 1966, *21,* 321–332.

ROSS, A. O., LACEY, H. M., & PARTON, D. A. The development of a behavior checklist for boys. *Child Development,* 1965, *36,* 1013–1027.

ROST, K. J., & CHARLES, D. C. Academic achievement of brain injured and hyperactive children in isolation. *Exceptional Children,* 1967, *34,* 125–126.

RUBIN, R., & BALOW, B. Learning and behavior disorders: A longitudinal study. *Exceptional Children* 1971, *38,* 293–299.

RYBACK, D., & STAATS, A. W. Parents as behavior therapy-technicians in treating reading deficits (dyslexia). *Journal of Behavior Therapy and Experimental Psychiatry,* 1970, *1,* 109–119.

SABATINO, D. A., & YSSELDYKE, J. E. Effect of extraneous "background" on visual-perceptual performance of readers and non-readers. *Perceptual and Motor Skills,* 1972, *35,* 323–328.

SAILOR, W., GUESS, D., & BAER, D. M. Functional language for verbally deficient children: An experimental program. *Mental Retardation,* 1973, *11* (3), 27–35.

SARASON, S. B. *Psychological problems in mental deficiency*. New York: Harper, 1949.

DESAUSSURE, F. *Cours de linguistique générale*. Paris: 1916. *Course in general linguistics*. (W. Baskin, trans.) New York: Philosophical Library, 1959.

SCHAEFER, E. S. Development of hierarchical, configurational models for parent behavior and child behavior. In J. P. Hill (Ed.), *Minnesota symposia on child psychology* (Vol. 5). Minneapolis: University of Minnesota Press, 1971.

SCHUTTE, R. D., & HOPKINS, B. L. The effects of teacher attention following instructions in a kindergarten class. *Journal of Applied Behavior Analysis*, 1970, *3*, 117–122.

SCHWARZ, R. H. Mental age as it relates to school achievement among educable mentally retarded adolescents. *Education and Training of the Mentally Retarded*, 1969, *4*, 53–56.

SCHWARZ, R. H., & COOK, J. J. Mental age as a predictor of academic achievement. *Education and Training of the Mentally Retarded*, 1971, *6*, 12–15.

SCHWEBEL, A. S. Effects of impulsivity on performance of verbal tasks in middle and lower class children. *American Journal of Orthopsychiatry*, 1966, *36*, 13–21.

SEKULER, R. W., & ROSENBLITH, J. F. Discrimination of direction of line and the effect of stimulus alignment. *Psychonomic Science*, 1964, *1*, 143–144.

SHERMAN, D. Review of "Goldman-Fristoe Test of Articulation." *Professional Psychology*, 1970, *1*, 493–494.

SHORES, R. E., & HAUBRICH, P. A. Effect of cubicles in educating emotionally disturbed children. *Exceptional Children*, 1969, *36*, 21–26.

SIDMAN, M., & WILLSON-MORRIS, M. Testing for reading comprehension: A brief report on stimulus control. *Journal of Applied Behavior Analysis*, 1974, *7*, 327–332.

SILVERMAN, M., DAVIDS, A., & ANDREWS, J. M. Powers of attention and academic achievement. *Perceptual and Motor Skills*, 1963, *17*, 243–249.

SKINNER, B. F. *Science and human behavior*. New York: Free Press, 1953.

SKINNER, B. F. *Verbal behavior*. Englewood Cliffs, N.J.: Prentice-Hall, 1957.

SLATER, B. R. Effects of noise on pupil performance. *Journal of Educational Psychology*, 1968, *59*, 239–243.

SLUYTER, D. J., & HAWKINS, R. P. Delayed reinforcement of classroom behavior by parents. *Journal of Learning Disabilities*, 1972, *5*, 20–28.

SMIRNOV, A. Psychology, pedagogy, and the school. *Soviet Education*, 1964, *7*(10), 22–30.

SMITH, D. D., & LOVITT, T. C. The educational diagnosis and remediation of written b and d reversal problems: A case study. *Journal of Learning Disabilities*, 1973, *6*, 356–363.

SMITH, D. D., LOVITT, T. C., & KIDDER, J. D. Using reinforcement contingencies and teaching aids to alter the subtraction performance of children with learning disabilities. In G. Semb (Ed.), *Behavior analysis and edu-*

*cation—1972.* Lawrence, Kans.: Kansas University Department of Human Development, 1972.

SOMMERVILL, J. W., WARNBERG, L. S., & BOST, D. E. Effects of cubicles versus increased stimulation on task performance by first-grade males perceived as distractible and nondistractible. *Journal of Special Education,* 1973, *7,* 169–185.

SPEARMAN, C. "General intelligence," objectively determined and measured. *American Journal of Psychology,* 1904, *15,* 201–293.

SPEARMAN, C. *The abilities of man.* London: Macmillan, 1927.

SPIVACK, G., & SPOTTS, J. The Devereux Child Behavior Scale: Symptom behaviors in latency age children. *American Journal of Mental Deficiency,* 1965, *69,* 839–853.

SPIVACK, G., & SPOTTS, J. *Devereux Child Behavior (DCB) Rating Scale.* Devon, Pa.: Devereux Foundation, 1966.

SROUFE, L. A., SONIES, B. C., WEST, W. D., & WRIGHT, F. S. Anticipatory heart rate deceleration and reaction time in children with and without referral for learning disability. *Child Development,* 1973, *44,* 267–273.

SROUFE, L. A. Drug treatment of children with behavior problems. In F. Horowitz (Ed.), *Review of child development research,* Vol. 4, University of Chicago Press, 1975.

STAATS, A. W. *Learning, language, and cognition.* New York: Holt, Rinehart, & Winston, 1968. (a)

STAATS, A. W. A general apparatus for the investigation of complex learning in children. *Behaviour Research and Therapy,* 1968, *6,* 45–50. (b)

STAATS, A. W. Behavior analysis and token reinforcement in educational behavior modification and curriculum research. In C. Thoresen (Ed.), *Behavior modification in education.* Seventy-second yearbook of the National Society for the Study of Education, Part I. Chicago: University of Chicago Press, 1973.

STAATS, A. W., BREWER, B. A., & GROSS, M. C. Learning and cognitive development: Representative samples, cumulative-hierarchical learning, and experimental-longitudinal methods. *Monographs of the Society for Research in Child Development,* 1970, *35*(8, Serial No. 141).

STAATS, A. W., & BUTTERFIELD, W. H. Treatment of nonreading in a culturally deprived juvenile delinquent: An application of reinforcement principles. *Child Development,* 1965, *4,* 925–942.

STAATS, A. W., FINLEY, J. R., MINKE, K. A., & WOLF, M. M. Reinforcement variables in the control of unit reading responses. *Journal of the Experimental Analysis of Behavior,* 1964, *7,* 139–149.

STAATS, A. W., MINKE, K. A., & BUTTS, P. A token-reinforcement remedial reading program administered by black therapy-technicians to problem black children. *Behavior Therapy,* 1970, *1,* 331–353.

STAATS, A. W., MINKE, K. A., FINLEY, J. R., WOLF, M. M., & BROOKS, L. O. A reinforcer system and experimental procedure for the laboratory study of reading acquisition. *Child Development,* 1964, *35,* 209–231.

STAATS, A. W., MINKE, K. A., GOODWIN, R. A., & LANDEEN, J. Cognitive behavior modification: 'Motivated learning' reading treatment with subprofessional therapy-technicians. *Behaviour Research and Therapy*, 1967, 5, 283–299.

STAATS, A. W., & STAATS, C. K. A comparison of the development of speech and reading behavior with implications for research. *Child Development*, 1962, 33, 831–846.

STAATS, A. W., & STAATS, C. K. *Complex human behavior*. New York: Holt, Rinehart, & Winston, 1963.

STAINBACK, W., PAYNE, J. S., STAINBACK, S. B., & PAYNE, R. A. *Establishing a token economy in the classroom*. Columbus, Ohio: Charles E. Merrill, 1973.

STEPHENS, B., McLAUGHLIN, J. A., HUNT, J. McV., MAHONEY, E. J., KOHLBERG, L., MOORE, G., & ARONFREED, J. Symposium: Developmental gains in the reasoning, moral judgment, and moral conduct of retarded and nonretarded persons. *American Journal of Mental Deficiency*, 1974, 79, 113–161.

STEVENSON, H. W. *Children's learning*. Englewood Cliffs, N.J.: Prentice-Hall, 1972.

STRANG, H. R. The automated instruction of practical reading skills to disadvantaged sixth grade children. *University of Virginia Education Review*, 1972, 10(1), 6–12. (a)

STRANG, H. R. An automated approach to remedial reading. *Psychology in the Schools*, 1972, 9, 434–439. (b)

STRANG, H. R., & WOLF, M. N. Automated reading instruction in the ghetto. *Child Study Journal*, 1971, 1, 187–201.

STRAUGHAN, J. M. Treatment with mother and child in the playroom. *Behaviour Research and Therapy*, 1964, 2, 37–41.

STRAUSS, A. A. Diagnosis and education of the cripple-brained, deficient child. *Journal of Exceptional Children*, 1943, 9, 163–168.

STRAUSS, A. A., & KEPHART, N. C. *Rate of mental growth in a constant environment among higher grade moron and borderline children*. Paper presented at American Association on Mental Deficiency, 1939.

STRAUSS, A. A., & KEPHART, N. C. *Psychopathology and education of the brain-injured child, (Vol. 2), Progress in theory and clinic*. New York: Grune & Stratton, 1955.

STRAUSS, A. A., & LEHTINEN, L. E. *Psychopathology and education of the brain-injured child*. New York: Grune & Stratton, 1947.

STRAUSS, A. A., & WERNER, H. Disorders of conceptual thinking in the brain-injured child. *Journal of Nervous and Mental Disease*, 1942, 96, 153–172.

SULZBACHER, S. I., & HOUSER, J. E. A tactic to eliminate disruptive behaviors in the classroom: Group contingent consequences. *American Journal of Mental Deficiency*, 1968, 73, 88–90.

SURRATT, P. R., ULRICH, R. E., & HAWKINS, R. P. An elementary student as a behavioral engineer. *Journal of Applied Behavior Analysis*, 1969, 2, 85–92.

TARAKANOV, V. B., & ZINCHENKO, V. P. Comparative analysis of touch and vision: Communication VI. Voluntary memory of form in preschool children. *Dokl. Akad. Pedagog.* NAUK RSFSR, 1960, *4*, 49–52.

TARVER, S. G., & HALLAHAN, D. P. Attention deficits in children with learning disabilities: A review. *Journal of Learning Disabilities,* 1974, *9*, 560–569.

TARVER, S. G., & HALLAHAN, D. P. Learning disabilities: An overview. In J. M. Kauffman & D. P. Hallahan (Eds.), *Teaching children with learning disabilities: Personal perspectives.* Columbus, Ohio: Charles E. Merrill, 1976.

TAWNEY, J. W. Training letter discrimination in four-year-old children. *Journal of Applied Behavior Analysis,* 1972, *5*, 455–465.

TEDESCHI, J. T., SMITH, R. B., & BROWN, R. C. A reinterpretation of research on aggression. *Psychological Bulletin,* 1974, *81*, 540–562.

THARP, R. G., & WETZEL, R. J. *Behavior modification in the natural environment.* New York: Academic Press, 1969.

THOMAS, A., CHESS, S., & BIRCH, H. G. *Temperament and behavior disorders in children.* New York: New York University Press, 1968.

THORESEN, C. E. (Ed.) *Behavior modification in education:* Seventy-second yearbook of the National Society for the Study of Education (Part 1). Chicago: University of Chicago Press, 1973.

THURSTONE, L. L. Primary mental abilities. *Psychometric Monographs,* 1938, *1*, 1–121.

TURIEL, E. Stage transition in moral development. In R. M. W. Travers (Ed.), *Second handbook of research on teaching.* Chicago: Rand McNally, 1973.

TURIEL, E. Conflict and transition in adolescent moral development. *Child Development,* 1974, *45*, 14–29.

ULLMANN, L., & KRASNER, L. *A psychological approach to abnormal behavior.* Englewood Cliffs, N.J.: Prentice-Hall, 1969.

United States Department of Health, Education, and Welfare. *Reading disorders in the United States: A report of the National Advisory Committee on Dyslexia and Related Reading Disorders.* Washington, D.C.: U.S. Government Printing Office, 1969.

United States Office of Education. *Estimated number of handicapped children in the United States, 1971–72.* Washington, D.C.: U.S. Office of Education.

VALETT, R. E. *A psychoeducational inventory of basic learning abilities.* Palo Alto: Fearon, 1968.

VANDENBERG, S. G. What do we know today about the inheritance of intelligence and how do we know it? In R. Cancro (Ed.), *Intelligence: Genetic and environmental influences.* New York: Grune & Stratton, 1971.

VYGOTSKY, L. S. *Thought and language.* New York: Wiley, 1962.

WAHLER, R. G. Child-child interactions in free field settings: Some experimental analyses. *Journal of Experimental Child Psychology,* 1967, *5*, 278–293.

WALKER, H. M. Empirical assessment of deviant behavior in children. *Psychology in the Schools,* 1969, *6,* 93–97.

WALKER, L., & COLE, E. M. Familial patterns of expression of specific reading disability in a population sample. *Bulletin of the Orton Society,* 1965, *15.*

WALLACE, G., & KAUFFMAN, J. M. *Teaching children with learning problems.* Columbus, Ohio: Charles E. Merrill, 1973.

WATT, N. F., STOLOROW, R. D., LUBENSKY, A. W., & McCLELLAND, D.C. School adjustment and behavior of children hospitalized for schizophrenia as adults. *American Journal of Orthopsychiatry,* 1970, *40,* 637–657.

WEBER, R. M. Grammaticality and the self-correction of reading errors. *Project Literacy Reports* (Cornell University), 1967, No. 8, 53–59.

WEDELL, K. Some aspects of perceptual-motor development in young children. In *Learning problems in the cerebral palsied.* London: Spastics Society, 1964.

WEDELL, K. Perceptual-motor difficulties. *Special Education,* 1968, *57,* 25–30.

WEDELL, K. *Learning and perceptuo-motor disabilities in children.* New York: Wiley, 1973.

WEPMAN, J. M. *Auditory Discrimination Test.* Chicago: Language Research Associates, 1958.

WEPMAN, J. M., CRUICKSHANK, W. M., DEUTSCH, C. P., MORENCY, A., & STROTHER, C. R. Learning disabilities. In N. Hobbs (Ed.), *Issues in the classification of children* (Vol. 1). San Francisco: Jossey-Bass, 1975.

WERNER, H. Process and achievement: A basic problem of education and developmental psychology. *Harvard Educational Review,* May, 1937.

WERNER, H. *Comparative psychology of mental development.* New York: International Universities Press, 1948.

WERNER, H., & STRAUSS, A. A. Problems and methods of functional analysis in mentally deficient children. *Journal of Abnormal and Social Psychology,* 1939, *34,* 37–62. (a)

WERNER, H., & STRAUSS, A. A. Types of visuo-motor activity in their relation to low and high performance ages. *Proceedings of the American Association on Mental Deficiency,* 1939, *44,* 163–168. (b)

WERNER, H., & STRAUSS, A. A. Causal factors in low performance. *American Journal of Mental Deficiency,* 1940, *45,* 213–218.

WERNER, H., & STRAUSS, A. A. Pathology of figure-background relation in the child. *Journal of Abnormal and Social Psychology,* 1941, *36,* 236–248.

WERNICKE, C. The symptom-complex of aphasia. In A. Church (Ed.), *Diseases of the Nervous System.* New York: Appleton, 1908.

WERRY, J. S. Organic factors in childhood psychopathology. In H. C. Quay & J. S. Werry (Eds.), *Psychopathological disorders of childhood.* New York: Wiley, 1972.

WHEELER, A. J., & SULZER, B. Operant training and generalization of a verbal response form in a speech-deficient child. *Journal of Applied Behavior Analysis,* 1970, *3,* 139–147.

WHELAN, R. J. The relevance of behavior modification procedures for teachers of emotionally disturbed children. In P. Knoblock (Ed.), *Intervention approaches in educating emotionally disturbed children.* Syracuse: Syracuse University Press, 1966.

WHELAN, R. J. Richard J. Whelan. In J .M. Kauffman & C. D. Lewis (Eds.), *Teaching children with behavior disorders: Personal perspectives.* Columbus, Ohio: Charles E. Merrill, 1974.

WHELAN, R. J., & HARING, N. G. Modification and maintenance of behavior through systematic application of consequences. *Exceptional Children,* 1966, *32,* 281–289.

WHITE, B. L., CASTLE, P., & HELD, R. Observations on the development of visually-directed reaching. *Child Development,* 1964, *35,* 349–364.

WHITE, G. D., NIELSON, G., & JOHNSON, S. M. Timeout duration and the suppression of deviant behavior in children. *Journal of Applied Behavior Analysis,* 1972, *5,* 111–120.

WHITE, M. A., & CHARRY, J. (Eds.) *School disorder, intelligence, and social class.* New York: Teachers College Press, 1966.

WIEDERHOLT, J. L., Historical perspectives on the education of the learning disabled. In L. Mann & D. Sabatino (Eds.), *The second review of special education.* Philadelphia: Journal of Special Education Press, 1974.

WOHLWILL, J. F. From perception to inference: A dimension of cognitive development. In W. Kessen and C. Kuhlman (Eds.), *Thought in the young child.* Chicago: University of Chicago Press, 1970.

WORELL, J., & NELSON, C. M. *Managing instructional problems: A case study workbook.* New York: McGraw-Hill, 1974.

YUSSEN, S. R. The effects of verbal and visual highlighting of dimensions on discrimination learning by preschoolers and second graders. *Child Development,* 1972, *43,* 921–929.

ZAPOROZHETS, A. V. The development of perception in the preschool child. In P. H. Mussen (Ed.), *European research in child development. Monographs of the Society for Research in Child Development,* 1965, *30* (Serial No. 100).

ZEAMAN, D., & HOUSE, B. J. The role of attention in retardate discrimination learning. In N. R. Ellis (Ed.), *Handbook of mental deficiency.* New York: McGraw-Hill, 1963.

ZEILBERGER, J., SAMPEN, S. E., & SLOANE, H. N. Modification of a child's problem behaviors in the home with the mother as therapist. *Journal of Applied Behavior Analysis,* 1968, *1,* 47–53.

ZIGLER, E. Developmental versus difference theories of mental retardation and the problem of motivation. *American Journal of Mental Deficiency,* 1969, *73,* 536–556.

ZIMMERMAN, E. H., & ZIMMERMAN, J. The alteration of behavior in a special classroom situation. *Journal of the Experimental Analysis of Behavior,* 1962, *5,* 59–60.

ZIMMERMAN, E. H., ZIMMERMAN, J., & RUSSELL, C. D. Differential effects of token reinforcement on instruction-following in related students instructed as a group. *Journal of Applied Behavior Analysis,* 1969, *2,* 101–112.

ZINCHENKO, V. P. Some properties of orienting movements of the hands and eyes and their role in the formation of motor habits. (Authorized summary of candidate's dissertation). Moscow: Institute of Psychology, 1957.

ZINCHENKO, V. P. Comparative analysis of touch and vision: Communication II. Properties of orienting-investigatory eye movements for preschool children. *Dokl. Akad. Pedagog.* NAUK RSFSR, 1960, *4,* 53–60.

ZINCHENKO, V. P., CHZHI-TSIN, V., & TARAKVANOV, V. V. Formation of and development of perceptive behavior. *Vop. Psikhol,* 1962, *8,* 1–14.

ZINCHENKO, V. P., LOMOV, B. F., & RUZSKAYA, A. G. Comparative analysis of touch and vision: Communication I. On so-called simultaneous perception. *Dokl. Akad. Pedagog.* NAUK RSFSR, 1959, *3,* 71–74.

ZINCHENKO, V. P., & RUZSKAYA, A. G. Comparative analysis of touch and vision: Communication III. Visual-haptic transfer in preschool age. *Dokl. Akad. Pedagog.* NAUK RSFSR, 1960, *4,* 95–98. (a)

ZINCHENKO, V. P., & RUZSKAYA, A. G. Comparative analysis of touch and vision: Communication VII. The observable level of perception of form in children of preschool age. *Dokl. Akad. Pedagog.* NAUR RSFSR, 1960, *4,* 85–88. (b)

ZUCKER, J. S., & STRICKER, G. Impulsivity-reflectivity in preschool Headstart and middle class children. *Journal of Learning Disabilities,* 1968, *1,* 578–583.

ZUSNE, L., MICHELS, K. M. Nonrepresentational shapes and eye movements. *Perceptual and Motor Skills,* 1964, *18,* 11–20.

# Index

academic retardation, 20, 21–22
  and educable mentally retarded children, 39–41
  and emotionally disturbed children, 39–41
  and IQ score, 21
  and learning disabled children, 39–41
  quantification of, 21
acetylcholine, 25
achievement tests, *see* tests
*Achieving Perceptual-Motor Efficiency* (Barsch), 133
Adams, P. A., 34
aggression
  control of, 256–63
  development and control of, 231–35
Ahrens, R., 79
American Academy for Cerebral Palsy, 136
American Academy of Physical Medicine and Rehabilitation, 136
American Congress of Rehabilitation Medicine, 136
angulation problems, 8
aphasia
  classification of, 8
  congenital, 186
  developmental, 19, 186
  work on, 186–87
applied behavior analysis, 12–18, 43, 57–74
  and arithmetic skills, 106
  of attention, 164–71
  characteristics of, 58
  defined, 14
  of distractibility, 164–71
  and educable mental retardation, 58

applied behavior analysis (*cont.*)
  and emotionally disturbed children, 18, 58
  ethical and moral aspects of, 265–66
  functional, 16
  of hyperactivity, 176–78
  and learning disabilities, 12–18, 58
  and measurement, 58–60
  and mentally retarded children, 18
  methods of, 17, 66–67
  and reading skills, 209–10
  recent developments in, 17–18
  of social behavior, 255–66
  in special education, 17
  and specification of abilities, 14
  and writing skills, 210–13
apraxia, 126, 200
arithmetic disorders, 19
arithmetic skills
  development of, 148–49
  training for, 106–8
Arlington County (Va.) Project, 15, 17
Association for Children with Learning Disabilities (ACLD), 11, 12
  and mental retardation, 11
Association Method, 202
attention
  applied behavior analysis of, 164–71
  assessment of, 153
  auditory, 154
  differential, 164
  in the disabled, 155–59
  importance in psychological theories, 151–52
  and the learning disabled, 156–59
  normal development of, 153–54
  in the retarded, 155–56